From Ideas to Action

From Ideas to Action

Governance Paths to Net Zero

JANIS SARRA

OXFORD
UNIVERSITY PRESS

OXFORD
UNIVERSITY PRESS

Great Clarendon Street, Oxford, OX2 6DP,
United Kingdom

Oxford University Press is a department of the University of Oxford.
It furthers the University's objective of excellence in research, scholarship,
and education by publishing worldwide. Oxford is a registered trade mark of
Oxford University Press in the UK and in certain other countries

First Edition published in 2020

Impression: 1

Published in the United States of America by Oxford University Press
198 Madison Avenue, New York, NY 10016, United States of America

British Library Cataloguing in Publication Data
Data available

Library of Congress Control Number: 2020942419

ISBN 978-0-19-885230-8

DOI: 10.1093/oso/9780198852308.001.0001

Printed and bound by
CPI Group (UK) Ltd, Croydon, CR0 4YY

Acknowledgements

My sincere thank you to Catherine McCall for her invaluable comments on the full draft of this book, and to Dr Ronald Davis and Eli Angen for each having provided comprehensive comments on two chapters. While this book project predates my work with the Canada Climate Law Initiative and the Commonwealth Climate and Law Initiative, in bringing the book to press I have benefited from the knowledge gained as principal co-investigator in those initiatives, which received financial support from my university and from the Ivey Foundation, McConnell Foundation, and North Growth Foundation under the auspices of the Clean Economy Fund. My sincere thanks also to the authors that have permitted me to quote from their published work, to Gregory Ronczewski for the book cover design, to MaryGrace Johnstone for her assistance with footnotes, to Helen Tooze for help with the subject index, and to the staff at Oxford University Press for their production assistance.

My heartfelt thanks to my partner Book and my children Samantha, Danielle, and Alexander for their continuing love and support. In particular, I have appreciated Samantha's diligence in sending me news items relating to climate corporate governance.

This book is dedicated to my four granddaughters, Amadea, Jolie, Carmen, and Magdalena - that they may grow up on a planet that is rich in biodiversity and that will sustainably, fairly, and equitably support their lives and the lives of future generations.

Table of Contents

List of Abbreviations

ABP	Pensioenfonds voor overheid en onderwijs (APB pension fund)
APRA	Australian Prudential Regulatory Authority
AIMCo	Alberta Investment Management Corporation
ASX	Australia Securities Exchange
CAB	climate awareness bond
CBA	Commonwealth Bank of Australia
CCGG	Canadian Coalition for Good Governance
CDPQ	Caisse de dépôt et placement du Québec
CEO	chief executive officer
CFRF	Climate Financial Risk Forum
CIF	Climate Investment Fund
CIO	chief investment officer
COP21	United Nations Conference of the Parties 21st meeting
CSA	Canadian Securities Administrators
CSR	corporate social responsibility
DICE	Dynamic Integrated Model of Climate and the Economy
EC	European Commission
ECCC	Environment and Climate Change Canada
ECHR	European Convention on Human Rights
EIB	European Investment Bank
EIF	European Investment Fund
E&P	exploration & production (companies)
EBRD	European Bank for Reconstruction and Developments
ERDF	European Regional Development Fund
EU	European Union
FSB	Financial Stability Board
FSCO	Financial Services Commission of Ontario
GHG	greenhouse gas
GDP	gross domestic product
GMST	global mean surface temperature
IAM	integrated assessment model
ICGN	International Corporate Governance Network
IEA	International Energy Agency
IFC	International Finance Corporation
IIGCC	Institutional Investors Group on Climate Change
IORP	institutions for occupational retirement provision
IOSCO	International Organization of Securities Commissions
IPCC	Intergovernmental Panel on Climate Change
ISPPBES	Intergovernmental Science-Policy Platform on Biodiversity and Ecosystem Services
MD&A	management disclosure and analysis
MSME	micro, small, and medium enterprises
NDC	nationally-determined contributions
NEEAP	national energy efficiency action plans

NGO	non-governmental organizations
OECD	Organization for Economic Co-operation and Development
PRA	Prudential Regulation Authority (UK)
RICE	Regional Integrated Model of Climate and the Economy
SASB	Sustainability Accounting Standards Board
SCC	Supreme Court of Canada
SFC	Securities and Futures Commission (Hong Kong)
SHARE	Shareholder Association for Research and Education
SIPP	Statement of Investment Policies and Procedures
SME	small and medium enterprises
SRI	sustainable and responsible investment
TCFD	Taskforce on Climate-related Financial Disclosures
tCO_2e	per tonne of carbon dioxide equivalent emissions
UK	United Kingdom
UN	United Nations
UN DRIP	United Nations Declaration on the Rights of Indigenous Peoples
UNEP	United Nations Environmental Programme
UN FCCC	United Nations Framework Convention on Climate Change
UN PRI	United Nations Principles for Responsible Investing
UNCTAD	United Nations Conference on Trade and Development
US	United States

1
Introduction

Climate change represents an urgent and potentially irreversible threat to human societies and to the planet. The science has been well-established for decades, and now, the financial analysis is equally well-established. It confirms that climate change poses a systemic threat to our economies, potentially disrupting the economic and social security of billions of people. Yet despite these clear signals, we are slow to act decisively, notwithstanding the evidence from countless recent acute events such as wildfires and flooding, and despite the fact that we have the legal, political, and technological tools to transition our economies to net zero carbon. Equally, we have been slow to acknowledge that climate change impacts disproportionately harm Indigenous peoples, racialized communities, and women. Thus, effective climate governance strategies need to be science-based and need to be grounded in a socio-economic framework that meaningfully addresses systemic risks and systemic harm.

While some businesses are reluctant to take significant steps to reduce their carbon footprint, many companies are well-intentioned but feel somewhat paralysed in the face of overwhelming data that portend a financially and environmentally devastating future. Yet the opposite is possible. We can still reverse the trajectory of climate change, but it requires bold and informed action to reduce our carbon footprint and accomplish that goal in a manner that embeds fairness in the transition.

This book offers a guide for companies, pension funds, asset managers, and other institutional investors to commence the legal, governance, and financial strategies needed for effective climate mitigation and adaptation, and to help distribute the economic benefits of these actions to their stakeholders. It takes the reader from ideas to action, from first steps to a more meaningful contribution to the move towards a net zero carbon, and ultimately, a climate positive, world.

However, this book is not only for corporate officers and pension fiduciaries. It can serve as a helpful guide to everyone implicated in a corporation's activities—employees, pensioners, consumers, banks and other lenders, policy-makers, and community members. It offers insights into what we should be expecting, and asking, of these individuals who have taken responsibility for effectively managing our savings, our retirement funds, our investments, and our tax dollars.

Immediate action is required from multiple actors—corporate directors and officers, institutional investors, governments, financial institutions, and ordinary citizens. Recognition of this imperative resulted in the overwhelming majority of countries globally adopting the United Nations ('UN') Framework Convention on Climate Change Paris Agreement in December 2015, the central aim of which is pursuing efforts to limit global temperature rise to 2° Celsius ("°C") above pre-industrial levels,

From Ideas to Action. Janis Sarra, Oxford University Press (2020). © Janis Sarra. DOI: 10.1093/oso/9780198852308.003.0001.

and to pursue efforts to limit it to 1.5°C.[1] The agreement adopted by the Conference of Parties ('COP 21') under the United Nations Framework Convention on Climate Change ('UN FCCC') set out a framework for reform initiatives.[2] One hundred and ninety-seven countries adopted an action plan to avoid dangerous climate change, agreeing that deep reductions in global emissions through both climate mitigation and adaption are urgently required.[3] As of December 2019, 189 states that were signatories to the Paris agreement have ratified the agreement in their home countries.[4]

In the five years since that agreement, progress has been slow and uneven. The Intergovernmental Panel on Climate Change ('IPCC') reported in 2018 that human-induced global warming has already reached approximately 1°C above pre-industrial levels, and is increasing at 0.2°C per decade.[5] If the current warming rate continues, the world could reach human-induced global warming of 1.5°C as early as ten years from now, with serious consequences for economic activity, water and food security, and the health and well-being of countless individuals.[6]

The IPCC represents the views of more than 800 scientists internationally, representing their national governments. The IPCC has recognized a strong scientific case for urgent and long term action on climate change, calling for fossil fuels to be phased out by 2100 and for immediate, substantial, and sustained reductions in greenhouse gas ('GHG') emissions.[7] The IPCC was created 'to provide policymakers with regular scientific assessments on climate change, its implications and potential future risks, as well as to put forward adaptation and mitigation options'.[8] It is the UN body for assessing the science related to climate change.[9] The IPCC utilizes evidence of the

[1] United Nations ('UN') Framework Convention on Climate Change ('FCCC') (COP21), 'Paris Agreement' (12 December 2015) FCCC/CP/2015/10/Add.1 at 1, <https://unfccc.int/resource/docs/2015/cop21/eng/10a01.pdf> (hereafter Paris Agreement). In October 2016, the country approval threshold for entry into force was achieved and the Paris Agreement entered into force on 4 November 2016. The UN tracks progress on implementation: see UN (Climate Change Secretariat), 'Progress Tracker: Work Programme Resulting from the Relevant Requests Contained in Decision 1/CP.21' (22 October 2018), <https://unfccc.int/sites/default/files/resource/Progress%20Tracker%20PAWP.pdf>.

[2] Paris Agreement, ibid.

[3] Ibid. UN FCCC, 'Paris Agreement: Status of Ratification' (2019), <https://unfccc.int/process/the-paris-agreement/status-of-ratification>.

[4] UN, 'Climate Change' (28 August 2019), <https://unfccc.int/process/the-paris-agreement/status-of-ratification>.

[5] More precisely, between 0.8°C and 1.2°C. By the decade 2006–2015, human activity had warmed the world by 0.87°C (±0.12°C) compared to pre-industrial times (1850–1900). See Intergovernmental Panel on Climate Change ('IPCC'), M Allen, O Dube, W Solecki, F Aragón-Durand, W Cramer, S Humphreys, M Kainuma, J Kala, N Mahowald, Y Mulugetta, R Perez, M Wairiu, and K Zickfeld, 'Framing and Context' (hereafter IPCC, 'Framing') in V Masson-Delmotte, P Zhai, H O Pörtner, D Roberts, J Skea, P Shukla, A Pirani, W Moufouma-Okia, C Péan, R Pidcock, S Connors, J B R Matthews, Y Chen, X Zhou, M I Gomis, E Lonnoy, T Maycock, M Tignor, and T Waterfield (eds), *Global Warming of 1.5°C: An IPCC Special Report on the Impacts of Global Warming of 1.5°C above Pre-industrial Levels and Related Global Greenhouse Gas Emission Pathways, in the Context of Strengthening the Global Response to the Threat of Climate Change, Sustainable Development, and Efforts to Eradicate Poverty* (IPCC 2019) at 51, <https://www.ipcc.ch/site/assets/uploads/sites/2/2019/05/SR15_Chapter1_Low_Res.pdf> (hereafter IPCC, Special Report 2018). See generally IPCC, 'Frequently Asked Questions' (2018), <https://www.ipcc.ch/site/assets/uploads/sites/2/2018/12/SR15_FAQ_Low_Res.pdf>.

[6] IPCC, 'Framing', ibid at 81.

[7] IPCC, *Climate Change 2014: Synthesis Report. Contribution of Working Groups I, II, and III to the Fifth Assessment Report of the Intergovernmental Panel on Climate Change* (hereafter IPCC 2014), <https://www.ipcc.ch/report/ar5/syr/>.

[8] IPCC, 'Home Page' (2019), <https://www.ipcc.ch/>.

[9] The IPCC is working on a Synthesis Report for 2022, to be released in time to inform the 2023 global stock-take by the United Nations Framework Convention on Climate Change ('UN FCCC') when

physical climate system and associated impacts and vulnerabilities of climate change; and knowledge drawn from perceptions of risk and experiences of climate impacts and governance systems. It utilizes scenarios and pathways to explore conditions enabling goal-oriented futures, while recognizing the significance of ethical considerations, the principle of equity, and the societal transformation needed.[10]

There is now a substantial body of literature on the scientific evidence regarding global warming and climate change, as well as the known and anticipated outcomes and the implications for social and economic security. This book directs its attention to one aspect of the tremendous challenges—the legal and governance strategies that businesses will have to adopt in order to effectively finance climate change mitigation and adaptation. These strategies require a serious departure from 'business as usual' and the book examines both the normative and financial imperatives that underpin the need for this transition.

The allocations of capital in business and investment have an impact on, and are impacted by, climate change.[11] This book examines why and how corporate directors and officers, pension trustees and their fiduciaries, as well as investment managers, asset managers, and other institutional investors can and should enhance their governance structures to exercise effective oversight of the transition to net zero carbon emissions and sustainable activities. It provides a timely analysis of how these corporate and financial decision-makers can shift their investment strategies to lower their carbon footprint, become more climate resilient, and how they can contribute their proportionate share of responsibility for reversing the current negative effects of climate change.

Climate change represents a significant risk in financial and other markets. It could substantially affect the valuation of many publicly held companies and place some investment portfolios at risk.[12] The challenges from delayed action to reduce GHG emissions include the risk of cost escalation, lock-in to carbon-emitting infrastructures, stranded assets, and reduced flexibility in future response options in the medium to long term.[13] In meeting the COP 21 goals, two-thirds of the world's fossil fuel reserves will not be used and are at risk of becoming stranded assets, placing trillions of dollars of investment at risk absent carefully planned transition.[14] Meaningful reduction

countries will review progress towards the Paris Agreement goal of keeping global warming to well below 2°C while pursuing efforts to limit it to 1.5°C; IPCC, 'AR6 Climate Change 2021: Impacts, Adaptation and Vulnerability' (Report) (2019), <www.ipcc.ch/report/sixth-assessment-report-working-group-ii>.

[10] IPCC, 'Framing' (n 5) at 51.

[11] Janis Sarra, *Fiduciary Obligations in Business and Investment: Implications of Climate Change* (CCLI, 2018) at 1, <https://law-ccli-2019.sites.olt.ubc.ca/files/2019/08/Janis-Sarra-Fiduciary-Obligation-in-Business-and-Investment.pdf>.

[12] World Economic Forum, *The Global Risks Report 2017*, <http://reports.weforum.org/global-risks-2017/> (hereafter WEF).

[13] IPCC, 'Summary for Policymakers' in IPCC, *Special Report 2018* (n 5) at 20, <https://www.ipcc.ch/site/assets/uploads/sites/2/2018/07/SR15_SPM_version_stand_alone_LR.pdf> (hereafter IPCC, 'Summary for Policymakers').

[14] Carbon Tracker Initiative, 'Unburnable Carbon' (2014), <http://www.carbontracker.org/wp-content/uploads/2014/09/Unburnable-Carbon-Full-rev2-1.pdf>; Cambridge Institute for Sustainability Leadership, 'Unhedgeable Risk: How Climate Change Sentiment Impacts Investment' (2015), <https://www.cisl.cam.ac.uk/publications/publication-pdfs/unhedgeable-risk.pdf>. Howard Covington and Raj Thamotheram, 'The Case for Forceful Stewardship', Pt 1 (10 January 2015), Working Paper: SSRN-id2551478.

of GHG emissions requires a shift from fossil fuels to renewable energy sources, as well as introduction of new technologies for energy efficiency and massive reduction of waste.

Cities generate 80 per cent of global gross domestic product ('GDP') and are home to more than half of the global population. One in ten people live in cities less than 10 metres above sea level and 40 per cent of the global population lives within 100 kilometres of a coast, which means that they are at serious risk of loss of life, homes, and businesses due to sea level rise and flooding, two chronic outcomes of climate change.[15] There are likely to be uneven distributional impacts between countries at different stages of development.[16]

Canada's Expert Panel on Sustainable Finance has observed that climate change is a macro disruptor across systems, industries, and geographies; it will have transformative economic impacts and require close assessment from both a prudential and systemic risk management perspective.[17]

A variety of concurrent strategies are required to achieve mitigation and adaptation internationally and domestically. This book draws on the best of current scholarly and business literature on effective governance of this transition, and offers a coherent normative and practical framework for moving forward. It explores both the risks and the opportunities for companies, and for pension funds, asset managers, and other institutional investors that support their economic activities.

This book firmly embeds principles of fairness and equity in examining the legal and governance frameworks that should inform corporate decision-making regarding climate change financial risk and the need to move towards a net zero carbon economy. It examines the governance questions that underpin business and investor support to meet the COP 21 goals, and to move beyond those goals towards a net zero carbon environmentally and financially sustainable future. It examines what drives corporate and investment decisions, the legal obligations of directors, officers and others entrusted with management of assets, the pressures for wealth maximization over different timeframes, and the growing social and economic pressures to address climate change risk. The law as currently framed is a driver for positive action on climate change, recognizing both the legal obligations and the potential risk and reward. Effective climate governance and finance could have a meaningful impact on our global sustainability.

The book suggests that to move from ideas to action on climate change and sustainable finance, we need to concurrently deploy a number of legal, governance, financial, and normative tools to change behaviour and encourage meaningful action in climate mitigation and adaptation. This text examines how each of these strategies are interlinked and can be advanced within corporate and business decision-making structures. It examines how multiple stakeholders have a role in shifting the

[15] Goldman Sachs Global Market Institute, *Taking the Heat: Making Cities Resilient to Climate Change* (4 September 2019) at 5, <https://www.goldmansachs.com/insights/pages/gs-research/taking-the-heat/report.pdf> (hereafter Goldman Sachs).

[16] IPCC, 'Summary for Policymakers' (n 13) at 20.

[17] Government of Canada, *Mobilizing Finance for Sustainable Growth* (Final Report of the Expert Panel on Sustainable Finance, June 2019) at 23, <http://publications.gc.ca/collections/collection_2019/eccc/En4-350-2-2019-eng.pdf>.

current trajectory of climate change in a way that is economically feasible, is just and fair, and meets individual and collective obligations to move towards net zero carbon economies.

I. The Need for Effective Climate Governance

Underpinning this transition by companies, pension funds, other institutional investors, and stakeholders generally is the need for effective corporate governance. We now know that anthropogenic climate change—climate change due to the activities of humans—presents the greatest challenge of this century. Governance, including how decisions are made, how they are effectively implemented, and how decision-makers are held accountable, needs to be responsive to the harms created by global warming.

Former Bank of England Governor Mark Carney has called climate change an 'existential' threat to humans and to business.[18] Recently, in respect of building a sustainable financial system, he observed:

> [T]he task is large, the window of opportunity is short, and the risks are existential.
> And like virtually everything else in the response to climate change, the development of this new sustainable finance is not moving fast enough for the world to reach net zero. To bring climate risks and resilience into the heart of financial decision-making, climate disclosure must become comprehensive, climate risk management must be transformed, and sustainable investing must go mainstream.[19]

One immediate imperative is the need to shift corporate and pension governance and investment practices. While regulatory oversight of efforts to address climate change is critically important, as discussed in Chapter 6, effective climate governance within companies and other organizations is fundamental to shifting the current trajectory of anthropogenic climate change. Essential to the responsibilities of corporate and financial actors is the notion of fiduciary obligation—the responsibility of directors and officers to oversee and manage their companies and organizations in a manner that takes responsibility for addressing climate change.

Fiduciary obligation and the duty of care, under both statutory provisions and the common law, require directors and officers to identify and address climate change risk in fulfilling their obligations to act in the best interests of the company. Fiduciary obligation also requires pension fund trustees and other investment and asset management fiduciaries to identify and act to address climate change risk in order to fulfil their obligations to beneficiaries. Recent developments regarding statutory disclosure are helpful in drawing the attention of fiduciaries to climate change risk, but are not, in themselves, sufficient.

[18] Bank of England Governor Mark Carney, 'Remarks given during the UN Secretary General's Climate Action Summit 2019' (23 September 2019) at 1, <https://www.bankofengland.co.uk/-/media/boe/files/speech/2019/remarks-given-during-the-un-secretary-generals-climate-actions-summit-2019-mark-carney.pdf?la=en&hash=C0D3A9F2C86647B04D88E7C0DC23264639D03BE2> (hereafter Carney 2019).

[19] Ibid.

To date, there is little jurisprudence internationally that expressly clarifies the relationship between fiduciary obligation, climate risk, and effective climate governance, but existing court judgments in many jurisdictions make clear that the obligations of fiduciaries are contextual and broad enough to recognize a duty of care in respect of climate change. Market actors and other stakeholders could benefit from further clarification by legislators regarding these obligations, and Chapters 4 and 5 of this book examine both obligations at common law and in statutory law that currently exist, as well as appropriate legislative frameworks and best practices that could be developed. What can, and should, fiduciaries do within the existing legal regime? What are the indicia of effective climate governance? How can governments support transition through public policy, legislation, and regulation to address barriers and drive greater action? This book offers insights on all these questions. Companies in countries that are highly dependent on fossil fuel production and export are particularly at risk financially, and hence require a comprehensive and timely strategy to shift governance of their economic activities.

Governor Carney has observed that climate risks have a number of distinctive elements, including: breadth of risk affecting multiple lines of business, sectors, and geographies; magnitude, as the full impacts of climate risks are large, potentially non-linear, and irreversible; foreseeable, in that the size of future impacts will be determined by the actions taken today; and an uncertain time horizon that stretches beyond traditional business planning cycles.[20] A significant challenge, therefore, is in assessing the resilience of firms' strategies to control transition risks, and in ensuring effective governance is in place.[21]

A growing number of studies emphasize the non-linearity of climate risks and impacts as temperature rises from 2°C to 4°C of warming, particularly in relation to water availability and heat extremes.[22] The resilience of ecosystems, meaning their ability to recover after a disturbance or acute event, may change, and often decline, in a non-linear way.[23] GHG emissions are a prime driver of rising global temperatures and, as such, are a key focal point of policy, regulatory, market, and technology responses to limit climate change.[24] Organizations with high levels of GHG emissions are likely to be impacted more significantly in the transition to net zero carbon, with current and future constraints placed on emissions, either by emission restrictions or through carbon budgets, which in turn will impact organizations financially.[25]

Jane Ambachtsheer, Global Head of Sustainability at BNP Paribas Asset Management, which has €399 billion in assets under management, has commented on the responsibility of long term investors in respect of climate governance:

[20] Bank of England Governor Mark Carney, 'A New Horizon', Presentation to European Commission Conference: A Global Approach to Sustainable Finance (21 March 2019) at 4–5, <https://www.bankofengland.co.uk/-/media/boe/files/speech/2019/a-new-horizon-speech-by-mark-carney.pdf?la=en&hash=F63F8064E0408F038CABB1F29C58FB1A0CD0FE25> (hereafter Carney, 'New Horizon').

[21] Ibid at 5.

[22] IPCC, 'Framing' (n 5) at 70.

[23] Ibid.

[24] Financial Stability Board Task Force on Climate-Related Financial Disclosures, *Final Report: Recommendations of the Task Force on Climate-Related Financial Disclosures* (15 June 2017) at 22, <https://www.fsb-tcfd.org/publications/final-recommendations-report/> (hereafter TCFD, *Final Report*).

[25] Ibid.

> We firmly believe that companies that adopt a sustainable approach are inherently more responsible and can therefore generate long-term value for customers. Beyond our fiduciary responsibility towards customers, our business allows us to influence decision-making bodies as well as the companies we invest in. This gives us an opportunity to take action for society as a whole with a view to creating sustainable, inclusive growth.
>
> If we are to successfully address the challenges of today—and secure a prosperous and sustainable economy for tomorrow—long-term investors must rise to the occasion as 'future makers', using the leverage that our investments and our voice bring to positively influence the world around us. We relish this opportunity and look forward to partnering with our clients and financial sector peers to achieve what should be a joint aim: a sustainable future.[26]

This notion of 'future makers' is gaining traction as institutional investors increasingly understand their responsibilities in respect of climate governance through their investment and engagement activities.

i. Overview of This Book

This book canvasses a number of issues that are critically important to developing a framework of legal and governance strategies to address climate change. 'Governance' in this book refers to the way that corporations, pension funds, institutional investors, and asset managers engage in oversight and management of companies, pension funds, and other investment funds. It includes the development of business plans, strategic planning, and oversight of the finances of the company. It refers to the systems used for communicating strategies for risk management throughout the organization, and for holding decision-makers accountable for their actions. It does not refer to the governance of climate change that focuses on the development of the international climate regime and its implementation, which is another important area of climate governance. While the book covers regulatory initiatives that directly address the obligations of corporations, pension funds, and other investment funds, it does not delve into best governance practices in respect of national and international governmental commitments to address climate change. These topics, which are vitally important, are beyond the scope of this book.

Equally, while there are a number of examples drawn from emerging and developing nations, this book is aimed at directors, officers, and fiduciaries in developed countries, as it is these fiduciaries that still lag considerably in their efforts to move the world to net zero carbon. There is much to learn from the global south, which is suffering the greatest impacts from climate change while having contributed the least to global warming, and the book offers examples of the circular economy and other initiatives in emerging countries. However, the text focuses primarily on the corporations and institutional investors and asset managers in the global north as the

[26] Jane Ambachtsheer (Global Head of Sustainability at BNP Paribas Asset Management), <https://www.bnpparibas-am.com/en/sustainability/as-an-investor/>.

primary beneficiaries of the economic activities that have created global warming. It is these companies and financial firms that need to take leadership. The legal obligations, the governance tools, and the technology already exist to shift governance to effectively meet the challenge of climate change. What is needed is the social and political will to shift trajectory.

This chapter, in addition to introducing the book, briefly discusses a few essential definitions related to the topic of climate governance. Too often these terms are used without clear explanation of what exactly they are referring to. Chapter 2 then offers a succinct analysis of the current state of the science, particularly as it relates to the impacts of climate change on businesses. It canvasses the physical impacts that are already being manifested. It explores the concept of 'climate tipping points', as well as discussing why mitigation is an essential part of the strategy to reduce the impacts of global warming. It explains the role of adaptation in these efforts.

Chapter 3 briefly examines what is already known about the financial impacts of climate change. In particular, it examines some of the costs to date of the increasing intensity and frequency of weather- and climate-related acute events. It examines the physical risks to business, as well as myriad transition risks. It highlights how women and Indigenous peoples are particularly impacted by climate change.

Chapter 4 undertakes an in-depth examination of fiduciary obligation and the oversight and management of climate change. It examines what fiduciary duty entails, and how it is conceptualized in law in terms of directors and officers of companies, pension trustees and their fiduciaries, asset managers, and investment funds. It examines where their duties align and where they involve nuanced differences. It examines the scope of the duties of care and prudence in respect of identifying and addressing climate-related risks. It looks at oppression remedies available in some jurisdictions. It examines how fiduciaries can fulfil their obligations through effective management of climate-related risks and opportunities. It introduces the reader to the new kinds of investment priorities of pension funds and other institutional investors regarding a commitment to moving to net zero carbon emissions.

Chapter 5 discusses the principles and frameworks that inform effective climate governance. It provides a roadmap on how boards can get started, and how they can move towards climate competence. It examines developments internationally in respect of disclosure of climate change as a governance tool, as well as other tools such as climate scenario analysis and integrated assessment models.

Chapter 6 undertakes the critically important discussion of regulatory oversight of climate governance. While there is global consensus on the need to act now to reduce GHG emissions, there is no consensus on the degree to which regulation of corporations and financial firms is necessary and what form it should take. This chapter explores some of the tools being used to focus corporate and financial managers' attention on climate-related financial risk and examines the challenges for regulating a global problem that requires individual nation attention. It examines regulatory initiatives in select jurisdictions, the United Kingdom ('UK'), the European Union ('EU'), Canada, and Australia, with references to how such regulation has stalled in countries like the United States ('US'). It examines capacity building in terms of gender roles in policymaking and discusses the need to observe legal requirements and normative imperatives in the duty to consult and work with Indigenous communities.

Chapter 7 then explores additional tools for holding corporate directors and officers accountable for their decisions and actions in respect of climate change. It analyses effects of direct engagement with companies, through proxy voting, direct engagement with corporate boards, policy engagement, and the use of divestment as a governance strategy. The chapter then examines early efforts at litigation seeking to force companies to take responsibility for their management, or lack thereof, of their carbon footprint and their carbon resilience.

Chapter 8 looks at the rapidly growing area of sustainable finance. There have been Expert Panels in the UK, EU, Canada, and China on how to create the infrastructure for a sustainable economy and how to build partnerships between the public and private sectors to shift financial activity towards a circular economy. While the strategies and tools are at a nascent stage, they are critically important to effective governance going forward. The chapter examines developments in green finance, Indigenous partnerships in sustainable finance, and gives examples of innovations in the transition towards zero carbon.

Chapter 9 is a concise but important consideration of the unique problems that micro, small, and medium enterprises ('MSME') face in the transition to a net zero carbon economy. Most of the literature on climate finance assumes that companies are publicly traded, well-resourced, and have an infrastructure that can undergird the transition. MSME face particular challenges in the transition away from carbon, as they often do not have the resources or infrastructure to develop strategies, metrics, and other tools. This chapter specifically addresses MSME, which comprise over 99 per cent of all business globally. It offers some practical insights into how to begin to effect climate mitigation and adaptation governance, given limited resources and infrastructure. This book also responds to differences in the economic, social, and legal circumstances of different countries.

Chapter 10 concludes with some final observations on charting a path forward from ideas to action. The Appendix offers a governance checklist for directors, officers, pension fiduciaries, and asset managers as they begin to embed effective climate governance in their management and oversight.

II. A Few Essential Definitions

While there are not yet universally accepted definitions of a number of climate-related terms, there is a developing consensus. It is important to set out several essential climate-related terms with respect to how they are used in this book. The definitions are drawn from sources in which there is a high degree of scientific and country consensus.

i. The Anthropocene

The 'Anthropocene' is the proposed geological epoch resulting from significant human-driven changes to the structure and functioning of the Earth System, including the climate system.[27] Proposed by the Earth System science community in 2000, almost twenty years later, the definition of the epoch is still undergoing a formalization process within the geological community based on the stratigraphic evidence that human activities have changed the Earth System with a signature that is distinct from those of the Holocene.[28] Its precise commencement date is yet to be determined, but the IPCC suggests that it is likely to be mid-twentieth century.[29]

'Anthropocene', as a term, has been used in a diversity of disciplines to denote the substantive influence humans have had on the state, dynamics, and future of the Earth System.[30] 'Anthropogenic climate change' thus refers to the climate change that is attributable to human activity. The IPCC observes that the Anthropocene offers a structured understanding of the culmination of past and present human-environmental relations and provides an opportunity to better visualize the future. Such visualization could minimize pitfalls, acknowledging the differentiated responsibilities and opportunities to limit global warming, and invest in prospects for climate-resilient sustainable development.[31]

ii. Global Warming and Climate Change

Scientists have known about the serious risks to our planet from anthropogenic climate change for more than thirty years.[32] Continued emissions of GHG will cause further warming of the Earth, and warming above 2°C, relative to the pre-industrial period, could lead to catastrophic economic and social consequences.[33]

The IPCC adopts a working definition of warming over the historical period based on an average of four global datasets that are supported by peer-reviewed publications.[34] 'Total warming' refers to the actual temperature change from all causes, while 'human-induced warming' refers to the component of that warming that is attributable to human activities.[35] The IPCC reports that human influence on climate has been the dominant cause of observed warming since the mid-twentieth century, and while global average surface temperature warmed by 0.85°C between 1880 and 2012, many regions of the world already have greater regional-scale warming, with 20–40 per cent of the global population having experienced over 1.5°C of warming in at least

[27] IPCC, 'Annex I: Glossary' in IPCC, *Special Report 2018* (n 5) at 543, <https://www.ipcc.ch/site/assets/uploads/sites/2/2019/06/SR15_AnnexI_Glossary.pdf> (hereafter IPCC, 'Glossary'). The Anthropocene Working Group ('AWG') established by the Sub-Commission on Quaternary Stratigraphy of the International Commission on Stratigraphy have agreed that: (i) the Anthropocene has a geological merit; (ii) it should follow the Holocene as a formal epoch in the Geological Time Scale; and (iii) its onset should be defined as the mid-twentieth century: IPCC, 'Framing' (n 5) at 54. See also <http://quaternary.stratigraphy.org/>.

[28] IPCC, 'Glossary', ibid at 543.

[29] Ibid.

[30] Ibid.

[31] IPCC, 'Framing' (n 5) at 54.

[32] IPCC, 'Climate Change 2014. Impacts, Adaptation and Vulnerability' at 9, <https://www.ipcc.ch/> (hereafter IPCC 2014). As discussed in Chapter 2, the earlier discovery of carbon dioxide and warming was more than 160 years ago.

[33] IPCC, *Fifth Assessment Report* (CUP, 2014).

[34] IPCC, 'Framing' (n 5) at 58.

[35] Ibid at 59.

one season.[36] 'Albedo' is the fraction of solar radiation reflected by a surface or object, often expressed as a percentage.[37] Snow-covered surfaces have a high albedo, soils' albedo range from high to low, and vegetation-covered surfaces and oceans have a low albedo.[38] Mitigation studies focus on human-induced warming, while studies of climate change impacts typically refer to total warming.[39]

The IPCC defines global warming as 'an increase in combined surface air and sea surface temperatures averaged over the globe and over a 30-year period', expressed relative to the period 1850–1900, used as an approximation of pre-industrial temperatures.[40] The IPCC notes that for periods shorter than thirty years, warming refers to the estimated average temperature over the thirty years, centred on that shorter period, accounting for the impact of any temperature fluctuations or trend within those thirty years.[41] For example, warming from preindustrial levels to the decade 2006–2015 is assessed to be 0.87°C (likely between 0.75°C and 0.99°C).[42] Warming greater than the global average has already been experienced in many regions and seasons, with higher average warming over land than over the ocean.[43]

If all anthropogenic emissions, including aerosol-related, were reduced to zero immediately, the IPCC suggests that any further warming beyond the 1°C already experienced would likely be less than 0.5°C over the next two to three decades. Thus, warming greater than 1.5°C is not geophysically unavoidable; and whether it will occur depends on future rates of emission reductions.[44]

The IPCC reports that all 1.5°C pathways involve limiting cumulative emissions of long-lived GHG, including carbon dioxide and nitrous oxide, and substantial reductions in other climate forcers.[45] Emissions pathways to 1.5°C are defined as those that, given current knowledge of the climate response, provide a one-in-two to two-in-three chance of warming either remaining below 1.5°C or returning to 1.5°C by around 2100 following an overshoot.[46] Overshoot pathways are characterized by the peak magnitude of the overshoot, which may have implications for impacts.[47] Limiting cumulative emissions requires either reducing net global emissions of long-lived GHG to zero before the cumulative limit is reached, or net negative global emissions after the limit is exceeded.[48] In other words, failing to reduce carbon emissions to zero by 2100 will mean that the only way to limit global warming to 1.5°C will be to have negative emissions for an extended period.

The IPCC in 2018 warned that current nationally-determined contributions ('NDC') made by countries as part of their commitments under the Paris Agreement,

[36] Ibid at 53.
[37] IPCC, 'Glossary' (n 27) at 542.
[38] Ibid.
[39] IPCC, 'Framing' (n 5) at 59.
[40] Ibid at 51.
[41] Ibid.
[42] Ibid.
[43] Ibid.
[44] Ibid.
[45] Ibid.
[46] Ibid.
[47] Ibid.
[48] Ibid.

which extend only to 2030, do not limit warming to 1.5°C. Depending on mitigation decisions after 2030, they cumulatively track toward a warming of 3°C to 4°C above pre-industrial temperatures by 2100, with the potential for further warming thereafter.[49] That means our current national plans for limiting global warming are woefully inadequate. Temperature rise, to date, has already resulted in profound alterations to human and natural systems, including increases in droughts, floods, and other types of extreme weather; sea level rise and inundation of salt water into fresh water; biodiversity loss; and unprecedented risks and losses to vulnerable persons and populations.[50]

The term 'climate' refers to the statistical mean and variability of temperature, precipitation, wind, and other variables over a period of months to decades to thousands or millions of years, with the classical period for averaging these variables being thirty years.[51] 'Weather' is the actual realization of the climatic process for a short period of time, for example, a day, a week, or a year.[52]

'Climate change' is the change in the state of the climate that can be identified using statistical analyses of changes in the mean and/or the variability of its properties and that persists for an extended period (decades or longer); and attributable to natural internal processes or 'external forcings' such as modulations of the solar cycles, volcanic eruptions, and persistent anthropogenic changes in the composition of the atmosphere or in land use.[53] The UN FCCC defines climate change as: 'a change of climate which is attributed directly or indirectly to human activity that alters the composition of the global atmosphere, and which is, in addition to natural climate variability observed over comparable time periods', distinguishing between climate change attributable to human activities altering the atmospheric composition and climate variability attributable to natural causes.[54]

iii. Greenhouse Gas Emissions and Carbon Intensity

'Greenhouse gases' ('GHG') are gaseous constituents of the atmosphere that absorb and emit radiation at specific wavelengths within the spectrum of terrestrial radiation emitted by the Earth's surface, the atmosphere, and by clouds, creating the 'GHG effect'.[55] Both natural processes and human activities release GHG to the atmosphere. Water vapour (H_2O), carbon dioxide (CO_2), nitrous oxide (N_2O), methane (CH_4), and ozone (O_3) are the primary GHG in the Earth's atmosphere, plus a number of human-made GHG in the atmosphere, such as the halocarbons and other substances containing chlorine and bromine.[56]

[49] Ibid at 56.
[50] Ibid at 51.
[51] IPCC, 'Glossary' (n 27) at 544.
[52] W D Nordhaus, *The Climate Casino: Risk, Uncertainty, and Economics for a Warming World* (Yale University Press, 2013) at 74 (hereafter Nordhaus, *Climate Casino*).
[53] IPCC, 'Glossary' (n 27) at 544.
[54] UN FCCC, Framework Convention on Climate Change, Article 1 (hereafter UN FCCC).
[55] IPCC, 'Glossary' (n 27) at 550.
[56] Ibid at 550–1.

Environment and Climate Change Canada ('ECCC') describes how GHG contribute to global warming:

> Greenhouse gases trap heat in the Earth's atmosphere, just as the glass of a greenhouse keeps warm air inside. Human activity increases the amount of GHGs in the atmosphere, contributing to a warming of the Earth's surface. This is called the enhanced greenhouse effect. Over the past 200 years in particular, humans have released GHG into the atmosphere primarily from burning fossil fuels. As a result, more heat is being trapped and the temperature of the planet is increasing. Sea levels are rising as Arctic ice melts, and there are changes to the climate, such as more severe storms and heat waves. All of this impacts the environment, the economy and human health.[57]

Scope 1 GHG emissions refer to all direct GHG emissions, and Scope 2 emissions refer to indirect GHG emissions from the company's consumption of purchased electricity, heat, or steam. Scope 3 GHG emissions refer to other indirect emissions not covered in scope 2 that occur in the value chain of the reporting company, including both upstream and downstream emissions.[58] Scope 3 emissions could include: the extraction and production of purchased materials and fuels, transport-related activities in vehicles not owned or controlled by the reporting entity, electricity-related activities such as transmission and distribution, outsourced activities, and waste disposal.[59]

'Carbon intensity' refers to the amount of emissions of CO_2 released per unit of another variable such as GDP, output, energy use, or transport.[60] A 'CO_2 equivalent emission' ('CO_2-eq') is the amount of CO_2 emissions that would cause the same integrated radiative forcing or temperature change, over a given time horizon, as an emitted amount of a GHG or a mixture of GHG.[61] Not all fossil fuels emit the same amount of carbon in the production process. For example, coal has approximately six times more CO_2 emissions per dollar of cost than natural gas and approximately twelve times more than that of petroleum.[62]

'Carbon footprint' is the total amount of GHG produced to support human activities directly and indirectly, usually expressed in equivalent tonnes of CO_2. For an individual person or business, the carbon footprint is the sum of all emissions that are induced by their activities in a given time frame, usually, per year.

[57] Environment and Climate Change Canada ('ECCC'), 'Canadian Environmental Sustainability Indicators Greenhouse Gas Emissions' (2017) at 5, <https://www.ec.gc.ca/indicateurs-indicators/default.asp?lang=en&n=F60DB708-1> (hereafter ECCC, 'Sustainability Indicators').

[58] TCFD, *Final Report* (n 24) at 63.

[59] Ibid.

[60] IPCC, 'Glossary' (n 27) at 544.

[61] Ibid at 546; there are a number of ways to compute such equivalent emissions and choose appropriate time horizons. Most typically, the CO_2 equivalent emission is obtained by multiplying the emission of a GHG by its global warming potential ('GWP') for a 100-year time horizon.

[62] Nordhaus, *Climate Casino* (n 52) at 163.

iv. Systemic Risk

Climate change is a systemic risk. A helpful definition of systemic risk is set out in an investor guidance issued by the International Corporate Governance Network ('ICGN'):

> The nature of systemic risk is that it builds over time, is interactive and synergistic and, once in play, is difficult to control. Systemic risk drivers tend to be cumulative and/or interdependent, resulting in far-reaching impacts, shocks, or even system-wide failure ... Systemic risks can often be neglected. On the one hand, they may be treated as immaterial by many investors with short-term horizons and market-relative benchmarks. On the other hand, they can go unaddressed by long-horizon investors who assume they will be protected through broadly diversified market exposure and the regulatory environment of the day in which political factors are less of a consideration. The ultimate costs of systemic risks are, by definition, undiversifiable and borne by all market participants, as well as by society more broadly. Ensuring that their fund's investment strategy is protected against systemic risk is a concern for investor fiduciaries.[63]

The ICGN guidance observes that climate change has emerged as a pressing higher order systemic financial risk, including physical weather-related impacts, resulting in property damage, insurance write-downs, and interruptions of global business operations; regulatory uncertainty across markets, with respect to countries' efforts to curb carbon emissions and take advantage of various tax incentives; and increased liability, with resultant reputational risks.[64] Accordingly, investor fiduciaries should be aware of the implications that climate change has for asset class risk, including commodity risk exposures, industry risk exposures, operational risk, country risk exposures, asset life projections, stranded asset risk, and heightened volatility of expected returns.[65]

v. Climate Mitigation and Adaptation

Climate mitigation refers to efforts to reduce the sources of GHG emissions and reduce actual emissions, or to enhance the absorption of gases already emitted, thus limiting the magnitude of future warming.[66] 'Mitigation requires the use of new technologies, clean energy sources, reduced deforestation, improved sustainable agricultural methods, and changes in individual and collective behaviour', which can also benefit biodiversity, air quality, and sustainable development.[67]

[63] ICGN, *Guidance on Investor Fiduciary Duties* (2018) at 10 and 11, <http://icgn.flpbks.com/icgn-fiduciary_duties/files/extfile/DownloadURL.pdf> (hereafter ICGN, *Guidance*).
[64] Ibid at 12.
[65] Ibid.
[66] IPCC 2014 (n 32); IPCC, 'Framing' (n 5) at 70.
[67] Ibid.

Removal of CO_2 can be accomplished by both natural and technological solutions. Technologies for carbon dioxide removal, to reduce concentrations already in the atmosphere, are in their infancy, but may become an important component of climate change mitigation.[68] Mitigation includes human intervention to enhance natural carbon sinks, such as forests, that absorb carbon.[69] Vegetation and oceans are natural carbon sinks that remove approximately one half of all emissions from human activities, but they are becoming less efficient at doing so, necessitating an urgent need to reduce deforestation and expand natural CO_2 sinks.[70] In addition to GHG, mitigation also applies to reducing emissions of other substances that have a warming effect on the climate.[71] There is a live question as to whether reforestation and ecosystem restoration can be massive-scale deployed to remedy the harms already caused.[72] Thus, both natural and technological solutions are likely necessary for meaningful climate mitigation pathways.

Reducing consumption of energy is also a major mitigation strategy. It requires urban design that reduces the need for private vehicles and encourages active mobility, such as walking and cycling. It means retrofitting buildings to be highly energy efficient, reducing the need to consume more energy for heating and cooling. Consumption of fuel products for electricity generation and transportation generates nearly 70 per cent of global GHG, which highlights the importance of corporations being instrumental in climate change mitigation.[73]

'Climate adaptation' refers to the actions taken to manage impacts of climate change and the process of adjustment to actual or expected changes.[74] The aim of adaptation is to reduce vulnerability and exposure to the harmful effects of climate change, such as sea level rise and more intense extreme weather events.[75] For example, in order for cities to reduce the impact of climate change, adaptation measures may include coastal protections, climate-resilient construction, urban planning to locate people and businesses away from rising sea levels, more robust infrastructure, and upgraded transportation systems.[76] Both adaptation and mitigation are required in the move towards a net zero carbon world.

[68] IPCC, 'Framing' (n 5) at 70.
[69] IPCC 2014 (n 32).
[70] Science Advisory Group of the UN Climate Action Summit 2019, *United in Science,* World Meteorological Organization (22 September 2019), <https://ane4bf-datap1.s3-eu-west-1.amazonaws.com/wmocms/s3fs-public/ckeditor/files/United_in_Science_ReportFINAL_0.pdf?XqiG0yszsU_sx2vOehOWpCOkm9RdC_gN> (hereafter *United in Science*).
[71] E Bush and G Flato, 'Chapter 1: About this report' in E Bush and D S Lemmen (eds), *Canada's Changing Climate Report* (Government of Canada 2019) at 13, <https://www.nrcan.gc.ca/sites/www.nrcan.gc.ca/files/energy/Climate-change/pdf/CCCR_FULLREPORT-EN-FINAL.pdf> (hereafter *Canada's Changing Climate Report* 2019).
[72] Ibid.
[73] Jacqueline Peel and Hari M Osofsky, *Climate Change Litigation: Regulatory Pathways to Cleaner Energy* (CUP, 2015) at 173–220.
[74] IPCC, 'Framing' (n 5) at 51, 70; IPCC 2014 (n 32).
[75] IPCC, March 2019, <https://www.ipcc.ch/site/assets/uploads/sites/2/2018/12/SR15_FAQ_Low_Res.pdf>.
[76] Goldman Sachs (n 15) at 5.

vi. Net Zero Carbon

'Net zero carbon' means that any GHG emissions are balanced by absorbing an equivalent amount from the atmosphere. In order to stabilize climate change, CO_2 emissions need to fall to net zero.[77] For example, the express aim of the UK Climate Change Act 2008 is to reach net zero emissions by 2050.[78] A recent study, *United in Science*, states that the net zero emissions needed to stabilize the climate requires both an acceleration in use of non-carbon energy sources and a rapid decline in the global share of fossil fuels in the energy mix.[79] 'Climate positive' is a reference to where a business' activity is absorbing more carbon emissions than it is creating, and thus it is a step better than net zero emissions.

vii. Climate Resilience

'Resilience', as a general concept, is the process of adapting well in the face of adversity, tragedy, and/or significant sources of stress; it is a capacity to 'bounce back' from difficult experiences.[80] Resilience can refer to a system's capacity to generate greater organization around challenges, particularly following a disruption, rather than simply a return to the pre-adversity state.[81] 'Climate resilience' is the ability to anticipate, prepare for, and respond to negative events or disturbances related to climate; and improving climate resilience involves assessing how climate change will create or alter climate-related risks and taking steps to better cope with these risks.[82] Climate resilience involves 'organizations developing adaptive capacity to respond to climate change to better manage the associated risks and seize opportunities, including the ability to respond to transition risks and physical risks. Opportunities include improving efficiency, designing new production processes, and developing new products'.[83]

viii. Circular Economy

The term 'circular economy' is relatively new and still evolving. A working definition for the purposes of this book is that a circular economy envisions a new approach to economic activity, in which the existing paradigm of produce/use/recycle or trash is

[77] Energy and Climate Intelligence Unit, 'Net zero, why is it necessary?' (2019), <https://eciu.net/briefings/net-zero/net-zero-why>.
[78] UK: *Climate Change Act* 2008, <https://www.legislation.gov.uk/ukpga/2008/27>.
[79] *United in Science* (n 70).
[80] American Psychological Association, 'The Road to Resilience' (2015), <http://www.apa.org/helpcenter/road-resilience.aspx>.
[81] Janis Sarra and Kim Berman, '*Ubuntu* as a Tool for Resilience: Arts, Micro Business and Social Justice in South Africa' (2017) 34 Conflict Resolution Quarterly 455 at 457.
[82] Center for Climate and Energy Solutions, 'Business Action on Resilience' (2019), <https://www.c2es.org/content/business-action-on-resilience/> (hereafter C2ES).
[83] TCFD, *Final Report* (n 24) at 7.

replaced with a much more sustainable framework that seeks to use only renewable energy and natural production components that can be returned to the earth after productive use, and designs the reduction and eventual elimination of waste into the system of production. It is aimed at net zero carbon emissions and the use of any production outputs (formerly waste) in new productive activities. The move to a circular economy is explored in Chapter 8.

The circular economy is the inspiration for the book cover, which, rather than a circle, is a Fibonacci Spiral, a logarithmic spiral whose shape is often found in nature. It inspires us to think about moving to net zero carbon emissions, renewable energy, and elimination of waste, each development bringing us closer to avoiding the devastating consequences of global warming and preserving the planet for future generations.

These terms are important to various aspects of climate governance and sustainable finance examined throughout this book. Equally important is to understand, at least on a basic level, what the science tells us about climate change, as this knowledge will also shape governance and finance strategies. The next chapter explores the science as it relates specifically to businesses, although there are many other excellent studies that examine the effects on morbidity and mortality, on water security, and other important impacts.

2
What the Science Tells Us about Climate Change

> Humans have altered the course of evolution. The pervasiveness of evolutionary impacts, from genome structure to dispersal rates, on species throughout the globe should make us take pause. Particularly troubling is the elevated extinction rate associated with human activities, which is disproportionately leading to the loss of large-bodied, specialist, narrow-ranged species, as well as species that are otherwise vulnerable to humans.
>
> Dr Sarah Otto[1]

In 1856—164 years ago—scientist Eunice Foote discovered that carbon dioxide ('CO_2') is a greenhouse gas; she was the first to link increased amounts of the gas to the heating up of our planet.[2] Foote isolated the component gases that make up the atmosphere, thus discovering that the gas that became the hottest in sunlight was carbon dioxide, and that the more CO_2 pumped into the atmosphere, the hotter it gets: 'if . . . at one period of time of the [Earth's] history the air had mixed with a larger proportion than at present, an increased temperature from its own action . . . must have resulted'.[3] Eunice Foote's work was presented to a national gathering of American scientists in 1856; however, Eunice was not allowed to present her own paper because of her gender. A male colleague had to present her findings, because women were not allowed to speak at the national scientific conference.[4] Three weeks later, *Scientific American* enthusiastically published the significance of her work in answering several scientific issues that had baffled her male peers, and her paper was published in the *American Journal of Science*.[5]

More than a century and a half later, the scientific evidence of climate change is now irrefutable. One of the most reliable sources of information is the Intergovernmental Panel on Climate Change ('IPCC'). The IPCC rates its predictions, based on consensus of more than 800 scientists, on levels of confidence. It defines 'confidence' as the robustness of a finding based on the type, amount, quality, and consistency of evidence,

[1] Sarah P Otto, 'Adaptation, Speciation and Extinction in the Anthropocene' (2018) 285 Proceedings of Royal Society 1 at 6, <https://doi.org/10.1098/rspb.2018.2047.

[2] John Perlin, 'A "Foote-Note" on the Hidden History of Climate Science: Why You Have Never Heard of Eunice Foote' (30 July 2019), Resilience, <https://www.resilience.org/stories/2019-07-30/a-foote-note-on-the-hidden-history-of-climate-science-why-you-have-never-heard-of-eunice-foote/>.

[3] Ibid.

[4] Ibid.

[5] Ibid.

From Ideas to Action. Janis Sarra, Oxford University Press (2020). © Janis Sarra. DOI: 10.1093/oso/9780198852308.003.0002.

such as mechanistic understanding, theory, data, models, expert judgment, and on the 'degree of agreement across multiple lines of evidence', usually expressed qualitatively.[6] While the many reports from the IPCC contain a wealth of information on climate change and its impacts, in this book, I address only the trends and impacts for which there are conclusions of 'high confidence' or 'very high confidence'.[7] That means this book highlights the greatest consensus of the scientific community. There are many additional negative impacts of climate change for which there is only consensus of 500 to 700 scientists, which are not discussed in this text; however, it is important to be cognizant of the fact that there is a relatively high degree of consensus on many additional impacts.

A recent report by the Science Advisory Group to the UN Secretary-General's Climate Action Summit documents that levels of the main long-lived greenhouse gases ('GHG'), carbon dioxide (CO_2), methane (CH_4), and nitrous oxide (N_2O) have reached new highs.[8] The last time that Earth's atmosphere contained 400 parts per million ('ppm') CO_2 was about 3–5 million years ago.[9] The amount of ice lost annually from the Antarctic ice sheet increased at least sixfold between 1979 and 2017. The report also found that there has been an overall increase of 26 per cent in ocean acidity since the beginning of the industrial era.[10]

As noted in the introduction, the IPCC reported in late 2018 that human activities have now caused approximately 1.0°C of global warming above pre-industrial levels.[11] While many countries have benefited tremendously from economic activities that generate carbon emissions—our means of transportation, the heating and cooling of our homes and businesses, our use of appliances, electronics and machinery, etc—the

[6] IPCC, 'Annex I: Glossary' in V Masson-Delmotte, P Zhai, H O Pörtner, D Roberts, J Skea, P Shukla, A Pirani, W Moufouma-Okia, C Péan, R Pidcock, S Connors, J B R Matthews, Y Chen, X Zhou, M I Gomis, E Lonnoy, T Maycock, M Tignor, and T Waterfield (eds), *Global Warming of 1.5°C: An IPCC Special Report on the Impacts of Global Warming of 1.5°C above Pre-industrial Levels and Related Global Greenhouse Gas Emission Pathways, in the Context of Strengthening the Global Response to the Threat of Climate Change, Sustainable Development, and Efforts to Eradicate Poverty* (IPCC, 2019) at 546, <https://www.ipcc.ch/site/assets/uploads/sites/2/2019/06/SR15_AnnexI_Glossary.pdf> (hereafter IPCC, *Special Report 2018*). 'Robust' is used here to mean that at least two thirds of climate models show the same sign of changes at the grid point scale, and that differences in large regions are statistically significant, at 178.

[7] IPCC, M Allen, O Dube, W Solecki, F Aragón-Durand, W Cramer, S Humphreys, M Kainuma, J Kala, N Mahowald, Y Mulugetta, R Perez, M Wairiu, and K Zickfeld, 'Chapter 1: Framing and Context' in IPCC, *Special Report 2018*, ibid at 71, <https://www.ipcc.ch/site/assets/uploads/sites/2/2019/05/SR15_Chapter1_Low_Res.pdf> (hereafter IPCC, 'Framing'). Five qualifiers are used to express levels of confidence in key findings, ranging from very low, through low, medium, high, to very high. The assessment of confidence involves at least two dimensions, one being the type, quality, amount, or internal consistency of individual lines of evidence, and the second being the level of agreement between different lines of evidence. In addition, a calibrated language scale is used to communicate assessed probabilities of outcomes, ranging from exceptionally unlikely (<1%), extremely unlikely (<5%), very unlikely (<10%), unlikely (<33%), about as likely as not (33%–66%), likely (>66%), very likely (>90%), extremely likely (>95%) to virtually certain (>99%), normally only applied to findings associated with high or very high confidence.

[8] Science Advisory Group to the UN Secretary-General's Climate Action Summit, 'United in Science' (22 September 2019), <https://www.ipcc.ch/2019/09/22/united-in-science-report-climate-summit/>.

[9] Ibid.

[10] Ibid.

[11] Ibid. IPCC, 'Summary for Policymakers' in IPCC, *Special Report 2018* (n 6) at 7, <https://www.ipcc.ch/site/assets/uploads/sites/2/2018/07/SR15_SPM_version_stand_alone_LR.pdf> (hereafter IPCC, 'Summary for Policymakers).

benefits from industrialization have been unevenly distributed. The individuals, companies, and countries that benefited most historically have also contributed the most to the current climate problem, and so should, arguably, bear greater responsibility.[12] The IPCC observes that one asymmetry is that the worst impacts of climate change tend to fall on those communities least responsible for the problem, within states, between states, and between generations.[13]

Global warming is likely to reach 1.5°C between 2030 and 2052 if it continues to increase at the current rate.[14] Warming from anthropogenic emissions from the pre-industrial period to the present will persist for centuries to millennia, and will continue to cause further long term changes in the climate system, such as sea level rise and associated impacts.[15] This evidence means that whatever we do now to try to remedy our carbon footprints, we will live with the consequences of our past emissions activities for the foreseeable future. However, the degree to which we exacerbate these risks and consequences will depend on implementation of mitigation and adaptation options, which will shape the resultant magnitude and rate of warming, geographic location, levels of development, and vulnerability.[16]

I. Reasons for Businesses to Be Concerned

In 2018, IPCC reported what it referred to as 'five reasons for concern':

> *Unique and threatened systems:* ecological and human systems that have restricted geographic ranges constrained by climate-related conditions and have high endemism or other distinctive properties. Examples include recent changes to Arctic sea ice and warm-water coral reef ecosystems, the Arctic and its Indigenous people, mountain glaciers and biodiversity hotspots.
>
> *Extreme weather events:* risks/impacts to human health, livelihoods, assets and ecosystems from extreme weather events such as heat waves, heavy rain, drought and associated wildfires, and coastal flooding.
>
> *Distribution of impacts:* risks/impacts that disproportionately affect particular groups due to uneven distribution of physical climate change hazards, exposure or vulnerability.
>
> *Global aggregate impacts:* global monetary damage, global-scale degradation and loss of ecosystems and biodiversity.
>
> *Large-scale singular events:* relatively large, abrupt and sometimes irreversible changes in systems that are caused by global warming. Examples include disintegration of the Greenland and Antarctic ice sheets.[17]

[12] IPCC, 'Framing' (n 7) at 55.
[13] Ibid at 55.
[14] Ibid at 6.
[15] Ibid at 7.
[16] Ibid.
[17] Ibid at 18–19.

Regions at disproportionately higher risk include Arctic ecosystems, dryland regions, coastal regions, small island developing states, and least-developed countries.[18] Poverty and disadvantage are expected to increase in a number of populations due to global warming.[19] Future climate-related risks can be reduced by the scaling-up and acceleration of far-reaching, multilevel and cross-sectoral climate mitigation, and by adaptation that is both incremental and transformational.[20] Limiting global warming to 1.5°C is projected to lower the impacts on terrestrial, freshwater, and coastal ecosystems, and to retain more of their services to humans.[21]

The IPCC's 2018 Special Report assesses current knowledge of the environmental, technical, economic, financial, socio-cultural, and institutional dimensions of a 1.5°C warmer world.[22] It reports that the rise in global CO_2 concentration since 2000 is about 20 ppm per decade, which is ten times faster than any sustained rise in CO_2 during the past 800,000 years.[23] The IPCC reports that detailed climate models have confirmed that current concentrations of CO_2 are far exceeding levels observed for at least 650,000 years.[24] The estimated global temperature increase from 1900 to 2100 is between 1.8°C, and 4.0°C, depending on the scenario, with temperatures rising more rapidly on land and in the Artic.[25] Also depending on the scenario, sea level rise this century will be between 7 and 23 inches (18 and 60 cm).[26] The Special Report alerted governments, companies, and investors to the fact that the changes evidenced are more rapid and drastic than previously believed.

Human-induced global warming has already caused multiple observed changes in the climate system, including increased land and ocean temperatures, increased frequency and duration of both land and marine heatwaves, and increased frequency and intensity of hurricanes.[27]

The global mean surface temperature ('GMST') has increased across the globe; however, global warming is not occurring uniformly. Thus, the IPCC observes that there is no single 1.5°C world.[28] Stabilization of an increase in GMST of 1.5°C means that a number of regions will have higher temperatures, affecting the resilience of human and natural systems, with accompanying regional and sub-regional risks.[29] Some of these risks are expected to be long-lasting and irreversible, such as the loss of some

[18] Ibid at 11.

[19] Ibid.

[20] Ibid at 7.

[21] Ibid at 10. Of 105,000 species studied, 9 per cent of insects, 8 per cent of plants, and 4 per cent of vertebrates are projected to lose over half of their climatically determined geographic range for global warming of 1.5°C, compared with double that amount for global warming of 2°C.

[22] Ibid at 53.

[23] Ibid.

[24] W D Nordhaus, *The Climate Casino: Risk, Uncertainty, and Economics for a Warming World* (Yale University Press, 2013) at 47 (hereafter Nordhaus, *Climate Casino*).

[25] Ibid at 47–8.

[26] Ibid at 48.

[27] IPCC, O D Hoegh-Guldberg, J M Taylor, M Bindi, S Brown, I Camilloni, A Diedhiou, R Djalante, K L Ebi, F Engelbrecht, J Guiot, Y Hijioka, S Mehrotra, A Payne, S Seneviratne, A Thomas, R Warren, and G Zhou, 'Chapter 3: Impacts of 1.5°C of Global Warming on Natural and Human Systems' in IPCC, *Special Report 2018* (n 6) at 177, <https://www.ipcc.ch/site/assets/uploads/sites/2/2019/05/SR15_Chapter3_Low_Res.pdf> (hereafter IPCC, 'Impacts of 1.5°C').

[28] Ibid at 177.

[29] Ibid.

ecosystems.[30] The IPCC concludes that in order to minimize the size and duration of these 'over-shooting temperatures', the remaining equivalent CO_2 budget available for emissions is very small, necessitating large, immediate, and unprecedented global efforts to mitigate GHG emissions.[31]

The IPCC also reports that climate models project robust differences in regional climate between present-day and global warming up to 1.5°C, and between 1.5°C and 2°C, depending on variables and regions.[32] Large, widespread differences are expected for temperature extremes. The strongest warming is expected to occur at mid-latitudes in the warm season, with increases of up to 3°C for 1.5°C of global warming, twice the global rate of warming. At high latitudes in the cold season, warming is expected to be three times the rate, with increases of up to 4.5°C at 1.5°C of global warming.[33] Extreme heatwaves are projected to emerge earliest in the tropical regions, becoming widespread at 1.5°C global warming.[34] The IPCC reports that *any* additional increase in global temperature from where we are today will negatively affect human health, including heat-related morbidity and mortality, and ozone-related mortality; and that 'urban heat islands' will amplify the impacts of heatwaves in cities.[35]

We see evidence of this warming already. In 2019, the UK Government's Meteorological Office ('MET Office') forecasted that temperatures could temporarily exceed 1.5°C above pre-industrial levels during the next five years.[36] Europe experienced record heatwaves in the summer of 2019, with many days at 42°C.[37] A group of European scientists observed that such heatwaves are likely to become more frequent and intense, and, absent action on climate change, such heatwaves will rise to frequent average days of 45°C before 2050.[38]

This warming affects businesses in myriad ways. There are significant new costs associated with changes in availability of sourcing and quality of water and other production inputs. Companies are experiencing financial strain from supply chain disruption, particularly where they are sourcing materials from regions or countries hard hit by the physical impacts of climate change. Wildfires have resulted in complete loss of capital assets such as factories and equipment. Extreme temperature changes have increased the costs of cooling in productive processes, as well as costs associated with employee health impacts.[39]

One scientific report suggests that even if the Paris Agreement target of a 1.5°C to 2°C rise in temperature is met:

[30] Ibid.
[31] Ibid.
[32] Ibid.
[33] Ibid.
[34] Ibid.
[35] IPCC, 'Framing' (n 7) at 180.
[36] MET Office, 'Forecast Suggests Earth's Warmest Period on Record' (Press release, 6 February 2019), <https://www.metoffice.gov.uk/about-us/press-office/news/weather-and-climate/2019/forecast-suggestsearths-warmest-period>. The Met Office is the UK's National Meteorological Service.
[37] France24, 'Scientists Link Europe Heat Wave to Man-Made Global Warming' (4 August 2019), <https://www.france24.com/en/20190802-scientists-europe-heat-wave-man-made-global-warming>.
[38] Ibid. See also R Vautard et al, 'Human Contribution to the Record-Breaking July 2019 Heat Wave in Western Europe' (2 August 2019), <https://www.worldweatherattribution.org/human-contribution-to-the-record-breaking-july-2019-heat-wave-in-western-europe/>.
[39] Met Office (n 36) at 6.

> we cannot exclude the risk that a cascade of feedbacks could push the Earth System irreversibly onto a 'Hothouse Earth' pathway. The challenge that humanity faces is to create a 'Stabilized Earth' pathway that steers the Earth System away from its current trajectory toward the threshold beyond which is Hothouse Earth. Creating such a pathway and basin of attraction requires a fundamental change in the role of humans on the planet. This stewardship role requires deliberate and sustained action to become an integral, adaptive part of Earth System dynamics.[40]

The IPCC observes that the extent of climate change effects depends on the pace of economic growth over the next century and beyond. Exposure to multiple and compound climate-related risks is projected to increase with additional global warming, with greater proportions of people exposed and susceptible to poverty in Africa and Asia, and in small island states.[41] Economically disadvantaged populations are particularly at risk.[42]

Mendelsohn et al observe that climate change is predicted to increase the frequency of high-intensity storms in selected ocean basins, depending on the climate model used, doubling economic damage.[43] They note that almost all of the tropical cyclone damage from climate change tends to be concentrated in North America, East Asia, and the Caribbean–Central American region. A North American tropical storm of 74 miles per hour or greater is labelled a hurricane; and the main factor generating hurricanes is warm water surface in oceans. Thus, as the areal extent of warm water increases with global warming, hurricanes will intensify and will increase the areas over which they commence.[44]

These outcomes are not linear in their development. Some decarbonization has occurred. For a number of products, less energy per unit of output is used than in previous years of their production. In addition, the sectors that continue to grow rapidly, such as electronics, use less energy per unit of output than industrial sectors that are shrinking.[45] Another source of decarbonization is the current shift in energy sources towards less carbon-intensive renewable sources.[46]

[40] Will Steffen, Johan Rockström, Katherine Richardson, Timothy Lentond, Carl Folke, Diana Liverman, Colin Summerhayes, Anthony Barnosky, Sarah Cornella, Michel Crucifix, Jonathan Donges, Ingo Fetzer, Steven Lade, Marten Scheffer, Ricarda Winkelmann, and Hans Joachim Schellnhuber, 'Trajectories of the Earth System in the Anthropocene' (August 2018) 115(33) National Academy of Sciences 8252 at 8254, <https://www.pnas.org/content/pnas/115/33/8252.full.pdf> (hereafter Steffen et al).

[41] Ibid.

[42] IPCC, 'Impacts of 1.5°C' (n 27) at 178.

[43] Robert Mendelsohn, Kerry Emanuel, Shun Chonabayashi, and Laura Bakkensen, 'The Impact of Climate Change on Global Tropical Cyclone Damage' (2012) Nature Climate Change, <https://arizona.pure.elsevier.com/en/publications/the-impact-of-climate-change-on-global-tropical-cyclone-damage>.

[44] Nordhaus, *Climate Casino* (n 24) at 117. See also William Nordhaus, 'The Economics of Hurricanes and Implications of Global Warming' (2010) 1 Climate Change Economics 1 (hereafter Nordhaus, Hurricanes); Kerry Emanuel, 'The Dependence of Hurricane Intensity on Climate' (1987) Nature 326 at 484; Thomas Knutso and Robert Tuleya, 'Impact of CO_2-induced warming in Simulated Hurricane Intensity and Precipitation Sensitivity to the Choice of Climate Model and Convective Parameterization' (2004) 17 Journal of Climate 3477–95.

[45] Nordhaus, *Climate Casino* (n 24) at 22.

[46] Ibid at 23.

II. The Physical Impacts of Climate Change Are Already Evident

Climate change impacts are directly related to how human activity is changing the planet. J Nyström et al have observed that the demand for harvestable biomass, food, fuel, and fibre by a growing and increasingly urbanized global human population is placing relentless pressure on the Earth's ecosystems; a demand that has been largely met by converting ecosystems into production ecosystems modified for production of one or a few harvestable species.[47] They note that humans have already altered more than 75 per cent of the world's terrestrial habitats.[48] Four per cent of all productive land has been converted into agricultural areas; two-thirds of all boreal forests are under some form of management, mainly for wood production; and 90 per cent of large industrial fisheries are either overexploited or fully exploited.[49]

William Nordhaus argues that for four specific areas of concern—sea level rise, hurricane intensification, ocean acidification, and loss of biodiversity—'the scale of the changes is at present beyond the capability of human efforts to stop'.[50] However, he points out that uncertainty, and the difficulty in managing it, does not mean that they can be ignored.[51]

i. Impacts on Human Health and Well-Being

A number of direct impacts on human health and well-being due to global warming are manifesting themselves in 2019. These impacts include malnutrition, breathing difficulties due to air pollution, and heat stress due to increasing number and duration of heatwaves.[52] There are direct human health effects related to changes in temperature and precipitation. In addition to tragic loss of human health and life, the impacts on human health and well-being have implications for business in terms of loss of employees, disruption of economic activity, reduced pools of customers, and rising health care costs.[53] Risks for some vector-borne diseases, such as malaria and dengue fever, are projected to increase with warming to 1.5°C, including potential shifts in their geographic range.[54] Some diseases will appear in regions that have never had exposure to them, because the warming allows the diseases to survive and spread. Risks vary based on the disease, region, extent of temperature change, and the degree of adaptation.[55] Within populations, women, the very young, the elderly, and the poor are

[47] J Nyström, J, B Jouffray, A V Norström, B Crona, P Søgaard-Jørgensen, S R Carpenter, Ö Bodin, V Galaz, C Folke, 'Anatomy and Resilience of the Global Production Ecosystem' (2019) 575 Nature, DOI: 10.1038/s41586-019-1712-3.

[48] Ibid.

[49] Ibid.

[50] Nordhaus, *Climate Casino* (n 24) at 144–5.

[51] Ibid at 145.

[52] Ibid at 91, citing IPCC, *Fourth Assessment Report: Climate Change* (2007) at 393.

[53] Ibid.

[54] IPCC, 'Impacts of 1.5°C' (n 27) at 180.

[55] Ibid at 180.

most at risk.[56] Indigenous and racialized communities are also highly at risk because they often live in low-lying lands that are prone to flooding, and the majority live in southern and mid-latitudes in which growing water scarcity and the rise of disease is profoundly increasing their morbidity and mortality.

The Lancet has reported that human health risks are becoming unacceptably high and that a lack of emission reductions threatens human life and health.[57] It observed that vector-borne diseases provide early warning of the compounded and overwhelming impact on public health, creating an unacceptably high level of risk for the current and future health of populations across the world.[58]

Any additional increase in global temperature will negatively affect human health, including heat-related and ozone-related morbidity and mortality.[59] Weather-related disasters in Europe caused a record €283 billion in economic damage in 2017.[60] Europe has experienced extreme heatwaves in four of the last five years.[61] The combination of acute weather events and extreme heat cycles has serious consequences for human health. They include direct impacts such as temperature-related illness and death, and indirect impacts such as illness from water- and food-borne diseases after acute events.[62] Air pollution in the European Union ('EU') now causes almost half a million premature deaths annually, with the main source of GHG emissions and air pollution being fossil fuels, industrial processes, agriculture, and waste.[63] Another study by the European Commission has estimated that the impacts of heatwaves on mortality and morbidity, including respiratory diseases, salmonellosis, and campylobacteriosis, will cause an acceleration of climate change-attributable deaths in Europe to approximately 40,000 additional annual deaths in the period to 2040, and more than 140,000 additional annual deaths in the decades prior to the end of this century.[64] It estimates that achieving net zero GHG emissions, in addition to existing air pollution measures, will reduce premature deaths caused by fine particulate matter by more than 40 per cent and reduce health damage by around €200 billion per annum.

The health impacts will disproportionately affect racialized peoples. The World Health Organization estimates that between 2030 and 2050, climate change will cause approximately 250,000 additional deaths per year from malnutrition, malaria,

[56] Ibid at 17.

[57] UN FCCC and World Health Organization, 'COP 24 Special Report Health & Climate Change' (2019) at 10, 333, N Watts et al, 'The 2018 report of *The Lancet* countdown on health and climate change', (2018) 392 The Lancet, 2479-2514 ((hereafter The Lancet); IPCC, *Fifth Assessment Report* (CUP, 2014).

[58] The Lancet, ibid.

[59] IPCC, 'Impacts of 1.5°C' (n 27) at 180.

[60] European Commission, 'A Clean Planet for All: A European Strategic Long-Term Vision for a Prosperous, Modern, Competitive and Climate Neutral Economy', COM/2018/773 final, (28 November 2018), Communication from the Commission to the European Parliament, the European Council, the European Economic and Social Committee, the Committee of the Regions and the European Investment Bank at 2, <https://ec.europa.eu/clima/policies/strategies/2050_en>.

[61] Ibid.

[62] European Commission, *Human Health Impacts of Climate Change in Europe*, <https://publications.jrc.ec.europa.eu/repository/bitstream/JRC86970/lfna26494enn.pdf> (hereafter *Human Health Impacts*).

[63] IPCC, 'Impacts of 1.5°C' (n 27) at 16.

[64] *Human Health Impacts* (n 62).

diarrhoea, and heat stress, the vast majority of deaths in the global south, given weak health infrastructures.[65]

Steffen et al report that there are numerous indirect effects with human health damaged by ecological disruptions due to climate change, such as displacement of populations following prolonged drought.[66] Poverty and disadvantage have increased with recent warming to 1°C, and the IPCC notes that an important information gap is an understanding of the link of 1.5°C and 2°C of global warming to human migration.[67]

Global warming poses particularly significant risks to human health in urban areas. Seventy-five per cent of natural resource consumption occurs in cities; with cities producing 50 per cent of global waste and 60 to 80 per cent of GHG emissions.[68] The extent of risk depends on human vulnerability and the effectiveness of adaptation in a specific city or region, as well as the existence of effective infrastructure such as energy, water, and transport.[69] Urban heat islands will amplify the impacts of heatwaves in cities.[70] Urban heat islands are created when vegetation is replaced by asphalt and concrete for roads, buildings, and other structures in cities. Such surfaces absorb, rather than reflect, the sun's heat, causing surface temperatures and overall ambient temperatures to rise well above surrounding rural areas.[71] Urban heat islands raise demand for electrical energy for air conditioning in summer, and dependence on fossils for that energy means increases in air pollutants and GHG emissions that are harmful to human health from complex air quality issues such as smog and fine particulate matter.[72]

In the United States, historical discrimination against black Americans in housing markets, referred to as 'redlining', meant that black Americans were relegated to buying or renting homes in city neighbourhoods that were overcrowded, lacked trees or other green space, and were proximate to industrial activity, with the consequence that these neighbourhoods have been exposed to more pollutants and have quickly become urban heat islands with global warming.

The New York City Panel on Climate Change has reported that climate change is already affecting New York and will have a significant impact in the future.[73] It is estimated that without a serious effort at mitigation, the hotter summers projected for 2020 could cause an estimated 30 to 70 per cent increase in heat-related deaths in New York City.[74] New York City, with 8.62 million inhabitants, declared a climate

[65] World Health Organization Regional Office for Africa, 'Facts' (2020), https://www.afro.who.int/health-topics/climate-change.

[66] W Steffen et al, (n 40). . The New York City Panel on Climate Change reported that the average annual temperature in New York City has increased at a rate of 0.79°F per decade over the last thirty years, New York City Panel on Climate Change, 'Special Issue: Advancing Tools and Methods for Flexible Adaptation Pathways and Science Policy Integration' (2019) New York Academy of Sciences (hereafter NPCC).

[67] IPCC, 'Impacts of 1.5°C' (n 27) at 180.

[68] Ellen MacArthur Foundation, 'Circular Economy in Cities: Project Guide' (March 2019), <https://www.ellenmacarthurfoundation.org/assets/downloads/CE-in-Cities-Project-Guide_Mar19.pdf>.

[69] IPCC, 'Impacts of 1.5°C' (n 27) at 180.

[70] Ibid at 11.

[71] UCAR Centre for Science Education, 'Urban Heat Islands' (2019), <https://scied.ucar.edu/longcontent/urban-heat-islands>.

[72] US Environmental Protection Agency, 'Heat Island Impacts' (2019), <https://www.epa.gov/heatislands/heat-island-impacts>.

[73] NPCC (n 66) at para 57.

[74] Ibid at para 61.

emergency in 2019 in an effort to mobilize local and national responses to stall global warming.[75] Cities around the world are doing the same.

ii. Impacts on Food Security and Food Production Systems

The people most affected by the rise in temperature live in low- and middle-income countries, some of which have experienced a decline in food security, which in turn is partly linked to rising migration and poverty.[76] The stability of food supply is projected to decrease as the magnitude and frequency of extreme weather events that disrupt food chains increases.[77] Acute events affect food security, including destruction of crops, loss of potable water, and destruction of fruit bearing trees. Small islands, megacities, and coastal regions are among the most affected.[78] In some instances, the community is barely recovering from one acute event when another hits, such as successive hurricanes in a region. As of 2016, 559 of the 6,190 domesticated breeds of mammals used for food and agriculture, more than 9 per cent, had become extinct and at least 1,000 more are threatened.[79]

As global warming becomes higher than 1.5°C, food scarcity will increase, with studies finding that there is likely to be substantial losses for coastal livelihoods.[80] There is clear evidence that ocean warming and acidification corresponding to 1.5°C of global warming will deplete coastal resources and impact a wide range of economic activities, reducing the productivity of fisheries and aquaculture.[81] Increasing risks to fisheries and aquaculture include impacts on the physiology, survivorship, habitat, reproduction, and disease incidence, as well as the risk of invasive species. The IPCC reports that the survival of a broad range of marine taxonomic groups, ranging from algae to fish, is at high risk. At 1.5°C of global warming, there will be substantially increased risks to marine biodiversity and its function and service to humans.[82]

Land use changes will emerge as critically important features of virtually all mitigation pathways that seek to limit global warming to 1.5°C.[83] The IPCC observes that even limiting global warming to 1.5°C, there will still be net reductions in yields

[75] New York City Council, 'Resolution 864: Resolution Declaring a Climate Emergency and Calling for an Immediate Emergency Mobilization to Restore a Safe Climate' (June 2019), <https://legistar.council.nyc.gov/LegislationDetail.aspx?ID=3940953&GUID=506493D1-9DF1-4289-8893-4AF892557355&Options=ID%7cText%7c&Search=>. See also Scottie Andrew and Saeed Ahmed, 'New York City Declares a Climate Emergency, the First US City with More than a Million Residents to Do So', *CNN News* (27 July 2019), <https://www.cnn.com/2019/06/27/us/new-york-city-declared-climate-emergency-trnd/index.html>.

[76] IPCC, 'Framing' (n 7) at 53.

[77] IPCC, *Special Report on Climate Change and Land, Summary for Policymakers* (7 August 2019) at 16, <https://www.ipcc.ch/site/assets/uploads/2019/08/Edited-SPM_Approved_Microsite_FINAL.pdf> (hereafter IPCC, Special Report on Climate Change and Land).

[78] Ibid.

[79] S Diaz et al, *The Global Assessment Report on Biodiversity and Ecosystem Services*, Intergovernmental Science-Policy Platform on Biodiversity and Ecosystem Services (May 2019) at 11, <https://ipbes.net/system/tdf/inline/files/ipbes_global_assessment_report_summary_for_polciymakers.pdf?file=1&type=node&id=36213>(hereafter ISPPBES).

[80] IPCC, 'Impacts of 1.5°C' (n 27) at 180.

[81] Ibid at 178.

[82] IPCC, 'Framing' (n 7) 10.

[83] IPCC, 'Impacts of 1.5°C' (n 27) at 180.

and quality of maize, rice, wheat, and other cereal crops, particularly in sub-Saharan Africa, Southeast Asia, and Central and South America.[84] In addition to growing food scarcity, many communities that depend on agriculture for their livelihoods are being deeply affected.

The deployment of carbon removal strategies could assist in controlling losses in food production, if implemented in a manner than helps restore natural ecosystems.[85] To date, however, diminished food production systems and increasing food insecurity are growing causes for concern in many regions globally.

The Intergovernmental Science-Policy Platform on Biodiversity and Ecosystem Services ('ISPPBES') notes that although food production today is sufficient to satisfy global needs, an estimated 11 per cent of the world's population is undernourished, and diet-related disease drives 20 per cent of premature mortality.[86] Once food production becomes incapable of meeting global needs, these impacts will be exacerbated.

iii. Impacts on Oceans and Their Ecosystems

In addition to the impacts of global warming on oceans as the habitat for food and thus key to food security, global warming is also seriously affecting oceans' capacity as carbon sinks. The accelerated rate in sea level rise as shown by altimeter satellites is attributed to the increased rate of ocean warming and land ice melt from the Greenland and West Antarctica ice sheets.[87]

To date, the ocean has taken up more than 90 per cent of the excess heat in the climate system; and by 2100, the ocean will take up two to four times more heat than between 1970 and the present, if global warming is limited to 2°C, and up to five to seven times more at higher emissions.[88] Ocean warming reduces mixing between water layers and, as a consequence, the supply of oxygen and nutrients for marine life. The ocean also absorbs nearly 25 per cent of the annual emissions of anthropogenic CO_2, which helps to alleviate the impacts of climate change on the planet; however, it also increases the acidity of the ocean.[89] The level of ocean acidification due to increasing CO_2 concentrations is amplifying the adverse effects of warming, impacting the growth, development, survival, and thus abundance of a broad range of species. The absorption of anthropogenic carbon dioxide and resultant ocean acidification and

[84] Ibid at 179–80.

[85] Ibid at 180.

[86] ISPPBES (n 79) at 10.

[87] Science Advisory Group of the UN Climate Action Summit 2019, *United in Science*, World Meteorological Organization (22 September 2019) at 5, <https://ane4bf-datap1.s3-eu-west-1.amazonaws.com/wmocms/s3fs-public/ckeditor/files/United_in_Science_ReportFINAL_0.pdf?XqiG0yszsU_sx2vOehOWpCOkm9RdC_gN> (hereafter United in Science).

[88] IPCC, *Special Report on the Ocean and Cryosphere in a Changing Climate* (September 2019) at 1–8, <https://www.ipcc.ch/site/assets/uploads/sites/3/2019/11/SROCC_FinalDraft_FullReport.pdf> (hereafter IPCC, *Cryosphere*).

[89] Science Advisory Group of the UN Climate Action Summit 2019, *United in Science*, World Meteorological Organization (22 September 2019) at 5, <https://ane4bf-datap1.s3-eu-west-1.amazonaws.com/wmocms/s3fs-public/ckeditor/files/United_in_Science_ReportFINAL_0.pdf?XqiG0yszsU_sx2vOehOWpCOkm9RdC_gN>.

changes to carbonate chemistry that the IPCC reports are unprecedented for at least the last 65 million years.[90]

Ocean ecosystems are already experiencing large-scale damage and other changes. The IPCC reports that critical thresholds are expected to be reached at 1.5°C of warming.[91] Currently, changes to water temperatures are expected to drive some species such as plankton and fish to relocate to higher latitudes and cause novel ecosystems to assemble.[92] Other ecosystems such as coral reefs and kelp forests are less able to move and are projected to experience high rates of mortality.[93] One example is the substantial evidence that 70 to 90 per cent of warm tropical coral reefs that exist today will disappear completely even if global warming is constrained to 1.5°C.[94]

The ISPPBES published a report in 2019 documenting that marine plastic pollution has increased tenfold since 1980, affecting at least 267 species, including 86 per cent of marine turtles, 44 per cent of seabirds, and 43 per cent of marine mammals, which in turn affect humans through food chains.[95] Plastics emit powerful GHG as they degrade, contributing to climate change.[96] Plastic microparticles and nanoparticles are entering food webs, with negative consequences for human health.[97]

There is substantial risk of declining ocean productivity and damage to ecosystems at low latitudes, and changes to ocean chemistry such as acidification, hypoxia, and dead zones.[98] All of these outcomes will be considerably magnified at 2°C of warming.

iv. Impacts on Land and Wetland Ecosystems

The *Special Report on Climate Change and Land* by the IPCC in 2019 demonstrates how keeping global warming to well below 2°C can be achieved only by reducing GHG emissions in all sectors, including land and food.[99] Human use directly affects more than 70 per cent of the global ice-free land surface.[100] Land is both a source and a sink of GHG and plays a key role in the exchange of energy, water, and aerosols between the land surface and atmosphere.[101] One study showed that of 105,000 species studied, 8 per cent of plants and 4 per cent of vertebrates are projected to lose over half of their climatically determined geographic range at global warming of 1.5°C.[102]

[90] IPCC, 'Impacts of 1.5°C' (n 27) at 178.
[91] Ibid at 179.
[92] Ibid.
[93] Ibid.
[94] Ibid.
[95] ISPPBES (n 79) at 13, 28.
[96] Sarah-Jeanne Royer, Sara Ferrón, Samuel Wilson, and David Karl, 'Production of Methane and Ethylene from Plastic in the Environment', University of Hawaii at Mānoa School of Ocean and Earth Science and Technology Study (1 August 2018), <https://journals.plos.org/plosone/article?id=10.1371/journal.pone.0200574>.
[97] ISPPBES (n 79) at 29.
[98] IPCC, 'Impacts of 1.5°C' (n 27) at 179.
[99] IPCC, Special Report on Climate Change and Land (n 77).
[100] Ibid at 2.
[101] Ibid.
[102] J T Houghton, Y Ding, D J Griggs, M Noguer, P J van der Linden, X Dai, K Maskell, and C A Johnson (eds), *Climate Change 2001: The Scientific Basis. Contribution of Working Group I to the Third Assessment Report of the Intergovernmental Panel on Climate Change* (CUP, 2001) (hereafter Houghton et al).

Depending on choices in future land use resulting from mitigation choices, there is a high likelihood of reduced food production and ecosystem diversity.[103] The IPCC reports risks of local species losses, and, consequently, risks of extinction.[104] There are risks associated with forest fires, extreme weather events, and the spread of invasive species, pests, and diseases.[105] The European Commission has observed that many terrestrial, freshwater, and marine species have already relocated, and that plant and animal species are at increased risk of extinction if global average temperatures continue to rise unchecked.[106] Yet, if we can constrain global warming, it could benefit terrestrial and wetland ecosystems and help preserve their services to humans.[107]

The ISPPBES reports that a million species of animals and plants are at risk of extinction.[108] As pollinator species disappear, reduced pollination may seriously affect crop productivity and the availability of medicines that benefit from such crops or other sources of nature. For example, an estimated 4 billion people rely on natural medicines for their health care; 70 per cent of drugs used for cancer are natural or products inspired by nature; and 75 per cent of global food crop types, such as coffee, cocoa, and almonds, rely on animal pollination.[109] The ISPPBES study revealed that land degradation has reduced productivity in 23 per cent of the global terrestrial area, and between US $235 billion and US $577 billion in annual global crop output is at risk as a result of pollinator loss.[110]

Reductions in the diversity of cultivated crops, crop wild relatives, and domesticated breeds mean that agroecosystems are less resilient against future climate change, pests, and pathogens. The ISPPBES reports that nearly one fifth of the Earth's surface is at risk of plant and animal invasions, impacting native species, ecosystem functions, and nature's contributions to people, in turn, negatively affecting economies.[111]

Since 1970, over 85 per cent of wetland area has been lost and an estimated one million species already face extinction, many within decades, unless action is taken to reduce the intensity of drivers of biodiversity loss.[112]

Natural CO_2 sinks, such as vegetation and oceans, currently remove approximately half of all emissions from human activities, but will become less efficient at doing so. Thus, there is urgent need to reduce deforestation and expand natural CO_2 sinks, particularly forests that can be improved by better management and habitat restoration.[113]

Increases in frequency and intensity of acute events has adversely impacted terrestrial ecosystems, as well as contributed to desertification and land degradation in many regions.[114] At the regional scale, changing land conditions can accentuate warming

[103] IPCC, 'Impacts of 1.5°C' (n 27) at 179.
[104] Ibid.
[105] Ibid.
[106] European Commission, 'Climate Change Consequences' (2019), <https://ec.europa.eu/clima/change/consequences_en>.
[107] IPCC, 'Impacts of 1.5°C' (n 27) at 179.
[108] ISPPBES (n 79) at 10.
[109] Ibid.
[110] Ibid at 11.
[111] Ibid.
[112] Ibid at 12.
[113] Global Carbon Project, 'Global Carbon Budget 2018' (5 September 2018), <https://www.globalcarbonproject.org/carbonbudget/>.
[114] IPCC, 'Impacts of 1.5°C' (n 27) at 251.

and affect the intensity, frequency, and duration of extreme events.[115] Climate change creates additional stresses on land, exacerbating existing risks to livelihoods, biodiversity, human health, ecosystem health, infrastructure, and food systems. Cascading impacts on multiple systems and sectors varies across regions.[116] Asia and Africa have the highest number of people vulnerable to increased desertification; and the tropics and subtropics are projected to be most vulnerable to crop yield decline.[117]

Land degradation resulting from the combination of sea level rise and more intense cyclones is jeopardizing lives and livelihoods in cyclone prone areas, and climate change is amplifying environmentally induced migration both within countries and across borders.[118]

There is also a deep interconnection between impacts of climate change on the ocean and on land systems. The IPCC reports that 'impacts associated with sea level rise and changes to the salinity of coastal groundwater, increased flooding and damage to infrastructure, are projected to be critically important in vulnerable environments, such as small islands, low-lying coasts and deltas.'[119] Small islands are projected to experience multiple interrelated risks at 1.5°C of global warming, including coastal flooding, loss of habitable land, infrastructures, and assets, and risks across marine ecosystems.[120]

The Solomon Islands are a case in point. Cyclones and other storms are increasing in frequency and intensity. Sea level rise from climate change has meant that many of the population of 560,000 people are being forced to leave their homes permanently.[121] Some of the islands are now permanently underwater due to sea level rise. That means families and entire tribes moving off islands that they have inhabited since the seventeenth century.[122] Pressure on the remaining land is causing tensions between local tribes that have not had to share land in the past. Salt water intrusion into fresh water supplies is deeply affecting the islands that are not yet underwater, and has destroyed the capacity to grow crops such as bananas and sweet potatoes.[123] The stones that the residents are using to try to reclaim land and build sea walls are killing the fish because the stones have been their natural feeding grounds.[124]

China's 'Third National Assessment Report on Climate Change' found that China's vulnerability to sea level rise is especially acute, as more than 550 million people live in China's coastal provinces on lands that face considerable risk of becoming uninhabitable.[125]

115 Ibid at 11.

116 Ibid at 15.

117 Ibid at 17.

118 Ibid.

119 *United in Science* (n 87) at 181.

120 IPCC, 'Impacts of 1.5°C' (n 27) at 181.

121 DW News, 'Climate Change Drives Solomon Islands' People of the Sea Ashore', <https://www.dw.com/en/climate-change-drives-solomon-islands-people-of-the-sea-ashore/a-40777201>.

122 Ibid.

123 Anna Watanabe, 'Solomon Island Villages Shrinking Due to Rising Sea Levels', *Kyodo News* (7 November 2017), <https://english.kyodonews.net/news/2017/11/9ef20f2d3394-focus-solomon-island-villages-shrinking-due-to-rising-sea-levels.html>.

124 Ibid.

125 David Sandalow, 'Guide to Chinese Climate Policy 2019', Columbia Center on Global Energy Policy (18 September 2019) at 26, <https://energypolicy.columbia.edu/sites/default/files/file-uploads/Guide%20to%20Chinese%20Climate%20Policy_2019.pdf>, citing Liu Zhenhe, 'Main Conclusions

Accumulated carbon in vegetation and soils is at risk of sink reversal, triggered by disturbances such as flood, drought, or pest outbreaks.[126] 'Sink reversal' means that carbon sinks that have stored carbon are now releasing it into the atmosphere. For example, NASA reports that record-breaking wildfires in Canada's Northwest Territories in 2014 burned more than 7 million acres of boreal forest and released nearly 104 million tonnes of carbon into the atmosphere.[127] Boreal forests in North America, Europe, and Canada store 30 to 40 per cent of all land-based carbon in the world. Canadian and US scientists from NASA's Earth Science Division took soil samples from more than 200 locations from the Canadian fires, finding that for old forests more than seventy years old and forests in wet locations, a thick layer of organic matter in the soil protected the oldest carbon, called 'legacy carbon'.[128] Yet in younger, drier forests, the shallower soil organic matter layer allowed fires to reach the legacy carbon, which had not previously burned in prior cycles of burn and regrowth, releasing it into the atmosphere. The study concluded that if bigger and more frequent fires start burning legacy carbon, these forests could start releasing more carbon than they store.[129]

In other words, acute events can release substantial amounts of carbon back into the atmosphere. Moreover, carbon sinks such as reforestation, agroforestry, soil carbon management on mineral soils, or carbon storage in harvested wood products do not continue to sequester carbon indefinitely.[130] When vegetation matures or when vegetation and soil carbon reservoirs reach saturation, the annual removal of CO_2 from the atmosphere declines towards zero.

Sea level rise also directly impacts the productive uses of land. For example, New York City is exceptionally vulnerable to sea level rise due to its long coastline and its large floodplain that is home to New York residents.[131] It has experienced loss of capital assets, disruption of business due to intrusion from sea level rise, and a huge increase in urban flooding that its sewer system has not had the capacity to effectively handle. After Hurricane Sandy, New York launched a US $20 billion multilayered investment programme in climate resiliency, including constructing levees and sea walls, elevating facilities and streets, and waterproofing and hardening infrastructure. The City is planning to enlarge existing storm and wastewater storage facilities, as well as associated infrastructure and pumping facilities, to prevent flooding in low-lying areas that are vulnerable to rising seas or increasingly severe downpours.[132] It filed a lawsuit against major fossil fuel companies for their contribution to these climate impacts, as discussed in Chapter 7.

of China's 3rd National Assessment on Climate Change,' 360doc.com (13 January 2016); Wang Jing, <第三次气候变化国家评估报告> 发布 (hereafter China's Third National Assessment on Climate Change Released) ScienceNet.cn (22 November 2015).

[126] IPCC, 'Impacts of 1.5°C' (n 27) at 219.

[127] Jessica Merzdorf, 'Boreal Forest Fires Could Release Deep Soil Carbon', NASA (22 August 2019), <https://climate.nasa.gov/news/2905/boreal-forest-fires-could-release-deep-soil-carbon/>.

[128] Ibid.

[129] Ibid.

[130] IPCC, 'Impacts of 1.5°C' (n 27) at 219.

[131] NPCC (n 66) at para 117.

[132] Ibid at para 119.

In addition to the physiological changes, there are direct economic consequences to changes in land ecosystems. Global warming has already affected tourism, with increased risks projected for seasonal tourism including sun, beach, and snow sports vacation destinations.[133] The downside risks for coastal tourism, particularly in subtropical and tropical regions, will increase with temperature-related degradation such as storms, heat extremes, and the resultant loss of beach and coral reef assets.[134]

v. Impacts on Fresh Water Resources

Fresh water is a fundamental resource for natural ecosystems and human livelihoods, and access to it is considered a universal human right.[135] About one half of the world's population is projected to face water shortages by 2030, when demand will exceed water supply by an estimated 40 per cent.[136] The global fresh water supply crisis poses a serious challenge to society, the World Economic Forum suggesting that it is the greatest economic challenge.[137] A third of the world's largest groundwater systems are already in distress.[138]

'Water scarcity' is the lack of sufficient available water resources to meet the demands of water usage. As of September 2019, 2.3 billion people already live in regions with water scarcity.[139] Climate change is resulting in increased frequency and magnitude of droughts in some regions.[140] The effects of climate change will intensify the risk of droughts, while at the same time, water use has grown at more than twice the rate of population increase globally, and it is still increasing in all sectors.[141] Increased water use by humans has profound negative effects on aquatic ecosystems and their species, causing severe environmental imbalance.[142] Increasing water scarcity is affecting human health and food security globally.

133 IPCC, 'Impacts of 1.5°C' (n 27) at 180.

134 Ibid.

135 United Nations Committee on Economic, Social and Cultural Rights, General Comment No 15, 'The Right to Water', UN Econ and Soc Council (2003) Geneva, Switzerland.

136 UN, 'Water Facts and Figures' (2019), <http://www.unwater.org/water-facts>.

137 World Economic Forum consistently ranks water crisis as top long-term risk in terms of impact in its report, see World Economic Forum, 'The Global Risks Report 2019', <www3.weforum.org/docs/WEF_Global_Risks_Report_2019.pdf>.

138 A S Richey et al, 'Quantifying renewable groundwater stress with GRACE' (16 June 2015), <https://doi.org/10.1002/2015WR017349>; A S Richey et al, 'Uncertainty in Global Groundwater Storage Estimates in a Total Groundwater Stress Framework' (16 June 2015), <https://doi.org/10.1002/2015WR017351>.

139 World Data Lab, 'Water Scarcity Clock' (14 September 2019), funded by the *Deutsche Gesellschaft für Internationale Zusammenarbeit* ('Federal Ministry for Economic Co-operation and Development of Germany) and International Institute of Applied Systems Analysis', <https://worldwater.io/?utm_source=google&utm_medium=search&utm_campaign=Waterscarcityclock&utm_term=sitelink&campaignid=6444167483&adgroupid=77198318295&adid=376808482554&gclid=Cj0KCQjwn_LrBRD4ARIsAFEQFKsEV41SIAb2FsyXWOwJ-I5dIMKu99iPgfvhXlj_zkd7w4NPLOfQak0aApelEALw_wcB> (hereafter World Data Lab).

140 IPCC, 'Impacts of 1.5°C' (n 27) at 179.

141 Ibid.

142 Ibid.

Lack of access to safe water has wide-ranging health implications. Eighty per cent of all illnesses in developing countries are attributable to unsafe drinking water and the spread of waterborne diseases.[143]

The CDP (formerly the Carbon Disclosure Initiative) Global Water Report in 2019 found that companies are not moving fast enough to reduce water consumption and responsibly manage water use within their operations.[144] It notes that with 19 per cent of water withdrawals coming from industry, and a further 70 per cent from agricultural supply chains, companies have a massive role in meeting global water goals. Seventy-five per cent of risks reported are physical, relating to water scarcity and declining water quality.[145] Companies are withdrawing more water year-on-year. Between 2015 and 2018, there has been an almost 50 per cent increase in the number of companies reporting higher water withdrawals, most pronounced in Asia and Latin America, particularly in the food and beverage, agriculture, manufacturing, and mineral extraction sectors.[146]

As water crises worsen, 'high impact companies are increasingly exposed to risks that could threaten their reputations, revenue, and financial stability'.[147] For example, for pharmaceuticals companies, fresh water plays a critical role as a reagent, solvent, and cleaning agent.[148] These companies often require high quality and ultra-pure water in production, requiring cooling systems that can vary in their water and energy efficiency.[149] In the agricultural sector, which accounts for almost 70 per cent of the world's water consumption, water is essential for growing crops and raising animals, and is used in the washing, boiling, packaging, and transportation of agricultural commodities.[150]

Water is also essential to the exploration, production, and refining of fossil fuels in most parts of the value chain, from construction to drilling, pumping, treatment, and cooling.[151] The International Energy Agency reports that coal production is one of the most-water intensive methods of generating electricity and accounts for 50 per cent of recent growth in fresh water use.[152] A major risk within the industry is water pollution, which can arise from spills, cross-aquifer mixing, drill muds, and cuttings, pollution of surface water and groundwater through water discharge, and contamination by pump leakages and oil spillages during transportation.[153] Lack of fresh water resources will place considerable pressures on these economic activities.

Other industries will also be affected by scarcity of fresh water resources. Light manufacturing includes the manufacture of metal parts, which has a water-intensive supply chain via mining; the manufacture of plastic and other products, with water

143 World Data Lab (n 139).

144 CDP, *Treading Water, Corporate Responses to Rising Water Challenges*, <https://www.cdp.net/en/research/global-reports/global-water-report-2018> (hereafter CDP, *Treading Water*).

145 Ibid at 4.

146 Ibid at 4.

147 Ibid at 11.

148 Ibid.

149 Ibid at 22.

150 Ibid at 23.

151 Ibid at 24.

152 Ibid.

153 Ibid.

used primarily for cooling and cleaning; and ultra-pure water required for some processes.[154] Auto manufacturing uses water for surface treatment and coating, paint spray booths, washing, rinsing, hosing, cooling, air-conditioning systems, and boilers. It also has a water intensive supply chain, as water is required to produce many auto components.[155] The chemicals manufacturing sector is also highly water intensive. Water is used for cooling purposes, as a raw material, in cleaning, transport, as a solvent, and as part of the final product.[156] When one thinks about impacts of climate change on fresh water sources, usually one thinks of drinking water, not the myriad economic activities that are dependent on access to clean water.

The 2018–2019 water crisis in South Africa involved a period of severe water shortage in the Western Cape region, particularly in Cape Town, where water levels dropped to between 15 per cent and 30 per cent of total dam capacity. The city of Cape Town implemented significant water restrictions to curb water usage. Its residents were required to limit themselves to 50 litres of water each day to avoid 'day zero'. These measures included completing an entire shower in sixty seconds, deferring laundry, and flushing their toilets only once a day.[157] Cape Town succeeded in reducing its daily water usage by more than half to around 500 million litres per day in March 2018.[158]

This severe water shortage is not confined to developing countries. The chief executive of the UK Environment Agency has warned that within twenty-five years, England will not have enough water to meet demand, observing that the country is facing an existential threat to water security.[159] With industry, power generation companies, and agri-businesses accounting for 50 per cent of water consumption in England and Wales, companies have a massive responsibility to help ensure a sustainable supply of fresh water.[160] In addition to finding ways to seriously reduce water consumption, rainwater and storm water retention technologies would relieve pressure on municipal infrastructure processing of water.

Since 2018, the CDP has asked companies to disclose their water usage and targets for usage. It is collecting metrics on water usage company-wide, by business activity, product, facility, country-level, and basin-level. It is asking companies to describe how they set targets for reduction of water usage. An analysis of the nearly 800 publicly held

[154] Ibid at 27.

[155] Ibid.

[156] Ibid.

[157] G York, 'Cape Town Residents Become "guinea Pigs for the World" with Water-Conservation Campaign', *The Globe and Mail* (8 March 2018), <https://www.theglobeandmail.com/news/world/cape-town-residents-become-guinea-pigs-for-the-world-with-water-conservationcampaign/article38257004/>.

[158] Z Cassim, 'Cape Town Could Be the First Major City in the World to Run Out of Water', *USA Today* (19 January 2019), <https://www.usatoday.com/story/news/world/2018/01/19/cape-town-could-first-major-city-run-out-water/1047237001>.

[159] Roger Harrabin, 'Climate Change: Water Shortages in England "Within 25 Years"', *BBC News* (19 March 2019), <https://www.bbc.com/news/uk-47620228>.

[160] Cate Lamb 'As Global Water Crisis Looms, Business as Usual Is No Longer an Option', Ethical Corporation (21 March 2019), <http://www.ethicalcorp.com/global-water-crisis-looms-business-usual-no-longer-option>.

companies that responded to CDP's investor request for water information in 2018 found that only 42 per cent have water targets at both the company and site level.[161]

vi. Impacts on the Cryosphere

The 'cryosphere' is defined as the components of the Earth System at, and below, the land and ocean surface that are frozen, including snow cover, glaciers, ice sheets, ice shelves, icebergs, sea ice, lake ice, river ice, permafrost, and seasonally frozen ground.[162] The IPCC reports that sea ice provides many critical functions. It provides essential habitat for polar species and supports the livelihoods of people in the Arctic, including Indigenous peoples; regulates climate by reflecting solar radiation; inhibits ocean-atmosphere exchange of heat, momentum, and gases; supports global deep ocean circulation via dense (cold and salty) water formation; and can aid (or hinder) transportation and travel routes in the polar regions.[163] As noted above, warming and changes in ocean chemistry are already disrupting species throughout the ocean food web, with impacts on marine ecosystems and people that depend on them.

Even if global warming is limited to well below 2°C, around 25 per cent of the near-surface permafrost (3–4 metre depth) will thaw by 2100. If GHG emissions continue to increase, potentially 70 per cent of near-surface permafrost could be lost. Arctic and boreal permafrost hold large amounts of organic carbon, almost twice the carbon in the atmosphere; thus, there is potential of significantly increased concentration of GHG in the atmosphere if they thaw.[164] The IPCC observes that it is unclear whether there is already a net release of carbon dioxide or methane due to the ongoing thaw of the Arctic permafrost.

III. Climate Tipping Points and Implications for Business

The overwhelming majority of the scientific community has concluded that if we reach 1.5°C above pre-industrial levels, we run a greater risk of passing through climate 'tipping points', thresholds beyond which certain impacts can no longer be avoided even if temperatures are later reduced.[165] Scientists have concluded that there may be as few as ten years to turn around the trajectory of global warming, without which we will have amplified risks of drought, floods, extreme heat, and poverty for hundreds of millions of people, in many cases causing irreversible and permanent harms.[166]

[161] Christina Copeland, 'Think Globally, Act Locally: New Guidance for Companies on Sustainable Water Use', CDP (20 August 2019), <https://www.cdp.net/en/articles/water/think-globally-act-locally-new-guidance-for-companies-on-sustainable-water-use>.

[162] Ibid at 1–9.

[163] IPCC, *Cryosphere* (n 88) at 7–8.

[164] Ibid.

[165] IPCC, 'Summary for Policymakers' (n 11) at 20: Pathways reflecting current nationally stated mitigation ambition until 2030 are broadly consistent with cost-effective pathways that result in a global warming of about 3°C by 2100. See also Jonathan Watts, 'We Have 12 Years to Limit Climate Change Catastrophe, Warns UN', *The Guardian* (8 October 2018), <https://www.theguardian.com/environment/2018/oct/08/global-warming-must-not-exceed-15c-warns-landmark-un-report>.

[166] IPCC, 'Summary for Policymakers', ibid at 20.

The IPCC defines a 'tipping point' as an abrupt and irreversible change in the climate system; noting that while the precise levels of climate change sufficient to trigger a tipping point remain uncertain, the risks associated with crossing multiple tipping points increases with rising temperature.[167] The threshold tipping point in the climate system, when exceeded, will lead to large changes in the state of the system.[168] There is growing recognition that climate impacts are hitting harder and sooner than climate assessments indicated even a decade ago.[169] The World Meteorological Association has stressed that if we are to avoid tipping points and meet the Paris Agreement goals, we need to take immediate and deep decarbonization action, complemented by ambitious policy measures that will protect and enhance carbon sinks and biodiversity.[170]

Tipping points are not always abrupt. For example, at the same level of temperature rise as currently, a large part of the Greenland ice sheet and/or West Antarctic ice sheet will inevitably melt; but the ice sheet itself may persist for many centuries.[171] The tipping point is gradually surpassed, beyond which Earth cannot recover. Some tipping elements, like the collapse of ecosystems, are irreversible. Houghton et al report that the Greenland ice sheet, consisting of layers of compressed snow from more than 100,000 years, contains, in its ice, today's most valuable record of past climates. The Greenland Ice Sheet has experienced record melting, and if the entire ice were to melt, global sea levels would rise 7.2 metres (24 feet).[172]

Nordhaus suggests that climate tipping points include the collapse of large ice sheets and large-scale changes in ocean circulation, observing that melting snow and ice exposes more land and ocean surface, which makes the earth darker, in turn absorbing more sunlight, warming the surface, and amplifying the greenhouse effect, known as the 'albedo effect'.[173]

Tipping points for impacts on natural and human systems from global warming have already been observed, with many land and ocean ecosystems compromised. A recent study found that since 1970, the number of birds in the United States and Canada has fallen by 29 per cent or nearly 3 billion.[174] The authors conclude that this loss of bird abundance signals an urgent need to address threats to future avifaunal collapse and associated loss of ecosystem integrity, function, and services.[175]

Another tipping point will be sea level rise that triggers massive loss of inhabitable land. A recent study documented that for a low emissions scenario, 190 million people currently occupy land below projected high tide lines for 2100.[176] Under the current

[167] IPCC, *Fifth Assessment Report* (CUP 2014).
[168] Ibid.
[169] *United in Science* (n 87) at 5.
[170] Ibid at 6.
[171] Houghton et al (n 102).
[172] Ibid.
[173] Nordhaus, *Climate Casino* (n 24) at 44, 56.
[174] Kenneth Rosenberg et al, 'Decline of the North American Avifauna' (4 October 2019) 366(6461) Science 120–4.
[175] Ibid.
[176] Scott A Kulp and Benjamin H Strauss, 'New Elevation Data Triple Estimates of Global Vulnerability to Sea-Level Rise and Coastal Flooding', *Nature Communications*, <https://www.nature.com/articles/s41467-019-12808-z> (hereafter Kulp and Strauss). See also Climate Central, 'Flooded Future: Global Vulnerability to Sea Level Rise Worse than Previously Understood' (29 October 2019), <https://climatecentral.org/pdfs/2019CoastalDEMReport.pdf>.

high emission scenario, up to 630 million people live on land below projected annual flood levels for 2100.[177] More than 70 per cent of the total number of people worldwide currently living on land at risk of becoming inhabitable due to climate impacts are in eight Asian countries: China, Bangladesh, India, Japan, Vietnam, Indonesia, Thailand, and the Philippines.[178] More than 600 million individuals having to relocate due to sea level rise alone seems almost unfathomable. The number of businesses that will have to be relocated has not yet been calculated, but the implications for business are huge. They include land use, loss of fixed capital assets such as production plants and office buildings, loss of access to power for production processes, loss of local populations to employ, loss of customers, and loss of infrastructure to transport production inputs and to deliver products to market.

IV. Mitigation is an Essential Part of a Climate Governance Strategy

Climate change mitigation includes efforts to reduce or prevent emission of GHG using new technologies and renewable energies, improving energy efficiency, and changing management practices and consumer behaviour.[179]

Mitigation pathways are typically designed to reach a predefined climate target.[180] There are a wide range of mitigation strategies. The International Energy Agency ('IEA') reports that to meet global emission-reduction goals, countries will need to transition a major percentage of their energy generation to low emission alternatives such as wind, solar, wave, tidal, hydro, geothermal, nuclear, biofuels, and carbon capture and storage.[181]

Other mitigation strategies include preserving and restoring natural ecosystems such as peatland, coastal lands, and forests, biodiversity conservation, fire management, and soil management, all of which have the potential to make positive contributions to sustainable development.[182] Sustainable land and forest management can prevent and reduce land degradation, maintain land productivity, and sometimes reverse the adverse impacts of climate change on land degradation. The IPCC reports that reducing and reversing land degradation, at scales from individual farms to entire watersheds, can provide cost effective, immediate, and long term benefits to communities, as well as supporting several UN Sustainable Development Goals.[183]

177 Kulp and Strauss, ibid.

178 Ibid.

179 UN, 'Environment Programme 2019', <https://www.unenvironment.org/explore-topics/climate-change/what-we-do/mitigation>.

180 IPCC, J Rogelj, D Shindell, K Jiang, S Fifita, P Forster, V Ginzburg, C Handa, H Kheshgi, S Kobayashi, E Kriegler, L Mundaca, R Séférian, and M V Vilariño, 'Chapter 2: Mitigation Pathways Compatible with 1.5°C in the Context of Sustainable Development' in IPCC, *Special Report 2018* (n 6) at 98, https://www.ipcc.ch/site/assets/uploads/sites/2/2019/05/SR15_Chapter2_Low_Res.pdf.

181 IEA, 'Global Energy Investment Down 8% in 2015 with Flows Signaling Move towards Cleaner Energy' (14 September 2016), <https://www.iea.org/newsroom/news/2016/september/global-energy-investment-down-8-in-2015-with-flows-signalling-move-towards-clean.html>.

182 IPCC, *Special Report on Climate Change and Land* (n 77) at 23.

183 Ibid at 24.

Sustainable forest management can maintain or enhance forest carbon stocks, including by transferring carbon to wood products, thus addressing the issue of carbon sink saturation.[184] The IPCC also notes that where wood carbon is transferred to harvested wood products, the products can store carbon over the long term. Where biomass is used for energy as a mitigation strategy, the carbon is released back into the atmosphere more quickly.[185]

Mitigation is essential because adapting to climate change will not in itself allow the planet to survive. Also of note is that the benefits of mitigation are shared globally, in the sense that it reduces carbon emissions overall, while adaptation is primarily beneficial locally. Moreover, we need to act now for mitigation to have meaningful effect in the long term. Even if emissions were reduced to zero now, Earth System model simulations show that global mean surface temperature will remain approximately constant for many centuries following cessation of GHG emissions.[186] In effect, regardless of when emissions cease, the current global mean surface temperature will continue to increase and then remain for the subsequent millennium.[187] Many scientists have concluded that aggressive mitigation efforts would need to achieve net zero CO_2 emissions within the decade, and even then, temperatures are likely to remain below the 1.5°C threshold only if the actual geophysical response ends up being towards the low end of the currently estimated uncertainty range.[188] The IPCC observes that mitigation needs to be substantially scaled-up and global emissions need to peak before 2030, with marked emissions shortly thereafter.[189] These estimates are well-founded on the science, but it merits noting again that the accuracy of these projections depends on whether we continue to increase our carbon emissions at the current rates. They will also be affected by what range of efforts, weak to forceful, are taken to limit emissions in the immediate and short term.

At least 118 countries have included forestry and land use mitigation measures as part of their pledges in their nationally-determined contributions to meet the goals of the Paris Agreement. The United Nations Environmental Programme ('UNEP') observes that fulfilment of these pledges could represent 162 million hectares of restored, reforested, and afforested land.[190]

Other policies that enable and incentivize sustainable land management for climate change mitigation include improved access to markets for inputs, outputs, and

[184] Ibid.

[185] Ibid.

[186] M Collins, R Knutti, J Arblaster, J L Dufresne, T Fichefet, P Friedlingstein, and M Wehner, 'Long-Term Climate Change: Projections, Commitments and Irreversibility in Climate Change' in T F Stocker, D Qin, G K Plattner, M Tignor, S K Allen, J Boschung, A Nauels, Y Xia, V Bex, and P M Midgley (eds), *The Physical Science Basis: Contribution of Working Group I to the Fifth Assessment Report of the Intergovernmental Panel on Climate Change* (CUP, 2013) at 1029–136 (hereafter Collins et al).

[187] E Bush, N Gillett, E Watson, J Fyfe, F Vogel, and N Swart, 'Understanding Observed Global Climate Change' in E Bush and D S Lemmen (eds), *Canada's Changing Climate Report* (Government of Canada, 2019) at 24–72, <https://www.nrcan.gc.ca/sites/www.nrcan.gc.ca/files/energy/Climate-change/pdf/CCCR_FULLREPORT-EN-FINAL.pdf> (hereafter *Canada's Changing Climate Report* 2019).

[188] IPCC, *Special Report* (n 6) at 97.

[189] Ibid at 95, 97.

[190] UN, Environment Programme 2019, 'Reducing Emissions from Deforestation and Forest Degradation' (2019), <https://www.unenvironment.org/explore-topics/climate-change/what-we-do/redd>.

financial services, reforming subsidies, and promoting an enabling trade system.[191] The effectiveness of decision-making and governance regarding mitigation strategies is enhanced by the involvement of local stakeholders, including women, Indigenous peoples, and local communities. They could have a significant role in decisions regarding the selection, evaluation, implementation, and monitoring of policy instruments for climate change mitigation.[192]

V. Adaptation is Necessary but Not Sufficient

Recall from Chapter 1 that 'climate adaptation' refers to the actions taken to manage the impacts of climate change, adapting business practices, and all other social and economic activity to cope with the disruptions and harmful effects. Adaptation takes place at international, national, and local levels, which the IPCC notes are key to developing and reinforcing measures for reducing climate-related risks.[193] There are many examples of adaptation. Countries are investing in coastal and riverbank flood defences such as building sea walls or restoring mangroves. They are making efforts to guide development away from high risk areas and retrofitting building structures to withstand flash flooding. They are modifying crops to avoid yield reductions and are using social learning that changes understanding on the community level to modify agricultural practices. Adaptation involves building capacity to respond better to climate change impacts, including making governance more flexible, and strengthening financing mechanisms, such as by providing different types of insurance. Adaptation measures include ecosystem-based adaptation, ecosystem restoration, strategies to avoid degradation and deforestation, biodiversity management, and sustainable aquaculture. These measures can benefit from using local knowledge and Indigenous knowledge. Adaptation measures also include efficient irrigation, disaster risk management, social safety nets, risk spreading and sharing with catastrophe funding for vulnerable populations, and community-based adaptation to reduce risks to health, food, water, and economic growth.[194]

Among the barriers to adaptation are lack of up-to-date and locally relevant information, lack of finance and technology, existing social values and attitudes that fail to understand the serious risks of climate change, and institutional constraints in terms of shifting resources to climate adaptation and mitigation.[195] Adaptation can be incremental or it can be transformational, meaning fundamental attributes of the system are changed.[196] Since different parts of the world are experiencing the impacts of climate change differently, there is similar diversity in how people in a given region are adapting to those impacts.

The IPCC *Special Report on Global Warming of 1.5 °C* makes clear that further global warming will take place given our historical use of fossil fuels.[197] It observes that we

[191] Ibid at 32.
[192] Ibid at 34.
[193] IPCC, 'Framing' (n 7) at 51.
[194] Ibid at 12.
[195] Ibid.
[196] Ibid at 70.
[197] Ibid at Chapter 1, 51.

are not yet experiencing the full warming effect of current CO_2 emissions as there is a delayed effect between carbon emissions and the resulting global warming.[198] However, it reports that limiting global temperature increase to 1.5°C is achievable if we act now and use every available tool. It observes that ecosystem-based adaptation can, in some contexts, promote nature conservation while alleviating poverty and providing co-benefits by removing GHG and protecting livelihoods.[199] For example, avoiding, reducing, and reversing desertification would enhance soil fertility and increase carbon storage in soils and biomass.[200] Preventing desertification is much preferable to trying to restore land that has already completely degraded. Currently, there is a lack of knowledge of adaptation limits and potential maladaptation to the combined effects of climate change and desertification, and the IPCC observes that in the absence of new or enhanced adaptation options, the potential for residual risks and maladaptive outcomes is high.[201]

The next chapter turns to the financial risks associated with climate change.

[198] Ibid at Chapter IV.5

[199] IPCC, *Special Report on Climate Change and Land* (n 77) at 20–1.

[200] Ibid at 22.

[201] Ibid at 23.

3
Financial Risks of Climate Change

> Climate change is the Tragedy of the Horizon. We don't need an army of actuaries to tell us that the catastrophic impacts of climate change will be felt beyond the traditional horizons of most actors—imposing a cost on future generations that the current generation has no direct incentive to fix.
>
> Mark Carney[1]

Climate-related financial risks and the transition to net zero carbon emissions affect most economic sectors and industries.[2] Former Bank of England Governor Mark Carney's reference to climate change as a tragedy of the horizon speaks directly to the fact that the most serious consequences of today's emissions will eventuate beyond the time-frame of current business and regulatory cycles.[3] Carney identified three types of financial risk: (1) physical risks that arise from increased frequency and severity of climate-related and weather-related events that damage property and disrupt trade; (2) transition risks resulting from adjustment towards a low carbon economy; and (3) liability risks from parties seeking compensation for suffering loss from the effects of climate change from those individuals, businesses, and other entities they hold responsible.[4] He noted that risks are a function of cumulative emissions, but that risks to financial stability will be minimized if the transition begins early and follows a predictable path.[5] Carney observed that there is still time to act, but the window of opportunity is finite and shrinking.

More recently, Carney has remarked on the breadth of climate risks as they affect multiple lines of business, sectors, and geographies.[6] The magnitude and full impacts of climate risks are large, non-linear, and irreversible, but they are foreseeable. Carney observed that given the dependency on short term actions, the size of future impacts will be determined by the actions taken today, thus, there is need to plan beyond

[1] Mark Carney, 'Breaking the Tragedy of the Horizon: Climate Change and Financial Stability' (29 September 2015) at 3, <https://www.bankofengland.co.uk/-/media/boe/files/speech/2015/breaking-the-tragedy-of-the-horizon-climate-change-and-financial-stability.pdf?la=en&hash=7C67E785651862457D99511147C7424FF5EA0C1A> (hereafter Carney, 'Tragedy').

[2] Financial Stability, 'Final Report: Recommendations of the Task Force on Climate-related Financial Disclosures' (15 June 2017) at iii, <https://www.fsb-tcfd.org/publications/final-recommendations-report/> (hereafter TCFD, 'Final Report').

[3] Carney, 'Tragedy' (n 1).

[4] Ibid.

[5] Ibid at 6.

[6] Mark Carney, 'TCFD: Strengthening the Foundations of Sustainable Finance', Speech delivered to Tokyo TCFD Summit (8 October 2019) at 4, <https://www.bankofengland.co.uk/speech/2019/mark-carney-speech-at-climate-related-financial-disclosure-summit>.

From Ideas to Action. Janis Sarra, Oxford University Press (2020). © Janis Sarra. DOI: 10.1093/oso/9780198852308.003.0003.

traditional business cycles.[7] The Reserve Bank of Australia observed in 2019 that the physical impacts of climate change and the transition are likely to have first-order economic effects.[8]

For example, in meeting the goals of the Paris Agreement, it is estimated that two-thirds of the world's fossil fuel reserves will not be used and are at risk of becoming stranded assets, placing trillions of dollars of shareholder and creditor value at risk.[9] Carney has observed that to hold global warming to even 2°C means that 80 per cent of coal assets, 50 per cent of gas assets, and one-third of oil assets are un-burnable and will be stranded.[10]

Mercer LLP has estimated that as much as 10 per cent of a fund's portfolio risk exposure within the next twenty years will arise from climate-related change and its technological, regulatory, and other impacts.[11] Important risk factors include the extent to which changes to the physical environment will affect investments, the implied cost of carbon, and the rate of development and opportunities for investment into low carbon technologies.

Four years later, Mercer updated its report, adding risk of reduced resource availability and chronic weather patterns to its list of significant sources of climate risk. It observed that climate change will unequivocally have an impact on investment returns such that it needs to be regarded as a new return variable.[12] Mercer observed that the two most significant categories of risk introduced by climate change are the physical risk of destroyed assets or assets with diminished value; and the regulatory risk associated with carbon policies that may lead to stranded assets or assets with diminished value. Traditional diversification across asset classes will be insufficient to mitigate the portfolio risks of climate change. Rather, diversification must take place across sources of risk, not just traditional asset classes, including increased allocation to climate positive assets as a potential hedge for risk.[13]

Both transition risks and physical risks may affect the price of and demand for products and services. Disruption of supply chains, loss of production inputs such as clean water, and other impacts discussed in Chapter 2 pose financial risks to businesses. Companies should consider the potential effect on revenues of the impacts

[7] Ibid.

[8] Deputy Governor Guy Debelle, 'Climate Change and the Economy', Speech delivered to the Centre for Policy Development, Sydney (12 March 2019), <https://www.rba.gov.au/speeches/2019/sp-dg-2019-03-12.html>.

[9] Cambridge Institute for Sustainability Leadership, 'Unhedgeable Risk: How Climate Change Sentiment IMPACTS investment', Cambridge Institute for Sustainability Leadership (2015), <https://www.cisl.cam.ac.uk/publications/publication-pdfs/unhedgeable-risk.pdf>. See also Carbon Tracker Initiative, 'Unburnable Carbon' (23 August 2017), <https://www.carbontracker.org/terms/unburnable-carbon/>.

[10] Mark Carney, 'Presentation to UK House of Lords Financial Affairs Sub-Committee', (18 March 2020), <https://www.parliamentlive.tv/Event/Index/c552cf86-c5e7-40a3-aaa5-9aecca4ee84a>.

[11] Mercer LLC, Carbon Trust and International Finance Corporation, 'Climate Change Scenarios: Implications for Strategic Asset Allocation' (February 2011) at 7,<http://www.mmc.com/content/dam/mmcweb/Files/Climate_Change_Scenarios_Implications_for_Strategic_Asset_Allocation.pdf>.

[12] Mercer LLC, International Finance Corporation and UK Department for International Development, 'Investing in a Time of Climate Change' (April 2015) at 14, <http://www.mercer.com/content/dam/mercer/attachments/global/investments/mercer-climate-change-report-2015.pdf>.

[13] Ibid at 2.

and identify potential opportunities for enhancing or developing new revenues. One example is the effect of carbon pricing mechanisms on revenue.

There is also risk of misallocation of capital. The Financial Stability Board's ('FSB') Taskforce on Climate-related Financial Disclosures ('TCFD') has observed that without the right information, investors and others may incorrectly price or value assets.[14] It suggests that:

> One of the most significant, and perhaps most misunderstood, risks that organizations face today relates to climate change. While it is widely recognized that continued emission of greenhouse gases will cause further warming of the planet and this warming could lead to damaging economic and social consequences, the exact timing and severity of physical effects are difficult to estimate. The large-scale and long-term nature of the problem makes it uniquely challenging, especially in the context of economic decision-making. Accordingly, many organizations incorrectly perceive the implications of climate change to be long term and, therefore, not necessarily relevant to decisions made today.[15]

The potential impacts of climate change are evident already and will be further manifested in the short, medium, and long term; thus management of the financial risks needs to commence now.

A major impact of climate change is on expenditures, which in turn may depend on a company's cost structure.[16] Suppliers may significantly raise prices in order to cope with their mitigation and adaptation needs. New suppliers may need to be sourced where supply chains are permanently disrupted. The TCFD observed that lower-cost suppliers may be more resilient to changes in cost resulting from climate-related issues and more flexible in their ability to address such issues.[17] In terms of the balance sheet assets and liabilities, the TCFD notes that supply and demand changes from changes in policy, technology, and market dynamics related to climate change could affect the valuation of organizations' assets and liabilities, particularly long-lived assets.[18]

Climate-related risks and opportunities may change the profile of an organization's debt and equity structure, either by increasing debt levels to compensate for reduced operating cash flows or because of the need for new capital expenditures to meet changing regulatory requirements for mitigation, such as reduction of waste and conversion to renewable energy sources. There are also likely to be costs associated with research and development, in order to adopt production processes and net zero emissions technologies.

The financial impacts of new technology required for climate mitigation and adaptation will depend on the sectors and regions in which companies operate. For example, substitution of existing products and services with lower emissions options may result in early retirement of existing assets, with some or all the value being

[14] TCFD, 'Final Report' (n 2) at 9.
[15] Ibid at ii.
[16] Ibid.
[17] Ibid at 9.
[18] Ibid.

written off. Some assets are likely to become stranded, such as coal or other fossil fuels left in the ground. There is likely to be reduced demand for carbon-intensive products and services, with financial implications for the companies that offer such products and services.[19]

The TCFD has reported that climate-related financial risks fall into two major categories: risks related to the transition to a low carbon economy and risks related to the physical impacts of climate change.[20] It suggested that transitioning to a low carbon economy may entail extensive policy, legal, technology, and market changes to address mitigation and adaptation requirements related to climate change; and such risks pose varying levels of financial and reputational risk to organizations.[21]

The TCFD also observed that policies are increasingly aimed at constraining actions that contribute to the adverse effects of climate change, or are aimed at promoting adaptation to climate change. They include implementing carbon-pricing mechanisms to reduce greenhouse gas ('GHG') emissions and promote more sustainable land-use practices.[22] As the value of loss and damage arising from climate change grows, litigation risk will also likely increase, as discussed in Chapter 7.

Financial risks to businesses are also deeply implicated in financial risks to individual communities and entire populations. Global asset manager BNP Paribas Asset Management has observed:

> Climate change is also a significant driver of inequality, hitting vulnerable populations the most and reversing hard-won development gains. It is critical to scale-up investing in adaptation, resilience and ensuring that the shocks of climate change do not disproportionally affect particular segments of society. This entails a stronger focus on the needs of the populations most affected by climate change, granting them access to the tools they need to adapt and cope with climate-related disasters. Disaggregated data on the anticipated local impacts of climate change and on the potential socio-ecological effects of responses to climate change (e.g. maladaptation risk) is a prerequisite for effective and just climate action.
>
> ...
>
> The shift to a zero-carbon and environmentally sustainable economic model is necessary, considering what is at stake. There is little doubt about the important economic and social benefits that the transition can deliver. The latest report of the New Climate Economy, for example, concludes that low-carbon growth could deliver economic benefits of USD 26 trillion by 2030 and generate over 65 million new low-carbon jobs. Investors will have a key role to play in enabling a just transition to low-emission, climate-resilient economies. Options for investor action include, *inter alia*, incorporating 'just transition' principles in their investment beliefs, climate action plans, investment research and strategies. Of equal importance is the need for

[19] Ibid.
[20] Ibid at 5.
[21] Ibid.
[22] Ibid.

investors to work with policymakers and governments to ensure inclusion of just transition principles in national plans and long-term climate strategies.[23]

The World Economic Forum observed in 2019 that 'we are in a new economic era: Globalization 4.0', in that major shifts underway in technology, environment, and society are combining in a new phase of globalization, whose trajectory will depend in large measure on how well corporations and governments adapt to these changes.[24] It observed that, given the urgency of global warming, change can only be achieved by mobilizing substantially increased amounts of private-sector financing for climate-related infrastructure, which will require deeper engagement, sustained dialogue, and heightened imagination by all stakeholders.[25] It reported that a new dimension of corporate governance requires attention by boards to the need to identify salient and just policies for climate change mitigation.[26]

I. The Physical Risks to Business

Financial impacts arising from physical risks resulting from climate change can be acute or longer term (chronic). Acute physical risk refers to risks that are event-driven, including increased severity of extreme weather events, such as cyclones, hurricanes, floods, or wildfires. Acute events create direct damage to assets: land, property and equipment, inventory, buildings, power lines, and assets or inventory held in storage. They create disruption of supply chains and reduce availability of water required for production processes. For example, severe storms, drought, and wildfires cost the United States ('US') more than US $91 billion in damage in 2018, according to the US National Oceanic and Atmospheric Administration.[27]

Future warming will be accompanied by increased frequency and severity of extreme weather events such as heatwaves, heavy rainfalls and related flooding, dry spells and/or droughts, and forest fires. All give rise to considerable risks to the value of capital and financial assets.

Chronic physical risks refer to longer-term shifts in climate patterns, such as sustained higher temperatures, which cause sea level rise and chronic heatwaves.[28] Extreme temperature changes may affect business operations, transportation needs, and employee health and safety. Physical risks, both acute and chronic, will inevitably have financial implications.

[23] BNP Paribas Asset Management, 'Global Sustainability Strategy' (2018) at 30–1, <https://docfinder.bnpparibas-am.com/api/files/1FC9FC6C-0DA8-468E-90B3-016DDB5CD270>.

[24] World Economic Forum, 'Globalization 4.0 Shaping a New Global Architecture in the Age of the Fourth Industrial Revolution' (April 2019), <http://www3.weforum.org/docs/WEF_Globalization_4.0_Call_for_Engagement.pdf>.

[25] Ibid at 15, 18.

[26] Ibid at 30.

[27] Phil McKenna, 'Hurricane Michael Cost This Military Base about $5 Billion, Just One of 2018's Weather Disasters', *Inside Climate News* (6 February 2019), <https://insideclimatenews.org/news/18122018/tyndall-military-hurricane-cost-2018-year-review-billion-dollar-disasters-wildfire-extreme-weather-drought-michael-florence>.

[28] TCFD, 'Final Report' (n 2) at 6.

All of the risks to land systems, food services, ocean systems, etc, discussed in the previous chapter, create financial risks to businesses. Companies need to rebuild after acute events. Insurance often does not fully cover losses to the business. Post acute events, the price of insurance may become unaffordable or insurers may decline to insure against some acute events.

The Insurance Bureau of Canada in 2019 reported that insurance payouts from extreme weather have more than doubled every five to ten years since the 1980s. For the nine years leading up to 2017, payouts for catastrophic losses averaged Cdn $1.8 billion per year in Canada, due to ice storms, floods, windstorms, and tornadoes, with implications for the cost and availability of insurance and reinsurance.[29] The Fort McMurry wildfire created Cdn $9.9 billion in damage and 88,000 people were evacuated from their homes and businesses. The Insurance Bureau of Canada is now working closely with governments to advocate for increased investment to mitigate the future impacts of extreme weather and build resiliency to its damaging effects, including investment in new infrastructure to protect communities from floods and fires, improved building codes, better land-use planning, and, increasingly, creating incentives to shift the development of businesses and homes away from areas of highest risk.

The mitigation required to minimize future acute and chronic events requires directing capital away from carbon-intensive activities towards more sustainable production. Equity investors will likely have to forgo some immediate returns in order that companies remain viable and can generate sustainable returns. Companies also need to introduce strategies to reduce the financial risks associated with chronic changes to the climate.

In 2019, Ernst & Young issued its 'Global Climate Risk Disclosure Barometer', providing a snapshot of climate disclosures of over 500 companies during the 2017–18 reporting period, across eleven highly impacted sectors in eighteen countries.[30] It concluded that almost all sectors of the economy face major disruption from climate transition and its physical impacts over the coming years. Yet a majority of companies in key economies are still not engaging seriously with these risks, which is likely to affect their valuation even before the impacts are fully realized.[31]

The Ernst & Young report observed that physical risk is the key risk to many high-risk sectors over the long term, and this lack of understanding and disclosure highlights a significant governance gap.[32] On average, it found that companies reported better on targets and metrics, mainly reporting on scope 1 and 2 GHG emissions and governance, whereas disclosures relating to strategy and risk management were the least developed.[33] Asset owners and asset managers were the underperformers, slower to respond to the systemic economic implications of climate change, and thus the report suggests are less likely to manage the required transition.[34] The study found that

[29] Insurance Bureau of Canada, 'Annual Report 2019'.

[30] Mathew Nelson, 'How Climate Change Disclosures Reveal Business Risks and Opportunities', Ernst & Young (9 January 2019), <https://www.ey.com/en_gl/assurance/climate-change-disclosures-revealing-risks-opportunities>.

[31] Ibid at 2.

[32] Ibid at 8.

[33] Ibid at 3.

[34] Ibid at 4–5.

while many companies are disclosing the transition risks, physical risks are often overlooked in valuation models and often completely omitted from forward-looking strategic and risk management disclosures.[35]

One inevitable financial impact of catastrophic events will be climate-related insolvencies and bankruptcies. In the United States, for example, California's largest utility corporation filed bankruptcy proceedings in 2019, with more than US $30 million in damage claims related to climate change.[36]

Nicholas Stern observes that delays in taking immediate action to mitigate climate change will amount to a decline of 5–10 per cent of worldwide GDP, but the reduction in GDP will only be 1–2 per cent if action is taken now.[37] Thus, any delay in acting poses a substantial financial risk.

The World Business Council for Sustainable Development notes that challenges for financial filings are that there is limited knowledge of climate-related issues within organizations; there is a tendency to focus mainly on near-term risks without paying adequate attention to risks that may arise in the longer term; and to date, there remains some difficulty in quantifying the financial effects of material climate-related issues.[38]

Former Governor Carney has called efforts to address climate change a new horizon, in that some sectors, such as insurance and reinsurance, are at the forefront of managing the financial risks from climate change by developing their modelling and forecasting capabilities, improving exposure management, and adapting coverage and pricing.[39]

i. Planetary Boundaries Have Been Crossed

Another way of considering the impacts of climate change is through the notion of planetary boundaries. A decade ago, the Stockholm Resilience Centre introduced the concept of 'planetary boundaries', which focuses on the nine systems that regulate the stability of the Earth.[40] Rockström et al report that there are nine planetary boundaries within which humanity can operate safely, suggesting that transgressing one or more planetary boundaries may be deleterious or catastrophic due to the risk of crossing thresholds that will trigger non-linear, abrupt environmental change within

35 Ibid at 3.

36 For a detailed discussion of insolvency issues, see Janis Sarra, 'Bad Moon Rising: New Dawn Ahead? Climate Change and Solvency Risk' in J Corraini and B Nixon (eds), *Annual Review of Insolvency Law 2019* (hereafter Sarra, 'Bad Moon').

37 Nicholas Stern (IPCC), 'Stern Review on the Economics of Climate Change' (2014), <http://www.ipcc.ch/pdf/assessment-report/ar5/syr/AR5_SYR_FINAL_SPM.pdf>.

38 World Business Council for Sustainable Development, 'Sustainability and Enterprise Risk Management: The First Step Towards Integration' (18 January 2017).

39 Mark Carney, 'A New Horizon', Bank of England, European Commission Conference: A Global Approach to Sustainable Finance (21 March 2019) at 5, <https://www.bankofengland.co.uk/-/media/boe/files/speech/2019/a-new-horizon-speech-by-mark-carney.pdf?la=en&hash=F63F8064E0408F038CABB1F29C58FB1A0CD0FE25> (hereafter Carney, 'New Horizon').

40 W Steffen et al, 'Planetary Boundaries: Guiding Human Development on a Changing Planet', Stockholm Resilience Centre (2015), <www.stockholmresilience.org/research/planetary-boundaries/planetary-boundaries/about-the-research/the-nine-planetary-boundaries.html> (hereafter Steffen et al, 'Planetary Boundaries').

continental- to planetary-scale systems.[41] Steffen et al report that four planetary boundaries have now been crossed: climate change, biosphere integrity, land-system change, and biogeochemical flows.[42] Renewable and non-renewable natural resources are also under severe threat. In crossing a planetary boundary, the world encounters high uncertainty and increasing risk, as the interactions of land, ocean, atmosphere, and life provide the conditions under which human societies depend.[43]

Rockström et al have quantified seven of the nine boundaries: climate change (CO_2 concentration in the atmosphere <350 ppm and/or a maximum change of +1 W m^{-2} in radiative forcing); ocean acidification; stratospheric ozone; biogeochemical nitrogen (N) cycle and phosphorus (P) cycle; global freshwater use; land system change; and the rate at which biological diversity is lost.[44] Their analysis of planetary boundaries lays the groundwork for shifting our approach to governance towards the estimation of the safe space for human development, as discussed in Chapter 6.

II. Transition Risks to Companies and Investors from Climate Change

Transition risks that can financially impact the business include technological innovations that support a net zero carbon economy, market risks, investor preference shifts, reputational risk, regulatory policies requiring business and consumers to shift to lower emissions in production and energy use, and the ability to attract and retain employees. There are likely to be increased production costs as prices of production inputs change and as carbon pricing alters the price at which the business sells its products or services. Climate change could substantially affect the valuation of assets of many companies globally. This part explores these financial risks.

i. Technology Risk

Existing technologies may become obsolete or written down in value because they no longer can be used in production processes where they generate GHG emissions beyond what is accepted by regulatory policy or the market. The pricing of carbon through carbon taxes or other mechanisms to internalize the cost of carbon may make the technologies too expensive to operate.

Technological innovations that support the transition to a low carbon, energy-efficient economic system can also have a significant financial impact on businesses.[45]

41 J Rockström et al, 'Planetary Boundaries: Exploring the Safe Operating Space' (2009) 14(2) Ecology and Society, <https://www.ecologyandsociety.org/vol14/iss2/art32/ (hereafter Rockström et al).

42 Stockholm University, 'Four of Nine Planetary Boundaries Now Crossed' (2019), <www.su.se/english/about/news-and-events/press/press-releases/four-of-nine-planetary-boundaries-now-crossed-1.218003>.

43 BNP Paribas Asset Management, 'Global Sustainability Strategy' (2018), <https://docfinder.bnpparibas-am.com/api/files/1FC9FC6C-0DA8-468E-90B3-016DDB5CD270> (hereafter BNP Global).

44 Ibid.

45 Janis Sarra, *Fiduciary Obligations in Business and Investment: Implications of Climate Change* (CCLI, 2018) at 60–8, <https://law-ccli-2019.sites.olt.ubc.ca/files/2019/08/Janis-Sarra-Fiduciary-Obligation-in-Business-and-Investment.pdf> (hereafter Sarra, *Fiduciary Obligations*).

New technologies in renewable energy and energy efficiency are all developing rapidly. These developments will affect the competitiveness of certain corporations, their production and distribution costs, and demand for their products and services.[46] Part of the risk is that new technology will displace or disrupt some parts of the existing economic system. The timing of technological developments and their deployment is a key uncertainty in assessing or quantifying technology risk.

To the extent that new technology displaces old systems, there will be successful businesses that benefit from the development, marketing, and use of innovative technologies. At the same time, there are financial risks to firms that are slow to adopt innovative technologies.

ii. Market and Investment Risk

Market risk is also a factor, in terms of shifts in supply and demand for certain commodities, products, and services, as market preferences shift and climate-related risks and opportunities are increasingly taken into account.[47] There may be a repricing of assets, such as oil reserves and land valuations.[48] The World Economic Forum observes that the average lifespan of a company listed in the S&P 500 index of leading US companies has shortened by more than fifty years in the last century, from an average lifespan of sixty-seven years to just fifteen years today.[49] That shift is likely to accelerate as new industries emerge in a net zero carbon economy and companies fail when they are unable to adapt.

Investment risks are arising from downward pressure on the value of carbon-linked assets during the transition towards a low carbon economy. Companies that fail to identify and manage risks as part of their business plans could face problems accessing capital. The risks and attendant costs associated with stranded assets, such as abandoned oil wells, can accrue not only to companies, but to particular industries. There may also be costs borne by governments and taxpayers as a whole, where there is no one else to pay for decommissioning, remediation, and reclamation of these stranded assets.[50]

Institutional investors are increasingly seeking additional information to quantify their exposure to carbon-linked assets. Pension funds and their investment managers, in particular, are fiduciaries charged with oversight and management of investment vehicles in the best interests of multiple generations of beneficiaries. They must therefore consider the intergenerational implications of their investment decisions and are now integrating climate change considerations in their management of investment portfolios.[51] Pension funds are major holders of long term assets globally. They are

[46] TCFD, 'Final Report' (n 2) at 6.

[47] Ibid.

[48] Ibid at 10.

[49] World Economic Forum, 'Two Degrees of Transformation: Businesses Are Coming Together to Lead On Climate Change. Will You Join Them?' (2018) at 4, citing a Yale University study by Richard Foster and Kim Gittleson, 'Can a Company Live Forever?', reporting that by 2020, more than three-quarters of the S&P 500 will be new companies.

[50] Sarra, 'Bad Moon' (n 36) at 12.

[51] Sarra, *Fiduciary Obligations* (n 45) at 69–70.

now stress testing their existing asset portfolios to quantify the potential impact of changes in carbon-based asset prices, in order to guide their investment decisions. A number have commenced shifting their investment activities.

For example, BNP Paribas Asset Management has adopted firm-wide targets for measuring and progressively aligning its investment portfolios with a sustainable future.[52] As of December 2018, it has directed €7.7 billion towards investments in energy transition, green bonds, water, the global environment, and climate change.[53] It is committed to aligning its investment portfolios with the goals of the Paris Agreement by 2025 and to encourage its investee companies to align their strategies with these goals.[54] Effective January 2020, it is divesting in coal-mining companies that derive more than 10 per cent of their revenue from mining thermal coal and/or account for 1 per cent or more of total global production. It will also stop investments in coal-power generators whose carbon intensity is above the 2017 global average of 491 gCO_2/kWh and will subsequently follow the Paris-compliant trajectory for the sector, requiring power generators' carbon intensity to fall to 327 gCO_2/kWh by 2025.[55] BNP Paribas Group has endorsed the zero net deforestation objective established by the Soft Commodities Compact, aimed at eliminating deforestation from the downstream and upstream supply chain no later than 2020.[56]

Climate Action 100+ is an investor initiative launched in 2017 to ensure the world's largest corporate GHG emitters take necessary action on climate change. More than 500 investors with over US $47 trillion in assets collectively under management are directly engaging with corporate boards, advising them to curb emissions, improve governance, and strengthen climate-related financial disclosures.[57] The targeted companies include 100 systemically important emitters that account for two-thirds of annual global industrial emissions, and sixty other companies that should be driving the clean energy transition.[58] Signatories have committed to phasing out investments in thermal coal mining and coal-fired power generation.[59] Their statement says:

> As institutional investors and consistent with our fiduciary duty to our beneficiaries, we will: ... work with the companies in which we invest to ensure that they are minimizing and disclosing the risks and maximizing the opportunities presented by climate change and climate policy.[60]

In addition to the shifts by equity investors, institutional lenders are also signalling that their lending practices will reflect the need to address climate-related financial risk. For example, RBC has reported that it will 'accelerate the flow of capital to clients engaged in efforts to mitigate and adapt to climate change, and to those providing

[52] BNP Global (n 43).
[53] Ibid at 14.
[54] Ibid at 25.
[55] Ibid at 26.
[56] Ibid at 28.
[57] Climate Action 100+, 'About Us', <https://climateaction100.wordpress.com/about-us/>.
[58] Ibid.
[59] The Investor Agenda, <https://theinvestoragenda.org/focus-areas/investment/>.
[60] Climate Action 100+, 'Facts', <https://climateaction100.wordpress.com/faq/>.

products and services that enable others to do so'.[61] In 2019, one third of global banks with more than US $47 trillion in assets under management adopted new United Nations-backed responsible banking principles to fight climate change, committing to shifting their loan portfolios away from fossil fuels and carbon-intensive activities and redirecting loans to lending capital to greener industries. They have committed to setting targets to increase positive impacts and reduce negative impacts on people and the environment.[62]

iii. Reputational Risk

Reputational risk is another transition risk, in terms of changing customer or community perceptions of a corporation's contribution to, or detraction from, the transition to a net zero carbon economy. There may be reduced demand for goods and services due to shifts in consumer preferences.

Companies that are 'consumer-facing' are particularly sensitive to social media and other reputational threats. Since the public face of climate activists are people between the ages 18 and 40, the ease with which they use and can mobilize social media to expose a company's poor climate governance is a serious risk. As more evidence becomes available regarding water scarcity, carbon emissions intensity reduction, effective climate risk management, and a range of other climate mitigation strategies, reputational risk will be become heightened.

However, the effectiveness of media campaigns in shifting governance is not entirely clear. In the context of human rights disclosures, Chilton and Sarfaty have observed that supply chain disclosures may be limited in their effectiveness because such disclosure does not necessarily have a large effect on consumer behaviour, suggesting that consumers have difficulty discerning levels of compliance and are thus not necessarily able to influence corporate behaviour.[63] At the same time, the negative social media exposure of major carbon emitters has arguably fueled recent public climate strikes, impacted some consumer and investor practices, and is clearly affecting recent national elections.

iv. Litigation Risk

Litigation risk is increasing, with a steady increase in climate-related litigation claims being brought before the courts by property owners, investors, municipalities, states,

[61] RBC, 'Climate Change Position & Disclosure Statement' (2017) at 2, <http://www.rbc.com/community-sustainability/_assets-custom/pdf/RBC_ClimateChangePosition_Disclosure_Statement_2017.pdf>.

[62] UN, 'The Principles for Responsible Banking' (22 September 2019), <https://www.unepfi.org/banking/bankingprinciples/>. See also M Green, '130 Banks Worth $47 Trillion Adopt New UN-backed Climate Policies to Shift their Loan Books Away from Fossil Fuels' (22 September 2019), *Reuters* <https://www.businessinsider.com/banks-worth-47-trillion-adopt-new-un-backed-climate-principles-2019-9?fbclid=IwAR0r6zeuPd9RKxiTeEWmsNpafzF5M4lF4Ozshl-_0zioH89HkxZ7lCdZEeg>.

[63] They cite the *California Transparency in Supply Chains Act*. Adam Chilton and Galit Sarfaty, 'The Limitations of Supply Chain Disclosure Regimes' (2016) Public Law Leg Theory 30–43.

insurers, shareholders, and public interest organizations.[64] Litigation risk arises from the failure of organizations to mitigate impacts of climate change, failure to adapt to climate change, and the insufficiency of disclosure around material financial risks. These lawsuits are discussed at length in Chapter 7.

v. Policy Risk

Policy actions that attempt to constrain business activities that contribute to the adverse effects of climate change or that promote climate mitigation and adaptation carry some financial risk for businesses, particularly where there is some uncertainty as to the scope of regulation that will be implemented. Policy uncertainties can include whether or not governments are going to adopt carbon-pricing mechanisms to reduce GHG emissions; require a shift in energy use toward low emission sources; require adoption of energy-efficiency solutions; and/or mandate greater water efficiency measures and more sustainable land-use practices.[65] All have a financial impact on businesses. The ongoing appellate litigation in Canada over the federal government's carbon pricing law is one example of policy uncertainty. While the issue will be resolved by the Supreme Court of Canada in 2020, businesses are left with some policy risk in the interim.

More than forty governments worldwide have now adopted a price on carbon, either through direct taxes on fossil fuels or through cap-and-trade programmes, including the United Kingdom ('UK'), Australia, the European Union ('EU'), and China. The financial impact will depend on the nature and timing of the policy changes, and in some cases, on the uncertainty generated as governments disagree or newly-elected governments alter carbon pricing policies.

Internationally, there are also policy shifts as governments try to find ways to implement the UN Social Development Goals. The IPCC notes that choices about mitigation portfolios for limiting warming to 1.5°C can positively or negatively impact the achievement of sustainable development.[66]

III. Women Are Disproportionally Affected

Globally, women are disproportionally affected by the impacts of climate change. Their traditional roles as the primary users and managers of natural resources, primary

[64] TCFD, 'Final Report' (n 2) at 5.

[65] Ibid.

[66] IPCC, J Rogelj, D Shindell, K Jiang, S Fifita, P Forster, V Ginzburg, C Handa, H Kheshgi, S Kobayashi, E Kriegler, L Mundaca, R Séférian, and M V Vilariño, 'Chapter 2: Mitigation Pathways Compatible with 1.5°C in the Context of Sustainable Development' in V Masson-Delmotte, P Zhai, H O Pörtner, D Roberts, J Skea, P Shukla, A Pirani, W Moufouma-Okia, C Péan, R Pidcock, S Connors, J B R Matthews, Y Chen, X Zhou, M I Gomis, E Lonnoy, T Maycock, M Tignor, and T Waterfield (eds), *Global Warming of 1.5°C: An IPCC Special Report on the Impacts of Global Warming of 1.5°C above Pre-industrial Levels and Related Global Greenhouse Gas Emission Pathways, in the Context of Strengthening the Global Response to the Threat of Climate Change, Sustainable Development, and Efforts to Eradicate Poverty* (IPCC, 2019) at 95, 97, <https://www.ipcc.ch/site/assets/uploads/sites/2/2019/05/SR15_Chapter2_Low_Res.pdf>.

caregivers, and keepers of the home, mean that they are involved in and depend on livelihoods and resources that are put most at risk by climate change.[67] For example, in Sub-Saharan Africa, where more than 600 million people have no access to electricity and over 700 million must rely on harmful fuels, it is women who bear the huge burden of energy poverty and who disproportionately shoulder the harmful effects of climate change.[68] As do women in Southeast Asia and South Asia, Sub-Saharan African women face both racial and gender discrimination, which creates additional barriers to being able to protect themselves and their families from the devastating consequences of climate change.

The World Economic Forum observes that with 70 per cent of women living in poverty, women are disproportionately affected by extreme weather events, loss of agricultural productivity, and destruction of life, property, and economic activity, all of which stem from the climate crisis.[69] It observes that women remain a largely untapped resource due to existing biases, including having restricted land rights in numerous jurisdictions, lack of access to training, technology, and financial resources, and limited access to political decision-making due to their under-representation in both elected leadership and in government bureaucracies.[70]

Women farmers currently account for between 45 and 80 per cent of all food production in developing countries, and the growing unpredictability of food sources because of climate change impacts their ability to feed and provide for their families.[71] Yet women are rarely at the policy decision-making table in most countries nationally and internationally, in terms of drawing attention to the impacts and having a meaningful voice in developing policies to mitigate risks and move to a net zero carbon economy.

One example pointed out by the United Nations ('UN') is the harvesting and processing of biomass, which is overwhelmingly performed by rural and Indigenous women, such as seaweed farmers in Zanzibar. Women are facing declines in the production of high-value seaweed as waters have become warmer due to climate change, and this reliance on climate-vulnerable biomass industries for their livelihoods gives their vulnerability a gender and ethnic dimension.[72]

The UN observes that as climate change reduces growing time and rainfall becomes scarce and unpredictable, tension arises over which crops to grow and prioritize, given the gendered nature of decision-making between men and women in many countries. Discrimination against women and girls is reinforced and the occurrence of domestic

[67] Government of Canada, 'Women and Climate Change' (2019) <https://www.canada.ca/en/environment-climate-change/services/climate-change/women.html>.

[68] Solar Sister, <https://solarsister.org/about-us/>.

[69] World Economic Forum, 'We Can Solve Climate Change—If We Involve Women' (16 September 2019), <https://www.weforum.org/agenda/2019/09/why-women-cannot-be-spectators-in-the-climate-change-battle/>.

[70] Ibid.

[71] Ibid.

[72] UN FCCC, 'Differentiated Impacts of Climate Change on Women and Men; the Integration of Gender Considerations in Climate Policies, Plans and Actions; and Progress in Enhancing Gender Balance in National Climate Delegations' (12 June 2019), at para 22, <https://unfccc.int/sites/default/files/resource/sbi2019_inf8.pdf> (hereafter UN, 'Differentiated Impacts').

violence increases during times of food scarcity.[73] When food is limited, women prioritize feeding their children and male spouses ahead of themselves, to the detriment of their overall nutrition and health.[74]

Indigenous women are particularly vulnerable to the impacts of climate change, primarily due to their reliance on natural resources for their livelihoods and the multiple forms of discrimination that they face due to their gender, ethnicity, and level of poverty.[75]

The Swedish International Development Co-operation Agency reports that, with fewer assets and heavier burdens, women are more vulnerable to shocks and less well positioned to respond to the effects of climate change.[76] Disasters, especially droughts and emergency situations, are the most common causes of food shortages in the world, and there is need to enhance resilience to climate change by diversifying production, as well as strengthening capacity to respond to challenges related to climate change.[77] Because of women's specific roles and experiences in food production and preparation, it is crucial to include them in emergency-related food security planning and decision making.[78]

Rural communities are in the front lines of efforts to improve food security. At the same time, these communities must cope with some of the harshest changing climate conditions.[79] For developing countries for which data are available, between 10 per cent and 20 per cent of all land holders are women, and countries having both the lowest and highest share of female land holders are in Africa.[80] Women that are holders of small land ('smallholders') have less access to loans, as they generally have less control over the types of fixed assets necessary as collateral for loans, and they face institutional discrimination in that they are offered smaller loans than male farmers.[81] Gender is one critical dimension that determines women's access to the resources and processes needed for dealing with climate change.

Atela et al examine women's microbusinesses in Kenya's semi-arid lands, which are climate change 'hot spots' where climate change is already having significant and documented impacts, such as longer and more frequent droughts.[82] They observe that Kenya as a whole lacks many of the conditions that support private sector adaptation, including gaps in data, capacity development, training, limited infrastructure,

[73] Swedish International Development Co-operation Agency, 'Women and Food Security' (2019) at 2, <https://www.sida.se/contentassets/bc3dc44b16c44725868e57125b9542e3/women-and-food-security.pdf> (hereafter SIDCA).

[74] UN, 'Differentiated Impacts' (n 72) at para 23.

[75] Ibid at para 26.

[76] SIDCA (n 73) at 2.

[77] Ibid at 2.

[78] Ibid.

[79] UN Food and Agriculture Organization and the CIGAR Research Programme on Climate Change, Agriculture and Food Security, *Gender and Climate Change Research in Agriculture and Food Security for Rural Development* (2013) at 1,<http://www.fao.org/3/i3385e/i3385e.pdf> (hereafter *Gender and Climate Change*).

[80] Ibid at 12.

[81] Ibid.

[82] Joanes Atela, Kate Elizabeth Gannon, and Florence Crick, *Climate Change Adaptation among Female-Led Micro, Small and Medium Enterprises in Semi-Arid Areas: A Case Study from Kenya*, Centre for Climate Change Economics and Policy (October 2018), <http://www.lse.ac.uk/GranthamInstitute/wp-content/uploads/2018/10/working-paper-338-Atela-et-al.pdf>

restricted access to new technologies, and the financial environment.[83] They point to evidence that some constraints, including access to finance and training opportunities, affect female-owned enterprises more severely than businesses owned by males. For example, when droughts reduce crops, many diversify into charcoal production and sale as they cannot see any other option; yet this short term coping strategy may weaken longer term resilience by destroying vegetation, exposing agricultural land to erosion, and further diminishing productivity, leading to loss of biodiversity.[84] Atela et al found that female-led micro businesses also face barriers to accessing new climate resilient technologies, finance, and other forms of business safety nets, such as climate insurance products.[85]

The UN Food and Agricultural Organization reports that food security consists of four components: availability, stability, utilization, and access. Gender issues impact food availability because asymmetries in ownership of, access to, and control of livelihood assets negatively affect women's capacity to produce food, and consequently, their ability to earn income.[86] Stability, in the sense of having access to adequate food at all times, has gender dimensions because when food becomes unavailable during acute climatic events, women are often forced to reduce their intake in favour of other household members.[87] Utilization of food refers to adequate diet, clean water, sanitation, and health care necessary to nutritional well-being where all physiological needs are met; key for women as they are typically responsible for food preparation and thus are crucially important to the dietary diversity of their households. Finally, food access refers to access by individuals to adequate resources for acquiring appropriate foods for a nutritious diet. Adequate amounts to maintain nutritional intake are often not as accessible for women compared to men based on hierarchy within the family.[88]

A study by the International Labour Organization found that outdoor air pollution in an urban environment due to emissions and other climate impacts also has a gendered effect on workers' absence from formal employment.[89] Drawing on twenty years of air pollution and employment data from Santiago, Chile—a highly polluted metropolis—the study found that air pollution reduces hours that women work, particularly women with children. During weeks with pollution at 100 μg/m3, the gender difference is doubled, as children are unable to go to school and mothers stay home and care for them, losing much needed income. These findings suggest that air pollution may contribute to gender inequality through the gender-biased distribution of childcare responsibilities.[90]

A report by McKinsey notes that under a 'women's full potential' scenario, in which women play an identical role in labour markets to men, as much as US $28 trillion, or 26 per cent, could be added to global annual gross domestic product ('GDP') by

[83] Ibid at 7.
[84] Ibid at 8.
[85] Ibid at 12.
[86] Ibid.
[87] Ibid at 14.
[88] Ibid.
[89] Guillermo Montt, *The Gendered Effects of Air Pollution on Labour Supply* (ILO, March 2018) at 1, 13–14, <https://www.ilo.org/wcmsp5/groups/public/---dgreports/---inst/documents/publication/wcms_625863.pdf>.
[90] Ibid.

2025.[91] It suggests that this augmentation of GDP could be sufficient to bridge the climate finance gap needed to fund the fight against climate change, which is estimated to be US $585 billion per year by 2020 and US $894 billion by 2030. Increasing the participation of women in the labour force could sufficiently increase the world's GDP for financing sustainable development.

IV. Indigenous Peoples Deserve Special Attention

Indigenous peoples globally deserve special attention and respect in the move to net zero carbon and a sustainable planet because of their longstanding and deep connections to land and water. This deep connection allows them to offer unique insights into how to conserve energy and biodiversity, and how to respect the Earth when conceptualizing economic development and climate resilience.

G L Terri-Lynn Williams-Davidson, of the Skedans Raven Clan of the Haida Nation, a lawyer and activist who works to arrive at environmental, cultural, and economic sustainability, observes:

> The process of colonization has displaced Indigenous Peoples from our territories worldwide. This legacy endures as colonial governments have yet to give legal effect to recognition and respect of Indigenous Title. Despite this history, Indigenous Peoples have deep and multi-faceted relationships with our territories, fostered throughout millennia. Territorial lands and waters have sustained us physically and spiritually, and our existence parallels the state of our territories. The importance of this sustenance is magnified in the absence of economic bases as many Indigenous Peoples depend upon their territories for daily sustenance.
>
> Climate change directly affects Indigenous Peoples. Drawing from the experience of the Haida Nation, rising ocean temperatures and ocean acidification have led to decreased marine life. Marine life is especially important as the islands of Haida Gwaii do not have significant terrestrial food sources. The natural balance has also been disrupted, with constantly changing natural cycles and significantly different seasonal times and quantities for harvesting from the land and sea. Hurricane force winds in Haida Gwaii are not unknown, but climate change has increased the frequency and severity of year-round storms. These storms lead to increased land erosion, power outages threatening preserved food stocks, extended communication blackouts, and damages to homes, roads and infrastructure.
>
> And yet, it is this living at the frontiers of climate change that strengthens Indigenous Peoples' resilience and commitment to protect the Earth. For example, even though Crown governments have not yet recognized Haida Title to Haida Gwaii, the Haida Nation has protected over 50% of the landbase and portions of the

[91] McKinsey Global Institute, *How Advancing Women's Equality Can Add $12 Trillion to Global Growth* (September 2015), <https://www.mckinsey.com/~/media/McKinsey/Featured%20Insights/Employment%20and%20Growth/How%20advancing%20womens%20equality%20can%20add%2012%20trillion%20to%20global%20growth/MGI%20Power%20of%20parity_Full%20report_September%202015.ashx>.

> marine territory, and jointly manages the rest of the landbase and other portions of the marine territory. Extractive industries, global climate crises and colonization have coalesced—and will continue to coalesce—to encourage the dire need for unprecedented governance models like those in Haida Gwaii that are environmentally, culturally and economically sustainable.[92]

The Haida Gwaii is a 10,180 km^2 archipelago of 150 islands approximately ninety nautical miles off British Columbia, Canada's coast. The Haida Nation have occupied traditional territory in and around Haida Gwaii for millennia and are co-managers in planning processes for the Pacific north coast, focused on capacity building and co-governance of resources, applying traditional knowledge and experience to marine-use planning and fisheries management, guided by fundamental Haida ethics and values such as respect, balance, and reciprocity.[93]

Negative climate impacts affecting Indigenous peoples are a global challenge. In high mountains and the Arctic, around 700 million people live in close contact with the cryosphere.[94] These people, including many Indigenous peoples, depend on snow, glaciers, and sea ice for their livelihoods, food and water security, travel and transport, and their cultural traditions. As the cryosphere changes, discussed in Chapter 2, Indigenous peoples are exposed to flood outbursts, landslides, and coastal erosion.[95] The shrinking cryosphere in the Arctic and high-mountain areas means that Indigenous peoples are suffering from the negative impacts on water resources, water quality, livelihoods, transportation, tourism, and recreation. Exposures to extreme warming, and continued sea-ice and permafrost loss in the Arctic challenge Indigenous communities' cultural identity, self-sufficiency, Indigenous knowledge, and health and well-being.[96]

Food and water security have been negatively impacted by changes in snow cover, lake and river ice, and permafrost in many Arctic regions, disrupting availability of food within herding, hunting, fishing, and gathering areas of Indigenous peoples.[97] Overall greening and browning of the tundra biome and boreal forest is changing the abundance and distribution of animals, including reindeer and salmon, impacting access to food.[98] In turn, it is harming the livelihoods and cultural identity of northern Indigenous peoples. Negative impacts of cryosphere change on human health have included increased risk of food and waterborne diseases, malnutrition, injury, and mental health challenges, especially among Indigenous peoples.[99] Glacier retreat and snow cover changes have contributed to localized declines in agricultural yields

[92] G L Terri-Lynn Williams-Davidson, email correspondence (on file with author, cited with permission).

[93] R Jones, C Rigg, and L Lee, 'Haida Marine Planning: First Nations as a Partner in Marine Conservation' (2010) 15(1) Ecology and Society 12.

[94] IPCC, *Special Report on the Ocean and Cryosphere in a Changing Climate* (September 2019), <https://www.ipcc.ch/site/assets/uploads/sites/3/2019/11/SROCC_FinalDraft_FullReport.pdf> (hereafter IPCC, *Cryosphere*).

[95] Ibid at 1–49.

[96] Ibid at 1–24.

[97] Ibid at 1–7.

[98] Ibid at 58.

[99] Ibid at 7.2.

in some high mountain regions, including Hindu Kush Himalaya and the tropical Andes.[100]

There are also serious impacts on Indigenous businesses and community infrastructures from melting permafrost. Local buildings and roads are collapsing in extraordinary numbers, and coastal communities in some cases have had to plan for complete relocation.[101] Estimates are that up to 70 per cent of infrastructure of businesses, residential, transportation, and industrial facilities in over 1,200 settlements will suffer damage due to projected permafrost thaw by 2050.[102]

Special attention is also needed in respect of development of pipelines and other economic activities that impinge on longstanding use of Indigenous territorial lands and waters. Larissa Crawford, of Métis and Jamaican ancestry, researcher on Indigenous renewable energy policy and independent business owner in Canada, has observed:

> We cannot speak to energy and land development—even in the interest of climate change—while removing the historical and present-day context of the violent and forced state-removal of Indigenous Peoples from their traditional lands. It is important, when reflecting on the urgency of climate change and the current RCMP raids on Wet'suwet'en territory, to understand that Indigenous Peoples all over the globe are using their ancestral wisdom in the interest of *all* of our future generations. We will not have climate justice with the absence of this understanding.[103]

Some advocates have observed that given the lack of economic security, the attraction of resource-related jobs is increasing, even where mining or transportation of fossil fuels negatively affect the land for which Indigenous peoples are stewards.[104] This economic pressure detracts from developing a broad consensus regarding the need to undertake economic development in partnership with Indigenous peoples, recognizing their hereditary and elected governance and decision-making structures. Co-management strategies developed collectively with Indigenous peoples can be highly effective in safeguarding nature and its contributions by incorporating Indigenous knowledge into project plans and their implementation.

The IPCC has reported on both the challenges and the potential for Indigenous peoples, noting that innovative tools and practices in polar resource management could enhance capacity to respond to climate change.[105] It calls for networks of protected areas and community-based ecological monitoring that draw on local and Indigenous knowledge to develop strategic plans for sustaining biodiversity and limiting risk to

[100] Ibid at 1–7.

[101] M Meredith, M Sommerkorn, S Cassotta, C Derksen, A Ekaykin, A Hollowed, G Kofinas, A Mackintosh, J Melbourne-Thomas, M Muelbert, G Ottersen, H Pritchard, and E Schuur, 'Polar Regions' in IPCC, *Cryosphere* (n 94) at 206, 260.

[102] Ibid at 260, citing J Hjort et al, 'Degrading Permafrost Puts Arctic Infrastructure at Risk by Mid-Century' (2018) 9(1) Nat Commun 5147.

[103] Larissa Crawford (public remarks and email exchange, on file with author, cited with permission).

[104] Melody Schreiber, 'The Race to Save Arctic Cities as Permafrost Melts', *Citylab* (10 May 2018), <https://www.citylab.com/environment/2018/05/the-race-to-save-arctic-cities-as-permafrost-melts/559307/>. See also Sheila Watt-Cloutier, *The Right to Be Cold: One Women's Story of Protecting Her Culture, the Artic and the Whole Planet* (Penguin, 2016) at 287.

[105] IPCC, *Cryosphere* (n 94) at 60.

human livelihoods and well-being.[106] The IPCC notes that strong multiscale linkages with Arctic local communities can benefit from including Indigenous knowledge in the formulation of adaptation strategies. It refers to Indigenous knowledge as the understandings, skills, and philosophies developed by societies with long histories of interaction with their natural surroundings, passed on from generation to generation, and highly adaptive in changing conditions.[107] The IPCC notes that Indigenous communities must be part of an integrated approach to disaster risk reduction in response to cryosphere hazards.[108]

The IPCC reports that Indigenous traditional knowledge systems and practices, including Indigenous peoples' holistic view of community and environment, are a major resource for adapting to climate change, but this knowledge has not been used consistently in existing efforts.[109] Integrating such forms of knowledge into practices can increase the effectiveness of adaptation; for example, Indigenous, traditional knowledge of water-saving, conservation agriculture, and food storage techniques.[110]

The Intergovernmental Science-Policy Platform on Biodiversity and Ecosystem Services ('ISPPBES') advocates recognizing the knowledge, innovations, practices, institutions, and values of Indigenous peoples and local communities, and ensuring their inclusion and participation in environmental governance.[111] Such inclusion can enhance their quality of life and help to generally advance conservation, restoration, and sustainable use of nature. These positive contributions of Indigenous peoples to sustainability can be facilitated through national recognition of land tenure, access and resource rights, improved collaboration, and fair and equitable sharing of benefits arising from use and co-management arrangements with local communities.[112]

There are numerous studies on why Indigenous peoples need special attention in the effort to address climate change, and it is important for companies, asset managers, and institutional investors to consider how they will integrate these considerations in their business plans.[113] As will be discussed in Chapter 8, which examines the Coastal

[106] Ibid at 60.

[107] Ibid at 1–36.

[108] Ibid at 1–38.

[109] IPCC, *Climate Change 2014: Synthesis Report. Contribution of Working Groups I, II, and III to the Fifth Assessment Report of the Intergovernmental Panel on Climate Change* (2014) at 80, <https://www.ipcc.ch/report/ar5/syr/>.

[110] Ibid at 96.

[111] S Diaz et al, *The Global Assessment Report on Biodiversity and Ecosystem Services*, Intergovernmental Science-Policy Platform on Biodiversity and Ecosystem Services (May 2019) at 18, <https://ipbes.net/system/tdf/inline/files/ipbes_global_assessment_report_summary_for_polciymakers.pdf?file=1&type=node&id=36213> (hereafter ISPPBES).

[112] Ibid.

[113] See for example, A Agrawal, 'Dismantling the Divide Between Indigenous and Scientific Knowledge (1995) 26 Development and Change 413–39; B Baptiste, D Pacheco, M Carneiro da Cunha, and S Diaz, 'Knowing Our Lands and Resources: Indigenous and Local Knowledge of Biodiversity and Ecosystem Services in the Americas' (2016) Knowledges of Nature 11; S Cassotta and M Mazza, 'Balancing de jure and de facto Arctic Environmental Law Applied to the Oil and Gas Industry: Linking Indigenous Rights, Social Impact Assessment and Business in Greenland' (2014) The Yearbook of Polar Law 63–119; S Crate et al, 'Permafrost Livelihoods: A Transdisciplinary Review and Analysis of Thermokarst-based Systems of Indigenous Land Use' (2015) 18 Anthropocene 89–104; J D Ford et al, 'Adaptation and Indigenous Peoples in the United Nations Framework Convention on Climate Change' (2016) 139 (3/4) Climatic Change 429–43; J Nalau et al, 'The Role of Indigenous and Traditional Knowledge in Ecosystem-based Adaptation: A Review of the Literature and Case Studies from the Pacific Islands' (2018) 10(4) Weather, Climate, and Society

First Nations Great Bear Initiative, there are successful models of conservation and economic development plans that build on Indigenous knowledge and offer economic models that empower Indigenous peoples in the protection of their traditional lands, while offering measurable co-benefits to businesses and the economy.

Having identified some of the financial risks, the next chapters begin to identify aspects of effective governance and climate resilience. Climate resilience involves organizations developing adaptive capacity to respond to climate change to better manage the associated risks and seize opportunities, including the ability to respond to transition risks and physical risks.[114] Opportunities include improving efficiency, designing new production processes, and developing new products. Opportunities related to resilience may be especially relevant for organizations that have long-lived fixed assets or extensive supply or distribution networks and businesses that depend critically on utility and infrastructure networks or natural resources in their value chain.[115]

851–65; M Roué and Z Molnar, 'Knowing Our Lands and Resources: Indigenous and Local Knowledge of Biodiversity and Ecosystem Services in Europe and Central Asia' (2017) Knowledges of Nature 9.

[114] TCFD, 'Final Report' (n 2) at 6–7.
[115] Ibid.

4
Fiduciaries' Obligations and Climate Governance

There is no more important or pressing issue of our time than climate change. The fundamental roles played globally by corporations and their investors means that their governance decisions will have profound consequences for whether we are able to meet the challenges confronting us.

Catherine McCall, Executive Director
Canadian Coalition for Good Governance ('CCGG')[1]

This chapter examines the nature of fiduciary obligation and the duty of care in respect of responsibility to address climate change. Given the importance of fiduciary obligation to understanding the obligations of directors and officers of companies, of pension trustees and other pension fiduciaries, and of asset managers and other individuals and entities managing the investments of others, it commences with a general discussion of duties imposed on each of these types of fiduciaries. The chapter draws on both common law and statutory law to examine why corporate law, pension law, trust law, and financial services law in most common law and civil law jurisdictions globally, as currently framed, already create obligations to take various kinds of action to address climate change.

The chapter then turns more specifically to each of these groups. It discusses the obligation of directors and officers of both publicly and privately held corporations to engage in effective climate governance as part of their obligation to act in the best interests of the company. It explains the notions of fiduciary obligation, the duty of care, and corporate citizenship. The chapter then examines how pension fund trustees, in fulfilling their obligations to invest and manage assets for multiple generations of beneficiaries, also have an obligation to identify and address climate-related financial risks. It then turns to asset managers and other managers of funds that invest for others, and analyses why they also have a duty of care in respect of their investment activities. The following part of the chapter then turns to what these obligations mean for each type of fiduciary in their effective management of climate-related risks. It explores how institutional investors are beginning to create new priorities for investments that aim towards moving to net zero carbon emissions. The chapter concludes with a discussion of why effective disclosure of climate risk is part of legal duties.

[1] Catherine McCall, Executive Director, Canadian Coalition for Good Governance, (December 2019). Quote on file with author and cited with permission.

From Ideas to Action. Janis Sarra, Oxford University Press (2020). © Janis Sarra. DOI: 10.1093/oso/9780198852308.003.0004.

The chapter is long and detailed because it is necessary to develop a deep understanding of the law in respect of the obligations of these different private actors to the organizations, beneficiaries, and clients over whose assets they have oversight and management responsibility. A comprehensive understanding of fiduciary and other obligations can facilitate, rather than constrain, the ability of directors, officers, and other fiduciaries to address the complex challenges of climate-related financial risk.[2] Such an understanding provides an answer to concerns that consideration of climate change somehow places social benefits before enterprise wealth maximization and maximization of the financial performance of a company's investments.[3] Fiduciary obligations require fiduciaries to make decisions based on a horizon longer than the financial quarter or year, and these decisions should not be limited to profit/return on investment for such limited periods. Fiduciaries have a duty to acknowledge, identify, and address the potential costs and benefits of climate change risk, even where those costs and benefits cannot be fully quantified immediately.[4] They have a responsibility to consider the benefits of investment in green adaption and mitigation technologies, and other products and services that are likely to have upside financial potential.

While the legislation governing corporate directors and officers, and that governing pension funds and other institutional investors, have different parameters, one point of commonality is the scope of duties of care and loyalty, and more specifically, how they create duties in respect of oversight and management of climate-related risk.

There are also significant opportunities for businesses and investors in the transition to a net zero carbon economy. Efforts to mitigate and adapt to climate change will produce new opportunities for organizations through resource efficiency and cost savings,[5] technological innovation, the adoption of low-emission energy sources,[6] the development of new low-emission products and services, and access to new markets as sectors shift to a net zero carbon economy and build resilience along the supply chain.[7] Good governance suggests that directors and other fiduciaries address these upside potential opportunities to offset transition risks and costs. Climate-related opportunities will vary depending on the region, market, and industry in which an organization operates.[8]

It is important to commence by examining what exactly a fiduciary is.

[2] Janis Sarra, *Fiduciary Obligations in Business and Investment: Implications of Climate Change* (CCLI, 2018) at 1, <https://law-ccli-2019.sites.olt.ubc.ca/files/2019/08/Janis-Sarra-Fiduciary-Obligation-in-Business-and-Investment.pdf> (hereafter Sarra, *Fiduciary Obligations*).

[3] Ibid.

[4] Ibid.

[5] UNEP and Copenhagen Centre for Energy Efficiency, 'Best Practices and Case Studies for Industrial Energy Efficiency Improvement' (February 2016); Environmental Protection Agency Victoria (EPA Victoria), 'Resource Efficiency Case Studies: Lower your Impact' (2013), <http://www.epa.vic.gov.au/business-and-industry/lower-your-impact/resource-efficiency/case-studies>.

[6] International Energy Agency, 'Global energy investment down 8% in 2015 with flows signalling move towards cleaner energy' (14 September 2016).

[7] G20 Green Finance Study Group, *G20 Green Finance Synthesis Report* (5 September 2016), <http://unepinquiry.org/wp-content/uploads/2016/09/Synthesis_Report_Full_EN.pdf>. See also Financial Stability Board, Task Force on Climate-related Financial Disclosures, *Final Report, Recommendations of the Task Force on Climate-related Financial Disclosures* (15 June 2017) at 6–7, <https://www.fsb-tcfd.org/publications/final-recommendations-report/> (hereafter TCFD, *Final Report*).

[8] Ibid.

I. What is a Fiduciary Duty?

The word 'fiduciary' is derived from the term *fiducia* in Roman law, which connotes a relationship of trust, confidence, and reliance.[9] For more than one hundred years, *Black's Law Dictionary* has defined a fiduciary as a relationship founded on trust, the fiduciary relationship arising where one person reposes faith, confidence, and trust in the other person to manage their money or other assets in good faith.[10] *Black's Law Dictionary* defines a fiduciary as 'a person holding the character of a trustee, or a character analogous to that of a trustee, in respect of the trust and confidence involved in it, and the scrupulous good faith and candor which it requires'.[11] It states that a fiduciary is:

> A person having duty, created by his undertaking, to act primarily for another's benefit in matters connected with such undertaking. The duty is to act primarily for another's benefit in matters connected with the undertaking ... A person or institution who manages money or property for another and who must exercise a standard of care in such management activity imposed by law or contract.[12]

Black's Law Dictionary goes on to specify that fiduciary relationships are marked with the obligation of the fiduciary to act in good faith, exercise fairness, and have due regard to the interests of the beneficiaries.[13]

Generally, a fiduciary relationship is 'a relationship in which one person is under a duty to act for the benefit of another person on matters within the scope of the relationship'.[14] The Supreme Court of Canada has held that a fiduciary obligation 'arises in a relationship in which the fiduciary has a discretion or power to exercise, the fiduciary can unilaterally exercise this discretion or power, and the beneficiary is vulnerable to, or at the mercy of, the fiduciary'.[15] The precise scope of a fiduciary's duties depends on the nature of the fiduciary's relationship with one or more beneficiaries.[16] Prior to modern corporations statutes, directors were found to be in a fiduciary relationship with the corporation and, therefore, required to exercise care in making management decisions with respect to the corporation.[17] The Supreme Court of Canada has held that there are certain common threads running through fiduciary duties that arise from relationships marked by discretionary power and trust, such as loyalty and the avoidance of a conflict of interest, and a duty not to profit at the expense of the beneficiary.[18]

[9] *Black's Law Dictionary* (West Publishing, 1971) at 563.
[10] Ibid at 564.
[11] Ibid at 563.
[12] Ibid.
[13] Ibid at 564.
[14] For a discussion see R Yalden, J Sarra, M Gillen, M Khimji, C Liao, P Patten, M Condon, G Campo, B Bryan, and M Deturbide, *Business Organizations: Practice, Theory and Emerging Challenges* (Emond Montgomery, 2017) (hereafter Yalden et al).
[15] *Lac Minerals Ltd v International Corona Resources Ltd* [1989] 2 SCR 574 (SCC) (hereafter *Lac Minerals*).
[16] *Guerin v The Queen* [1984] 2 SCR 335 at 384.
[17] *Lac Minerals* (n 15).
[18] Ibid.

In common law jurisdictions, fiduciary duties are the key framework governing the discretion of corporate directors and investment decision-makers, duties originally developed by the courts and enhanced by statute.[19] In the United Kingdom ('UK'), for example, a fiduciary is 'someone who has undertaken to act for or on behalf of another in a particular matter in circumstances that give rise to a relationship of trust and confidence'.[20]

In jurisdictions where civil law applies, for example, Brazil, China, Japan, and countries in the European Union ('EU') such as France and Germany, the obligations equivalent to fiduciary duties are set out in statutory provisions regulating the conduct of investment decision-makers and directors of companies, and in the governmental guidelines that assist in the interpretation of these provisions.[21] For example, for investment fiduciaries, the obligations differ slightly between jurisdictions and type of fiduciary, but common features include: the duty to act conscientiously in the interests of beneficiaries; the duty to seek returns; recognition of the portfolio approach to modern investment, either in express terms or implicitly in the form of requirements to ensure adequate diversification; and other duties relating to liquidity and limits on the types of assets that may be selected for certain categories of funds.[22] These fiduciaries have discretion as to how they invest the funds they control, but the scope of that discretion varies.[23]

Fiduciary duties or their equivalent obligations exist to ensure that those individuals or organizations that manage other people's money act in the interests of beneficiaries and do not serve their own interests. A important aspect is the duty of loyalty, i.e. that fiduciaries must act honestly and in good faith in the interests of their beneficiaries, impartially balance the conflicting interests of different beneficiaries, avoid conflicts of interest, and they must not act for the benefit of themselves or a third party.[24] Another important obligation is the duty of care or duty of prudence, i.e. that fiduciaries must act with due care, skill, and diligence, managing or investing as an 'ordinary prudent person' would.[25]

II. The Duties of Directors and Officers of Companies

In most countries globally, the statutory framework that governs corporations specifies that, in exercising their duties under corporate law, directors and officers must act in the best interests of the company.[26] As with fiduciary obligations generally, the

[19] UN PRI, Fiduciary Duty in the 21st Century Final Report (October 2019) at 11, <https://www.unpri.org/download?ac=9593> (hereafter UN PRI, *Fiduciary Duty in the 21st Century*).

[20] Alexia Staker and Alice Garton, 'Directors' Liability and Climate Risk: United Kingdom—Country Paper' (CCLI, 2018), <https://ccli.ouce.ox.ac.uk/wp-content/uploads/2018/04/CCLI-UK-Paper-Final.pdf> (hereafter UK CCLI Country Paper). See also *Bristol and West Building Society v Mothew* [1998] Ch 1 at 16, which held that the 'principal is entitled to the single-minded loyalty of his fiduciary'.

[21] UN PRI, *Fiduciary Duty in the 21st Century* (n 19) at 11.

[22] Ibid.

[23] Ibid.

[24] Ibid at 12.

[25] Sarra, *Fiduciary Obligations* (n 2).

[26] For an in-depth discussion in the Canadian context, see ibid.

fiduciary duty to act in the best interests of the company is often framed as both a duty of care and a duty of loyalty. In some countries, such as Canada, the court has ruled that the statutory fiduciary obligation refers to the duty of loyalty part of a director's duty and that the duty of care is separate, as discussed below.

In the EU, as in most jurisdictions globally, directors' duties are owed to the company, rather than to its shareholders.[27] The company's interest is to survive in the long term in order to achieve the purpose for which it was incorporated, taking into consideration the economic, social, and environmental issues to which its activities give rise.[28] For example, in the Netherlands, directors are to act in the best interests of the company and its enterprise, which includes all its stakeholders.[29] The duties and responsibilities of company directors in the Netherlands are regulated the Dutch Civil Code and by the respective company's articles of association.[30] The Civil Code requires directors to serve the best interest of the company, and when managing the company, the interests of all the persons involved in the company should be considered. Directors are to act with due care and attention, and a company director should make sure that the company complies with existing laws and regulations.[31] Directors are also to behave towards others in the company in accordance with what is required by standards of reasonableness and fairness.[32] The Supreme Court of the Netherlands has held that shareholder interests do not take priority over the interests of other stakeholders.[33] The Netherlands Corporate Governance Code also requires that the management board pay attention to environment, social, and employee-related matters, the supply chain within which the enterprise operates, respect for human rights, and fighting corruption and bribery.[34]

In jurisdictions where specific duties are imposed on directors, a core duty is to promote and protect the interests of the company, often expressed as a duty of care and duty of loyalty.[35]

In the UK, under company law and common law, directors of companies have a duty to promote the success of the company, to exercise independent judgment, and to exercise reasonable care, skill, and diligence.[36] The UK courts have held that the scope, scale, and probability of a particular risk will determine the extent to which directors must consider and address that risk in order to fulfil their due diligence obligations.[37]

[27] Claire Jeffwitz, 'Redefining Directors' Duties in the EU to Promote Long-Termism and Sustainability', <https://frankbold.org/sites/default/files/publikace/redefining_directors_duties_in_the_eu_to_promote_long-termism_and_sustainability_paper_frank_bold.pdf> (hereafter Jeffwitz).

[28] Ibid at 2.

[29] B Sjåfjell, A Johnston, L Anker-Sorensen, and D Millon, 'Shareholder Primacy: The Main Barrier to Sustainable Companies' in B Sjåfjell and B Richardson (eds), *Company Law and Sustainability* (CUP, 2015) at 104 (hereafter Sjåfjell et al).

[30] Book 2 of the Dutch Civil Code, <http://www.dutchcivillaw.com/civilcodebook022.htm>.

[31] Section 2:9 of the Dutch Civil Code.

[32] Section 2:8 of the Dutch Civil Code. The Netherlands has strict rules regarding personal liability of directors of limited companies ('BV') and public limited companies ('NV').

[33] Jeffwitz (n 27) at 15.

[34] Sjåfjell et al (n 29) at 104.

[35] Beate Sjåfjell and Linn Anker-Sørensen, 'The Duties of the Board and Corporate Social Responsibility' (9 September 2013), <https://papers.ssrn.com/sol3/papers.cfm?abstract_id=2322680.

[36] UK, Companies Act 2006, ss 172, 173, and 174.

[37] UK 'CCLI Country Paper' (n 20) at 19.

Directors have 'a continuing duty to acquire and maintain a sufficient knowledge and understanding of the company's business to enable them to properly discharge their duties'; and any delegation of functions to managers does not absolve a director from the duty.[38]

More recently, the UK has adopted an 'enlightened shareholder value' approach. Section 172 of the UK Companies Act 2006, titled 'Duty to promote the success of the company', specifies that a company director must act in the way he or she considers, in good faith, would be most likely to promote the success of the company for the benefit of its members as a whole, and in doing so have regard, amongst other matters, to the likely consequences of any decision in the long term; the interests of the company's employees; the need to foster the company's business relationships with suppliers, customers, and others; the impact of the company's operations on the community and the environment; the desirability of the company maintaining a reputation for high standards of business conduct; and the need to act fairly as between members of the company.[39] One study has observed that this phrasing is confusing because stakeholder interests may materialize in the longer term, while shareholder interests are often short term, and thus the guidance may not achieve its objective of a broader consideration of interests implicated in the company's activities.[40]

In Australia, the duties of directors of publicly held companies are codified in the Corporations Act, as well as existing at common law.[41] The principal duties are the duty of trust and loyalty, including the obligation to act in the best interests of the corporation, honestly, and good faith, and for proper purposes, and to avoid material conflicts of interest. There is also the duty of competence and attentiveness, including duties to act with prudence, due care, skill, and diligence.[42]

In Japan, the Civil Code of Japan requires a person who is under a duty to manage another person's affairs under an agreement, to perform his or her duties with the care required of a 'good and conscientious manager', including a duty of loyalty.[43] The Government has adopted a voluntary Corporate Governance Code,[44] which sets out fundamental principles for effective corporate governance for publicly held companies in Japan, including a requirement that companies should take appropriate measures to address sustainability issues.[45] The United Nations Principles for Responsible Investing ('UN PRI') note that although the term fiduciary duty is commonly translated by legal

[38] Ibid, citing *Re Barings plc (No 5)* [1999] 1 BCLC 433.

[39] UK, Companies Act 2006, s 172.

[40] EU High Level Expert Group on Sustainable Finance 2018, 'Financing a sustainable European economy' (December 2018) at 45–6, <https://ec.europa.eu/info/publications/180308-action-plan-sustainable-growth_en>.

[41] Australia, Corporations Act 2001 (Cth). Section 185 of the Act clarifies that the common law continues to exist, an addition to duties set out in ss 180–184.

[42] Sarah Barker, 'Directors' Liability and Climate Risk: Australia—Country Paper' (CCLI, 2018), <https://ccli.ouce.ox.ac.uk/wp-content/uploads/2018/04/CCLI-Australia-Paper-Final.pdf> (hereafter Barker, 'Australia'), citing *Invensys Australia Superannuation Fund Pty Ltd v Austrac Investments* (2006) 198 FLR 302 at 324.

[43] Article 644 of the Civil Code of Japan, <http://www.japaneselawtranslation.go.jp/law/detail/?id=2057&vm=02&re=02>.

[44] UN PRI, *Fiduciary Obligation in the 21st Century* at 61–2, <https://www.unpri.org/download?ac=1378> citing Japan Corporate Governance Code, effective 2015.

[45] Ibid at 61.

scholars in Japan as 'Jyutakusha-Sekinin' and is a widely-recognized concept among regulators, investors, and companies, the term fiduciary duty is not explicitly stated in Japanese laws and regulations.[46] Japanese law refers to duties of care and of loyalty, which broadly correspond to the duties encompassed by fiduciary duty as defined in other countries.[47]

In South Africa, there are two general duties of directors—fiduciary duties of good faith, honesty, and loyalty; and the duty to exercise reasonable care, skill, and diligence.[48] The fiduciary duties of directors, partially codified in the South African Companies Act, are mandatory and apply to all companies.[49] Directors must exercise their powers and perform their functions in good faith and for a proper purpose in the best interests of the company.[50]

These examples illustrate that while the statutory frameworks differ between jurisdictions, and between common law and civil law legal systems, there are recurring themes of due diligence, loyalty, reasonable care, and acting in the best interests of the company.

III. Obligations of Pension Fiduciaries, Their Investment Managers, and Service Providers

Pension trustees and their investment and engagement fiduciaries have a fiduciary obligation to their pension beneficiaries, which include active employee members currently contributing money, former employees who have vested rights to receive a pension on retirement, and retirees. Pension fund trustees have a fiduciary obligation to pension beneficiaries to act prudently in their best interests in making investment decisions regarding fund portfolios.[51] A fiduciary's duties to beneficiaries are two-fold: to act prudently and with care, and the duty of loyalty. These duties are remarkably similar across many jurisdictions.

Pension trustees' duties are assessed based on the express language in the pension plan, the constating documents of the pension fund, and the relevant pension and trust legislation.[52] For example, for a defined benefit pension plan, the objective is to build a life income for the future retirees. Pension plans have an obligation to make investment decisions that create sustainable pension funds, addressing intergenerational pressures such as the need to fund pensions in the short to medium term, and the need to look ahead to future generations of beneficiaries.[53]

[46] Ibid at 62.

[47] Ibid.

[48] Christine Reddell, 'Directors' Liability and Climate Risk: South Africa—Country Paper' (CCLI, April 2018), <https://ccli.ouce.ox.ac.uk/wp-content/uploads/2018/04/CCLI-South-Africa-Paper-Final.pdf> (hereafter Reddell, 'South Africa').

[49] South Africa, Companies Act, s 76.

[50] Ibid.

[51] Sarra, *Fiduciary Obligations* (n 2) at 45.

[52] *Burke v Hudson's Bay Co* [2010] 2 SCR 273 (SCC) at para 41; *Nolan v Kerry (Canada) Inc* [2009] 2 SCR 678 (SCC) at para 187.

[53] Sarra, *Fiduciary Obligations* (n 2). See also Ronald B Davis, *Democratizing Pension Funds, Corporate Governance and Accountability* (UBC Press, 2008) at 175 (hereafter Davis, *Democratizing Pension Funds*).

Beneficiaries rely on these fiduciaries to act in their best interests, typically defined exclusively in financial terms.[54] Within the scope of the investment decision-maker's discretion, fiduciary duties and equivalent obligations in civil law jurisdictions require that those individuals who manage other people's money act responsibly in the interests of beneficiaries or investors.[55] These duties are particularly important in relationships where there is imbalance in expertise or where the ability of the beneficiary to monitor decisions of the fiduciary or hold them accountable is limited.[56] Investor fiduciaries with obligations to different generations of beneficiaries should make decisions in a manner that balances intergenerational wealth maximization. They need to be cognizant of the potential transfer of risks between generations.

Waitzer and Sarro argue that there is now broad-based acceptance of the idea that most investment returns come from general exposure to the market (*beta*), rather than from seeking market benchmark outperformance strategies (*alpha*).[57] Thus, systemic market factors are critically important to fiduciary responsibility in assessing the impact of investment decisions on intergenerational beneficiaries. In this respect, the definition of prudence in the duty of care has evolved as understanding of investment risk has changed.[58] Under modern portfolio theory, fiduciaries must weigh risk by looking at the portfolio as a whole, to ensure that it is appropriate for beneficiaries and designed to generate a suitable rate of return without creating an undue risk of loss.[59] Asset classes of higher duration often yield the highest private and societal returns.[60] Decisions regarding investments must look beyond current market benchmarks and consider questions of future value, including systemic governance and market risks, as well as potential benefits to current and future generations.[61]

Fiduciaries charged with managing and advising investment vehicles that are exercising stewardship for multiple generations of beneficiaries, like pension plans, must therefore consider the intergenerational implications of their decisions or advice, importing the principle of intergenerational fairness and equity into the duty of loyalty.[62] Pension fiduciaries need to take proactive steps to invest and to encourage investment for the long term, serving the best interests of their beneficiaries by charting a course whereby investment decisions take account of important social and economic challenges, including sustainable development.[63]

In delegating investment decisions to investment managers and proxy voting to service providers, pension trustees cannot delegate their fiduciary obligations. Moreover, in accepting these engagements, the investment managers and services providers

[54] UN PRI, *Fiduciary Duty in the 21st Century* (n 19) at 10.

[55] Ibid.

[56] Ibid at 11.

[57] E Waitzer and D Sarro, 'Fiduciary Society Unleashed: The Road Ahead for the Financial Sector' (2014) Business Lawyer 1081 at 1093 (hereafter Waitzer and Sarro)

[58] Ibid at 1091.

[59] Ibid at 1092.

[60] Ibid at 1093–4, citing Roger Ibbotson, 'The Importance of Asset Allocation' (Mar/Apr 2010) Financial Analysts Journal 18 at 20.

[61] Steve Lydenberg, 'Reason, Rationality and Fiduciary Duty' (2014) 119 Journal of Business Ethics 365 at 375.

[62] Waitzer and Sarro (n 57) at 1096.

[63] Ibid at 1097.

also acquire a fiduciary obligation to act in the best interests of multigenerational beneficiaries.

IV. Fiduciary Obligations of Asset Managers and Investment Funds

Many institutional investors and asset managers are not fiduciaries in the same sense as pension funds, in that they do not have a prudential obligation to act in the interests of multiple generations of beneficiaries to deliver the pension promise. However, they do have fiduciary obligations.

Asset managers and investment managers, in this context, refer to individuals and firms that manage the investments of others on behalf of those individuals and organizations, working towards appreciation of a client's assets over time while mitigating risk. They have a fiduciary obligation to act in the best interests of those persons that have entrusted the asset manager with managing their investment funds. The asset manager owes duties of good faith, care, diligence, and trust, and is bound ethically to act in the others' best interests.

Turning back to *Black's Law Dictionary* for a moment, it specifies that a relation between two persons in regard to a business, contract, or property of such character that trust has been reposed in the other, requires the person with control and management of the assets to exercise a 'corresponding degree of fairness and good faith' and not to engage in self-dealing with regard to the assets.[64] The undertaking of the asset manager is to invest the assets in a prudent and reasonable manner in the interests of clients.

In 2019, in the final report of the 'Fiduciary Obligation in the 21st Century' programme, 'modern fiduciary obligation' was defined as follows:

> Fiduciary duties (or equivalent obligations) exist to ensure that those who manage other people's money act in the interests of beneficiaries, rather than serving their own interests. The most important of these duties are:
>
> Loyalty—Fiduciaries should:
>
> - Act honestly and in good faith in the interests of their clients or beneficiaries.
> - Understand and incorporate into their decision making the sustainability preferences of clients and beneficiaries, whether or not these preferences are financially material.
> - Impartially balance the conflicting interests of different beneficiaries and clients.
> - Avoid conflicts of interest.
> - Not act for the benefit of themselves or third parties.
>
> Prudence—Fiduciaries should act with due care, skill and diligence, investing as an 'ordinary prudent person' would. This includes:

[64] *Black's Law Dictionary* (n 9) at 564.

> - Incorporating financially material ESG [environmental, social and governance] factors into their investment decision making, consistent with the timeframe of the obligation.
> - Being an active owner, encouraging high standards of ESG performance in the companies or other entities in which they are invested.
> - Supporting the stability and resilience of the financial system.
>
> Fiduciaries should disclose their investment approach to clients and/or beneficiaries including information on how preferences are incorporated into the scheme's investment strategy and the potential risks and benefits of doing so.[65]

The International Corporate Governance Network ('ICGN') reports that producing investment returns to meet fund liability obligations, within a prudent level of risk, is the core obligation of investor fiduciaries, and thus, consideration of systemic risk is embedded in fiduciary duty.[66] Investor fiduciaries must take both a fact-based and a longer term holistic view in balancing how their investment practices affect the short and long term interests of their beneficiaries.[67] Over the long term, unsustainable investment practices that carry material systemic risks or impose negative externalities on society may have adverse financial consequences for beneficiaries; thus, mitigating any potential effects from systemic risk may be considered part of fiduciary duty.[68]

This brief summary helpfully synthesizes the collective insights of jurisdictions across the world in terms of the fiduciary obligations of investors, equally applicable to investors that are not pension fiduciaries. The next two parts analyse how these general obligations apply in respect of climate change financial risk.

V. The Duties of Company Directors and Officers in Respect of Climate Change Governance

As noted in the previous chapter, climate-related financial risk will continue to increase as countries transition to a net zero carbon economy. Directors and officers have a duty to identify the risks, and where these risks are material, they have an obligation to develop strategies to address those risks in the best interests of the company. Duly diligent efforts by these fiduciaries are not likely to be second-guessed by the courts, and thus, the best strategy to avoid liability risk is by acting now.

One of the most challenging aspects of effective climate governance is to address the tension between moving the business towards climate resilience and the need to produce returns in the short term for equity investors.[69] For publicly traded companies, reporting financial results on a quarterly, biannual, and annual basis exacerbates pressures for short term returns. Yet while there appears to be mismatched timelines between capital markets' need for profit, given directors' and officers' obligations to act

[65] UN PRI, *Fiduciary Duty in the 21st Century* (n 19) at 21.

[66] ICGN, *Guidance on Investor Fiduciary Duties* (2018) at 12, <http://icgn.flpbks.com/icgn-fiduciary_duties/files/extfile/DownloadURL.pdf> (hereafter ICGN, *Guidance*).

[67] Ibid.

[68] Ibid.

[69] Sarra, *Fiduciary Obligations* (n 2) at 10.

in the best interests of the company, and the need for long term sustainability of a company,[70] such mismatches are neither necessary nor inevitable, as addressed in this part.

The statutory obligations, and for common law countries, the statutory and common law obligations, that directors act honestly and in good faith, and act with care and diligence in supervising and managing the corporation's affairs, necessarily means that they must engage with the issues of physical and transition climate change risks.[71] While in the immediate term, the risks may range from minor to major, there is no business now immune from the effects of global warming. The US Sustainability Accounting Standards Board reports that seventy-two of seventy-seven industry subsectors are materially affected by climate change and that climate risks affect 93 per cent of US equity markets.[72] Thus, there is a direct economic link between directors' and officers' duties and effective climate governance. In acting in best interests of the company, directors and officers have a duty to be proactive and critically evaluate and address the material financial and other risks and opportunities associated with climate change. There are a wide range of issues for boards to address, depending on the location of the company's operations and assets. Moreover, as governments move towards enhanced standards to achieve net zero carbon emissions, all businesses will have to act to meet these evolving targets.

On a practical level, the exercise of corporate duties can be complex. Climate-related risk is one of many risks that directors must identify and plan for in exercising oversight of the company, along with other emerging risks such as cybersecurity risk, fintech financing, insurance pricing and availability, and health pandemics. Part of directors' responsibility is to assess the materiality of these risks and work to address material risks to the extent that they can. In this respect, they need to ensure that managers are providing them with the information and technical expertise to allow the directors to make effective decisions about business strategies and responses to myriad risks, allocating resources as appropriate.

In the UK, a study by the Commonwealth Climate and Law Initiative has observed that the scope of directors' duties and the extent to which they require directors to address climate risk will evolve to reflect increasing awareness of climate change and its potential impact on business.[73] Lord Sales, Justice of the UK Supreme Court, recently observed that the duties of directors of companies in relation to climate change are threefold: they have obligations to comply with various regulatory and legal disclosure requirements now implemented; directors have a responsibility to take account of climate change effects and their financial impacts on their companies in so far as the law imposes fines in relation to polluting activities or creates tax incentives to encourage a shift to low carbon activity; and third, the general obligations of directors owed to their company permits directors to have regard to climate change effects as a factor in

[70] Janis Sarra, 'The Anthropocene at the Time of Trump' (2018) 51 UBC Law Review 489–547 (hereafter Sarra, 'Anthropocene').

[71] Sarra, *Fiduciary Obligations* (n 2) at 5–6.

[72] SASB, 'Annual Report 2015', <https://www.sasb.org/wp-content/uploads/2016/07/SASB-AnnualReport-071316-web-spreads.pdf>.

[73] UK CCLI Country Paper (n 20) at 11.

their decision-making.[74] Lord Sales observed that under certain circumstances, directors' general fiduciary and due care obligations require them to cause their companies to take action to reduce their contribution to climate changing activity, noting that the 'climate change horizon' is getting closer.[75]

In Canada, there are both statutory provisions and a highly developed jurisprudence on director and officer duties in the business context that are sufficient to ground a duty to address climate-related financial risk.[76] Codified fiduciary duty provisions operate in tandem with common law obligations. Corporate law specifies that directors and officers of corporations have a duty to act in the best interests of the corporation.[77] The corporate statutory duty of loyalty requires that the directors and officers of a corporation 'act honestly and in good faith with a view to the best interests of the corporation'.[78] The statutory duty of care requires that the directors and officers 'exercise the care, diligence and skill that a reasonably prudent person would exercise in comparable circumstances'.[79] The Supreme Court of Canada ('SCC') has held that: 'In considering what is in the best interests of the corporation, directors may look to the interests of, inter alia, shareholders, employees, creditors, consumers, governments and the environment to inform their decisions.'[80] In executing its duty of loyalty to the corporation, the board of directors is required to reflect on the interests of the corporation both as an economic actor and as a 'good corporate citizen'.[81]

In Canada, while early court decisions on the common law fiduciary obligation found the obligation includes both the duty of care and the duty of loyalty, under statutory corporate law, almost twenty years ago the SCC separated the duties into the duty of loyalty (calling it the statutory fiduciary obligation) and the duty of care. While the substance of the duties did not change, to whom the duty was owed was distinguished. The duty of loyalty is to the corporation; the duty of care is broader. The SCC held that the duty of care does not specifically refer to an identifiable party as the beneficiary of the duty.[82] Thus, the identity of the beneficiary of the duty of care is more open-ended,[83] which may mean that other stakeholders could seek remedies from the company for directors' failure to act on climate change. The SCC held that the statutory duty of care requires more of directors and officers than the traditional common law duty of care.[84] A director's duties implicate considerations of what good corporate citizenship requires in the context of climate change.

[74] Lord Sales, Justice of UK Supreme Court, 'Directors' duties and climate change: Keeping pace with environmental challenges' (27 August 2019) at 3–4, <https://www.supremecourt.uk/docs/speech-190827.pdf>.

[75] Ibid at 2.

[76] For a comprehensive analysis, see Sarra, *Fiduciary Obligation* (n 2).

[77] See, for example, the Canada Business Corporations Act, RSC 1985, c C-44, as amended (hereafter CBCA), s 122(1).

[78] CBCA and its sister provincial and territorial corporations statutes.

[79] *Peoples Department Stores Inc (Trustee of) v Wise*, 2004 SCC 68, [2004] 3 SCR 461 (hereafter *Peoples Department Stores*).

[80] Ibid; *BCE Inc v 1976 Debentureholders*, 2008 SCC 69 at para 39, [2008] 3 SCR 560 (hereafter *BCE*).

[81] BCE, ibid at para 66.

[82] Ibid at para 57.

[83] Ibid.

[84] Ibid.

Effective November 2019, the Canada Business Corporations Act ('CBCA') codified the common law to state that, when acting with a view to the best interests of the corporation, the directors and officers of the corporation may consider, but are not limited to, the interests of different stakeholders, the environment, and the long term interests of the corporation. The amendments apply to 350,000 Canadian companies.

Globally, the risks posed by climate change, the broad scientific consensus on the impacts of climate change, and recent governmental commitment to its remediation create reasonable expectations by citizens that legal and other processes will advance these public policy objectives.[85] Reasonable expectations have been used to achieve objectives that are remarkably consistent across nation states, requiring the fair treatment of others and upholding the integrity of legal or regulatory regimes by closing the gaps and loopholes that allow avoiding the obligations associated with these regimes.[86]

A focus on systemic risks acknowledges the interdependencies of companies, financial organizations, and civil society. It requires that decision-makers act with reference to others in society and to the principles that inform reasonable expectations. These principles—fair treatment of others, as well as upholding the integrity of legal regimes—are concerned with the protection or enhancement of the public good.[87] These expectations can also inform a judgment as to what constitutes good corporate citizenship in the context of climate change when evaluating whether directors have fulfilled their duties.

Such an inclusive view of corporate decision making is not new. John Rawls envisioned society as a fair system of social co-operation over time that reflects a notion of reciprocity or mutuality, passed inter-generationally, guided by publicly recognized rules and agreed upon standards.[88] He observed that if individuals had to determine distribution of goods or treatment of others ignorant of where they would fall within that distribution, they would strive for a more equitable distribution for everyone.[89] Viewing climate change in this way, the SCC's direction that fiduciaries are to act as good corporate citizens has relevance for the allocation of both the benefits and costs of addressing climate-related financial risk equitably across society.

i. Directors' Duty of Care Requires Action on Climate Change

As part of their mandate to manage risk in the best interests of the company, corporate directors and officers must turn their minds to climate-related risk. Give the wide acknowledgement of the risks by governments and courts, directors can no longer claim not to be aware of climate change. The duty of care requires directors and officers to exercise the care, diligence, and skill that a reasonably prudent person would exercise in the circumstances. This duty requires directors and officers to identify and develop

85 Ibid.
86 Ibid.
87 John Rawls, *Political Liberalism* (Harvard University Press, 1966).
88 John Rawls, *Justice as Fairness: A Restatement*, E Kelly (ed.) (Harvard University Press, 2001).
89 John Rawls, *A Theory of Justice* (Harvard University Press, 1971, revised 1999).

strategies to supervise and manage the transition that will address the specific material risks posed by climate change. It also requires ongoing monitoring and adjusting of climate-related strategies to ensure they continue to be responsive to the risks. Neglect of their duty may increase financial risks for the corporation. To the extent that the failure to act causes foreseeable harm to third parties, the corporation may be held liable through a tort action.

The crucial question of 'what are the best interests of the company' in respect of climate change risk requires directors and officers to directly engage with developments in knowledge regarding physical and transition risks and how that information may impact their corporation. As discussed above, fiduciaries can consider the interests of numerous types of stakeholders and the environment when determining how to act in the corporation's best interest in respect of climate-related risks and opportunities. Directors and officers who engage in good governance practices already take account of socio-economic conditions and the diverse and sometimes conflicting interests of all the stakeholders with an interest in the company. Ronald Davis has observed that:

> While shareholder wealth maximization as a goal of corporate activity has an appealing simplicity to it, the simplicity is deceiving. Conceptually it contains a level of indeterminacy that continues to raise issues of the proper exercise of corporate power, the balance between interests of investors with differing time horizons, and the appropriate concern to be shown to stakeholders other than shareholders by corporate management ... the range of options on corporate management's desk rarely involves the following decision pairs—profit, only if socially irresponsible versus no profit, only if socially responsible. Providing one takes into account all consequences that can reasonably be expected to occur over the foreseeable future, having only these choices before one is rare. These rare choices will be provided only if one is focused solely on the immediate cost and benefit, to the exclusion of all other costs and benefits.[90]

Director oversight involves balancing multiple considerations, different types of risk, over different timelines, and the interests of a range of stakeholders, including debt and equity investors, employees, consumers, and suppliers. Oversight of managers means that directors need to be alert to how risks specifically impact their company, sector, and region, how it may affect supply chains or distribution of products and services, and what strategies can be deployed to manage that risk. They can rely on managers and professionals to advise them, but cannot delegate their duties.

In two legal opinions on climate change and directors' duties in Australia, Noel Hutley SC and Sebastian Hartford Davis in 2016 and 2019 found that Australian companies are exposed to material physical and transition risks of climate change.[91] In their first

[90] Davis, *Democratizing Pension Funds* (n 53) at 175.

[91] Noel Hutley SC and Sebastian Hartford Davis, 'Climate Change and Directors' Duties, Supplementary memorandum of Opinion' (26 March 2019), Australia Centre for Policy Development (hereafter Hutley and Hartford Davis 2019). See also Noel Hutley SC and Sebastian Hartford Davis, 'Climate Change and Directors Duties, Memorandum of Opinion' (7 October 2016), commissioned by the Future Business Council and the Centre for Policy Development, <https://cpd.org.au/wp-content/uploads/2016/10/Legal-Opinion-on-Climate-Change-and-Directors-Duties.pdf> (hereafter Hutley and Hartford Davis 2016).

opinion, they considered the extent to which the duty of care and diligence imposed on company directors by s 180(1) of the Australia Corporations Act 2001 permits Australian company directors to respond to climate change risks. Their opinion was that, as matter of Australian law, company directors can, and in some cases should, be considering the impact on their business of climate change risks, to the extent they intersect with the interests of the firm, and that climate-related risks are foreseeable risks of harm to Australian businesses.[92] They advised that prudent directors should take positive steps: to inform themselves, disclose the risks as part of financial reporting, and take such steps as they may see fit, with due regard to gravity and probability of the risk, and the burden and practicality of available steps in mitigation.[93] In their view, company directors who fail to consider climate change risks could be found liable for breaching their duty of care and diligence in the future.[94] In the subsequent 2019 opinion, Hutley and Hartford Davis opine:

> The developments that have occurred suggest that we are now observers of a profound and accelerating shift in the way that Australian regulators, firms and the public perceive climate risk. There has been a series of coordinated interventions by Australian regulators, which will require in practice that increased attention be given to both the assessment and disclosure of climate risk. There has been acute interest in these issues from investor groups. There have been developments in the state of scientific knowledge. In our opinion, these matters elevate the standard of care that will be expected of a reasonable director.[95]

Hutley and Hartford Davis observed that company directors should be assessing the impact on their business if concerted decarbonization efforts do not occur.[96] Specifically, directors must assess what steps are necessary or appropriate to adapt to global warming of 1.5°C, possibly within five years; what steps are necessary to predict, influence, and respond in the short to medium term to the unprecedented transitions that will be required in order to avoid global warming of 1.5°C, particularly in the resource, energy, transport, and industrial sectors; and what the impact on their business will be as a result of the escalating physical changes.[97] They noted that the significant and well-publicized risks associated with climate change and global warming would be regarded by a court as foreseeable, therefore requiring engagement by company directors.[98] Regulators and investors now have an expectation of rigorous financial analysis, targeted governance, comprehensive disclosures, and ultimately, sophisticated corporate responses at the individual firm and system level; and large firms will be expected to invest seriously in capabilities to monitor, manage, and respond to climate change risks.[99] Hutley and Hartford Davis suggest that the exposure

[92] Ibid (2016) at 2.
[93] Ibid.
[94] Ibid at 6–8.
[95] Hutley and Hartford Davis 2019 (n 91) at 2.
[96] Ibid at 6.
[97] Ibid at 6–7.
[98] Ibid at 8.
[99] Ibid.

of individual directors to climate change litigation will increase, probably exponentially, with time.[100]

The Hutley and Hartford Davis legal opinion has been cited with approval by the Australian Prudential Regulatory Authority ('APRA'), the Australian Securities and Investment Commission, the Australian Stock Exchange, the Reserve Bank of Australia, and both Australian accounting and auditing/assurance standards boards.

In October 2019, there was also a legal opinion out of New Zealand that reached many of the same conclusions, opining that directors and pension scheme managers must assess and manage climate risk as they would any other financial risk, pursuant to their obligation to act with reasonable care.[101]

One tool that corporate stakeholders may have to encourage directors to act on climate change is a derivative action under corporate law, in which a complainant 'steps into the shoes of the corporation' and brings an action in the name of the company against directors and officers personally for harms caused to the corporation. Arguably, stakeholders of a company could establish that the failure of directors to act on climate change has caused harm to the financial viability of the company. In many jurisdictions, complainants need the approval of the court to commence a derivative action. The courts generally serve a gatekeeping role in determining leave to commence a derivative action, and thus, only meritorious cases are likely to proceed. Some jurisdictions require that the complainant first ask the directors to act, which creates another opportunity for the directors to turn their minds to the risks. One barrier to bringing such lawsuits, however, is the cost of litigation. Courts have generally been reluctant to order corporations to cover the costs of derivative actions until a judgment on the merits is obtained, creating a considerable cost barrier to their pursuit for anyone without deep resources.[102] The recent development of litigation financing for public interest lawsuits may change that situation.[103]

ii. Oppression Remedies in Some Countries

A further avenue for holding directors accountable for failing to address climate adaptation and mitigation in countries such as Canada is the statutory corporate law oppression remedy, available where directors act in a manner that is oppressive, unfairly prejudicial to, or unfairly disregards the interests of specified stakeholders. For example, under Canadian corporate statutes, the oppression remedy is a potentially powerful tool to press directors and officers to take action on climate change. The oppression remedy under Canadian corporate law focuses on harm to the legal and equitable interests of stakeholders when directors act oppressively, unfairly prejudicially or they unfairly disregard the interests of securityholders.[104] If the court finds

[100] Ibid at 8–9.

[101] Chapman Tripp, 'Climate Change Risk—Implications for New Zealand Company Directors and Managed Investment Scheme Providers' (October 2019) Legal Opinion.

[102] Janis Sarra, '*Review of the Derivative Action Provisions of the Canada Business Corporations Act, Policy Implications and Options*' (Report for Corporations Canada, 30 April 2005).

[103] There are both positive and negative aspects of the rise of such financing, beyond the scope of this book.

[104] *Wilson v Alharayeri*, 2017 SCC 39 (SCC) (hereafter *Wilson*). See also *BCE* (n 80) at para 45.

that the directors acted in a manner that is oppressive, unfairly prejudicial, or unfairly disregarding, an extraordinarily broad set of remedies is available to complainants bringing such claims. The oppression remedy 'seeks to ensure fairness—what is just and equitable'.[105]

In establishing that directors have breached their obligations such that the oppression remedy is available, the complainant must first identify the stakeholder expectations that he or she claims have been violated by the conduct at issue and establish that the expectations were reasonably held.[106] Second, the complainant must show that these reasonable expectations were violated by corporate conduct that was oppressive, or unfairly prejudicial to, or unfairly disregarded the interests of 'any security holder, creditor, director or officer'.[107] The scope of the remedy is broad, but it must be tailored to remedy only the specific conduct. Possible remedies include orders restraining conduct, replacing directors, setting aside transactions, and compensating aggrieved persons.[108] The oppression remedy seeks to apply a measure of corrective justice, but it should go no further than necessary to correct the injustice or unfairness of the directors' action or inaction.[109]

The SCC has held that the concept of reasonable expectations is objective and contextual. Fair treatment—a central theme running through the oppression jurisprudence—is most fundamentally what stakeholders are entitled to 'reasonably expect'.[110] There need not be any bad faith or an intention to harm the complainant.[111] The SCC held that where conflicts among corporate stakeholders involve the interests of the corporation, 'it falls to the directors of the corporation to resolve them in accordance with their fiduciary duty to act in the best interests of the corporation, viewed as a good corporate citizen'.[112]

In *Wilson v Alharayeri*, the SCC reaffirmed that a corporation's directors may be found personally liable in an oppression action under Canadian corporate law.[113] The test for personal liability requires that the 'oppressive conduct must be attributable to the individual director because of his or her action or inaction' and imposition of personal liability 'must be fit in all of the circumstances'.[114] It held that four general principles should guide the courts in fashioning a remedy.[115] The remedy requested must, in itself, be a fair way of dealing with the situation.[116] Fairness is central to the inquiry.

105 *BCE*, ibid at para 81; *Wilson*, ibid at para 23.
106 *BCE*, ibid at para 70; *Wilson*, ibid at para 24.
107 *Wilson*, ibid at para 24.
108 CBCA, s 241(3) (n 77).
109 *Wilson* (n 104) at para 27. See also *Naneff v Con-Crete Holdings Ltd* (1995) 23 OR (3d) 481 (Ont CA).
110 Ibid at paras 62–4.
111 *Downtown Eatery (1993) Ltd v Ontario* (2001) OJ No 1879, 200 DLR (4th) 289 (Ont CA), leave to appeal refused (2001) SCCA No 397 (SCC) (hereafter *Downtown Eatery*). See also *Ferguson v Imax Systems Corp* (1983) OJ No 3156, 150 DLR (3d) 718 at 727 (Ont CA), leave to appeal refused (1983) 2 OAC 158 (note) (SCC) (hereafter *Ferguson*); *Brant Investments Ltd v KeepRite Inc* (1991) OJ No 683, 3 OR (3d) 289 (Ont CA); *UPM-Kymmene Corp v UPM-Kymmene Miramichi Inc* (2002) OJ No 2412, 214 DLR (4th) 496 (Ont SCJ), additional reasons at 2002 CarswellOnt 3579 (Ont SCJ (Commercial List)), aff'd (2004) OJ No 636 (Ont CA) (hereafter *UPM-Kymmene Corp*).
112 *BCE* (n 80) para 81.
113 *Wilson* (n 104).
114 Ibid at para 31.
115 CBCA, s 241 (n 77). All the provincial corporate law statutes also have oppression remedy provisions.
116 *Wilson* (n 104).

The Court held that it may be fair to hold a director personally liable where a remedy against the corporation would unduly prejudice other security holders. While personal benefit and bad faith are hallmarks of conduct attracting personal liability, they are not necessary preconditions to imposing personal liability.[117] Fairness must be assessed in light of all the circumstances of a particular case. Any order should go no further than necessary to rectify the oppression.[118] Any order may serve only to vindicate the reasonable expectations of corporate stakeholders.[119] A court should consider the general corporate law context in exercising its remedial discretion.[120] Director liability cannot be a surrogate for other forms of statutory or common law relief.[121]

Applying these standards to conduct in respect of climate change risk, 'unfair disregard' of interests extends the remedy to where directors have ignored an interest as being of no importance, contrary to the stakeholders' reasonable expectations. Directors and officers are arguably at risk of personal liability if a complainant had a reasonable expectation that directors and officers would address climate change risks, and they disregarded the risks. Once recognized, the court has broad authority to craft a remedy to address the risk or the harm caused. However, directors' due diligence in addressing climate risk will protect them from personal liability.

The Court has held that the oppression remedy is designed to address the imbalance of power on the part of those directors in control with the vulnerability on the part of those individuals who have a genuine stake in the affairs of the corporation, but no control over its conduct.[122] But it does not mean that those individuals with a genuine stake will not be adversely affected as the corporation adapts to climate change. Claimants seeking to assert that climate mitigation strategies are oppressive because of the effect on immediate returns are liable to be thwarted by the reasonable corporate citizen view of the corporation's best interests as the lens through which the reasonableness of expectations will be evaluated.

iii. Responsible Action on Climate Change Will Be an Effective Defence

The best defence for a company and its directors and officers in meeting their corporate law duties is for the corporate board to be proactive in its efforts to move the company to net zero carbon. In Canada and other jurisdictions, courts have held that the business judgment rule accords deference to a business decision, so long as it lies within a range of reasonable alternatives.[123] This deference reflects the reality that directors, who are mandated to manage the corporation's business and affairs, are often better suited to determine what is in the best interests of the corporation, including

[117] Ibid at paras 41 and 51.
[118] Ibid at para 53.
[119] Ibid at para 54.
[120] Ibid at para 55.
[121] Ibid.
[122] *1413910 Ontario Inc (cob as Bulls Eye Steakhouse & Grill) v McLennan* (2009) OJ No 1828 (Ont SCJ Div Ct).
[123] *BCE* (n 80).

decisions on the appropriate balance among stakeholders' interests, as well as other directorial decisions.[124] With respect to climate-related financial risk, the court would likely look to see that the directors made a reasonable decision, not a perfect decision. Provided that the decision made, and the actions taken to monitor, mitigate, and adapt with respect to climate risk are within a range of reasonable strategies, the courts will not substitute their opinion for that of the directors.

Canadian courts have held that many decisions made in the course of business, although ultimately unsuccessful, are reasonable and defensible at the time they are made. Provided the decision taken is within a range of reasonableness, courts are unlikely to substitute their opinion for that of the board, even though subsequent events may have cast doubt on the board's determination.[125] However, Canadian courts have held that they 'are capable, on the facts of any case, of determining whether an appropriate degree of prudence and diligence was brought to bear in reaching what is claimed to be a reasonable business decision at the time it was made'.[126]

Corporate directors are responding to the challenges of climate change. There is evidence that an increasing number of corporate directors and officers are identifying and addressing climate-related financial risk. For example, Teck Resources Ltd, has identified as one of its four primary sustainability goals, a focus on taking 'urgent action to combat climate change and its impacts'.[127] It expressly recognizes that its 'activities consume energy and generate significant greenhouse gas (GHG) emissions'.[128] Its four pillars of tackling climate change include: setting ambitious targets to reduce its carbon footprint, which it is working to achieve through innovation, improved efficiency, and adoption of low carbon technologies; an express commitment to achieving carbon neutrality by 2050; positioning Teck for a net zero carbon economy in terms of products; advocating for climate action, including effective carbon pricing;[129] and adapting to the physical impacts, increasing the resilience of its operations by incorporating forecasted climate scenarios into project design and mine closure planning.[130] Since 2011, Teck has implemented initiatives reducing GHG emissions at its operations by 289,000 tons, the equivalent to taking over 88,000 combustion engine cars off the road.[131]

A second example is TransAlta Corporation, a large publicly-traded corporation owning, operating, and managing a diversified portfolio of sixty-nine power generating facilities that use a variety of fuels, including coal, natural gas, hydro, and

[124] Ibid. See also *1688782 Ontario Inc v Maple Leaf Foods Inc et al* 2019 CanLII 7964 (SCC) (hereafter *Maple Leaf Foods*); *Kerr v Danier Leather Inc* [2007] 3 SCR 331 (SCC); and *UPM-Kymmene Corp* (n 111) at para 152.

[125] *BCE* (n 80) at para 64.

[126] Ibid.

[127] Teck Resources Ltd, 'Sustainability Report 2016' (April 2017), <http://www.teck.com/media/2016-Teck-Annual-Report.pdf>.

[128] Teck Resources Ltd, 'Taking Action on Climate Change', <http://www.teck.com/responsibility/featured-topics/taking-action-on-climate-change/>. See also Teck Resources Ltd, 'Teck Announces Goal of Carbon Neutrality by 2050' (2 February 2020), <https://www.teck.com/media/20-8-TR.pdf> (hereafter Teck, Carbon Neutrality)

[129] For example, Teck supported development of the SunMine—Western Canada's largest solar power facility and the first owned and operated by a municipality, see ibid.

[130] Ibid.

[131] Teck, Carbon Neutrality (n 128).

wind.[132] It is converting coal plants to gas plants to significantly reduce GHG emissions before 2030.[133] In addition to being the largest hydro producer in Alberta, it is now the largest wind energy producer in Canada.[134] Its disclosures reveal that its goal, in line with a commitment to the UN Sustainable Development Goals, is to reduce its total GHG emissions in 2021 to 30 per cent below 2015 levels, and 60 per cent below 2015 levels by 2030.[135] It is working towards optimizing its plants to reduce energy consumption and GHG emissions. It seeks to generate offset and renewable energy credits from its renewable energy portfolio and emissions trading, and participates in carbon pricing structures in California, Alberta, Ontario, and Australia. It reports annually on climate change strategy, risk, opportunities, and emissions database. These examples reveal proactive strategies by directors and officers that are likely to be given broad deference by the courts.

The United States is the largest carbon emitter globally, yet the Trump administration has rolled back the US' commitment to the Paris Agreement, as well as other environmental and climate-based initiatives.[136] However, state and municipal governments are continuing to develop effective policy; see for example, California's climate strategy.[137] In this context, US companies that comply with regulatory developments at the state and municipal level are likely to have a strong legal defence to stakeholder litigation alleging that directors failed to meet their duties to address climate change risk. They may still be vulnerable to tort and investor claims if they fail to engage in effective climate governance, as discussed in Chapter 7. While to date, there has not been a final court judgment rendered on the duties of directors in respect of climate change in the US, there is a line of recent cases on directors' general '*Caremark*' duties (named after a 1996 US judgment), in which the Delaware Court has allowed cases to proceed against directors personally, alleging they failed to make a good faith effort to monitor corporate risk and sustainability, including where the Court held that directors have 'a duty to exercise oversight and to monitor the corporation's operational viability, legal compliance, and financial performance' and the particularized facts supported a reasonable inference that directors failed to implement any system to monitor.[138]

In 2019, the US Business Roundtable issued a statement on the purpose of a corporation, signed by 181 leading chief executive officers of US companies generating

[132] TransAlta, 'Action on Climate Change', 2017, <http://www.transalta.com/sustainability/climate-change-action-and-strategy/> (hereafter TransAlta, 'Action on Climate Change').

[133] Ibid. See also TransAltsa, 'Statement on Coal to Gas Conversion' (29 November 2016), <http://www.transalta.com/statement-on-coal-to-gas-conversion/>.

[134] TransAlta, 'Action on Climate Change' (n 132).

[135] Ibid.

[136] For a discussion, see Sarra, 'Anthropocene' (n 70).

[137] Government of California, 'California Climate Strategy' (2019), <https://www.climatechange.ca.gov/>.

[138] *Marchand v Barnhill*, 212 A 3d 805 (Del 2019); the case settled for US $60 million. See also two cases that survived early attempts to dismiss and are ongoing: *Hughes v Hu* (Del Ch 27 April 2020), No 2019-01112-JTL, alleging lack of financial oversight and monitoring, and *Inter-Marketing Group USA Inc v Armstrong* (Del Ch 31 January 2020) for alleged failure to oversee pipeline operations, leading to a significant spill in an environmentally sensitive coastal area, where the court granted leave to amend on the basis of several felony and misdemeanor criminal convictions related to the spill in California that postdated the filing of the complaint and that could allow the plaintiff to show a tighter nexus between the directors and the actions subject to the complaint.

US $488 billion in revenues annually.[139] While not specifically mentioning climate change, the statement specifies that the signatories share a fundamental commitment to all of their stakeholders, and that they commit to, among other things, protecting the environment by embracing sustainable practices across their businesses; investing in their employees, including training to develop new skills for a rapidly changing world; fostering diversity, inclusion and respect; dealing fairly and ethically with suppliers; and generating long term value for shareholders, stating that 'each of our stakeholders is essential'.[140]

VI. Obligations of Pension Fiduciaries, Other Institutional Investors, and Asset Managers in Respect of Climate Change

This part discusses the prudential and fiduciary obligations of pension trustees and other pension fiduciaries, as well as the fiduciary obligations of non-pension investment managers and asset managers, to engage in effective governance and investment practices in respect of climate-related financial risk. It draws on examples from different jurisdictions globally. It explores how these duties largely align for different types of institutional investors. Climate change will substantially affect the valuation of assets of both investors and the companies in which they invest.

Climate change presents both risks and opportunities across asset classes. There are clear benefits to investing in companies that prioritize energy efficiency and reduction of GHG emissions and that develop sustainable business models. Institutional investor action on climate change can help to minimize risk and ensure that portfolio companies are working towards cost-effective and innovative climate solutions. Pension funds, in particular, are now engaging with companies in their portfolios in respect of climate risk. Pension funds and other institutional investors will potentially lose significant value of their investments if they do not act as prudent investors by recognizing climate change financial risk.

Institutional investors have an important role to play in facilitating an overall strategy to move to net zero carbon and to advance the goal of financial sustainability. To date, business enterprises have externalized the negative environmental effects of their economic activities that generated GHG emissions. One reason is because of pressure to exhibit short term returns to capital market investors, resulting in pressures to issue dividends rather than reinvest a significant amount of profits into ensuring the sustainability of the business over the medium and long term. Another reason is that pollution regulation by national governments has not historically required firms to internalize the costs of carbon emissions, and thus, organizations and their investors have benefitted from externalizing these costs to society at large.

[139] Business Roundtable, 'Statement on the Purpose of a Corporation' (19 August 2019), <https://opportunity.businessroundtable.org/wp-content/uploads/2019/09/BRT-Statement-on-the- Purpose-of-a-Corporation-with-Signatures-1.pdf>.

[140] Ibid.

Yet, in order to move swiftly to net zero carbon emissions and mitigate the devastating impacts discussed in Chapters 2 and 3, the cost of carbon needs to be internalized, measured, and paid for. Institutional investors globally have the economic power to push businesses to shift trajectory and take meaningful action on climate change. For example, the Bank of Canada reports that the eight largest Canadian public pension funds are major investors domestically and globally, with net assets under management of more than Cdn $1 trillion.[141] They have the financial power to influence how quickly strategies to address climate change could be integrated into investment decision-making.

Internationally, institutional investors have increased their attention to climate risk management. For example, in the Netherlands, nine large Dutch pension funds with €800 million in assets under management,[142] as well as asset managers, insurers and banks, for a total of signatories representing €3.3 trillion in assets under management, signed the government's national Climate Accord in 2019.[143] The Dutch government's goal is to reduce the Netherlands' GHG emissions by 49 per cent by 2030, with a 95 per cent reduction by 2050, compared to 1990 levels.[144] Participation by the forty-five signatories was voluntary, but implementation is binding.[145] Its Platform for Sustainable Financing is developing a uniform method for measuring carbon emissions.[146]

Institutional investors, as fiduciaries, could be held accountable for failing in their obligations if they do not address the issues discussed in earlier chapters regarding climate-related financial risk.[147] As noted in the introduction to this chapter, a fiduciary's duties to beneficiaries are twofold: the duty to act prudently and with care, and the duty of loyalty.[148] It is the prudential obligation that necessitates fiduciaries paying attention to climate change risk, for the same reasons that directors and officers of corporations must. The ICGN recommends that the investor fiduciary should attempt to reconcile considerations of systemic economic, social, and financial stability across the total fund with risk and return objectives, having regard for inputs from various stakeholders.[149]

The European Commission's High Level Expert Group on Sustainable Finance reported that failure to consider climate-related risks may breach fiduciary duties and potentially lead to claims for damages by beneficiaries and clients of financial

[141] Bank of Canada, 'Large Canadian Public Pension Funds: A Financial System Perspective' (2016), <https://www.bankofcanada.ca/wp-content/uploads/2016/06/fsr-june2016-bedard-page.pdf>. See also Bank of Canada, 'Financial System Review 2019' <https://www.bankofcanada.ca/wp-content/uploads/2019/05/Financial-System-Review—2019-Bank-of-Canada.pdf>.

[142] Frank van Alphen (IPE), 'Largest Dutch pension schemes commit to national climate agreement' (11 July 2019), <https://www.ipe.com/countries/netherlands/largest-dutch-pension-schemes-commit-to-national-climate-agreement/www.ipe.com/countries/netherlands/largest-dutch-pension-schemes-commit-to-national-climate-agreement/10032251.fullarticle> (hereafter van Alphen).

[143] CIO, 'Dutch Pension APG Signs Government Climate Agreement' (16 July 2019) <https://www.ai-cio.com/news/dutch-pension-apg-signs-government-climate-agreement/>.

[144] Government of the Netherlands, 'Climate Policy' (2019), <https://www.government.nl/topics/climate-change/climate-policy>.

[145] van Alphen (n 142) quoting Wopke Hoekstra, the Dutch Finance Minister.

[146] Ibid.

[147] Sarra, *Fiduciary Obligations* (n 2) at 3.

[148] *Hodgkinson v Simms*, [1994] 3 SCR 377 (SCC) at 419.

[149] ICGN, *Guidance* (n 66) at 12.

institutions.[150] Its 2018 report clarified that the fiduciary duty of investors should explicitly integrate material environmental, social, and governance ('ESG') factors and long term sustainability.[151] It recommended establishing a single set of principles describing the content of what a fiduciary duty and all its related concepts entail, which can then feed into the respective relevant laws according to the specificities of market participants, observing that regulatory authorities need to make clear to all parties in the investment and lending chain that managing ESG risks is integral to fulfilling fiduciary duty, acting loyally to beneficiaries, and acting in a prudent manner.[152] As noted in Chapter 6, new regulations in 2019 specify that institutional investors must disclose material ESG factors and impacts.

i. Pension Fiduciaries' Duties of Care and Prudence Require Attention to Climate Change

Pension funds are large institutional investors in global financial markets. Pension trustees, and their investment and engagement fiduciaries, must address the full range of considerations relevant to both risk and return. As Ronald Davis noted more than a decade ago, pension fund fiduciaries must make their investment strategy decisions based on a time frame commensurate with the pension plan's liabilities.[153] While there is always a risk of loss, trustees are to make decisions in a manner that avoids undue loss. Prudential obligations require fiduciaries to undertake a careful and thorough evaluation of climate change risk prior to making decisions, and to act on information generated by that process, including understanding the rationale for their decisions.[154]

Many smaller pension funds entrust decisions on investing the pension fund's assets to investment managers. The pension fund's investment manager, if one is used, is in a fiduciary relationship with the beneficiaries of the trust.[155] Another long-accepted fiduciary relationship is that of an agent to the agent's principal. An agent is expected to act with care and in the best interests of the principal. In terms of individuals and firms who manage other people's money, their fiduciary obligation requires them to act in the interests of beneficiaries, rather than serving their own interests, including a duty of prudence and loyalty.[156] The duty of loyalty requires fiduciaries to act in good faith in the interests of their beneficiaries, impartially balance the conflicting interests of different beneficiaries, avoid conflicts of interest, and includes a duty not to act for the benefit of themselves or a third party.[157] While the definitions vary slightly in different countries, a common understanding is that the prudential obligation

[150] European Commission, 'High Level Group on Sustainable Finance Early Recommendations' (13 July 2017), <https://ec.europa.eu/info/sites/info/files/170713-sustainable-finance-report_en.pdf>.

[151] Financial Stability, Financial Services, and Capital Markets Union, *Final report of the High-Level Expert Group on Sustainable Finance* (31 January 2018) <https://ec.europa.eu/info/sites/info/files/c-sustainable-finance-final-report_en.pdf>.

[152] Ibid at 25.

[153] Davis, *Democratizing Pension Funds* (n 53) at 54.

[154] Sarra, *Fiduciary Obligations* (n 2).

[155] Ibid at 3.

[156] Davis, *Democratizing Pension Funds* (n 53) at 54.

[157] Sarra, *Fiduciary Obligations* (n 2).

requires fiduciaries to act with the care, diligence, and skill in the administration and investment of the pension fund that a person of ordinary prudence would exercise in dealing with the property of another person.[158]

A pension fund trustee's fiduciary duty is to provide oversight of those fiduciaries making investment decisions on the fund's behalf, with the objective of trying to ensure that there are funds to pay the promised pension benefits owing to members currently and in the future. Pension fund trustees' fiduciary duty requires them to take into account any material risks, within their portfolios, of climate change, as well as investment opportunities. Climate change can no longer be considered a non-financial risk, as the costs of climate-related acute and chronic events are now foreseeable and costly.

In Germany, while fiduciary duty is not a clear legal term, duties to pursue the best interests of the end investor exist in the Capital Investment Code (*Kapitalanlagegesetzbuch-KAGB*) and the prudent person principle is embedded in the Pension Insurance Act (*Versicherungsaufsichtsgesetz-VAG*).[159]

In Australia, a 2017 legal opinion published by Noel Hutley and James Mack discussed the obligations of trustee directors of registrable superannuation (pension) entities in Australia in respect of climate change.[160] In Australia, trustees' obligations are set out in the Superannuation Industry (Supervision) Act ('SISA'),[161] which regulates individual trustees, groups of individual trustees, corporate trustees, and directors of corporate trustees (referred to as 'trustee directors').[162] Hutley and Mack concluded that climate change risks should be considered by trustee directors to the extent that those risks intersect with the financial interests of beneficiaries.[163] Trustee directors should source, consider, and weigh relevant information relating to climate change risk and record their decision-making processes.[164] They observed that a trustee director must act in the best interest of beneficiaries, must exercise due care, skill, and diligence in relation to all matters affecting a registrable superannuation entity, and must comply with the 'enhanced director obligations' in relation to 'MySuper products'.[165] Corporate trustees must adhere to the investment covenants and must exercise a reasonable degree of care and diligence to ensure that they carry out investment and other covenants.[166] Thus, climate change risks should be considered by trustee directors to the extent that those risks may intersect with the financial interests of beneficiaries of a superannuation fund, particularly when making a significant decision related to investments that are exposed to climate change risk. They note that it is incumbent upon a trustee director, in an appropriate case, to consider climate

[158] See for example, the Ontario *Pension Benefits Act*, RSO 1990, c P 8, as amended, s 22(1).

[159] UN PRI, *Fiduciary Duty in the 21st Century* (n 19) at 40.

[160] Noel Hutley and James Mack, 'Superannuation Fund Trustee Duties and Climate Change Risk', legal opinion to Market Forces (15 June 2017) (hereafter Hutley and Mack).

[161] Superannuation Industry (Supervision) Act 1993 (Cth) ('SISA').

[162] Hutley and Mack (n 160) at 1.

[163] Ibid at 2.

[164] Ibid at 3.

[165] Ibid, citing s 52A(2)(c) and (b), and s 29VO. Legislation providing for default superannuation products called 'MySuper' was enacted in 2012.

[166] Ibid at 4, citing s 52A(2)(f).

change risk, in order to satisfy the requirements of due care, skill, and diligence in relation to the best interests of beneficiaries.[167]

Hutley and Mack opined that although the Australian Prudential Regulatory Authority's ('APRA') investment prudential standard does not define risk, it provides a framework for determining when the financial effect of climate change risks may warrant consideration, and that when formulating an investment and diversification strategy, the foreseeable financial effect of climate change risk factors may need to be identified.[168] The due diligence involved in an investment selection process should be commensurate with any financial effect of climate change risks related to an investment.[169] Trustee directors can avoid liability by establishing a defence that they complied with the law, which, in their opinion, imposes a higher standard than the business judgment rule in the Australian corporations law.[170] The SISA requires that trustee directors use their acumen, knowledge, and judgment in weighing all relevant factors, including professional advice.[171] Hutley and Mack concluded that if a trustee director were confronted with a significant investment decision that involved a substantial exposure to climate change risks, it would be prudent to seek out information in relation to the risk and obtain advice on the risk, as well as keep a record of why a trustee director was satisfied that any investment was in the best interests of beneficiaries notwithstanding the risks.[172]

The legal opinion aligns with statements by APRA that it will conduct its regulatory functions conferred by the SISA on the basis that climate change presents a financial risk.[173]

Trustees can take climate change into account as a legitimate investment issue, which may be short or long term or both, because once climate change becomes material to the investment decision, it is part of trustees' fiduciary obligation.[174] If trustees fail to act to address material climate change risk, they are liable for breach of their fiduciary obligation. Inaction is no longer acceptable, given all the evidence that climate change risk is material across the entire economy.[175] Trustees can also take climate change into account because they have duties as public fiduciaries additional to their financial duty to beneficiaries.[176]

For many years, the 1984 English judgment Cowan *v Scargill*[177] was cited in England, Canada, and Australia as limiting the scope of conduct of pension

[167] Ibid at 5.

[168] Referring to APRA's prudential standard SPS 530 Investment Governance, ibid at 5.

[169] Ibid at 5–6.

[170] Ibid at 6. Section 55 of SISA governs the liability of a trustee director for loss or damage for breaches of covenants such as provided at s 52A(2)(a), (b), and (f) of SISA.

[171] Ibid, citing *VBN and Australian Prudential and Regulation Authority* (2006) 92 ALD 259, (2006) AATA 710 at (469).

[172] Ibid at 6–7.

[173] APRA Member Geoff Summerhayes to the Australian Senate, 'Economic References Committee: Carbon risk disclosure' (8 March 2017), citing *Hansard* at 38, 'APRA sees climate related risks as distinctly financial in nature and likely to be relevant and important for all APRA regulated entities.'

[174] Sarra, *Fiduciary Obligations* (n 2).

[175] Ibid at 47.

[176] Ibid.

[177] *Cowan v Scargill* [1985] Ch 270, [1984] 3 WLR 501, [1984] 2 All ER 750, [1984] ICR 646, [1984] IRLR 260, 128 SJ 550 (hereafter *Cowan v Scargill*).

fiduciaries.[178] Elsewhere I have analysed this judgment in detail and concluded that a careful reading of the judgment reveals that it is entirely compatible with pension fiduciaries having an obligation to address climate-related financial risk.[179] The Court held that the trustees are to exercise their powers in the best interests of present and future beneficiaries, holding the scales impartially between different classes of beneficiaries.[180]

The UNEP Finance Initiative report on fiduciary responsibilities, in commenting on *Cowan v Scargill*, observed that all factors relevant to risk and return should be considered by fiduciaries in investment decisions, and it may be a breach of fiduciary duties not to take into account ESG considerations that are relevant.[181] Climate change risk involves both material financial and non-financial risks, both relevant to fiduciaries.

Pension funds, which safeguard the financial security of aging populations, will potentially lose significant value of their investments if they do not more effectively manage their carbon-intensive investments.[182] Pension fund fiduciaries must act in the best interests of pension fund beneficiaries in accordance with the terms of the trust.[183] This fiduciary obligation is evident in both statutory and common law, requiring positive actions on the part of the fiduciaries. In determining asset allocation between short term and long term investments, the duty of care precludes those short term investments that prejudice long term investments, as the pension fund must be sustained over the long term. Thus, trustees must take account of systemic risks.[184] Climate change is one such risk. The duty of impartiality requires trustees and fund managers to balance intergenerational interests in their investment decisions, in that the time horizon for older workers and retirees is very different than for workers just entering the workforce.[185]

Failure to consider climate change could constitute a breach of fiduciary duty 'where it is determined that trustees ought to have had a reasonable expectation that such factors could influence materially the long term performance of plan investments'.[186] Materiality is important in assessing the likelihood of the risk materializing and the downside financial risk if it does. Pension trustees and other fiduciaries must evaluate the market and regulatory risks that are likely to depress market prices or restrain fossil fuel production and consumption, adjusting their investment strategies

[178] See, for example, *Boe v Alexander*, 1987 CanLII 2596 (BC CA); *Bathgate v National Hockey League Pension Society*, 1994 CanLII 1427 (Ont CA).

[179] For an extensive discussion, see Sarra, *Fiduciary Obligations* (n 2).

[180] Ibid at 286.

[181] UNEP Finance Initiative ('UNEP FI'), 'A Legal Framework for the Integration of Environmental, Social, and Governance Issues into Institutional Investment' (Freshfields Bruckhaus Deringer LLP, 2005).

[182] Sarra, *Fiduciary Obligations* (n 2).

[183] *Galambos v Perez* [2009] 3 SCR 247 at para 69.

[184] James Hawley, Keith Johnson, and Ed Waitzer, 'Reclaiming Fiduciary Duty Balance' (2011) 4 Rotman International Journal of Pension Management 2 at 13.

[185] Davis, *Democratizing Pension Funds* (n 53) at 54.

[186] Shareholder Association for Research and Education, 'Fiduciary Duties, Investment Screening and Economically Targeted Investing: A Flexible Approach for Changing Times' (SHARE, 2005) at 9, <http://www.share.ca/files/Fiduciary_Duties,_Investment_Screening_and_ETI.pdf>. See also Gil Yaron, 'Acting Like Owners: Proxy Voting, Corporate Engagement and the Fiduciary Responsibilities of Pension Trustees', <https://papers.ssrn.com/sol3/papers.cfm?abstract_id=772184>.

appropriately.[187] One question that pension fiduciaries should be asking is: how does materiality of climate change manifest itself in pension fund investments?

The Shareholder Association for Research and Education ('SHARE') suggests that pension trustee decision-making should be aimed at protecting the long term interests of investors, working people, communities, and society, which in turn will help improve outcomes for pension plan members and other beneficiaries of trusts.[188]

ii. The US Employee Retirement Income Security Act ('ERISA') and Acting on Climate-Related Financial Risk

A brief note on pension fiduciary obligation in the United States is warranted here, given that political shifts have raised a question in respect of fiduciary obligation, climate change, and litigation risk. The US accounts for the largest share of pension assets globally, and private sector retirement plans are subject to the provisions of the US Employee Retirement Income Security Act ('ERISA').[189] The overall trend in US private sector pension plans is a move to self-directed defined contribution plans, if any pension plan is offered to employees at all. The result is one of risk transfer from pension plan sponsors to the beneficiaries, as companies seek to avoid the liability associated with providing a promised level of pension.[190] As a result, beneficiaries of defined contribution pension plans carry all the downside risks of the pension funds neglecting to consider climate change factors and the need for long term sustainability, while the pension fiduciaries do not bear the risks from the failure to respond to climate-related financial risks.

The ERISA sets standards for fiduciaries of defined benefit and defined contribution plans based on a 'prudent person standard'.[191] Pursuant to the ERISA:

> a fiduciary shall discharge his [her] duties with respect to a plan solely in the interest of the participants and beneficiaries and—
> (A) for the exclusive purpose of:
> (i) providing benefits to participants and their beneficiaries; and
> (ii) defraying reasonable expenses of administering the plan;

[187] Damian Carrington and Caelainn Barr, 'Coal Crash: How Pension Funds Face Huge Risk from Climate Change', The Guardian (15 June 2015), <www.theguardian.com/environment/2015/jun/15/coal-crash-how-pension-funds-face-huge-risk-from-climate-change>. UNEP FI, 'Portfolio Carbon: Measuring, Disclosing and Managing the Carbon Intensity of Investments and Investment Portfolios', UNEP FI Investor Briefing, A document of the UNEP FI Climate Change Advisory Group and Investment Commission (July 2013) at 3, <http://www.unepfi.org/fileadmin/documents/UNEP_FI_Investor_Briefing_Portfolio_Carbon.pdf>.

[188] SHARE Annual Report, <https://share.ca/?s=annual+report>.

[189] US, Employee Retirement Income Security Act, 29 USC ch 18 § 1104.

[190] UNEP, UN PRI, The Generation Foundation, and Godeke Consulting, *Untangling Stakeholders for Broader Impact: ERISA Plans and ESG Incorporation*, UN Fiduciary Duty in the 21st Century Programme, (September 2018) at 6, <https://www.unepfi.org/wordpress/wp-content/uploads/2018/09/ERISA-plan-and-ESG-integration_Sept-2018.pdf>(hereafter UNEP et al, *Untangling Shareholders*).

[191] US Department of Labor, *Employee Retirement Income Security Act (ERISA)* (2019), <https://www.dol.gov/general/topic/retirement/erisa>.

(B) with the care, skill, prudence, and diligence under the circumstances then prevailing that a prudent man [woman] acting in a like capacity and familiar with such matters would use in the conduct of an enterprise of a like character and with like aims;
(C) by diversifying the investments of the plan so as to minimize the risk of large losses, unless under the circumstances it is clearly prudent not to do so; and
(D) in accordance with the documents and instruments governing the plan insofar as such documents and instruments are consistent with the provisions of this subchapter and subchapter III.[192]

The US Department of Labor's guide to pension fiduciaries states: 'Fiduciaries have important responsibilities and are subject to standards of conduct because they act on behalf of participants in a retirement plan and their beneficiaries'.[193] These responsibilities include: acting solely in the interest of plan participants and their beneficiaries and with the exclusive purpose of providing benefits to them; carrying out their duties prudently; following the plan documents (unless inconsistent with the ERISA); diversifying plan investments; and paying only reasonable plan expenses.[194] Plan sponsors that breach any of these fiduciary duties can be held personally liable. The ERISA expressly confers on the Department of Labor direct responsibility and authority to investigate fiduciary violations of the ERISA.[195]

Over the years, the language of the provision, to exercise duties 'solely' in the interests of participants and beneficiaries has been interpreted to allow consideration of climate and ESG factors more generally only where the pension fund could establish the decision was solely in the interests of pension plan participants and beneficiaries. A number of pension funds interpreted these provisions more purposively, concluding that ESG factors are important to consider in acting with care, skill, prudence, and diligence.

This unevenness in interpretation has not been assisted by US regulators, who seem to change views as governments change. In 2015, a guidance was issued to say that 'if a fiduciary prudently determines that an investment is appropriate based solely on economic considerations, including those that may derive from environmental, social and governance factors, the fiduciary may make the investment without regard to any collateral benefits the investment may also promote', stating that where competing investments serve the plan equally well, 'collateral considerations' can serve as a 'tie-breaker'.[196] Then in 2018, the Employee Benefits Security Administration issued another bulletin that states that ERISA fiduciaries may not sacrifice investment returns

[192] Ibid.
[193] US Department of Labor, 'Meeting Your Fiduciary Responsibilities' (2019) at 2, <https://www.dol.gov/sites/dolgov/files/EBSA/about-ebsa/our-activities/resource-center/publications/meeting-your-fiduciary-responsibilities.pdf>.
[194] US Department of Labor, 'Fiduciary Investigations Program' (2019), <https://www.dol.gov/agencies/ebsa/about-ebsa/our-activities/enforcement/oe-manual/chapter-48>.
[195] Ibid.
[196] DOL Employee Benefits Security Administration, Bulletin No 2015-01.

or assume greater investment risks as a means of promoting collateral social policy goals:[197]

> plan fiduciaries are not permitted to sacrifice investment return or take on additional investment risk as a means of using plan investments to promote collateral social policy goals ... Fiduciaries must not too readily treat ESG factors as economically relevant to the particular investment choices at issue when making a decision. It does not ineluctably follow from the fact that an investment promotes ESG factors, or that it arguably promotes positive general market trends or industry growth, that the investment is a prudent choice for retirement or other investors. Rather, ERISA fiduciaries must always put first the economic interests of the plan in providing retirement benefits. A fiduciary's evaluation of the economics of an investment should be focused on financial factors that have a material effect on the return and risk of an investment based on appropriate investment horizons consistent with the plan's articulated funding and investment objectives.[198]

With respect to shareholder engagement, including proxy voting, the 2018 guidance said that the Employee Benefits Security Administration's policy 'was not meant to imply that plan fiduciaries, including appointed investment managers, should routinely incur significant plan expenses to, for example, fund advocacy, press, or mailing campaigns on shareholder resolutions, call special shareholder meetings, or initiate or actively sponsor proxy fights on environmental or social issues relating to such companies ... plan fiduciaries may not increase expenses, sacrifice investment returns, or reduce the security of plan benefits in order to promote collateral goals.'[199] Also in 2018, a US Government Accountability Office publication examined the use of ESG factors by US retirement plans and made recommendations to the Department of Labor to 'clarify whether the liability protection offered to qualifying default investment options allows use of ESG factors'.[200]

Increasingly, US investors are incorporating ESG factors into their investment decisions; however, because of these regulatory uncertainties, the US lags in private sector retirement assets that are managed with explicit regard for climate change.[201] Most recently, in 2019, President Trump issued an 'executive order on energy infrastructure', directing the US Department of Labor to consider the role that funds governed by the ERISA play in energy as a critical element of the US economy and national security.[202] The executive order states in part that 'to advance the principles of objective materiality and fiduciary duty', the Secretary of Labor was to report on whether there are discernible trends in retirement plans subject to the ERISA with respect to investments

[197] DOL Employee Benefits Security Administration, Bulletin No 2018-01 (23 April 2018), <https://www.dol.gov/agencies/ebsa/employers-and-advisers/guidance/field-assistance-bulletins/2018-01> (hereafter Bulletin 2018-01).

[198] Ibid.

[199] Ibid.

[200] United States Government Accountability Office, 'Retirement Plan Investing: Clearer Information on Consideration of Environmental, Social and Governance Factors Would Be Helpful' (May 2018) (hereafter GAO Report).

[201] UNEP et al, *Untangling Shareholders* (n 190) at 4.

[202] President Trump, Executive Order on Energy Infrastructure (10 April 2019).

in the energy sector and whether existing Department of Labor guidance on the fiduciary responsibilities for proxy voting should be rescinded, replaced, or modified to ensure consistency with current policies that promote long term growth and maximize return on ERISA plan assets.

Ceres responded by saying that President Trump's executive order on the ERISA was aimed at expediting the processes for building oil and gas pipelines:

> President Trump's executive order directing the US Department of Labor to look into whether private pension funds that have engaged with oil and gas companies on climate change are complying with federal law is misguided and ignores the very clear information related to the financial risks of climate change . . . With this executive order, the Trump Administration misses the mark and ignores the financial data. ERISA aims to ensure that pension funds represent the best interest of their beneficiaries, and that investors who are asking oil and gas companies to consider financial and material issues, such as climate-related risks, are doing just that—protecting their investments. The financial risks, which impact every sector of our economy, are jeopardizing share value. Investors should not only have the right to review these risks, they must do so to assure judicious financial decision making.[203]

Neil Minow observes that pension funds and other institutional investors want the Department of Labor to keep the standard that they can meet their fiduciary obligation to consider all elements of investment risk and return 'for the exclusive benefit of plan participants', as the ERISA requires, which a number interpret as being required to consider climate-related financial risk.[204]

As this book goes to press, the US Department of Labor has proposed a new rule that ERISA plan fiduciaries may not invest in ESG vehicles if doing so reduces risk-adjusted return for the purpose of non-financial objectives.[205] The proposal adds new regulatory text to codify that the ERISA requires plan fiduciaries to select investments and investment courses of action based on financial considerations relevant to the risk-adjusted economic value of a particular investment or investment course of action; an express regulatory provision prohibiting fiduciaries from subordinating the interests of plan beneficiaries to 'non-pecuniary goals'; and a new provision that requires fiduciaries to consider other available investments to meet their prudence and loyalty duties under the ERISA.[206] The proposal acknowledges that ESG factors can be pecuniary factors, but only if they present economic risks or opportunities that

[203] Mindy Lubber, 'Trump's Executive Order on ERISA is "misguided and ignores the data"' Ceres (11 April 2019), <https://www.ceres.org/news-center/press-releases/trumps-executive-order-erisa-misguided-and-ignores-data-ceres-says>.

[204] Nell Minow, 'President Trump's Executive Order and Shareholder Engagement on Climate Change' (25 May 2019), Harvard Law School Forum on Financial Regulation, <https://corpgov.law.harvard.edu/>.

[205] US Department of Labor, 'US Department of Labor Proposes New Investment Duties Rule' (June 2020), < HYPERLINK "https://www.dol.gov/newsroom/releases/ebsa/ebsa20200623" https://www.dol.gov/newsroom/releases/ebsa/ebsa20200623>.

[206] Ibid.

qualified investment professionals would treat as material economic considerations under generally accepted investment theories.[207]

These developments in the US mean that while pension fiduciaries can consider climate and other ESG factors, they must be able to directly attribute any decisions or engagement activities to their direct duties to plan participants and beneficiaries. It is unfortunate that the Trump administration has set up this 'looking over the shoulder' framework of decision making. Fortunately, other jurisdictions have not followed suit.

An important point is made by Ronald Davis—that acting 'solely for plan members and beneficiaries' is not a bar at all to pension fiduciaries actively considering climate-related financial risk.[208] If the market believes that climate change factors are affecting the value of assets in the market, which they are, then it will price the risk in; and if these factors are being priced into the price of assets, fiduciaries must take climate factors into account.

Davis notes that there is clear case law in the US that permits pension fund trustees to undertake novel investment strategies where they were able to demonstrate careful consideration of all the relevant factors before deciding on the strategy.[209] He gives the example of *Donovan v Walton*, in which the US Secretary of Labor charged union trustees with breach of their fiduciary and statutory duties as union-appointed pension fund trustees in their approval of construction of a building on property owned by the pension fund and leasing part of it to the union, as well as providing mortgages with the fund's assets to plan participants at rates below bank rates.[210] The Court found that the building project was thoroughly researched and that the rental to the union was designed to obtain a reasonable rate of return, while the benefits to the union were merely the result of a mutually beneficial transaction.[211] Davis observes that with respect to the mortgage loans, the Court noted that plan participants had to be creditworthy and that the ERISA provided only that loans to plan participants had to receive a reasonable rate of interest, not the prevailing rate. In addition, the mortgage loans earned the highest rate of return of the assets in the portfolio.[212]

Davis cites another example in which US pension trustees voted to divest from business in South Africa during the apartheid era. The Maryland Court of Appeals approved a plan by the City of Baltimore to require the trustees of its employee pension plans to divest their investments in companies that did business in South Africa during apartheid.[213] The Court found no violation of the trustees' fiduciary duties by using social criteria as the basis for excluding investments, providing the costs

[207] Ibid. The Department of Labor is also proposing a new provision on selecting designated investment alternatives for 401(k)-type plans; the prudence and loyalty standards set forth in the ERISA apply to a fiduciary's selection of an investment alternative to be offered to plan participants and beneficiaries in an individual account plan. The proposal describes the requirements for selecting investment alternatives for such plans that purport to pursue one or more ESG-oriented objectives in their investment mandates or that include such parameters in the fund name.

[208] Ronald Davis email correspondence (December 2019), on file with author, cited with permission.

[209] Davis, *Democratizing Pension Funds* (n 53).

[210] Ibid, citing *Donovan v Walton* (1985) 609 F Supp 1221 (DC Fla), aff'd per cur *Brock v Walton* 794 F 2d 586 (CA 11th Cir, 1986), *reh denied*, 802 F 2d 1399 (1986, CA 11).

[211] Ibid, citing *Donovan v Walton* (1985) 609 F Supp 1221 at 1244–5.

[212] Ibid, citing *Donovan v Walton*, ibid at 588.

[213] Ibid, citing *The Board of Trustees of the Employees' Retirement System of the City of Baltimore v Mayor and Council of Baltimore City* (1989) 562 A 2d 720 (Maryland CA).

for doing so were minimal, despite the need to divest 47 per cent of the plans' equity portfolios and 10 per cent of their fixed income portfolios.[214] The Court emphasized that the plans' trustees were given the power to suspend divestment if they believed that it was becoming imprudent to continue to divest. It accepted evidence that it was possible to construct a portfolio of South Africa-free investments with a comparable risk-return profile at minimal costs.[215] Davis notes that key to such judgments in US pension law is that courts have been clear that divestment decisions must expressly consider the best interests of the beneficiaries, although it need not be the decision that is most profitable, and that the advice of experts can be important in arriving at such decisions.[216]

Davis observes, therefore, that divestment is not per se a breach of trust for US pension trustees, provided that the best interests of the beneficiaries are considered and protected in both the divestment decision and procedure.[217] His careful analysis of the case law offers important insights for US pension fiduciaries and their consideration of climate-related financial risks and opportunities.

iii. The Duty of Care of Asset Managers and Other Non-Pension Investment Managers in Respect of Climate Change

For many of the same reasons set out immediately above, asset managers and investment managers have a duty of care in respect of climate change. As discussed earlier, a person or institution who manages assets for others must exercise a standard of care, skill, and due diligence in such management activity. Where the asset manager or investment manager is investing funds on behalf of a pension fund or endowment fund, it acquires a fiduciary obligation to invest those assets in the best interests of the pension fund and its beneficiaries or the endowment fund.

However, even where the investment manager is not working for pension fiduciaries, they still have a duty of care to the individuals and entities on whose behalf they are acting. Given all the information in respect of climate-related financial risk, it is reasonable that investors who entrust their assets to these managers will expect that they take account of the risks and opportunities presented by climate change in their investment and management decisions. Courts are likely to find that such expectations are reasonable given the urgency and importance of climate change and the financial risks that it is generating.

Mercer has suggested that 'it is in investors' best interests and therefore consistent with fiduciary duty to actively support the low carbon transition to avoid the worst physical damages scenarios, which will have almost entirely negative impacts across sectors and asset classes'.[218] Mercer points to the growing number of

[214] Ibid.

[215] Ibid, citing *The Board of Trustees of the Employees' Retirement System of the City of Baltimore v Mayor and Council of Baltimore City* (1989) 562 A 2d 720 at 85–7.

[216] Ibid.

[217] Ibid.

[218] Mercer LLC, International Finance Corporation, and UK Department for International Development, *Investing in a Time of Climate Change* (April 2015) at 16–17, <http://www.mercer.com/content/dam/

financial regulators indicating that investors need to consider and manage climate-related risks in order to comply with their existing fiduciary duties.[219] Asset managers and other investment fiduciaries that fail to consider, manage and disclose their potential portfolio-specific risks may be susceptible to legal challenges in the future.[220]

VII. Fulfilling Fiduciary Obligations and Duties of Care through Effective Management of Climate-Related Risks and Opportunities

From the above discussion, it is clear that there is a legal duty placed on institutional investors to effectively manage climate-related risks in complying with their obligations to manage assets in the best interests of beneficiaries and investors. This part discusses the contours of such duties.

The 2015 *Fiduciary Duty in the 21st Century* report sets out a number of recommendations for institutional investors and asset managers, including that they should publish commitments to integrate climate change risk in their responsible investing, and provide explanations of how these commitments align with their fiduciary duties.[221] It recommended that investors implement these commitments in all their investment processes; monitor how investment managers are implementing these commitments; and report to beneficiaries and clients on how these commitments have been implemented and the resultant outcomes. They should ensure that trustees, corporate boards, and executives have the resources and knowledge to hold investment managers and advisers accountable for their handling of climate-related issues; requiring investee companies to provide robust, credible, and detailed accounts of their management of climate risk.[222] Asset owners have significant freedom to decide how they wish to take account of ESG issues in their investment practices and processes, but they should pay close attention to decisions that can skew portfolios and may negatively affect the overall risk profile of the fund.[223]

Another study has suggested that the fiduciary duties of investors include: a duty of care/prudence, duty of loyalty, a precautionary 'do no harm' duty, a duty of impartiality, a duty to maintain adequate diversification at the total fund level, a duty to incur only reasonable costs to achieve investment objectives, a duty to inform and consult with beneficiaries, clients and other stakeholders, and a duty to comply with governing documents.[224] The ICGN observes:

mercer/attachments/global/investments/mercer-climate-change-report-2015.pdf> (hereafter Mercer, *Investing*).

[219] Ibid at 17.
[220] Ibid.
[221] UN PRI, *Fiduciary Duty in the 21st Century* (n 19) at 20.
[222] Ibid.
[223] Ibid.
[224] ICGN, *Guidance* (n 66) at 7–8.

> The concepts of guardianship and trust lie at the heart of fiduciary duty. The fiduciary relationship between those to whom power is entrusted to invest (the 'investor fiduciaries') and the fund beneficiaries sets the stage for developing stewardship policies and practices. Asset owners have fiduciary obligations to their end beneficiaries. Fiduciary duties exist to safeguard the current and future interests of fund beneficiaries, both to enhance value and to protect them from potential misuse of their assets, owing to negligence, conflicts of interest (or agency issues) and/or incompetence of their investor fiduciaries.[225]

The ICGN observes that asset owners, as investor fiduciaries, cannot discharge their fiduciary obligations simply by hiring an asset manager; they may delegate investment tasks to asset managers, who themselves have a fiduciary duty to their client, but fiduciary duty itself is a core governance concept that cannot be delegated by the asset owner.[226] It suggests that stewardship expectations should be clearly articulated in the written mandate between asset owners and asset managers. There should be periodic evaluation of its terms, to assist with clarity of expectations and promote mutual understanding between parties.[227]

Institutional investors should ensure they are appropriately informed and that they understand the implications of their instructions to investment managers, as articulated in their statement of investment policies, including instructions in respect of climate-related asset allocation, market exposures, and investment parameters.[228] The ICGN observes that an investor fiduciary cannot act in the best interests of the client or beneficiary without informing the client or beneficiary of the risk-return implications of any investment strategy, and should consult with them periodically for input.[229] Investor fiduciaries must consider whether fund assets are invested over an appropriate time horizon to meet current and future liabilities, are appropriately diversified, and adequately consider climate and other ESG factors.[230] Their investment strategies should be aligned with mitigation of systemic risk. Investor fiduciaries should be engaging in stakeholder relations to communicate their investment policies in respect of climate-related risk in order to inspire client and beneficiary confidence.[231]

Integrating climate considerations into investment decisions will allow investors to improve investment performance consistent with their fiduciary duties, in turn, allocating capital towards well-governed companies. The ICGN observes that investors can embed concern about climate change in their investment processes by analysing risks and opportunities over the longer term and by encouraging companies to adopt higher standards and better practices in controlling their carbon emissions, consistent with their fiduciary duties.[232] Investors should engage with investee companies to influence them to allocate capital in a manner that will address climate change risks,

225 Ibid at 4.
226 Ibid at 9.
227 Ibid.
228 Ibid.
229 Ibid.
230 Ibid at 10.
231 Ibid.
232 Ibid at 18.

contributing to 'the goals of a greener economy and a more sustainable society'.[233] Engagement is discussed in Chapter 7.

The ICGN observes that 'even investors with shorter term time horizons can benefit from improving the longer term prospects for portfolio companies, which leads to more sustainable business plans, future cash flows, and higher current valuations. Investor fiduciaries should consider the unintended consequences of short-termism and its impact on how systemic, environmental, financial, and social risks are identified, understood, and integrated in the investment process'.[234]

However, the *Fiduciary Obligation in the 21st Century Final Report* notes that:

> As currently defined, fiduciary duties do not require a fiduciary to account for the sustainability impact of their investment activity beyond financial performance. In other words, fiduciary duties require consideration of how sustainability issues affect the investment decision, but not how the investment decision affects sustainability. More fundamental changes—to incentives, to structures, to duties, to obligations and to the broader legal frameworks within which investors operate—are needed if the financial sector is to enable economic activities and societies to prosper in a sustainable manner. Wider public policy, more explicitly on real-economy outcomes, is the key next step in moving towards a more sustainable economy.[235]

Harmes observes that investment managers have strong incentives to maintain or increase asset value in the short term, and may be reluctant to promote climate change mitigation, in part because the funds they are investing on behalf of tend to not link their generally sustainability statements and policies with short term investment decisions.[236]

In March 2019, a coalition of groups led by Majority Action delivered over 129,000 petition signatures to BlackRock, the world's largest asset manager and the world's largest investor in fossil fuels, calling on BlackRock, Vanguard, and Fidelity to use their immense voting power responsibly to support key climate-related shareholder resolutions and vote against directors who are not serving long term investors' best interests at nine major upcoming shareholder meetings.[237]

The 'Global Statement on Investor Obligations and Duties' signed by 122 investors from twenty-two countries has called on international policymakers and national governments to clarify the obligations and duties of investors and other organizations

[233] Ibid.

[234] Ibid at 14–15.

[235] UN PRI, *Fiduciary Duty in the 21st Century* (n 19) at 23.

[236] A Harmes, 'The Limits of Carbon Disclosure: Theorizing the Business Case for Investor Environmentalism' (2011) Global Environmental Politics 11 at 98–119.

[237] MarketWatch, 'United States: Groups Deliver 129,000+ Signatures Demanding BlackRock Act on Climate' *MarketWatch* (3 May 2019), <https://www.marketwatch.com/press-release/united-states-groups-deliver-129000-signatures-demanding-blackrock-act-on-climate-2019-05-03>. Majority Action is a non-profit, non-partisan organization that empowers shareholders to hold corporations accountable to high standards of corporate governance, social responsibility, and long term value creation, <https://www.majorityaction.us/about>.

in the investment system.[238] It asked governments to clarify that investors must act with due care, skill, and diligence, must act in good faith in the interests of their clients, and must take account of ESG issues in their investment processes and in their engagement with the companies and issuers in which they invest.[239] Governments have begun to respond to these calls, as discussed in Chapter 6.

Jagannathan et al observe that the largest institutional investors are 'universal owners', as they own a slice of the world economy through their sizeable holdings, and thus, they are more exposed to externalities from climate change.[240] Many institutional investors with highly diversified and more passively managed portfolios have a higher risk exposure, as they have less scope to divest assets with large climate-related financial risk.[241] Even smaller pension funds may have similar exposures through their participation in pooled investment vehicles.

A number of reports have concluded that managing climate change is part of fiduciary duties. A report issued by UN PRI in 2015, in collaboration with the UN Global Compact and UNEP Finance Initiative, analysed investment practice and fiduciary obligation in eight countries.[242] It offered insights for thinking about climate change risk, noting that failing to consider long term investment value drivers is a failure of fiduciary duty.[243] Asset owners may take account of climate risk issues where there is a clear focus on beneficiaries' interests. Thus, a decision not to invest in coal mines because of risk of stranded assets can be a decision in the best interests of beneficiaries.[244] Such a decision is consistent with fiduciary duties as long as the decision is based on credible assumptions and a robust decision-making process, including clear decisions on investment objectives, reviewing outcomes achieved, and willingness to change if the data change or if it is clear that the decision is causing significant damage to the beneficiaries' financial interests.[245]

The *Fiduciary Duty in the 21st Century* report also observed that fiduciaries need to be able to show that they have identified and assessed the risks of climate change to companies and to their investment portfolios.[246] Fiduciaries should disclose that they have recognized relevant risks, even if they are sceptics on the issue of climate change. They should demonstrate that they have analysed how climate change might affect investment returns over the short, medium, and long term.[247] They should also

[238] UN PRI, UNEP, and Generation Foundation, 'Global Statement on Investor Obligations and Duties' (29 June 2016), <http://www.fiduciaryduty21.org/uploads/8/0/3/0/80301594/pri_fiduciary-duty-21st-century-statement.pdf>.

[239] Ibid.

[240] Ravi Jagannathan, Ashwin Ravikumar, and Marco Sammon, 'Environmental, social and governance criteria: Why investors are paying attention', NBER Working Paper No 24063 at 19, <https://ssrn.com/abstract=3082225> (hereafter Jagannathan et al).

[241] Ibid at 19.

[242] UN PRI, UN Global Compact, and UNEP Finance Initiative, *Fiduciary Duty in the 21st Century* (Eight Country Study), <https://www.unpri.org/download?ac=1378> (hereafter *Fiduciary Duty*, Eight Countries). Its precursor, a 2005 report commissioned by UNEP FI from Freshfields Bruckhaus Deringer concluded that integrating ESG considerations into investment analysis is clearly permissible and is arguably required, ibid.

[243] Ibid at 9.

[244] Ibid.

[245] Ibid at 9 and 16.

[246] Ibid at 16.

[247] Ibid.

have explicitly managed the risks, and not assumed that the risks are automatically managed by other risk management strategies.[248] Fiduciaries need to demonstrate that they have questioned their investment managers and engagement services providers, to ensure that climate change risks are being effectively managed. They must have established processes that enable them to demonstrate the actions they have taken.[249] Failure to consider long term environmental and social goals is a failure of the investor's fiduciary duty.[250]

In October 2019, in the final instalment of the four-year *Fiduciary Duty in the 21st Century* programme, the *Fiduciary Duty in the 21st Century Final Report* affirmed that fiduciary duty requires the incorporation of ESG issues into investment analysis and decision-making processes.[251] The report notes that in the modern investment system, organizations and individual fiduciaries manage money or other assets on behalf of beneficiaries and investors. It suggests that the consideration of ESG issues has become a core characteristic of a prudent investment process.[252]

Investors can reduce portfolio risk by incorporating climate criteria into their investment decision making.[253] Studies on asset pricing models have pointed to the importance of climate risks as a long-run risk factor, including carbon risks in respect of returns on equity.[254]

The Taskforce on Climate-related Financial Disclosures ('TCFD') framework, discussed in Chapter 5, contains recommendations for improving investors' ability to appropriately assess and price climate-related risk and opportunities.[255] One of its goals is to 'help companies understand what institutional investors want from disclosure in order to measure and respond to climate change risks, and encourage firms to align their disclosures with investors' needs'.[256] The TCFD concluded that assessing climate change risk is complex, partly because there are not yet uniform risk assessment tools or disclosure standards, and because the interaction of climate science, financial markets, and regulatory frameworks is complex in determining downside risks of particular strategies.[257] However, there is global consensus in the scientific community that there is an urgent need for mitigation and adaptation, which can be guideposts for fiduciaries. Given this need for action by institutional investors, what steps should be taken?

248 Ibid.
249 Ibid at 17.
250 Ibid.
251 UN PRI, *Fiduciary Duty in the 21st Century* (n 19).
252 Ibid at 8.
253 Jagannathan et al (n 240).
254 Ravi Bansal, Marcelo Ochoa, and Dana Kiku, 'Climate Change and Growth Risks', Duke University Working Paper (2015), <https://pdfs.semanticscholar.org/4705/4048806550cdf35da70f764b7d1d930acb9b.pdf>. See also Po-Hsuan Hsu, Kai Li, and Chi-Yang Tsou, 'The Pollution Premium', Asian Bureau of Economic Finance and Research, University of Hong Working Paper (2019), <http://abfer.org/working-papers/search-result?filter_tag=Chi-Yang%20Tsou%20(Hong%20Kong%20University%20of%20Science%20and%20Technology>.
255 TCFD, *Final Report* (n 7) at iii.
256 Financial Stability Board, 'Introduction to the Task Force on Climate-related Financial Disclosures', <https://www.fsb-tcfd.org/about/#>.
257 TCFD, *Final Report* (n 7) at ii.

One 2019 survey of 439 institutional investors found that investors generally believe that climate risks have important financial implications for their portfolio firms, and the majority believe that climate risks have already started to materialize.[258] It found that the vast majority expect a significant rise in global temperature by the end of this century, and most have taken at least first steps towards managing climate risks, primarily analyses of carbon footprints and stranded asset risks, while divestment is the least frequently used approach to date.[259]

The Economic Intelligence Unit reports that climate change is likely to represent an obstacle for many asset owners and managers to fulfil their fiduciary duties to deliver the best, risk-adjusted returns possible.[260] It observes that too many investors currently over-emphasize short term performance at the expense of longer term returns. It suggests that investment managers should be aware of the extent of climate risk to the long term value of the portfolios they manage; and to ignore them is arguably a breach of their fiduciary duty.[261] It recommends that pensioners should insist that the fund managers responsible for their retirement savings seriously address the full spectrum of long term risks they are facing, and that they reduce the climate risk embedded in their portfolios.[262]

Pension fiduciaries are now explicitly recognizing their fiduciary obligations in respect of climate-related financial risk. For example, the University of Toronto Asset Management Corporation has expressly recognized that its fiduciary obligations include addressing climate change, stating that its approach to responsible investing recognizes that ESG factors, including climate change, can have a material impact on the long term risk and return of a given investment, and that incorporating relevant and material ESG issues into its decision-making processes is consistent with its fiduciary duty.[263]

VIII. New Investment Priorities for Pension Funds and Other Institutional Investors Regarding Climate Change

Pension funds are major holders of long term assets. They are now stress testing their existing asset portfolios to quantify the potential impact of changes in carbon-based asset prices, in order to guide their investment decisions. A number have now commenced shifting their investment activities.[264]

[258] P Krueger, Z Sautner, and L T Starks, 'The Importance of Climate Risks for Institutional Investors' (2019) ECGI Working Paper No 610/2019 at 19, <https://ecgi.global/sites/default/files/working_papers/documents/finalkruegersautnerstarks.pdf>.

[259] Ibid at 36–7.

[260] Economist Intelligence Unit. *The Cost of Inaction: Recognizing the Value at Risk from Climate Change* (EIU, 2015) at 3, <https://eiuperspectives.economist.com/sites/default/files/The%20cost%20of%20inaction_0.pdf>.

[261] Ibid.

[262] Ibid at 30.

[263] University of Toronto Asset Management Corporation, 'UTAM Responsible Investing Policy' (2019), <https://utam.utoronto.ca/responsible-investing/utam-responsible-investing-policy/>.

[264] See for example, bcIMC, submission to the Federal Department of Finance statements on climate change, Canada, Review of the Federal Financial Sector Framework (October 2017), <https://www.bcimc.com/newsroom/pdf/Submissions/2017/bcIMC%20response%20to%20Review%20of%20Federal%20Finanical%20Sector%20Framework%20Second%20Consultation.pdf>; SHARE, *Canada's Lobbyist*

In 2016, the large Dutch pension fund, Pensioenfonds voor overheid en onderwijs ('APB'), launched a programme to invest sustainably.[265] ABP targets for 2020, in comparison with 2015, are that its investments that contribute to the UN Sustainable Development Goals double to €58 billion; it will invest €5 billion in renewable energy such as wind energy, solar energy, and geothermal energy; and invest €1 billion in education and communication technology.[266] By the end of 2018, it had carried out sustainability and responsible business practices assessments for 7,700 of the over 10,000 companies in which ABP invests via shares or bonds, comprising approximately 90 per cent of the value of its investments.[267] As a result, it sold seven coal companies in 2018 that were assessed as laggards, the value of these coal investments in the portfolio amounted to € 71.8 million.[268] At the end of 2018, ABP had realized its target of 25 per cent reduction in the CO_2 footprint of its overall equity portfolio.[269] It had invested €55.5 billion in companies that contribute to the UN Sustainable Development Goals.[270] It had invested € 4.96 billion in renewable energy.[271] The ABP reports that as a supporter of the Dutch National Climate Agreement, it has voluntarily committed to the target of a 49 per cent emissions reduction in 2030 for its whole portfolio, not just equities.[272]

Institutional investors globally are beginning to protect their portfolios from the risks associated with global warming and climate change. For example, the Fourth Swedish National Pension Fund, Fjärde AP-Fonden ('AP4') will invest US $3.2 billion in passive investment funds, tracking low carbon benchmarks.[273] The SEK 391 billion (US $42 billion) pension scheme intends to decarbonize its US $14.7 billion global equity portfolio by 2020. During 2018, AP4 divested holdings in companies with substantial operations in thermal coal and oil sands, reducing the carbon footprint in its equity portfolio, which is now 37 per cent lower than a broad-based global market index.[274] AP4 will drastically cut exposure to companies that pollute with fossil fuels and is increasing investment in companies with low carbon emissions.

PKA, Denmark's fourth-largest pension fund, with €35.5 billion in assets, asked fifty-three companies that generate between 25 and 50 per cent of their revenues from coal to provide plans on how they will reduce their exposure to the fossil fuel, and has

Registries: What Can They Tell Investors about Corporate Lobbying? SHARE (5 September 2017), <https://share.ca/documents/investor_briefs/Governance/2017/Lobbyist_Registry_Scorecard.pdf>.

[265] ABP, Pensioenfonds voor overheid en onderwijs, 'ABP on course with sustainable investments' (8 May 2017), <https://www.abp.nl/images/press-release-sustainable-and-responsible-investment-report%20-2016.pdf>. The General Pension Fund for Public Employees ('ABP') has 2.9 million participants and €388 billion in available assets as at 31 March 2017.

[266] ABP, 'Sustainable and responsible investment 2018' (2019) at 17, <https://www.abp.nl/images/responsible-investment-report-2018.pdf>.

[267] Ibid at 12.

[268] Ibid at 18.

[269] Ibid at 35.

[270] Ibid at 24.

[271] Ibid at 34.

[272] Ibid at 60.

[273] AP4, <https://www.ap4.se/en/>.

[274] AP4, 'Climate & Environment part of sustainability focus' (2019), <https://www.ap4.se/en/about-ap4/>.

announced that it will pull money from businesses that lack plans or provide inadequate proposals for the shift to a low carbon future. PKA also divested itself of thirty-one coal-only companies in 2015.[275]

In Canada, Caisse de dépôt et placement du Québec ('CDPQ') is factoring climate change into every investment decision. It is increasing its low carbon investments by Cdn $10 billion by 2020, having already invested Cdn $18 billion in low carbon investments.[276] It is aligning compensation of its portfolio managers with reaching low carbon investment targets.[277] CDPQ is committed to reducing its carbon footprint by 25 per cent per dollar invested by 2025; and setting a carbon target covering all of its asset classes.[278]

The Alberta Investment Management Corporation ('AIMCo') is one of Canada's largest and most diversified institutional investment managers with more than Cdn $108.2 billion of assets under management, responsible for the investments of thirty-one pension, endowment, and government funds in Alberta.[279] Its investment strategy explicitly recognizes that addressing climate change risk is part of its fiduciary obligations and commits to integrating consideration of climate risk and resiliency into its investment decision making and voting its proxies to limit carbon emissions and facilitate the transition to a lower carbon economy.[280]

Another example is the California Public Employees Retirement System ('CalPERS') board, which adopted ten 'investment beliefs' that acknowledge the need for a broad set of investment and actuarial risk measures and clear processes for managing risk, specifying that as a long term investor, CalPERS must consider risk factors such as climate change that could have a material impact on company or portfolio returns.[281]

As of September 2019, the UN PRI had over 2,500 signatories representing US $86.3 trillion in assets under management, including 465 asset owners and 1,823 asset managers that are committed to integrating ESG issues into corporate and investment analysis and decision-making processes. However, the approaches are not yet consistent.[282] The UN PRI reports that 69 per cent of asset owners disclose that they include ESG-related factors when appointing asset managers, and 62 per cent stated that they consider ESG-related factors in all stages of asset manager selection, appointment, and monitoring.[283] In 2019, the UN PRI found that 90 per cent of surveyed respondents explicitly acknowledged the consideration of ESG issues in their investment processes as component of their fiduciary duties.[284] The vast majority regarded

[275] Chris Flood, 'Sweden's AP4 Pension Fund Avoids Fossil Fuels in Landmark Move', *Financial Times* (18 July 2016).

[276] Caisse de dépôt et placement du Québec ('CDPQ'), '2018 Stewardship Investing' (2019) at 10–12, <https://www.cdpq.com/sites/default/files/medias/pdf/en/ra/id2018_rapport_investissement_durable_en.pdf> (hereafter CDPQ, '2018 Stewardship').

[277] CDPQ has investment strategies to address climate change, built on four pillars; CDPQ, 'Climate Change' (2019), <https://www.cdpq.com/en/investments/stewardship-investing/climate-change>.

[278] CDPQ, '2018 Stewardship' (n 276) at 10–12.

[279] Alberta Investment Management Corporation ('AIMCo'), 'Who We Are' (2019), <https://www.aimco.alberta.ca/Who-We-Are/At-a-Glance>.

[280] AIMCo, 'Investment Philosophy' (2019), <https://www.aimco.alberta.ca/How-We-Think/Investment-Philosophy>.

[281] Ibid.

[282] UN PRI, *Fiduciary Duty in the 21st Century Final Report* (n 19) at 19.

[283] Ibid.

[284] Ibid at 20.

the consideration of ESG factors as a necessary to fulfilling their fiduciary duty towards their clients or beneficiaries.[285]

Thus far, this chapter has revealed how directors, officers, pension fiduciaries, and asset managers have duties in respect of managing climate risk. While there are not yet consistent standards globally against which their conduct will be assessed, there is growing consensus regarding the obligation to assess materials risks, to manage those risks, to set targets for reduction of emissions, and to disclose their effects to their stakeholders. The next part turns to disclosure requirements under securities and financial services law.

IX. Disclosure as Part of Legal Duties

Corporate stakeholders, both equity and debt investors, require transparency from directors and officers in respect of their oversight and management of climate-related financial risks and opportunities. For privately held companies, that disclosure is to investors in the form of disclosures at annual general meetings of the company and in loan documents requiring disclosure on an ongoing, periodic, or change of circumstances basis. For publicly held companies, there is an extensive disclosure regime under national securities and financial services legislation. For both privately and publicly held companies, directors have an obligation to disclose material information so that investors can make informed decisions. Transparency requirements draw fiduciaries' attention to climate risk and serve as a normative influence on fiduciaries to take action.

There is growing consensus that companies, investors, and asset managers should expressly report on their strategies to address how they are meeting their climate risk mitigation responsibilities.[286] The Canadian Coalition for Good Governance ('CCGG') has observed that financial reporting should convey key considerations related to governance, strategy, and risk management with the right level of detail, context, supporting information, and metrics, so that investors can make better informed decisions.[287] Boards should have the necessary controls in place, whether internal or external, to provide reasonable verification and assurance of the disclosure. The CCGG observes that corporate social responsibility reports are often not subject to board oversight or approval and do not give investors or other corporate stakeholders the same assurances as processes that support financial reporting.[288] As a result, boards of directors are often not paying attention to climate and other ESG factors. Incorporating climate-related financial disclosures into financial statements would address this deficiency in current reporting.

[285] Ibid.

[286] Taskforce on Climate-related Financial Disclosures, *Phase I Report of the Task Force on Climate-Related Financial Disclosures* (March 2016), <https://www.fsbtcfd.org/wp-content/uploads/2016/03/Phase_I_Report_v15.pdf>.

[287] CCGG, *The Directors' E&S Guidebook* (May 2018) at 4, <https://admin.yourwebdepartment.com/site/ccgg/assets/pdf/The_Directors__E_S_Guidebook.pdf>.

[288] Ibid.

As discussed in the following two chapters, there are both private and public initiatives to further embed climate-related disclosure as an obligation of companies and financial firms. Integrating climate-related financial risk in corporate financial statements will allow greater transparency and accountability. The notes to the financial statements can make clear the basis on which any metrics are being reported or which metrics have changed year over year.[289] It would also allow for reporting of currently known risks and opportunities, as well as forward-looking information.

i. An Important Note on Materiality

In most G20 jurisdictions, publicly held companies have a legal obligation to disclose material information in their financial filings.[290] The TCFD recognized that most information included in financial filings is subject to a materiality assessment; however, because climate-related risk is a non-diversifiable risk that affects nearly all industries, it requires special attention.[291] It reported that effective management of financially material, climate-related risks and opportunities requires direct oversight and executive leadership because climate risk is material.[292] The TCFD recommended that disclosures related to the company's governance and risk management of climate change should be included in annual financial filings. In respect of disclosures related to the strategy, metrics, and targets, the TCFD recommended that companies provide such information in annual financial filings when the information is deemed material. Organizations should describe their processes for prioritizing climate-related risks, including how materiality determinations are made within their organizations.[293]

Essentially, the materiality requirement enables investors and other stakeholders to see major trends and significant events related to climate change that affect, or have the potential to affect, the company's financial condition and its ability to achieve its business plan or strategy. The TCFD also suggested that organizations in four non-financial groups that have more than US $1 billion equivalent in annual revenue should consider disclosing such information in other reports when the information is not deemed material and not included in financial filings, as they are more likely to be financially impacted.[294]

Mercer has observed that financial regulators are increasingly formalizing the expectation that investors should consider the materiality of these risks and manage them accordingly as part of their fiduciary duties—particularly for pension funds.[295] It suggests that financial materiality of transition risk, including technology and policy

[289] Dr Janis Sarra and Professor Cynthia Williams, *Time to Act: Response to Questions Posed by the Expert Panel on Sustainable Finance on Fiduciary Obligation and Effective Climate-related Financial Disclosures* (CCLI, 2019) at 69.

[290] Ibid.

[291] TCFD, *Final Report* (n 7) at 17.

[292] Ibid.

[293] Ibid at 21.

[294] The TCFD noted that it chose the US $1 billion annual revenue threshold because it captures organizations responsible for over 90 per cent of Scope 1 and 2 GHG emissions in the industries represented by the four non-financial groups (about 2,250 organizations out of roughly 15,000), ibid at 17.

[295] Mercer, *Investing* (n 218) at 16.

changes necessary to transform the economy away from fossil fuels, have significant implications for all energy-dependent and high-emitting sectors of the economy.[296] Material physical risk captures the damage arising from temperature increases, increasing frequency and severity of storms, wildfires, and floods, Mercer noting that investors with real asset exposures will need to increasingly review insurance coverage and uninsured loss implications, together with additional capital expenditure requirements.[297]

The Sustainability Accounting Standards Board ('SASB') identifies financially material issues as issues that are reasonably likely to impact the financial condition or operating performance of a company and therefore are most important to investors.[298] SASB's Materiality Map identifies sustainability issues that are likely to affect the financial condition or operating performance of companies within an industry.[299] For example, its map shows that GHG emissions are likely to be material for more than 50 per cent of industries in the extractive and minerals processing sector, including oil and gas, coal, and metals mining; the transportation sector, including air, marine, and rail travel; and the food and beverage sector, including agricultural production.[300]

The Australian Accounting Standards Board in 2017 issued a practice guidance on making materiality judgments, which provides guidance on climate-related disclosures and financial statement materiality assessments when preparing general financial statements in accordance with Australian accounting standards.[301] When making materiality judgments, directors need to take into account how information could reasonably be expected to influence the primary users of its financial statements when they make decisions on the basis of those statements.[302] Materiality is an entity-specific aspect of relevance based on the nature or magnitude, or both, of issues such as climate-related risk to which the information relates to an individual entity's financial report.[303] The Board emphasized that the objective of financial statements is to provide financial information about a reporting entity that is useful to existing and potential investors, lenders, and other creditors, in making decisions about providing resources to the entity, necessitating appropriate materiality judgments.[304]

The Australian Accounting Standards Board's guidance notes that even where carbon emissions regulations have not yet been enacted, a company should determine the likelihood of national enactment of regulations to reduce the use of carbon-based energy, and whether it could reasonably be expected to influence decisions by primary users of the entity's financial statements so that they can understand the impact

[296] Ibid.

[297] Ibid, citing IIGCC and PRI investor guides, which can be found at <http://www.iigcc.org/publications/category/investor-guides> and <https://www.unpri.org/esg-issues/environmentalissues/climate-change>.

[298] SASB, 'Why is Financial Materiality important?' (2019), <https://www.sasb.org/standards-overview/materiality-map/>.

[299] Ibid.

[300] Ibid.

[301] Australian Accounting Standards Board ('AASB'), 'Practice Statement 2: Making Materiality Judgments' (2017) at 4, <https://www.aasb.gov.au/admin/file/content102/c3/AASBPS2_12-17.pdf>. See also the guidance issued by the International Accounting Standards Board ('IASB') in 2020, discussed in Chapter 6.

[302] Ibid.

[303] Ibid.

[304] Ibid at 7.

of the impairment on the entity's financial position, financial performance, and cash flows.[305] If it constitutes material information, the board must disclose those assumptions in its financial statements.[306]

The Canadian Securities Administrators ('CSA') acknowledge that climate change-related risks and their potential financial impacts are now mainstream business issues, and that despite the potential uncertainties and longer time horizon associated with climate change-related risks, boards and management should take appropriate steps to understand and assess materiality.[307] In 2019, the CSA issued a notice regarding climate-related financial risk, clarifying that it considers information to be material if a reasonable investor's decision whether or not to buy, sell, or hold securities of the issuer would likely be influenced or changed if the information was omitted or misstated.[308] That information should be in the annual information form ('AIF') and the management disclosure and analysis ('MD&A') as part of financial statements. The CSA acknowledged that securities law tests may differ from other legal tests and that companies should consider the applicable test when preparing disclosure in respect of climate change-related information. The board needs sufficient information, including management's materiality assessments in respect of the company's climate change-related risks, to appropriately oversee these risks. The board must be comfortable with the methodology used by management to capture the nature of climate change-related risks and assess the materiality of such risks.[309]

The CSA notice also states that management should have, or have access to, appropriate expertise to understand and manage material climate change-related risks that may affect the company.[310] There should be clear responsibility for identifying, disclosing, and managing material climate-related risks and reporting lines to senior management, and these responsibilities should be integrated with mainstream business processes. Management should be assessing the current and future financial impacts of material climate-related risks on the company's assets, liabilities, revenues, expenses, and cash flows over the short, medium, and long term.[311] Regulatory filings should contain the required disclosures in respect of material climate change-related risks, avoiding boilerplate disclosure.[312] The CSA states that materiality is the determining factor in any assessment of whether information is required to be disclosed in a company's continuous disclosure.

The CSA notes that there is no 'bright line test', i.e. uniform quantitative threshold at which a particular type of information becomes material.[313] The materiality of certain information may vary between industries. In assessing materiality, a company should consider whether the impact of an environmental matter might reasonably be

[305] Ibid.
[306] Ibid.
[307] CSA, 'Staff Notice 51-358 Reporting of Climate Change-related Risks' (1 August 2019) at 4, <https://www.osc.gov.on.ca/en/SecuritiesLaw_csa_20190801_51-358_reporting-of-climate-change-related-risks.htm> (hereafter CSA August 2019).
[308] Ibid at 7.
[309] Ibid at 5.
[310] Ibid at 6.
[311] Ibid.
[312] Ibid.
[313] Ibid at 7.

expected to grow over time, in which case early disclosure of the matter might be important to reasonable investors, particularly relevant where the public company is in an industry with a longer investment cycle or where new technologies are going to be required. The disclosure should reflect a thoughtful assessment by directors and officers of the information available as to the materiality of climate change-related risks affecting their business and the impact of such risks. The CSA observed that most industries and companies have some exposure to these types of risks, even if they are not directly involved in a carbon-intensive industry.[314] It suggests that an assessment of materiality in relation to climate-related risks may require companies to adapt their existing approaches to risk assessments, including adjusting their approaches to consider the longer time horizon associated with climate change.

A publicly held company should not limit its materiality assessment to near-term risks, and it should disclose climate-related matters, even if they may only crystallize over the medium or long term or if there is uncertainty whether they will actually occur.[315] The CSA directs that, where practicable, the company should quantify and disclose the potential financial and other impacts of such climate-related risks, including their magnitude and timing. The CSA acknowledges that the precise impacts of climate change-related risks may be difficult to quantify or measure, yet companies should consider both quantitative and qualitative factors in making their materiality assessments and may consider using assumptions and estimates that have a reasonable basis and are within a reasonable range.[316]

As this book goes to print, a landmark legal opinion by distinguished Canadian corporate lawyer Carol Hansell, commissioned by the Canada Climate Law Initiative, makes clear that Canadian directors and officers have an obligation to put climate change on the board agenda.[317] Hansell observes that directors 'must require reports and recommendations from management and external sources as necessary, and be satisfied that the corporation is addressing climate change risk appropriately'.[318] In respect of potential civil liability for failure to disclose climate-related financial risks, Hansell notes that directors of publicly listed companies should be aware that disclosure is a legal obligation and directors are not protected by the business judgment rule.[319] She suggests that claims regarding disclosure breaches, anchored in operational failures to adequately assess and manage climate risk, may have a reasonable possibility of success.[320] Hansell opines:

> Since there can be little doubt that directors are aware of climate change risk, they must inform themselves of the risk that climate change poses to the corporation and how that risk is being managed. If this information is not already included in

314 Ibid at 8.
315 Ibid at 9.
316 Ibid at 9.
317 Carol Hansell, 'Putting Climate Change Risk on the Boardroom Table', <https://law-ccli-2019.sites.olt.ubc.ca/files/2020/06/Hansell-Climate-Change-Opinion-1.pdf?file=2020/06/PUTTING-CLIMATE-CHANGE-RISK-ON-THE-BOARDROOM-TABLE.pdf>.
318 Ibid at 1.
319 Ibid at 20, citing the Supreme Court of Canada in *Kerr v Danier Leather Inc*, 2007 SCC 44 at para 54.
320 Ibid at 21.

> management reports to the board, the board should direct management to deliver the necessary information to them ...
>
> As is the case for any disclosure, misrepresentations about climate change risk can expose the corporation, its officers and its directors to both regulatory and civil liability. In respect of potential civil liability, an important factor for directors is that investors need not be aware of a misrepresentation about climate change to seek damages based on it; securities law deems them to have relied on the misrepresentations.
>
> Directors should also be aware that their decisions about disclosure are not protected by the business judgment rule.
>
> Making room in the board agenda for regular reports from management on climate change risk is an important part of the board's oversight of risk, but also sends a clear message to management that climate change risk is a priority. The board might consider conducting an internal assessment or inventory to see how the corporation is currently engaging with climate change as an issue ... [Directors] must then receive reports and recommendations from management and reports from external sources as necessary, to be satisfied that the corporation is addressing climate change risk appropriately.[321]

Also of note is that internationally there are efforts to build consensus on disclosure obligations. In addition to the TCFD framework, discussed in this chapter and several others, the World Economic Forum has published a white paper in collaboration with the four major accounting firms globally that proposes a common, core set of metrics and recommended disclosures that corporate directors and officers could use to align their mainstream reporting to measure and disclose meaningful and relevant aspects of their performance on environmental, social, and governance matters, and their actions on a consistent and comparable basis, perhaps moving to a generally accepted international accounting standard.[322]

The World Economic Forum is proposing metrics and disclosures aligned with the UN Sustainable Development Goals and principal ESG factors, pulling together the standards and metrics of the TCFD, SASB, and the Global Reporting Initiative. It is based on four highly interdependent pillars: principles of governance, planet, people, and prosperity, each of which the World Economic Forum reports has an important bearing on the capacity of a firm to generate shared and sustainable value.[323] The principles of good governance include principles of agency, accountability, and stewardship. 'Planet' refers the goal of protecting the planet from degradation, through sustainable consumption and production, sustainably managing natural resources, and 'taking urgent action on climate change, so that it can support the needs of the present and future generations'.[324] 'People' refers to an ambition to end poverty and hunger in all their forms and to ensure that all human beings can fulfil their potential

[321] Ibid at 20 and 22–4.

[322] World Economic Forum, *Toward Common Metrics and Consistent Reporting of Sustainable Value Creation* (January 2020) at 5, <https://www.weforum.org/whitepapers/toward-common-metrics-and-consistent-reporting-of-sustainable-value-creation>.

[323] Ibid at 10.

[324] Ibid at 10 and 44, noting that the definitions of these pillars were taken from UN, 'Transforming Our World: The 2030 Agenda for Sustainable Development (2015).

in dignity and equality and in a healthy environment. 'Prosperity' is the objective of ensuring that all human beings can enjoy prosperous and fulfilling lives and that economic, social, and technological progress occurs in harmony with nature.[325]

The World Economic Forum proposes two related sets of metrics. First are core metrics, a set of twenty-two well-established metrics and reporting requirements that are primarily quantitative metrics for which information is already being reported by many firms or can be obtained with reasonable effort.[326] They focus primarily on activities within an organization's own boundaries. Second are expanded metrics, currently less well-established standards that have a wider value chain scope or convey impact in a more sophisticated way, including in monetary terms. The World Economic Forum notes that the enhanced metrics represent a more advanced way of measuring and communicating sustainable value creation, encouraging companies to report against them as well.[327]

Disclosure is discussed further in the next chapter, which explores the contours of effective climate governance practice.

325 Ibid at 10.
326 Ibid at 7.
327 Ibid.

5
Effective Climate Governance

A key aspect of moving from ideas to action on climate change is for organizations to examine all aspects of their business plan, economic activities, and risk management strategies to identify how climate change is affecting, and is likely to affect, their assets and operations. 'Corporate governance' refers to how directors exercise their oversight authority in terms of the company and its activities, including strategic planning, independent oversight of management, monitoring their performance, and management of risk. Effective corporate governance is important to creating long term sustainable value and reducing investment risk.[1] The Canadian Coalition for Good Governance ('CCGG') has observed that effective governance means high performance boards that are accountable and independent; have experienced, knowledgeable, and effective directors with the highest level of integrity, who have clear roles and responsibilities, and engage with shareholders and other stakeholders.[2] As part of their responsibilities, each director should 'carefully examine the ethical implications of the corporation's strategies, policies, initiatives, and activities'.[3] These observations regarding best governance practice, plus the legal duties of corporate officers, discussed in Chapter 4, make clear that companies, pension funds, and other institutional investors need to have a governance structure that is responsive to existing and emerging risks—climate change is one such material risk.

In acting in the best interests of the company, directors and officers have a duty to be proactive and critically evaluate and address the material financial and other risks to the organization, including risks and opportunities associated with climate change. Companies are moving strategically to create value over short, medium, and long term, and as they transition, are engaging in a thorough discussion about risks, disruptors, and upside opportunities for the company. Best practices include that directors and officers have undertaken efforts to identify risks and opportunities to their business from climate change; have developed appropriate strategies to manage risks; and have mechanisms in place to respond rapidly to changes in the company's risk profile, including oversight and monitoring of the actions of individuals charged with managing these risks. They should be considering the benefits of adopting green mitigation technologies, products, and services likely to have upside financial potential.

[1] Canadian Coalition for Good Governance, *Building High Performance Boards* (2020), <https://ccgg.ca/wp-content/uploads/2019/03/building_high_performance_boards_branding-update_2020.pdf> (hereafter *High Performance Boards*).

[2] Ibid at 5.

[3] Ibid at 9.

From Ideas to Action. *Janis Sarra*, Oxford University Press (2020). © Janis Sarra. DOI: 10.1093/oso/9780198852308.003.0005.

I. Principles and Frameworks That Inform Effective Climate Governance

There is a huge literature on effective corporate governance.[4] However, one aspect of effective governance that is still developing is 'effective climate governance'. This part suggests that fairness and public interest doctrines can serve as guideposts and principles for effective climate governance of companies, institutional investors, and the national authorities that regulate their activities.

John Rawls observed that one way of testing for fairness of a law or policy is to regard it as fair insofar as it treats the interests of all those individuals subject to it with equal concern.[5] It should not countenance favourable treatment simply on the basis of wealth, gender, race, ethnicity, tribe, family, sexual orientation, social status, or political affiliation.[6] In the same spirit, effective climate governance should aspire, in good faith, to treat consumers, investors, and citizens with equal concern. Such an approach aligns with the United Nation's Sustainable Development Goals.

Elsewhere, I have suggested that 'fairness' as a general concept can be viewed as the capacity to take the perspective of another and to adjust our conduct and decisions to take account of others' perspectives in order to achieve more equitable outcomes.[7] Perspective-taking can deepen our understanding of climate change and its relationship to corporate governance and financial markets, and encourage a substantive aspirational goal of more equitable treatment of individuals differently situated.[8] Currently, the notion of fairness in financial markets is limited primarily to creating 'equal opportunity to participate in the market'.[9] Yet current rules and practices have direct and indirect distributive consequences, widening wealth disparities and disparities in climate outcomes.[10] We know, for example, that the impacts of warming

[4] See for example, Lynne Dallas, 'Is There Hope for Change? The Evolution of Conceptions of Good Corporate Governance' (2017) 54 San Diego Law Review 491; CCGG, *Building High Performance Boards* (2013), <https://www.ccgg.ca/wp-content/uploads/2019/03/building_high_performance_boards_august_2013_v12_formatted__sept._19_2013_last_update_-1-1.pdf>; ICGN, *Global Governance Principles*, <http://icgn.flpbks.com/icgn_global_governance_principles/> (hereafter ICGN, *Global Governance Principles*); CCGG, *The Directors' E&S Guidebook* (May 2018) at 20, <https://admin.yourwebdepartment.com/site/ccgg/assets/pdf/The_Directors__E_S_Guidebook.pdf> (hereafter CCGG, *Directors' E&S Guidebook*); CCGG, *Best Practices for Proxy Circular Disclosure* (2018), <https://www.ccgg.ca/wp-content/uploads/2019/03/2018_best_practices-ccgg-1-1.pdf>; Aaron Dihr, *Homogeneous Corporate Governance Cultures* (CUP, 2015); Cheryl L Wade, 'Fiduciary Duty and the Public Interest' (2011) 91 Boston University Law Review 1191.

[5] John Rawls, *A Theory of Justice* (Harvard University Press, 1971) (hereafter Rawls, *Theory of Justice*); John Rawls, *Political Liberalism* (Columbia University Press, 1996). See also Janis Sarra, 'Embedding Fairness as a Fundamental Norm in Financial Markets' in J Sarra (ed.), *An Exploration of Fairness, Interdisciplinary Inquiries in Law, Science and the Humanities* (Carswell, 2013) at 193–240 (hereafter Sarra, 'Embedding Fairness in Financial Markets').

[6] Ronald Davis, Stephan Madaus, Alberto Mazzoni, Irit Mevorach, Rizwaan J Mokal, Barbara Romaine, Janis Sarra, and Ignacio Tirado, *Micro, Small, and Medium Enterprise Insolvency* (OUP, 2018) at 29 (hereafter Davis et al).

[7] Sarra, 'Embedding Fairness in Financial Markets' (n 5) at 193–240.

[8] Ibid.

[9] Janis Sarra, *Modernizing Disclosure in Canadian Securities Law: An Assessment of Recent Developments in Canadian and Selective Jurisdictions* (Report to the Task Force to Modernize Securities Law in Canada, 2006).

[10] Sarra, 'Embedding Fairness in Financial Markets' (n 5) at 194.

are disproportionately affecting disadvantaged and vulnerable populations in Africa, Asia, and Latin America, through food and water insecurity, higher food prices, lost livelihood opportunities, adverse health impacts, and population displacements.[11] Within these populations, racialized and Indigenous peoples are experiencing some of the worst harms.

Financial markets are part of a complex system of social, political, and economic influences and historical inequitable endowments of wealth.[12] In 2016, 13 economists, including four former chief economists of the World Bank, issued a statement of consensus that advanced notions of fairness.[13] They agreed that it is now evident that some recommendations of more traditional economics were not valid, and that while policies to promote gross domestic product ('GDP') growth are needed, GDP cannot be an end in itself, but a means to create the resources needed to achieve a range of societal objectives, including improved health, education, employment, and security.[14] The economists agreed that climate change is a long term threat to the viability of the planet and, equally, a short to medium term threat to livelihoods, agriculture, and habitat in many countries. Policy should help ensure that development is socially and economically inclusive, and does not leave behind groups of the population — whether identified by gender, ethnicity, or other social indicators.[15] The statement says that development policy has to build on a judicious balance among market, state, and community, and that macroeconomic policies need to ensure financial sustainability.[16] It observes that a fall in the share of wages must not be treated as an inevitable consequence of the rise of new technologies, and that new technology that is linking up the global labour market should make it possible for workers in developing countries to work for global markets and consumers without having to relocate themselves.[17] These developments should advance equality, not detract from it.[18]

The Intergovernmental Panel on Climate Change ('IPCC') notes that 'distributive equity' refers to sharing the burdens and benefits of climate mitigation and adaptation, recognizing that women are often more vulnerable to the impacts of climate change and may be disadvantaged in outcomes of climate policy.[19] It advocates

[11] Intergovernmental Panel on Climate Change ('IPCC'), J Roy, P Tschakert, H Waisman, S Abdul Halim, P Antwi-Agyei, P Dasgupta, B Hayward, M Kanninen, D Liverman, C Okereke, P Pinho, K Riahi, and A Suarez Rodriguez, 'Sustainable Development, Poverty Eradication and Reducing Inequalities' in V Masson-Delmotte, P Zhai, H O Pörtner, D Roberts, J Skea, P Shukla, A Pirani, W Moufouma-Okia, C Péan, R Pidcock, S Connors, J B R Matthews, Y Chen, X Zhou, M I Gomis, E Lonnoy, T Maycock, M Tignor, and T Waterfield (eds), *Global Warming of 1.5°C: An IPCC Special Report on the Impacts of Global Warming of 1.5°C above Pre-industrial Levels and Related Global Greenhouse Gas Emission Pathways, in the Context of Strengthening the Global Response to the Threat of Climate Change, Sustainable Development, and Efforts to Eradicate Poverty* (IPCC, 2019) at B5.1, <<https://www.ipcc.ch/site/assets/uploads/sites/2/2019/05/SR15_Chapter5_Low_Res.pdf>. (hereafter IPCC, *Special Report 2018).*

[12] Ibid at 195.

[13] 'Stockholm Statement: Towards a New Consensus on the Principles of Policy-Making for the Contemporary World' (2016), <https://www.wider.unu.edu/sites/default/files/News/Documents/Stockholm%20Statement.pdf>.

[14] Ibid at 2.

[15] Ibid at 2–3.

[16] Ibid at 3–4.

[17] Ibid at 4.

[18] Ibid at 4.

[19] IPCC, H de Coninck, A Revi, M Babiker, P Bertoldi, M Buckeridge, A Cartwright, W Dong, J Ford, S Fuss, J C Hourcade, D Ley, R Mechler, P Newman, A Revokatova, S Schultz, L Steg, and T Sugiyama,

intergenerational equity that explicitly acknowledges that the effects of past and present emissions, vulnerabilities, and policies impose costs and benefits for people in the future.[20]

Immanuel Kant advanced the idea that each individual's actions should be guided by the notion that such actions would become a universal law or norm; that what can be determined as fair is the result of that universal perspective-taking.[21] Yet perspective-taking alone will not allow for a fundamental shift in climate governance to embed fairness norms, as the decision-makers continue to be the most economically privileged in our society.[22] Even if they try to be other-regarding, directors may not have the insight or capacity to fully understand fair or unfair outcomes of particular governance choices in respect of climate change or to shift fundamental norms. Just as markets are dynamic, our conception of how fairness values should be inculcated into the governance of climate change needs to be dynamic and responsive to problems identified. Markets are socially constructed, but their norms and standards are the result of a complex interplay between the most powerful market actors, corporate officers, supervisory authorities, elected representatives, and the judiciary and other adjudicators. It is these inputs that need retooling to advance our collective notions of what is fair or just.[23]

Economist Amartya Sen observed that in fashioning principles of justice, one cannot ignore the 'inescapable plurality of competing principles' of social justice that may conflict with one another, and the possible adverse effects on peoples beyond the borders of each country from specific actions and choices.[24] It must permit partial agreements or resolution of issues of justice, making room for incompleteness, tentativeness, and diversity of inputs.[25] Sen suggested an important role for public reasoning, including questioning the normative standing of preferences, understanding demands for fairness, and the necessity of scrutinizing or reexamining norms and choices.[26] We are increasingly linked by our social and economic relations, but also 'by vaguely shared but far-reaching concerns about injustice and inhumanity that challenge our world'.[27]

Drawing on these ideas, we know that corporate governance in respect of climate change is evolving, shifting away from notions that best interests of the company is concerned only with direct investors. Directors can face complex decisions as they exercise their duties, and there are no 'correct answers' in terms of the actual decisions they must make in the specific circumstances in which the company is operating. It is also increasingly evident that corporate decisions can no longer be made devoid of consideration of the impacts of carbon emissions on humans and ecosystems.

'Chapter 4: Strengthening and Implementing the Global Response' in IPCC, *Special Report 2018* (n 11) at 549 (hereafter IPCC, 'Global Response 2018').

[20] Ibid at 549.
[21] Immanuel Kant, *Kant: Political Writings* (CUP, 1991).
[22] Sarra, 'Embedding Fairness in Financial Markets' (n 5) at 200.
[23] Ibid at 203.
[24] Amartya Sen, *The Idea of Justice* (Harvard University Press, 2009) at 57 (hereafter Sen).
[25] Ibid at 90, 107–9.
[26] Ibid at 110–11.
[27] Ibid at 173.

Moreover, emissions and the effects of climate change are not restricted to any one region or country, and thus corporate decisions in respect of high emissions scenarios versus strategies to move to net zero are no longer confined to a single government's regulatory oversight. It reminds us that norms of fairness in respect of climate governance and climate action are continually developing and there is no global consensus on the most effective way to manage climate-related financial risk, a challenge for governance. Being guided by principles of fairness and justice can assist directors navigate oversight of management of climate risks, and is a reminder of the need for flexibility as governments, large institutional investors, and civil society develop new consensus on priorities for the distribution of the costs and benefits of managing risks and opportunities, and, ultimately, on saving the planet.

Like Sen, philosopher Martha Nussbaum's scholarship did not specifically address climate change, but her analysis offers additional theoretical insights that may inform climate governance. She advocated for basic social minimums under a policy approach that focuses on 'human capabilities', what people are actually able to do and be.[28] Acknowledging that the concept can be complex, she argued that human capabilities can serve as the objects of overlapping consensus among people who otherwise have different conceptions of the public good.[29] Nussbaum observed that creating an international overlapping consensus around ideas of mutual respect, sensitive to cultural differences, is the most urgent task for the world community during this century, and that notions of fairness from many countries and cultures can inform our approaches to justice and fairness.[30] A basic tenant of Nussbaum's conception of fairness is the 'principle of each person as end', which means that each society secures a threshold level of the basic goods of life to each person and, to that end, law should foster human capabilities and basic principles of justice.[31]

In many respects, Nussbaum's ideas reflect some of the principles underlying the UN Sustainable Development Goals, in that they challenge us to think about the unfair impacts of current carbon emissions and encourage corporations, in their actions to reverse global warming, to take some responsibility for decisions that are fair to stakeholders, to the environment, and to the public interests that underpin many of the international agreements on climate action.

Beate Sjåfjell and Christopher Bruner suggest that corporate governance and the regulatory infrastructure for corporate decision-making should support the achievement of regulatory goals to facilitate the internalization of society's sustainability goals.[32] In order to be sustainable, corporate governance must engage with the implementation of international human rights, and with the regeneration and preservation of ecosystems.[33] Sjåfjell and Bruner observe that it involves business and finance

[28] Martha C Nussbaum, *Women and Human Development: The Capabilities Approach* (CUP, 2000) at 5 (hereafter Nussbaum, *Capabilities*).

[29] Ibid at 5.

[30] Ibid at 8, 51.

[31] Ibid at 247, 270.

[32] Beate Sjåfjell and Christopher Bruner, 'Corporations and sustainability' in Beate Sjåfjell and Christopher Bruner (eds), *Cambridge Handbook of Corporate Law, Corporate Governance and Sustainability* (CUP, 2019) at 9 (hereafter Sjåfjell and Bruner).

[33] Ibid at 10.

creating value in a manner that is environmentally sustainable, ensuring long term stability and resilience of the ecosystems that support human life; socially sustainable, facilitating the achievement of human and other basic social rights; and economically sustainable governance that satisfies the economic needs necessary for stable and resilient societies.[34]

Waitzer and Sarro argue that future corporate governance needs to be ethical, recognizing responsibility to preserve and build on a natural environment capable of sustaining a company's operations, and a stable, equitable economy capable of sustaining a strong consumer base for the enterprise's products or services.[35] They suggest that it implies a normative duty to ensure that externalities are properly priced and moral failures are addressed, by taking a more integrative approach to investment.[36] Waitzer and Sarro argue that it will require a shift from the zero-sum culture that has crept into finance, towards a fiduciary culture where service providers place a premium on treating clients fairly.[37]

These principles assist in informing the contours of effective climate governance.

II. Effective Climate Governance

As discussed in Chapter 4, directors and officers should understand that their duty to the company requires that they have undertaken efforts to identify any material risks to their business from climate change and climate-related policies and that they have appropriate strategies in place to manage these risks. Effective climate governance practice suggests that directors and officers undertake efforts to identify benefits and risks of investing to support a net zero carbon infrastructure. Directors should take account of the business sector, sources of energy, direct and indirect carbon emissions, best environmental practices in terms of regulatory compliance, and integration of asset climate risk and resiliency in the firm's investment decision making. There should be mechanisms in place to respond rapidly to changes in the company's risk profile, including oversight and monitoring of the actions of individuals charged with managing these risks. Boards should consider the benefits of adopting net zero carbon technologies, products, and services likely to have upside financial potential. Fiduciary duty concepts are fundamental to informing board views of risk and materiality, with a view to sustainability of the company.

Going further than these concepts are the notions of fairness, good faith, and being 'other-regarding', creating governance structures aimed at moving towards net zero carbon and operating within planetary boundaries. While a full exploration of this latter notion is beyond the scope of this book, it merits deep consideration going forward.

[34] Ibid.

[35] E Waitzer and D Sarro, 'Fiduciary Society Unleashed: The Road Ahead for the Financial Sector' (2014) 69(4) Business Lawyer 1081 at 1096.

[36] Ibid at 1098–9, citing UN Environmental Programme Fin Initiative, 'Integrated Governance: A new Model for Sustainability' (2014), <http://goo.gl/AiZJou>.

[37] Ibid at 1098.

i. Getting Started

For the corporate board, pension fund board, or asset manager that has not yet taken action on climate change, there are a number of questions that directors and trustees should immediately ask themselves and their senior management. These questions or issues will allow the board to begin to identify strategies to move to net zero. A detailed list of questions for directors, officers, and pension fiduciaries is included in the appendix to this book.

Effective oversight means ensuring that directors have the information and skills to satisfy themselves that their managers are addressing climate-related risks and opportunities. The board needs to identify what information directors need in order to understand impacts on the business and to prioritize strategies to mitigate or control risks, directing managers to gather the appropriate information.

Directors should be asking their officers if the company has a climate plan that allows the company to survive in a 1.5°C or net zero carbon world. Critically important is the corporate board's effective oversight of its climate strategy, including identifying climate-related risks that are emerging or increasing in significance for the company and all its stakeholders. Given the urgency of climate-related financial risk, a climate plan needs to be developed that is tied directly to strategies to be sustainable under a range of likely scenarios, including a high-carbon scenario and net zero carbon scenario. As part of the company's, pension fund's, or asset manager's climate plan, the board needs to identify organization-wide material risks and strategic opportunities for the business over the short, medium, and long term as an integral part of its accountability for the long term stewardship of the organization. The board needs a robust understanding of how climate change may affect the company.[38]

The board's deliberations should be integrated into strategic planning, business models, financial planning, and other decision-making processes across the organization. Directors, officers, asset managers, and pension fiduciaries need to embed climate opportunity priorities in their strategic planning, performance objectives, policies, annual budgets, business plan, and enterprise risk management system.[39] Directors need to clearly communicate to their executive team and investment managers their expectations as to how climate-related materiality assessments are to be conducted and integrated into budget or operating cycle planning.

The board needs clearly defined processes by which it and its board committees are informed on a timely basis about new or emerging climate-change-related issues facing the company. There must be effective monitoring of implementation of the strategy against goals and targets. It is also important that the board has identified the senior executives responsible and accountable for oversight of climate policies, strategy, and information. The board needs to make clear how it is holding management accountable for implementing the regulatory requirements for climate-relevant disclosure and for maintaining oversight of emerging regulation. Scenario analysis,

[38] Janis Sarra, 'Canadian Climate Governance Experts (2019) (on file with author) (hereafter Climate Governance Experts).

[39] Ibid.

discussed below, can be very helpful in informing the corporate board about risks and opportunities.

The above steps for getting started are agreed on by many financial market participants. However, effective climate governance should go a step further and consider how fairness to all beneficiaries and stakeholders can be embedded in governance decisions. Moreover, how can the notion of planetary boundaries offer a meta-framework for governance decisions on long term sustainability? While corporate and pension boards need to consider the interests of their stakeholders, they can have regard for how those interests support the UN Sustainable Development Goals.[40] Numerous corporations have expressly embraced these additional governance considerations. For example, BNP Paribas Asset Management has stated that institutional investors, including both asset managers and asset owners, have the obligation to take action to help achieve the UN Sustainable Development Goals.[41]

ii. Climate Competent Directors and Pension Fiduciaries

Underpinning effective climate action is the need to have climate competent directors and pension fiduciaries. The board needs to ensure that it has climate expertise and knowledge in its matrix of board composition, and director and executive officer skills.[42] The CCGG suggests that companies should ensure that directors are highly competent and bring the requisite knowledge and experience to the board, defining competent directors as individuals with integrity, expert knowledge, business, industry or other relevant experience, and with the time and motivation to understand and carry out their fiduciary duties in the long term best interests of the corporation and all its stakeholders.[43] It notes that an effective governance system ensures that a significant number of directors on a board have experience and expertise relevant to the corporation's industry, financial responsibilities, and risk profile, and other directors bring specific expertise, such as accounting, law, or other relevant professional knowledge.[44]

Ideally, among the skills matrix of directors, there would be one or more directors that have expertise and knowledge regarding how climate change will impact the particular sector the company is operating in. However, an alternative to having a director highly knowledgeable in climate risk management on the board is to ensure that at least one director is paying serious attention to oversight of the climate strategy and ensuring that the board is receiving the professional advice needed to make informed decisions in respect of climate risk, essentially a 'lead climate director'. There should be a designated board committee to take responsibility for climate-related issues. Climate governance training for board members is important, so that they have

[40] UN Sustainable Development Goals, <https://sustainabledevelopment.un.org/?menu=1300>. See Chapter 8 for a discussion of the link between the Sustainable Development Goals and climate change.

[41] BNP Paribas Asset Management, 'Global Sustainability Strategy' (2019) at 17, <https://docfinder.bnpparibas-am.com/api/files/1FC9FC6C-0DA8-468E-90B3-016DDB5CD270>.

[42] Climate Governance Experts (n 38).

[43] *High Performance Boards* (n 1) at 8.

[44] Ibid at 9.

sufficient knowledge to ask questions of their managers regarding risk management, strategies, and potential opportunities. The board also needs to ensure that internal evaluations of the board include whether directors and officers are meeting their responsibilities to oversee climate risk management.

The CCGG suggests that boards should ask themselves whether and how the nomination process ensures the company has the right mix of climate-related experience, skills, and perspectives, and it should consider the qualities that will enable open, constructive dialogue on new and evolving topics.[45] If climate change has emerged as highly important for company strategy, investors would expect the board to have the requisite skills or expertise to address it, and climate-focused capabilities should be captured in the board skills matrix.[46]

Climate competence suggests that the board should be displaying a fundamental understanding of climate change and sustainability issues material to its business, having regard also to notions of fairness and good faith. Directors and pension trustees should integrate climate-related issues into board oversight and strategic and financial decisions, including looking specifically at the financial impacts of climate risk as it relates to revenues, expenditures, assets, liabilities, and financial capital.[47] Given the reputational risks, consumer-facing organizations should be assessing expectations of their clients, consumers, and beneficiaries.

The board's audit and risk committees should have clear responsibility for considering climate change risks and opportunities and their impact on operations, assets, and people over various timeframes and scenarios, making recommendations to the board. The obligation of directors on the audit committee is to be responsible for financial reporting by the company. Given that climate change poses risk of significant financial impacts on many businesses, as discussed in earlier chapters, the audit committee has a responsibility to assess the risk to capital. Committee members should acquire knowledge to understand the potential financial impacts of climate change on its assets, operations, and third parties. The committee should be asking if management and the board itself have strategies to mitigate and/or adapt to climate impacts. Climate change requires consideration of a longer term horizon that quarterly or annual reporting. Just as financial literacy is a requirement for audit committee members, there should be efforts to acquire climate competence or literacy in respect of risk exposure, including being able to estimate financial impacts across a range of scenarios and to assess whether the company's financial disclosures are accurate. The role of the audit committee in respect of climate risk will develop as knowledge about impacts grows.

The International Accounting Standards Board ('IASB') has observed that the international financial reporting standards ('IFRS') require audit committees to undertake a series of assessments of climate-related risk, including impairments to or changes in the useful life of assets.[48] If the information is material, the audit committee should be

[45] CCGG, *Directors' E&S Guidebook* (n 4) at 14.
[46] Ibid at 15.
[47] Ibid.
[48] International Accounting Standards Board, 'IFRS Standards and climate-related disclosures' (November 2019), <https://cdn.ifrs.org/-/media/feature/news/2019/november/in-brief-climate-change-nick-anderson.pdf?la=en>. See also the discussion in Chapter 6 of its guidance on climate and financials.

monitoring it, ensuring their risk assessment metrics accurately capture risk and are linked to existing financials, and that their metrics are accurately disclosed.

If oversight of climate risks is given to several board committees such as the risk committee, the audit committee, and the governance committee, then an effective governance tool is to appoint one director to be a lead climate director, as discussed above, to ensure that there are no gaps in oversight, given the importance of effective climate governance to the company's sustainability.

Also critically important is that the strategies to address climate change are cascading down to integrated management processes, operations, and value chain. A designated officer should be responsible for climate-related risk and accountable for implementing the company's strategy. That designated manager should be responsible for communicating climate-related issues effectively to the board, so that directors or trustees can undertake decisions that are informed by the best available information on climate risks and opportunities.

UK Supreme Court Justice Lord Sales has suggested that there should perhaps be introduction of a legislative or regulatory best practice requirement to appoint a designated board member for environmental impact issues, a dedicated voice on the board to ensure that climate issues are taken into account by directors when the board acts.[49] A designated board member would give climate change due prominence in the decision-making process of the board *as a whole*, rather than siphoning off responsibility for these important issues to one particular board member.[50]

The International Corporate Governance Network's ('ICGN') Global Stewardship Principles suggest that asset owners should ensure that their investment managers, advisors, consultants, and professional staff are fully competent and trained to take ESG factors, including climate change, into account across investment decision-making and reporting; and that the chief executive officer and chief investment officer of the investor fiduciary should provide assurance that ESG is adequately reflected in internal governance processes.[51]

Once climate change is identified as a strategic governance priority, it becomes easier to integrate climate risk into other business factors, such as risk management and compensation. Climate-related material value or risk to the organization should be thoughtfully incorporated into long term strategic objectives, with oversight by the board. The board should allocate sufficient time to reviewing priorities as an evolving component of the strategic plan. Periodic focus sessions should be held, at least annually, to allow the board and management to jointly assess whether the strategy captures changes in drivers, experience, and knowledge.[52] The board is responsible for monitoring performance against the strategic plan, using appropriate metrics and milestones, and climate priorities that are part of the strategic plan should be captured in performance evaluation and management compensation structures.[53]

[49] Lord Sales, Justice of UK Supreme Court, 'Directors' Duties and Climate Change: Keeping Pace with Environmental Challenges' (27 August 2019) at 13, <https://www.supremecourt.uk/docs/speech-190827.pdf> (hereafter Lord Sales).

[50] Ibid at 14.

[51] ICGN, *Global Stewardship Principles* (n 4).

[52] CCGG, *Directors' E&S Guidebook* (n 4) at 14.

[53] Ibid at 19.

The CCGG observes that corporate boards are accountable as fiduciaries for an organization's effective management of material environmental and social business issues, and as such, communication of these matters should be held to the same standards of accountability as any other material operational or risk issues.[54] Approval for climate-related reporting should be under the mandate of the board committee charged with oversight, and the board should have the necessary controls in place, whether internal or external, to provide reasonable verification and assurance of the facts and assumptions relied on by management in preparing the reports.[55]

In 2019, the World Economic Forum published eight principles for effective climate governance.[56] It reports that the board should be accountable for the company's long term resilience to potential shifts in the business landscape from climate change. The board should ensure that its composition is sufficiently diverse in knowledge, skills, experience, and background to effectively debate and take decisions informed by an awareness and understanding of climate-related threats and opportunities.[57] Directors are stewards for long term performance, so they need to determine the most effective way to integrate climate considerations into the board's structure and committees.

The World Economic Forum's fourth principle is that the board should ensure that management assesses the short, medium, and long term materiality of climate-related risks and opportunities for the company on an ongoing basis, and ensure the company's responses to climate are proportionate to the materiality of climate to the company.[58] The board should ensure that climate systemically informs strategic investment planning and decision-making processes and is embedded into the management of risk and opportunities across the organization. The board should ensure that executive incentives are aligned to promote climate-related targets and the long term prosperity of the company.[59] The board should ensure that material climate-related risks, opportunities, and strategic decisions are consistently and transparently disclosed to all stakeholders in financial filings. Finally, Board should maintain regular exchanges and dialogues with peers, policy-makers, investors, and other stakeholders to encourage the sharing of methodologies and to stay informed about the latest climate-relevant risks and regulatory requirements.[60] These principles offer a comprehensive guide to how boards can enhance their governance processes in respect of oversight of climate governance.

[54] Ibid at 23. See also Guide for General Counsel on Corporate Sustainability, <https://www.gsb.stanford.edu/sites/gsb/files/publication-pdf/ cgri-closer-look-68-building-better-board-book.pdf>.

[55] CCGG, *Directors' E&S Guidebook* (n 4) at 23.

[56] World Economic Forum, 'How to Set Up Effective Climate Governance on Corporate Boards, Guiding principles and questions' (2019), http://www3.weforum.org/docs/WEF_Creating_effective_climate_governance_on_corporate_boards.pdf.

[57] Ibid at 12.

[58] Ibid at 13.

[59] Ibid at 15.

[60] Ibid at 17.

iii. Effective Governance and Fiduciary Obligation in Engaging Asset Managers and Engagement Service Firms

Pension trustees and other investment fiduciaries may be held accountable by fund beneficiaries, even when they choose to hire external investment and asset managers and service providers to manage a portion or all of fund assets.[61] Smaller pension boards often hire outside expertise in the form of investment managers to make decisions on investment and management of funds, particularly where the trustees do not have the expertise and resources to do so themselves. Similarly, they may hire service firms to exercise their proxy-voting and/or direct engagement with investee companies. In such instances, the pension fiduciaries need to select these outside services in a manner that allows them to fulfil their fiduciary obligations. Not only can they not delegate their fiduciary obligations to third-parties, but the third-party asset managers or service providers also acquire fiduciary obligations.

In order to fulfil their fiduciary obligations in respect of engaging asset managers and engagement services firms, pension trustees need to select investment managers and service providers that have investment and engagement goals and practices that align with the pension fund's intergenerational goals and responsibilities. Arguably, climate competence is now a material factor in selecting such managers and service providers. Any contracts for engagement should articulate these objectives or standards and the pension trustees need to monitor the services of the asset manager or service provider to ensure that they are complying with the written mandate or direction given. Pension trustees should require that investment managers and service providers have clearly articulated climate action plans themselves and that they align with the climate-related objectives of the pension fund. They should require ongoing disclosure in respect of meeting targets in their climate action plan.

The ICGN suggests that the investment and risk management policies and processes agreed on between pension fiduciaries and their service providers should include objectives with respect to time horizons, risk tolerances, stewardship responsibilities, and ESG considerations, including in proxy voting and in company engagements, as well as clear understanding of how responsible investment activities will be reported to the board as principal investor fiduciary.[62] It recommends that metrics used for monitoring investment portfolios should seek to balance short and long term performance indicators, including systemic risk, stewardship, and ESG measures, and that decisions requiring approval or meriting notification to the investor fiduciary are appropriately specified, including circumstances allowing a revocation of the delegation.[63] It also recommends that compensation and remuneration paid to third parties contracted or employed by the investment fiduciary should be aligned with beneficiaries' interests, including appropriate incentives for the services providers to act in accordance with the principles and objectives set by the investment fiduciary with regard to climate and other ESG stewardship matters.[64]

[61] ICGN, *Global Governance Principles* (n 4) at 19.
[62] Ibid at 20.
[63] Ibid.
[64] Ibid.

iv. Monitoring Progress against Goals

The board should ensure that implementation of the climate strategy is being monitored effectively against goals and targets. Critical to the success of a climate strategy is that the board is confident that the company or pension fund is positioned and has dedicated sufficient resources to effectively identify, mitigate, manage, and monitor material climate-related risks. The board should be approving the disclosure of the company's efforts to manage climate change to investors and stakeholders, including integrating disclosure in its financial reporting. The company should report on the financial risks and opportunities associated with climate change. The directors should have a strategy to verify that the company has embedded effective materiality assessment processes in relation to climate risks and opportunities. The board must be aware and informed about potential mandatory climate-related reporting requirements in jurisdictions in which it has operations. It also needs to be prepared to explain its disclosures on climate in response to investor-led challenges.

The company's climate plan should link the company's management compensation incentivization scheme to reward sustainable value creation over time. Remuneration policies need to reflect progress towards net zero carbon emissions, with the metrics and targets applied.[65]

Sarah Barker has recommended that directors update their standing declarations to identify extraneous interests that may compromise their ability to exercise independent judgment on climate-related governance issues in the best interests of the corporation.[66] She asks whether the board's variables, assumptions, parameters, benchmarks, and methodologies have been updated to reflect scientific, economic, and financial developments, with the board asking what impact do these developments have for the company's strategy, risk management, and disclosure?[67] Barker recommends that assessments of remuneration structures should be conducted by management and the board compensation committee to ensure that no perverse incentives exist that may undermine climate policies or progress, such as incentives that may favour capex or investment in assets at risk of being stranded.[68]

Measuring progress on climate action against specific goals will assist in advancing the integrity of an organization's climate plan. For example, on the asset management side, the University of Toronto Asset Management Corporation ('UTAM') measures its ESG governance against the UN Principles for Responsible Investment.[69] In terms of incorporating ESG issues into investment analysis and decision-making processes, it evaluates ESG-related risks across all portfolios, integrates consideration of ESG

[65] Sarah Barker, 'The Climate Risk Reporting Journey: A Corporate Governance Primer', Centre for Policy Development, Commonwealth Climate and Law Initiative and Minter Ellison (June 2018) at 5, <https://ccli.ouce.ox.ac.uk/wp-content/uploads/2018/11/CCLI-Climate-Risk-Reporting-Journey-vFINAL.pdf> (hereafter Barker).

[66] Ibid at 3.

[67] Ibid at 5.

[68] Ibid.

[69] University of Toronto Asset Management Corporation, 'UTAM Responsible Investing Policy' (2019), <https://utam.utoronto.ca/responsible-investing/utam-responsible-investing-policy/>.

factors into its investment and operational due diligence policies, incorporates ESG considerations into manager selection and monitoring processes, supports development of ESG-related tools, metrics, and analyses, and provides ESG training for its investment professionals.[70] It is an active owner, in that it has a proxy voting policy that integrates ESG considerations and, where possible, applies this integrated policy to all public equity segregated account mandates, as well as to public equity funds in which its client's portfolios are the only investors.

UTAM encourages its investment managers to adopt voting policies that integrate ESG considerations, supports corporate and regulatory proposals that contribute to improved governance practices and more effective boards, and participates in collaborative engagement initiatives.[71] It asks its managers to undertake and report on ESG-related engagements with companies in their portfolios, and supports regulatory or policy developments that enable implementation of the principles for responsible investing.[72] UTAM also discloses how ESG issues are integrated in its investment process, its active ownership activities, its progress in effective ESG, including climate, governance.[73] UTAM was recently formally assessed by the UN PRI, receiving four A+ marks and one A for its responsible investing activities in managing the University of Toronto's pension and endowment assets, higher than the median PRI signatory in all relevant categories.[74]

v. Broadening Climate Expertise

Investors are also combining resources to broaden training and opportunities to advance climate governance expertise. In 2018, the OTPP, AIMCo, Allianz, Aviva, CalPERS, CDPQ, Generali, Natixis Investment Managers, OPTrust, CPPIB, and PGGM, together representing more than US $6 trillion in assets under management, joined to pledge resources, expertise, and networks to enhance expertise in infrastructure financing and development in emerging and frontier economies, to open opportunities for women in finance and investment worldwide, and to speed up the implementation of uniform and comparable climate-related disclosures.[75] They have committed to launching an infrastructure fellowship programme for senior public sector infrastructure managers that includes an intensive business school programme with their organizations. They are advocating for increased career opportunities in finance for women by implementing best practices in diversity and establishing and supporting an internship programme that encourages university women studying in

[70] University of Toronto Asset Management Corporation, 'A Closer Look: Applying an ESG Lens to Our Investment Decisions' (UTAM Responsible Investing Report 2018) at 12, <https://utam.utoronto.ca/wp-content/uploads/2019/05/UTAM017-Interactive_V3_Singles.pdf>.

[71] Ibid at 12.

[72] Ibid at 13.

[73] Ibid.

[74] Ibid at 14.

[75] OTPP, 'Leading Canadian and G7 Investors Come Together in Support of Global Development Initiatives' (6 June 2018), <https://www.otpp.com/news/article/-/article/790381>.

developing markets to learn about, prepare for, and gain experience in the investment industry.[76]

In Canada, the Canadian Climate Governance Experts is an initiative of the faculties of law at the University of British Columbia and York University, supported by funding from five foundations under the auspices of the Clean Economy Fund.[77] The Experts engage with corporate and pension boards to enhance the effectiveness of their climate governance. More than fifty-five governance and capital markets experts are donating their time *pro bono* over the next two years to the Canadian Climate Governance Experts programme, part of the Canada Climate Law Initiative, to conduct educational and information exchange sessions with directors and officers in all sectors of the economy. The goal is to support a serious enhancement of effective climate governance and climate competent directors on Canadian corporate and pension boards.

vi. Due Diligence is Both Good Governance and a Strong Defence to Decisions Made

As discussed in Chapter 4, given the broad mandate of directors, officers, and pension fiduciaries under their statutory fiduciary obligation and their duty of care, specific decisions made to address climate change are unlikely to give rise to personal liability. It is important to mention this due diligence once again because of the importance of understanding due diligence is an integral part of effective climate governance. Failure to act to manage climate-related risk is likely to attract liability, given the reasonable expectations of stakeholders, either through derivative actions on behalf of the company or personal actions against directors and officers. Courts will examine directors' decisions that balance competing interests, yet in many jurisdictions, once a decision is found to be reasonable, it will likely be upheld. Measuring fulfilment of directors' duties against reasonable expectations serves not only as an accountability check, but may also provide evidence that directors have met their statutory and common law obligations, and thus provide a defence against shareholder and other claims of breach of those obligations.

III. The Taskforce on Climate-related Financial Disclosure ('TCFD') Framework

To date, the greatest advances in respect of transparency and climate governance have been generated by the voluntary private sector initiative, the Financial Stability Board's Taskforce on Climate-related Financial Disclosures ('TCFD'). The TCFD recommendations aim to remedy the growing demand for decision-useful, climate-related

[76] Ibid.

[77] Canadian Climate Governance Experts, Canada Climate Law Initiative, <https://ccli.ubc.ca/>.

information by a range of participants in financial markets.[78] Creditors and investors require information on financial risk, and how it is being managed, in a form that is consistent, comparable, reliable, and clear.[79] There have been issues in respect of failure to disclose climate-related risks, inconsistent disclosure by companies year over year, and lack of comparability within and across sectors. Users of climate-related disclosures commonly cite the lack of information on the financial implications of the climate-related aspects of an organization's business and assets as a key gap. Users also cite inconsistencies in disclosure practices, a lack of context for information, use of boilerplate language, and non-comparable reporting as major obstacles to incorporating climate-related risks and opportunities as considerations in their investment, lending, and insurance underwriting decisions over the medium and long term.[80] One study found that inconsistent climate-related risk information hinders investors and creditors from considering climate-related issues in their asset valuation and allocation processes.[81] Cash flows from operations, net income, and access to capital could all be impacted by the effects of climate-related risks and opportunities.[82]

Realistically, the only way that corporations will fully take account of climate-related financial costs and benefits is to require that they include them in the company's financial statements.[83] Financial statements are a fundamental component of continuous disclosure. Financial statements provide equity and debt investors with the information to make informed choices whether to buy, sell, or hold their investment.[84] They can assist consumers in making product choices. They provide the information necessary for regulatory oversight. Financial reporting generally discloses the company's record of past transactions that have contributed to climate change or continue to emit GHG, and their impact on the company's financial position.[85] In order for the disclosure to be meaningful, it needs to be comparable year over year, or the notes to the financials need to reconcile and explain any differences.

Climate-change financial reporting has, to date, been either non-existent or inconsistent. If companies have separate reports on climate risk or embed discussions of climate change in non-financial corporate social responsibility ('CSR') reports, they can easily change the metrics from one year to the next if they do not like the results, and there is nothing that requires them to explain the changes. Thus, there is

[78] Financial Stability Board Task Force on Climate-related Financial Disclosures, 'Final Report, Recommendations of the Task Force on Climate-related Financial Disclosures' (15 June 2017) at 1, <https://www.fsb-tcfd.org/publications/final-recommendations-report/> (hereafter TCFD, *Final Report*).

[79] Ibid.

[80] Sustainability Accounting Standards Board ('SASB'), SASB Climate Risk Technical Bulletin No TB001-10182016 (October 2016).

[81] Mercer LLC, International Finance Corporation, and UK Department for International Development, 'Investing in a Time of Climate Change' (April 2015) at 16–17, <http://www.mercer.com/content/dam/mercer/attachments/global/investments/mercer-climate-change-report-2015.pdf>.

[82] Dr Janis Sarra and Professor Cynthia Williams, *Time to Act: Response to questions posed by the Expert Panel on Sustainable Finance on Fiduciary Obligation and Effective Climate-related Financial Disclosures* (CCLI, 2019) at 37–8 (hereafter Sarra and Williams, *Time to Act*).

[83] Ibid at 68.

[84] See for example, in Canada, National Instrument 51-102, *Continuous Disclosure Obligations* (12 June 2018), s 4.1 (hereafter NI 51-102).

[85] Mary Condon, Anita Anand, Janis Sarra, and Sarah Bradley, *Securities Law in Canada: Cases and Commentary* (3rd edn, Emond Montgomery, 2017) at 401 (hereafter Condon et al).

no comparability or consistency in reporting year over year.[86] The CCGG notes that siloed, non-integrated, CSR and environmental reporting can be viewed as greenwashing.[87] Integration into financial statements requires companies to measure climate-related factors, including the value of potentially stranded assets, costs of regulatory implementation of carbon pricing or new climate standards such as emissions reduction, and other impacts on financials.

It is also helpful for investors to understand capital expenditure plans. The level of debt or equity financing needed to fund climate resilience plans will depend on the willingness of capital markets to fund organizations exposed to significant levels of climate-related risks.[88]

Barker observes that directors must exercise due care and diligence in assuring that the company's disclosures present a true, fair, and balanced view of financial performance and prospects, and that they have been prepared on the basis of a robust process.[89] When climate reports are not part of financial statements, they tend not to be considered and approved by boards. If the board is not engaging in oversight of climate risks, then they are not being effectively managed. Failure to gather, analyse, and act on climate-related information means that the board is failing in its oversight obligations. The CCGG observes that key performance indicators and metrics used to convey environmental issues are most useful when they are well-defined, objective, and comparable, calling for better standardization, uniformity, and comparability.[90] The standards developed by the Sustainability Accounting Standards Board ('SASB') are aimed at creating consistent application of metrics that correspond to material risks and cross-cutting issues that can be compared across companies over time.[91]

Embedding climate-related disclosure in financial statements enhances corporate governance as it allows directors and officers to report how they view climate as material in the reporting period and how they have addressed it to date. It can embed sustainability thinking in core financial reporting and allow investors to measure progress year over year.[92] Requiring climate disclosure in financial statements would require corporate officers to explain changes in methodology of measuring material risks and opportunities, and would provide transparency and comparability in the market across corporations.[93] Changes in metrics because of developing information, such as climate-related financial risk, would be explained in the notes to the financial statements, leading to increased transparency.[94]

Requiring all companies to disclose how they have considered climate change, whether they consider it to be material over the short, medium, and long term, and how they are addressing both risks and opportunities, will create a more level playing field in terms of information for investors and other stakeholders. It should enhance

[86] Sarra and Williams, *Time to Act* (n 82) at 68.
[87] Ibid.
[88] TCFD, *Final Report* (n 78) at 9.
[89] See Barker (n 66).
[90] CCGG, *Directors' E&S Guidebook* (n 4) at 20.
[91] SASB, 'Why is Financial Materiality important?' (2019), <https://www.sasb.org/standards-overview/materiality-map/>.
[92] Sarra and Williams, *Time to Act* (n 82) at 68.
[93] Ibid.
[94] Ibid.

transparency regarding resources that companies are expending to assess and address these risks and opportunities. It will encourage directors' and officers' best thinking in respect of material climate risks and opportunities.

The TCFD core principles for effective disclosure are that disclosures should represent relevant information; be clear, specific, and complete; balanced and understandable; consistent over time; comparable among companies within a sector, industry, or portfolio; reliable, verifiable, and objective; and should be provided on a timely basis.[95]

The TCFD's recommendations centre on four thematic areas: governance, strategy, risk management, and metrics and targets. The figure below is now an increasingly familiar visual on its core elements of climate-related financial disclosures.

Core Elements of Recommended Climate-Related Financial Disclosures

Governance
The organization's governance around climate-related risks and opportunities

Strategy
The actual and potential impacts of climate-related risks and opportunities on the organization's businesses, strategy, and financial planning

Risk Management
The processes used by the organization to identify, assess, and manage climate-related risks

Metrics and Targets
The metrics and targets used to assess and manage relevant climate-related risks and opportunities

Figure 1 Core elements of recommended Climate-related Financial Disclosures
Source: TCFD, 'Core Elements of Recommended Climate-related Financial Disclosures 2017'[96]

i. Disclosure of Governance of Climate Risk

The TCFD recommends that organizations should provide information specific to their governance oversight of the potential impact of climate-related risks and opportunities in their financial statements and future cash flows, and that climate-related financial disclosures should be included in annual financial filings.[97] Specifically, it reports that 'asset impairments may result from assets adversely impacted by the effects of climate change and/or additional liabilities may need to be recorded to account for regulatory fines and penalties resulting from enhanced regulatory standards.'[98]

In disclosing board oversight of climate-related issues, the TCFD recommends that organizations should include discussion of the processes and frequency by which the board and/or board committees are informed about climate-related issues; whether the board and board committees consider climate-related issues when reviewing and

[95] Ibid at 18.
[96] TCFD, *Final Report* (n 78) at v.
[97] Ibid at 18.
[98] Ibid at 18, 37–8.

guiding strategy, major plans of action, risk management policies, annual budgets, and business plans. Organizations should disclose how they have set climate-related performance objectives, and how they are monitoring implementation and performance, and overseeing major capital expenditures, acquisitions, and divestitures.[99] The board should disclose how it monitors and oversees progress against goals and targets for addressing climate-related issues. Making these governance practices transparent will enhance investor and consumer confidence and assist with regulatory oversight.

In disclosing the role of management, the TCFD recommends that boards describe management's role related to the assessment and management of climate-related issues, including whether the organization has assigned climate-related responsibilities to management-level positions or committees; and, if so, whether such management positions or committees directly report to the board or a board committee. There should be disclosure of whether those managers' responsibilities include assessing and managing climate-related issues; a description of the associated organizational structures; the processes by which management and the board is informed about climate-related issues; and how management monitors climate-related issues.[100] Flowing from these recommendations are that companies allocate sufficient resources to allow corporate officers to effectively develop, implement, manage, and evaluate climate plans.

ii. Disclosure of Climate Strategy

In terms of disclosure of climate strategy, the TCFD recommends that companies disclose the impacts of climate change on the organization's business strategy and financial planning where such information is material.[101] They should describe the climate-related risks and opportunities that the organization has identified, as well as disclose the board's view of the resilience of the organization's strategy, taking into consideration different climate-related scenarios, including a 2°C or lower scenario.[102] In disclosing relevant short, medium, and long-term time horizons, boards should take into consideration the useful life of the organization's assets or infrastructure and the fact that climate-related issues often manifest themselves over the medium and longer term.[103] They should also describe the specific climate-related issues for each time horizon and the process used to determine which risks and opportunities could have a material financial impact on the organization.[104]

Also in terms of climate strategy, the TCFD recommends that boards describe the impact of climate-related risks and opportunities in terms of products and services, supply chain and/or value chain, adaptation and mitigation activities, investment in research and development, and in operations.[105] They should describe how climate-related issues serve as an input to their financial planning process, the time periods

[99] Ibid at 19.
[100] Ibid.
[101] Ibid at 11.
[102] Ibid at 14.
[103] Ibid at 20.
[104] Ibid.
[105] Ibid.

used, and how priorities are established.[106] The TCFD recommends that the 'disclosures should reflect a holistic picture of the interdependencies among the factors that affect their ability to create value over time'.[107] There should also be disclosure of climate financial planning in respect of operating costs and revenues, capital expenditures and capital allocation, acquisitions or divestments, access to capital, and any climate-related scenarios used to inform the organization's strategy and financial planning.[108]

iii. Disclosure of Risk Management

With respect to risk management, the TCFD recommends disclosure of processes for identifying, assessing, and managing climate-related risks, disclosing how these processes are integrated into the organization's overall risk management.[109] It observes that an important aspect is disclosure of how organizations determine the relative significance of climate-related risks in relation to other risks.[110] Corporate boards should describe whether they consider existing and emerging regulatory requirements related to climate change; their processes for assessing the potential size and scope of identified climate-related risks; and the definitions of risk terminology used or references to existing risk classification frameworks used. They should disclose their processes for how they make decisions to mitigate, transfer, accept, or control risks; their processes for prioritizing climate-related risks, including how materiality determinations are made within their organizations; and how their processes for identifying, assessing, and managing climate-related risks are integrated into their overall risk management.[111]

Climate-related financial disclosures should be subject to appropriate internal governance processes, and as part of annual financial filings, involve review by the chief financial officer and audit committee, as appropriate.[112]

Lord Sales of the UK Supreme Court has observed in respect of managing climate risks:

> This kind of tailored approach to corporate disclosure and reporting on environmental issues, amongst other environmental, social and governance factors, has been promoted by leading academics in Canada, Dr Janis Sarra and Professor Cynthia Williams, in a paper of January 2019 entitled *Time to Act*. The idea would be to require specific reporting, with the relevant legislation or a supplementary best practice code providing clear parameters for which aspects of environmental impact should normally be covered. Examples include reporting on supply chain management,

[106] Ibid at 20.
[107] Ibid.
[108] Ibid.
[109] Ibid at 14.
[110] Ibid at 21.
[111] Ibid at 21–2.
[112] Ibid at 18.

corporate waste disposal, company investment profiles, environmental impact assessments for major projects, and energy consumption.[113]

iv. Disclosure of Metrics and Targets

As the fourth part of the TCFD disclosure framework, metrics and targets, the TCFD recommends disclosure of the metrics the company's uses to assess climate-related risks and opportunities in line with its strategy and risk management process. In most G20 jurisdictions, public companies have a legal obligation to disclose material climate-related information in their financial filings, and climate-related financial disclosure is compatible with national disclosure requirements for financial filings.[114] The TCFD observes that its 'disclosure recommendations should result in more quantitative financial disclosures, particularly disclosure of metrics, about the financial impact that climate-related risks have or could have on an organization.'[115]

The TCFD recommends that companies should disclose in their financial statements how they govern climate risk, carbon emissions, emissions intensity, and metrics and targets to decrease emissions over time.[116] When climate risks are material, disclosures related to metrics and targets should be quantified in annual financial filings.[117] Disclosure should include existing and committed future activities and decisions requiring new investment, restructuring, impaired assets, or assets that need to be written down.[118]

The goal of financial reporting is to allow corporate stakeholders, including equity investors, debt investors, regulators, and other corporate stakeholders, to understand the financial performance of the corporation. Accounting for ESG factors, including climate-related financial risk and return, in financial reporting must allow corporate stakeholders to understand the corporation's economic performance in respect of these issues. Metrics need to be clear and measurable. Financial reporting metrics continue to be refined by a number of organizations in Canada and internationally. The reporting framework a company chooses to follow, and its rationale, should be described in the company's management discussion and analysis ('MD&A'), allowing investors and others to assess how the financials have been measured and verified.

The board should disclose metrics and targets for scope 1, scope 2, and over time, scope 3, GHG emissions, and the related risks; and describe the targets used by the organization to manage climate-related risks and opportunities and performance against targets.[119] The TCFD recommends that companies consider including metrics on climate-related risks associated with water usage, energy usage, land use, and waste management where relevant and applicable.[120]

113 Lord Sales (n 49) at 13.
114 TCFD, *Final Report* (n 78) at 17.
115 Ibid at 18, 37–8.
116 Ibid at 37–8.
117 Sarra and Williams, *Time to Act* (n 82).
118 TCFD, *Final Report* (n 78) at 9.
119 Ibid at 14. See Chapter 1 for the definition of scope 1, 2, and 3 GHG emissions.
120 Ibid at 22.

Companies should disclose a description of the methodologies used to calculate or estimate climate-related metrics. GHG emissions should be calculated in line with the GHG Protocol methodology or a consistent methodology to allow for aggregation and comparability across organizations and jurisdiction, the TCFD noting that while challenges remain, the GHG Protocol methodology is the most widely used international standard for calculating GHG emissions.[121] The GHG Protocol is aiming for global standardized frameworks to measure and manage GHG emissions from private and public sector operations, value chains, and mitigation actions, a collaboration of the CDP, World Resources Institute, and the World Business Council for Sustainable Development.[122]

Of note is that scope 1 and scope 2 emissions are easier to quantify because the company has direct control over that information. Scope 3 emissions will be more difficult to measure until many of the companies delivering supplies or other inputs or supplying services under contract to the reporting company are also measuring their emissions. Quite aside from future regulatory requirements, such reporting is likely to become part of the terms of supply and other contracts between the parties to such commercial relationships.

Where climate-related issues are material, organizations should describe how related performance metrics are incorporated into their remuneration policies.[123] Companies should provide their internal carbon prices, as well as climate-related opportunity metrics such as revenue from products and services designed for a low carbon economy.[124]

The TCFD further recommends that 'as appropriate, organizations should consider providing related, generally accepted industry-specific GHG efficiency ratios.'[125] It observed that for industries with high energy consumption, metrics related to emission intensity are important to provide, such as emissions per unit of economic output.[126] Its implementation Annex gives examples of metrics.[127] Companies should describe their key climate-related targets, including GHG emissions, in line with anticipated regulatory requirements, efficiency or financial goals, financial loss tolerances, or net revenue goals for products and services designed for a low carbon economy.[128] In describing targets, companies should specify whether the target is absolute or intensity based, time frames over which the target applies, base year from which progress is measured, and key performance indicators used to assess progress against targets.[129]

Patrick Bolton and Marcin Kacperczyk have examined whether carbon risk is currently reflected in asset prices, and whether a carbon risk factor or carbon-emission characteristics affect cross-sectional US stock returns.[130] They found that carbon

121 Ibid.

122 Greenhouse Gas Protocol (2019), <http://ghgprotocol.org/corporate-standard>.

123 TCFD, *Final Report* (n 78) at 22.

124 Metrics should be provided for historical periods to allow for trend analysis, ibid.

125 Ibid.

126 Ibid.

127 TCFD, 'Annex: Implementing the Recommendations of the TCFD' (2017), <https://www.fsb-tcfd.org/publications/final-implementing-tcfd-recommendations/>.

128 TCFD, *Final Report* (n 78) at 23.

129 Ibid.

130 Patrick Bolton and Marcin Kacperczyk, 'Do Investors Care about CARBON risk?' (Working paper, Columbia University and Imperial College, 16 July 2019), <https://ssrn.com/abstract=3398441>.

emissions do affect returns on equity investment. They note that current reporting standards of carbon emissions distinguish between scope 1, 2, and 3 emissions.[131] Bolton and Kacperczyk found that for scope 1, 2, and 3 emissions, there is a positive and statistically significant effect on firms' stock returns and that carbon emissions are associated with higher returns, after controlling for size, book-to-market, momentum, and other well-recognized variables.[132] They found that, in aggregate, institutional investors hold a smaller fraction of companies with high scope 1 and 2 emissions, and in particular, insurance companies, pension and investment advisors are underweight in companies with scope 1 and 2 carbon emissions with the rise in sustainable investment and negative exclusionary screening investment strategies. However, they found that institutional investors are not underweight in scope 3 emissions, which they say may be attributable to lack of reliable scope 3 information.[133] They conclude that firms can increase their value by reducing their exposure to scope 3 emissions, which has the added benefit of lowering their cost of capital[134]

The TCFD maintains an online knowledge platform designed to help organizations implement the TCFD recommendations, providing over 400 relevant insights, tools, and resources.[135] It includes case studies, articles on best practices, online educational programmes, and implementation guidance being issued by regulators in different countries.

v. Adoption of the TCFD Framework

The TCFD voluntary framework has had remarkable pick-up in a very short timeframe. As of 2019, three-quarters of the world's globally systemic banks, leading pension funds and insurers, eight of ten largest global asset managers, and the four largest accounting firms support the TCFD framework, collectively they manage almost US $110 trillion in assets.[136] 785 companies have committed to using the TCFD disclosure framework.[137]

Leading reporting frameworks and standards organizations, including the Sustainability Accounting Standards Board, the Global Reporting Initiative, and the Carbon Disclosure Standards Board are working to align their guidance to the TCFD framework, to minimize the reporting burden on publicly traded companies.

In 2019, the UN Principles for Responsible Investment announced that TCFD-based reporting would become mandatory in 2020 for signatories to the Principles for Responsible Investment, comprising investors with over US $80 trillion in

[131] Ibid.
[132] Ibid.
[133] Ibid.
[134] Ibid.
[135] TCFD, 'Knowledge Hub' (2020), <https://www.fsb-tcfd.org/tcfd-knowledge-hub/>.
[136] Financial Stability Board, 'TCFD Supporters', <https://www.fsb-tcfd.org/tcfd-supporters/; Task Force on Climate-related Financial Disclosures (2018).
[137] TCFD, '2019 Status Report Taskforce on Climate Related Financial Disclosures' (June 2019) at vi, <https://www.fsb-tcfd.org/wp-content/uploads/2019/06/2019-TCFD-Status-Report-FINAL-053119.pdf>

funds under management.[138] In Australia, the Australian Prudential Regulatory Authority ('APRA'), the Reserve Bank, and the Australian Securities and Investments Commission have endorsed the TCFD framework.[139] In March 2019, APRA said it 'expects that disclosure that is specific, comprehensive and considers climate change risks distinctly will progress in the future', noting that the TCFD recommendations provide an established, voluntary framework for this disclosure.[140]

The Bank of England has also endorsed the TCFD framework. Former Bank Governor Carney stated that the financial sector must help the transition to a net zero carbon footprint, and to support meaningful disclosure, the TCFD should share best practices to increase the quantity and quality of climate-related disclosures, give a definitive view on what is high quality disclosure, spread knowledge on how to measure and use information on strategic resilience more widely, and consider how asset owners should disclose how well their portfolios are placed for the transition to net zero carbon.[141]

The Network for Greening the Financial System, a group of 36 central banks and supervisors, has encouraged companies to disclose in line with the TCFD recommendations.[142] The International Organization of Securities Commissions ('IOSCO'), an association of regulators of the world's securities, while not expressly endorsing the TCFD, names it as one framework in encouraging companies to consider and disclose the materiality of ESG matters to their business and to assess risks and opportunities in light of their business strategy and risk assessment methodology.[143]

One study recently asked survey participants to rate the financial materiality of three sources of climate risks: physical risks, regulatory risks, and technological disruption risks.[144] The survey found that long term investors believe climate-related physical and technological risks are substantially more financially material than do other investors. Large institutions consider physical risks as more financially material, which the authors note is consistent with the idea that such investors bear greater costs related to climate change.[145] The study also found that investors who consider

[138] United Nations Principles for Responsible Investment, 'TCFD-based Reporting to Become Mandatory for PRI Signatories in 2020' (19 February 2019), <https://www.unpri.org/news-and-press/tcfdbased-reporting-to-become-mandatory-for-pri-signatories-in-2020/4116.article>.

[139] Deputy Governor Guy Debelle, 'Climate Change and the Economy', Speech delivered at Centre for Policy Development, Sydney (12 March 2019), <https://www.rba.gov.au/speeches/2019/sp-dg-2019-03-12.html>. See also John Price, ASIC Commissioner, 'Climate Change', Speech delivered at Centre for Policy Development, Sydney (18 June 2018), <https://asic.gov.au/about-asic/news-centre/speeches/climate-change/>.

[140] Australian Prudential Regulation Authority ('APRA'), 'Climate Change: Awareness to Action' (20 March 2019) at 17, <https://www.apra.gov.au/sites/default/files/climate_change_awareness_to_action_march_2019.pdf>.

[141] Mark Carney, 'TCFD: Strengthening the Foundations of Sustainable Finance', Speech delivered to Tokyo TCFD Summit (8 October 2019), <https://www.bankofengland.co.uk/speech/2019/mark-carney-speech-at-climate-related-financial-disclosure-summit>.

[142] Ibid.

[143] International Organization of Securities Commissions, 'Statement on Disclosure of ESG Matters by Issuers' (18 January 2019) at 3, <https://www.iosco.org/library/pubdocs/pdf/IOSCOPD619.pdf>.

[144] Philipp Krueger, Zacharias Sautner, and Laura Starks, 'The Importance of Climate Risks for Institutional Investors', ECGI Finance Working Paper No. 610/2019 (June 2019), <http://ssrn.com/abstract_id=3235190>.

[145] Ibid at 20–1.

the effects of climate change to be more financially material use more engagement channels.[146] Survey respondents generally believed that climate risks have important financial implications for their portfolio firms.[147] The vast majority expected a significant rise in global temperature by the end of this century and have deep concerns about the effects of climate change on their portfolios.[148]

IV. Climate Scenario Analysis as a Potential Governance Tool

The science of climate change makes clear that the risks are urgent and foreseeable, and the ecosystem and financial impacts are large, but there is no precise way to predict their magnitude. Given that immediate action is needed, even in the face of uncertainty on magnitude and exact timing, a number of different tools are being developed to assist companies and investors.

For example, companies and institutional investors are now using scenario analysis as a tool to test their strategic resilience to different climate outcomes. Scenario analysis can broaden directors' thinking across a range of plausible scenarios in which climate-related impacts are likely to be significant but there is uncertainty as to future pathways.[149] Scenarios can be qualitative or quantitative information, relying on numerical data and models, or a combination of qualitative and quantitative information.[150] Climate scenarios are data-driven narratives that help companies and investors think through different possible futures.[151]

Companies can assess a range of plausible business, strategic, and financial impacts from climate change and actions that are needed to manage the company's strategic, business, and financial plans.[152] Scenario analysis can assist companies in recognizing when the environment is moving toward a different scenario, encouraging reassessment and adjustment of strategies and financial plans accordingly.[153]

In 2017, the TCFD released three key documents that support implementation of its recommendations, 'Final Report: Recommendations of the Task Force on Climate-related Financial Disclosures; Annex: Implementing the Recommendations of the TCFD', which provides detail to help companies implement the recommendations, described as a 'living document' that will be refined as companies gain more experience

[146] Ibid at 30.

[147] Ibid at 36.

[148] Ibid at 36.

[149] Ibid at 26.

[150] See TCFD, *Final Report* (n 78) at 25–6, citing Mark Rounsevell and Marc Metzger, 'Developing Qualitative Scenario Storylines for Environmental Change Assessment', (2010) WIRE Climate Change 606–19; and Oliver Fricko et al, 'Energy Sector Water Use Implications of a 2°C Climate Policy' (2016) 11 Environmental Research Letters 1–10.

[151] Mark Carney, 'A New Horizon', Speech delivered to European Commission Conference 'A Global Approach to Sustainable Finance' (21 March 2019) at 7, <https://www.bankofengland.co.uk/-/media/boe/files/speech/2019/a-new-horizon-speech-by-mark-carney.pdf?la=en&hash=F63F8064E0408F038CABB1F29C58FB1A0CD0FE25> (hereafter Carney, New Horizon).

[152] Ibid.

[153] Ibid, citing J N Maack, 'Scenario Analysis: A Tool for Task Managers, Social Analysis—Selected Tools And techniques', Social Development Papers Number 36 (World Bank, 2001).

preparing climate-related financial disclosures; and a 'Technical Supplement: The Use of Scenario Analysis in Disclosure of Climate-Related Risks and Opportunities', which provides a further level of detail that can assist companies in scenario analysis.[154] The TCFD reports that scenario analysis can be very helpful to fiduciaries in determining climate-related financial risk, as well as strategies to respond. It can also assist in identifying upside investment opportunities in developing technologies for climate adaptation.

The TCFD recommends that organizations use climate-related scenarios to disclose how resilient their strategies are to climate-related risks and opportunities.[155] Boards should disclose how climate-related scenarios and associated time horizons are influencing directors' decisions on strategies to address such potential risks and opportunities.[156]

Scenario analysis can also assist investors in understanding the robustness of a company's forward-looking strategies and financial plans.[157] It can be important for investors and other stakeholders in understanding how vulnerable individual organizations are identifying transition and physical risks, and how such vulnerabilities are, or would be, addressed.[158] Organizations should disclose scenario analysis information in their annual financial filings.[159]

Selection of different scenarios should cover a reasonable choice of favourable and unfavourable future outcomes, and the TCFD recommends organizations use a 2°C above pre-industrial levels or lower scenario in addition to two or three other scenarios most relevant to their circumstances.[160] One potential scenario is to link the company's activities to their home jurisdiction's nationally-determined contributions under the Paris Agreement. The TCFD suggests that companies in the initial stages of implementing scenario analysis should disclose how resilient, qualitatively or directionally, the organization's strategy and financial plans may be to a range of relevant climate change scenarios.[161]

For companies with significant exposure to climate-related issues, directors should disclose key assumptions and pathways related to the scenarios they use, in order to allow users to understand the analytical process and its limitations.[162] The TCFD observes that the information should include critical input parameters across different assets and regions of activity, assumptions, and analytical choices for the scenarios used; assumptions about possible technology responses, and timing and costs to implement, including short, medium, and long term milestones. It should include information about the resiliency of the organization's strategy, including implications for the organization's value chain, capital allocation decisions, research and development

[154] Technical Supplement, 'The Use of Scenario Analysis in Disclosure of Climate-Related Risks and Opportunities' (December 2016), <https://www.fsb-tcfd.org/wp-content/uploads/2016/11/TCFD-Technical-Supplement-A4-14-Dec-2016.pdf>.

[155] TCFD Annex (n 127); TCFD, *Final Report* (n 78) at 20.

[156] TCFD, *Final Report*, ibid.

[157] Ibid at 26.

[158] Ibid at 25.

[159] Ibid.

[160] Ibid at 27.

[161] Ibid at 28.

[162] Ibid.

focus, and potential material financial implications for the organization's operating results and financial position.[163]

The TCFD further recommends that in conducting scenario analysis, organizations should strive to achieve transparency; comparability of results across different scenarios and analytical approaches; adequate documentation for the methodology, assumptions, data sources, and analytics; consistency of methodology year over year; sound governance over scenario analysis conduct, validation, approval, and application; and effective disclosure of scenario analysis that will inform a constructive dialogue between investors and organizations on the range of potential impacts and resilience of the organization's strategy under various plausible climate-related scenarios.[164]

Climate scenario analysis is not intended to forecast the future, it is aimed at examining the exposure and vulnerability of long term business strategy and performance to various hypothetical climate change pathways, and their associated physical, transition, and litigation risk potential.[165] The Canadian government has observed that while Earth system models can simulate the climate system's response to human emissions of GHG, they cannot predict future human decisions and activities; thus, projections are made using various scenarios or pathways of future GHG concentrations, aerosol loading, and land-use change.[166] The tools to assess climate-related financial risks are just emerging; however, tools to assess the changing climate, temperature, and other scientific aspects have been used for decades and are very well developed.

The Bank of England expects UK firms to consider scenario analysis as part of their assessment of the impact of climate risks on their balance sheet and business strategies.[167] Carney observed that scenarios should be comprehensive, rigorous, and challenging; and that the assumptions and methodologies in the models, such as the assumed global temperature rise, the energy mix, or whether the transition happens smoothly or abruptly, should be sufficiently transparent to allow for comparisons across businesses and sectors.[168] Best practice suggests that scenarios should be implemented consistently across the business, linking identification of risks and opportunities to governance strategy and disclosure.[169]

The Bank of England's biennial scenario testing will allow the Bank to examine how major financial firms expect to adjust their business and risk management models to respond to climate-related risks.[170] The Bank will test the resilience of UK's largest banks and insurers to climate-related risks and the financial system as a whole to three

[163] Ibid at 28.

[164] Ibid at 29.

[165] Government of Canada, 'Final Report of the Expert Panel on Sustainable Finance: 'Mobilizing Finance for Sustainable Growth' (June 2019) at 19, <http://publications.gc.ca/collections/collection_2019/eccc/En4-350-2-2019-eng.pdf> (hereafter Canada Expert Panel).

[166] Government of Canada, 'Canada's Changing Climate Report 2019' at 122, <https://www.nrcan.gc.ca/sites/www.nrcan.gc.ca/files/energy/Climate-change/pdf/CCCR_FULLREPORT-EN-FINAL.pdf>.

[167] Carney, 'New Horizon' (n 151).

[168] Ibid at 7.

[169] Ibid.

[170] Bank of England Discussion Paper, 'The 2021 Biennial Exploratory Scenario on the Financial Risks from Climate Change' (18 December 2019) at 1, <https://www.bankofengland.co.uk/paper/2019/biennial-exploratory-scenario-climate-change-discussion-paper>.

climate scenarios.[171] The Bank will use an extended modelling horizon of 30 years because climate change will occur over a much longer timeframe than the normal horizon for stress testing. To make these scenarios credible and tractable, the Bank will examine firms' resilience using fixed balance sheets, focusing on sizing the risks and the scale of business model adjustment required to respond to these risks, rather than testing the adequacy of firms' capital to absorb those risks. The Bank will provide pathways for temperature, emissions, and climate policies to capture the underlying physical and transition risks in each scenario, providing a consistent set of macrofinancial variables to enable firms to model the impact of the scenarios.[172] Firms are also to assess the vulnerability of individual counterparties' business models to the underlying climate-related risks in each scenario.

The IPCC observes that climate change scenarios need to be an 'internally consistent, plausible, and integrated description of a possible future of the human–environment system, including a narrative with qualitative trends and quantitative projections'.[173] It notes that scenarios provide a framework for developing and integrating projections of emissions, climate change, and climate impacts, including an assessment of their inherent uncertainties.[174] It reports that the multifaceted nature of climate change requires climate scenarios to describe how socio-economic trends in the 21st century could influence future energy and land use, resulting emissions, and the evolution of human vulnerability and exposure. In turn, scenarios can inform policy choices.

Canada's Expert Panel on Sustainable Finance observed that while no single scenario will be universally applicable, a starting point for comparability would help create incentives for financial analysis and avoid myriad companies 'reinventing the wheel', and from there, individual companies and industry groups can customize the scenarios and build out proprietary analysis.[175]

Recognizing its fiduciary obligation to address climate change, the Ontario Teachers' Pension Plan ('OTPP'), with almost Cdn $310 billion in assets under management, has implemented a Low Carbon Economy Transition Framework, in which it is integrating climate change considerations across its entire investment cycle, from the opportunities, to assessment and decision-making processes before acquiring an asset, to how it manages an asset once it owns it.[176] Its Low Carbon Economy Transition

[171] Ibid. Insurers will participate via a BES-aligned Insurance Stress Test in 2021.

[172] Ibid.

[173] IPCC, M Allen, O Dube, W Solecki, F Aragón-Durand, W Cramer, S Humphreys, M Kainuma, J Kala, N Mahowald, Y Mulugetta, R Perez, M Wairiu, and K Zickfeld, 'Chapter 1 Framing and Context' in V Masson-Delmotte, P Zhai, H O Pörtner, D Roberts, J Skea, P Shukla, A Pirani, W Moufouma-Okia, C Péan, R Pidcock, S Connors, J B R Matthews, Y Chen, X Zhou, M I Gomis, E Lonnoy, T Maycock, M Tignor, and T Waterfield (eds), *Global Warming of 1.5°C: An IPCC Special Report on the Impacts of Global Warming of 1.5°C above Pre-industrial Levels and Related Global Greenhouse Gas Emission Pathways, in the Context of Strengthening the Global Response to the Threat of Climate Change, Sustainable Development, and Efforts to Eradicate Poverty* (IPCC, 2019) at 63, <https://www.ipcc.ch/site/assets/uploads/sites/2/2019/05/SR15_Chapter1_Low_Res.pdf> (hereafter IPCC, *Special Report 2018*).

[174] Ibid.

[175] Canada Expert Panel (n 165) at 19.

[176] OTPP, '2018 Climate Change Report' (2019) at 11,<https://www.otpp.com/documents/10179/859251/2018+Climate+Change+Report/152d6724-3d35-4f69-8971-641ec13ed737> (hereafter OTPP, '2018 Climate Change Report'). At the core of the framework are three scenarios that describe what the

Framework is a guide to a more systematic approach to understanding the potential impacts of climate change. OTPP's framework is aimed at allowing the pension fund to make more informed decisions on individual public and private investments and its portfolio as a whole.[177] At the core of OTPP's framework are three scenarios that describe what the future could look like in 2030, as well as processes in place that consider material climate change impacts in its investments.[178] The scenarios range from an orderly transition to a low carbon economy, to a middle scenario extrapolating from current climate policies/actions, to a high-carbon world where fossil fuels dominate until 'drastic and disruptive action is taken'.[179] The scenarios are defined with respect to five key catalysts: policy, technology, consumer preference, capital, and physical impacts, using the scenarios as signposts in respect of climate developments and future investment.[180]

Caisse de dépôt et placement du Québec ('CDPQ') is another example of an institutional investor that undertakes scenario analyses. CDPQ has established probability measures, which are then considered in depth in order to understand the impact the scenarios will have on its portfolios, facilitating decisions on how to position its investments.[181] CDPQ analyses climate risk by considering a number of unknowns and possible scenarios that examine medium and long term systemic risks, with the express objective of increasing its low carbon assets and reducing the carbon intensity of it overall portfolio by 25 per cent by 2025.[182] Scenarios are used by CDPQ when necessary to analysing the impact of transitioning to more sustainable forms of energy based on key performance indicators, with CDPQ reporting based on the TCFD recommendations.[183]

The Institutional Investors Group on Climate Change ('IIGCC') has published a guide to help asset owners and managers use scenario analysis to understand how climate change drives financial impact across their portfolios.[184] It observes that understanding the assumptions behind scenarios and the methodologies used to apply them to investments is critically important, as they drive the results. The IIGCC suggests that scenario analysis should be viewed as a dynamic process that is repeatable; it should be embedded into mainstream risk management and investment functions.[185]

future could look like in 2030. OTPP has processes in place that consider material climate change impacts in its investments.

[177] Ibid.

[178] Ibid.

[179] Ibid at 1.

[180] Ibid.

[181] Claude Bergeron, 'Managing Risks in a World of Uncertainty' (CDPQ 2017), <https://www.cdpq.com/en/news/articles/managing-risks>.

[182] CDPQ, 'Stewardship Investing 2018' (April 2019), Appendix 2, <https://www.cdpq.com/en/news/pressreleases/la-caisse-publishes-its-2018-annual-report> (hereafter CDPQ, 'Stewardship Investing').

[183] Ibid.

[184] Institutional Investors Group on Climate Change, 'Navigating Climate Scenario Analysis: A Guide for Institutional Investors' (4 February 2019), <https://www.iigcc.org/download/navigating-climate-scenario-analysis-a-guide-for-institutional-investors/?wpdmdl=1837&refresh=5dc829feea23e1573399038> (hereafter IIGCC).

[185] Ibid.

It can provide a starting point for investors to monitor the early warning signs about which scenario is most likely to materialize and to take action accordingly.[186]

While some companies may be large enough to generate their own climate transition scenarios, many companies will need to build on commonly available models. In the UK, the Climate Financial Risk Forum, co-chaired by the UK Prudential Regulation Authority and Financial Conduct Authority, is working towards standardization of scenario tools, including assumptions and metrics.[187]

In 2019, the International Actuarial Association commenced an initiative to advance the public interest by developing actuarial approaches in climate-related financial risk management and reporting.[188] It will assist other organizations, such as the TCFD, in selecting climate-dependent risk scenarios and applying them to the appropriate risk management methods such as the development of event frequency and severity for actual liabilities in insurance and pensions; provide educational material on current and future impacts on categories of assets of various climate-related risk scenarios; and monitor how climate change financial and insurance risks assist in responding to modifications in regulatory requirements and disclosure systems that arise from changes in the outlook or strategies to control the evolution of climate-related risks, with special reference to maintaining access to equitable risk pooling.[189]

Climate-related scenario analysis has challenges. There is need for greater transparency in the range of data inputs and outputs and the functionality of tools. The availability and granularity of data can be a challenge for companies assessing various energy and technology pathways or carbon constraints in different jurisdictions and geographic locations.[190] The TCFD observes that use of climate-related scenario analysis to assess potential business implications is still at an early stage, and there is need to share experiences in order to advance use of these tools, data sets, and methodologies.[191]

The UN PRI has observed that scenario analysis considers how a company might perform in response to a range of hypothetical outcomes and that it can help to assess the awareness of risks by bond issuers. However, it points out that scenario analysis has its limitations when it comes to ascertaining plausibility, as well as comparability and how many scenarios to consider overall.[192] It suggests incorporating other forms of 'what-if' analysis, such as sensitivity analysis, which involves assessing the impact on the cash flow and balance sheet of a change of variable such as emissions reductions, noting that while estimates of sensitivities are not new to credit risk analysis, they are typically conducted through financial variables, as opposed to treating climate factors as independent variables. It also suggests that stress testing, currently used for macroprudential oversight of the banking sector, could help test a company's

[186] Ibid.

[187] Climate Financial Risk Forum, 'Minutes of July 2019 Meeting', <https://www.bankofengland.co.uk/minutes/2019/pra-fca-joint-climate-financial-risk-forum-july-2019>.

[188] International Actuarial Association, 'Draft Statement of Intent (SOI) for IAA Activities on Climate-related Risks' (2019) at 1–3.

[189] Ibid at 4.

[190] TCFD, *Final Report* (n 78) at 29.

[191] Ibid at 30.

[192] UN PRI, 'Credit Ratings' (2019), <https://www.unpri.org/credit-ratings/statement-on-esg-in-credit-risk-and-ratings-also-available-in-chinese/77.article>.

cash flow and balance sheet resilience under one extreme scenario or a combination of severe scenarios that are not necessarily correlated, and thus help with climate-related planning.[193] It notes that the analytical tools will improve over time and models are likely to become more user-friendly.

As helpful as scenario testing may be, Kevin Anderson and Alice Bows offer a cautionary note regarding the scenario approaches that are being used to map corporate and regulatory climate strategies.[194] Assessing the methodology of a number of scenarios, they conclude that emissions data on future emission pathways need to be more consistent and accurate, that many used a global emissions peak in 2010, for which there is now irrefutable evidence to the contrary, and many counted on significant biomass with carbon capture and storage, which has not yet been realized.[195] They suggest that making explicit the implications of particular assumptions such as peak emission dates would provide insights intelligible to wider groups of stakeholders and decision-makers, and provide contextual parameters and constraints to more complex modelling approaches.[196]

Anderson and Bows observe that differences in predictions as to how best to avoid 'dangerous climate change' relate less to different interpretations of the science underpinning climate change and much more to differing assumptions related to five fundamental and contextual issues: what delineates dangerous from acceptable climate change; what risk of entering dangerous climate change is acceptable; what is the reasonable assumption regarding when global emissions will peak; what reduction rates in post-peak emissions is it reasonable to consider; and can the primacy of economic growth be questioned in attempts to avoid dangerous climate change?[197] Their message is, essentially, use scenario testing, but be very clear on the accuracy of the data, the assumptions underpinning targets, and the normative question of what is acceptable.

V. Integrated Assessment Models and Climate Change Financial Risk

Scientists are evaluating the effects of the various mitigation pathways on sustainable development using integrated assessment models ('IAM') that provide relevant information on land-use changes, and biodiversity, food security, and air quality.[198] IAM combine insights from various disciplines in a single framework, allowing scientists to describe energy–economy–land-climate systems that cover the largest sources of anthropogenic GHG emissions from different sectors, studying energy and land

[193] Ibid.

[194] Kevin Anderson and Alice Bows, 'Beyond "Dangerous" Climate Change: Emission Scenarios for a New World' (2011) 369 Philosophical Transactions of the Royal Society 20 at 24.

[195] Ibid at 26, 38.

[196] Ibid at 39.

[197] Ibid.

[198] IPCC, J Rogelj, D Shindell, K Jiang, S Fifita, P Forster, V Ginzburg, C Handa, H Kheshgi, S Kobayashi, E Kriegler, L Mundaca, R Séférian, and M V Vilariño, 'Chapter 2: Mitigation Pathways Compatible with 1.5°C in the Context of Sustainable Development' in IPCC, *Special Report 2018* (n 12) at 98, <https://www.ipcc.ch/site/assets/uploads/sites/2/2019/05/SR15_Chapter2_Low_Res.pdf>.

systems, air pollutants, and water uses.[199] The difficulty, however, is that many unknown political, economic, and social factors can affect outcomes of these models and are not easily predictive.

Economists are also trying to estimate impacts of climate change using IAM. The baseline scenario William Nordhaus uses in his Dynamic Integrated Model of Climate and the Economy ('DICE') model is where per capita consumption continues to rise rapidly over the coming decades with the projected growth in global per capita output a little under 2 per cent per year for the twenty-first century.[200] While it is difficult to estimate impacts as they combine the uncertainties of emissions projections and climate models, there are now many IAM of climate change used to advise companies and investors in respect of climate-related risk. Essentially, IAM, in this context, are simplified representations of complex economic and geophysical realities, and while comprehensive on variables, they are in the nascent stage for predicting financial outcomes. Nonetheless, they are another tool for assessing both climate-related risk and opportunity.

For example, a 2019 Mercer Report found potential gain or loss of value and transition opportunities by sector under a 2°C scenario to 2030, emphasizing why a below 2°C scenario is most beneficial.[201] Mercer's IAM results include the per annum cumulative effect to 2050, where, notably, it found annual loss/growth impacts for that oil and gas is −95.1 per cent, coal −100 per cent, renewables +177.9 per cent, infrastructure +39.4 per cent, and sustainability infrastructure +67.1 per cent.[202] It observed that expected annual return impacts have significant variations, particularly for energy, utilities, materials, consumer staples, and telecoms; and that variations in results between asset classes and across regions, cumulative impacts, and the emphasis on sustainable opportunities provide multiple portfolio construction possibilities for investors.[203] Mercer combined IAM with climate scenarios that provide investors with analysis of asset-class and industry-sector sensitivities to climate risk factors to quantify a forward-looking climate impact on return.[204] The model contains a short term stress-testing component, enabling some assessment of present-value impacts for sudden market repricing events.[205]

William Nordhaus, winner of the Noble Prize for his DICE IAM, observes that environmental predictions have been subject to little revision as IAM models have developed, as they have been found to be relatively accurate, whereas economic projections are the least precise parts.[206] Nordhaus observes that economic growth is producing unintended but perilous changes in climate and Earth systems, and financial

[199] Ibid.

[200] W D Nordhaus, *The Climate Casino: Risk, Uncertainty, and Economics for a Warming World* (Yale University Press, 2013) at 79 (hereafter Nordhaus, *Climate Casino*).

[201] Mercer Report, 'Investing in a Time of Climate Change: The Sequel 2019' (2019), <https://www.mercer.com/content/dam/mercer/attachments/private/nurture-cycle/gl-2019-wealth-climate-change-the-sequel-full-report.pdf>.

[202] Ibid.

[203] Ibid.

[204] Ibid.

[205] Ibid.

[206] William Nordhaus, 'Integrated Assessment Models of Climate Change' (2017) NBER Reporter No 3, <https://www.nber.org/reporter/2017number3/nordhaus.html> (hereafter Nordhaus, 'IAM').

predictions are complex.[207] He observes that there are dozens of IAM today, a handful of which have a track record of at least a decade. Nordhaus suggests that IAM are an important approach for analysis of climate change as they try to represent the entire process of emissions in terms of the science, the economics, and the effects of policies for slowing climate change.[208] The DICE model calculates damages, depending on the increase in temperature and the size of the economy.[209]

Nordhaus notes that IAM range from small ones like the DICE model to enormous ones that may have as many as a half-million variables.[210] The DICE and the Regional Integrated Model of Climate and the Economy ('RICE') have gone through several revisions since their initial development in 1990.[211] DICE is a globally aggregated model. RICE is essentially the same, except that output and abatement have structures for twelve regions. A run of 1,000 years takes five seconds, so it can be used for projects with multiple states.[212] The DICE model views the economics of climate change from the perspective of neoclassical economic growth theory, extending it by including the 'natural capital' of the climate system as an additional kind of capital stock.[213] The premise is that through emissions reductions, economies reduce consumption today but prevent economically harmful climate change and thereby increase consumption possibilities in the future.[214] Nordhaus advises that the international goal of 2°C is not feasible with current DICE estimates without technologies that allow negative emissions by mid-twenty-first century.[215]

Nordhaus has observed that a high-level approximation of the capital requirements underpinning the proposed Mid-Century Transition Path offers a credible line of sight to the necessary type, scale, and pace of investment and innovation required between now and 2050, with 2030 as an important milestone.[216] It helps draw attention to critical industry funding gaps that inform requirements for public-private co-investment to address climate change and placement of incentives.[217] Using buildings as an example, a capital plan would articulate the capital needs and potential sources to move major building types, such as commercial, residential, and governmental, to net zero emissions.[218] The DICE model has twelve behavioural equations, two variables to be optimized, and several identities.[219] In the GAMS version, the simplest model has about 240 lines of operational code, and Nordhaus notes that while small comprehensive models have many advantages, they also have major shortcomings because of their simplifications.[220]

207 Nordhaus, *Climate Casino* (n 200) at 20–8.
208 Ibid at 28.
209 Ibid at 29.
210 Nordhaus, 'IAM' (n 206).
211 Ibid.
212 Ibid.
213 Ibid.
214 Ibid.
215 Ibid.
216 Ibid.
217 Ibid.
218 Ibid at 11.
219 Ibid.
220 Ibid.

Nordhaus suggests that an important finding of IAM models is that policies to slow emissions should be introduced as soon as possible across sectors, regions, and countries.[221] In his book, *The Climate Casino*, Nordhaus compares the results of a number of IAM surveyed under a Stanford University study as illustrative of what he calls the 'climate casino at play'.[222] He observes that all of the various trajectories project continued increase in CO_2 emissions, although projected growth rates vary for the period 2000 to 2100, confirming that the emissions issue is not going to resolve itself in the market.[223]

Nordhaus also observes how the various IAM illustrate great uncertainties on both the physical and economic impacts the further out in time that the projection goes, due to great uncertainty regarding future growth of the world economy.[224] Yet the uncertainty does not mean waiting until results are certain, as it will be too late; and Nordhaus likens failing to act on climate change to driving in the dark at 100 miles an hour with the headlights off on a foggy night and hoping there are no curves.[225] IAM at least offer some best-guess scenarios for output, populations, emissions, and climate change, developing policies and insurance to meet these high consequence outcomes, regardless of probability and timelines.[226]

The IPCC reports that based on the IAM literature, climate policies in line with limiting warming to 1.5°C require a marked upscaling of supply-side energy system investments between now and mid-century, possibly up to US $3.8 trillion per year globally from 2016 to 2050.[227] It suggests that current IAM may underreport the potential for supply-side technological change assumed in 1.5°C-consistent pathways, but may be more optimistic about the systemic ability to realize incremental changes in reduction of emission intensity as a consequence of favourable energy efficiency returns.[228] The IPCC reports that studies have compared nationally-determined contributions pathways with emissions pathways produced by IAM, assessing the contribution against the objective of achieving the 1.5°C target, with high agreement that current emissions levels are not in line with pathways to limit warming to 1.5°C by the end of the century.[229]

Having canvassed the various indicia of effective climate governance and the tools that can enhance it, the next chapter examines regulatory oversight of climate governance, in terms of international developments and continuing 'governance gaps'.

[221] Nordhaus, *Climate Casino* (n 200) at 7.

[222] Ibid at 32, citing L Clarke, C Bohringer, and T Rutherford, 'International, US and EU Climate Change Control Scenarios: Results from EMF 22' (2009) Energy Economics 31, Supp 22.

[223] Ibid at 32–3.

[224] Ibid at 33–4.

[225] Ibid at 34.

[226] Ibid at 34–5.

[227] IPCC, 'Global Response 2018' (n 19).

[228] Ibid at 322.

[229] Ibid at 358.

6

Regulatory Oversight of Climate Governance of Companies and Institutional Investors

An entire book could easily be written on regulatory oversight of climate governance and this chapter does not attempt a comprehensive analysis of regulatory efforts in this respect. However, it does provide a snapshot of various regulatory initiatives aimed at supporting more effective climate governance for companies, investors, and financial institutions.

Most companies respond positively to legislative standards, as they create a level playing field across all businesses and because they serve as a counter-balance to investor pressure for short term returns. What companies and institutional investors want, however, is clarity and certainty in respect of regulators' expectations. In respect of climate change, while many organizations are directing their attention towards risks and opportunities, absent regulatory requirements to reduce emissions, companies are unlikely to direct sufficient resources to move the world to net zero carbon. Former Bank of England Governor Mark Carney has observed that by the time climate change becomes a clear danger to financial stability, it may already be too late to stabilize the atmosphere.[1]

Across the world's fifty largest economies, there are now over 730 hard and soft law policy revisions across 500 policy instruments that support investors in their consideration of long term value drivers, including climate factors.[2] Forty-eight of these economies now have policy designed to help investors consider sustainability risks, opportunities, or outcomes.[3] At a multilateral level, the central banks' Network for Greening the Financial System has acknowledged that climate change is a source of financial risk.[4] The Network has the objective of promoting practices to smooth the reallocation of capital to a low carbon economy. In 2020, it published a guide to climate scenario analysis for central banks and supervisors.[5] The guide provides practical

[1] Mark Carney, 'Resolving the Climate Paradox', Arthur Burns Memorial Lecture, Berlin (22 September 2016) at 9, <http://www.bankofengland.co.uk/publications/Documents/speeches/2016/speech923.pdf>.

[2] UN PRI, *Fiduciary Duty in the 21st Century Final Report* (October 2019) at 13, <https://www.unpri.org/download?ac=9593> (hereafter UN PRI, *Fiduciary Duty in the 21st Century*).

[3] Ibid.

[4] Network for Greening the Financial System, *A Call for Action, Climate Change as a Source of Risk* (2019), <https://www.banque-france.fr/sites/default/files/media/2019/04/17/ngfs_first_comprehensive_report_-_17042019_0.pdf>.

[5] Network for Greening the Financial System, 'Guide to climate scenario analysis for central banks and supervisors' (2020), <https://www.ngfs.net/sites/default/files/medias/documents/ngfs_guide_scenario_analysis_final.pdf>. The Expert Group on Climate Obligations of Enterprises has legal experts and judges involved in the drafting of the Principles on Climate Obligations for Enterprises: see Expert Group on Climate Obligations of Enterprises, *Principles on Climate Obligations of Enterprises* (Eleven International Publishing, 2018).

From Ideas to Action. Janis Sarra, Oxford University Press (2020). © Janis Sarra. DOI: 10.1093/oso/9780198852308.003.0006.

advice on using scenario analysis to assess climate risks to the economy and financial system, including to stress test financial firms and the financial system; explore structural changes to the economy and/or assess risks to central banks' own portfolios; and allowing comparability across different jurisdictions. The guidance will allow central banks to assess the impact of climate risks on a wide-ranging set of economic and financial variables; communicate results; and use them to inform whether existing regulatory policies such as capital treatment and approaches such as economic forecasting are fit for purpose.[6]

In 2019, the World Bank and finance ministers from more than twenty countries launched a coalition to promote climate action through national financial policies. Also in 2019, the International Organization of Securities Commissions ('IOSCO') and the international pension supervisors' organization launched consultations on environmental, social, and governance ('ESG') integration and disclosure for companies and pension fund regulators.[7] IOSCO has emphasized that ESG matters such as climate change may have a material short term and long term impact on the business operations and on risks and returns for investors and their investment decisions.[8]

Clearly, these international and voluntary collaborations have advanced governance of climate-related risk. However, they raise the important question of the extent to which climate governance should be driven by voluntary standards, such as the Financial Stability Board's Taskforce on Climate-related Financial Disclosures ('TCFD') framework, and the extent to which governments should step in to regulate standards. While the TCFD framework has enhanced the climate governance conversation tremendously, it continues to be framed through the securities law and financial services lens of transparency for debt and equity investors, so that capital owners can make decisions as to whether to buy, sell, or hold their investments. That investor-centric view, while important, can obscure the need for governance best practices aimed at a broader set of society's stakeholders. Lövbrand et al suggest that voluntary pledges submitted by states and non-state actors to meet the conditions of the Paris Agreement will need to be much more firmly co-ordinated, evaluated, and upscaled.[9]

While there is growing consensus internationally regarding the need for transparency of climate-related risks and opportunities, there continues to be deep divisions as to regulation that is needed in respect of actually requiring reductions to achieve net zero carbon within specified timeframes. This chapter provides a qualitative snapshot of some of the regulatory efforts to date, and then considers what is missing from the regulatory discussion internationally. It commences, however, with a discussion of how fairness principles can inform regulatory policy regarding climate change.

[6] Ibid at 4–5.

[7] IOSCO, 'Statement on Disclosure of ESG Matters by Issuers (19 January 2019), <https://www.iosco.org/library/pubdocs/pdf/IOSCOPD619.pdf>.

[8] Ibid at 1.

[9] E Lövbrand, M Hjerpe, and B O Linnér, 'Making Climate Governance Global: How UN Climate Summitry Comes to Matter in a Complex Climate Regime' (2017) 26(4) Environmental Politics 580–99 (hereafter Lövbrand et al).

I. Fairness and Equity Should Inform Regulation

While it is unlikely that domestic regulation on climate change will harmonize, it is possible that the principles informing that regulation could be harmonized, such that different approaches are informed by the same fundamental ideas. Fairness and equity are arguably two such principles.

In thinking about regulatory oversight of the transition to net zero carbon, as well as the move to a circular economy, discussed in Chapter 8, it is important to return again to the concepts of fairness and equity. The IPCC has observed that equity is the principle of fairness in burden sharing and is a basis for understanding how the impacts and responses to climate change, including costs and benefits, are distributed in and by society.[10] Given that climate change represents an urgent and potentially irreversible threat to human societies and the planet, responding to anthropogenic climate change will require approaches that integrate multiple levels of co-operation, including public regulatory and private sector co-operation globally. Equity involves notions of justice and fairness in the responsibility for climate impacts and policies and distribution of climate positive benefits across society, including different generations, racialized peoples, and genders, all of whom should be able to participate and exercise some control in the decision-making processes.[11]

The IPCC defines governance capacity as the 'ability of governance institutions, leaders, and non-state and civil society to plan, co-ordinate, fund, implement, evaluate, and adjust policies and measures over the short, medium, and long term, adjusting for uncertainty, rapid change, wide-ranging impacts, multiple actors, and complex demands'.[12] Governance should facilitate direct public engagement in decision-making using a variety of techniques, for example, referenda and community deliberation.[13] The IPCC reports that while efforts in energy efficiency, carbon intensity of fuels, electrification, and land-use change are underway in various countries, limiting warming to 1.5°C will require a greater scale and pace of change for an effective transition.[14] It argues that all countries need to significantly raise their level of ambition, including enhancing strategies in all countries, building international capability to utilize Indigenous and local knowledge, offering financial, technological, and other forms of

[10] IPCC, 'Annex I: Glossary' (hereafter IPCC, 'Glossary') in V Masson-Delmotte, P Zhai, H O Pörtner, D Roberts, J Skea, P Shukla, A Pirani, W Moufouma-Okia, C Péan, R Pidcock, S Connors, J B R Matthews, Y Chen, X Zhou, M I Gomis, E Lonnoy, T Maycock, M Tignor, and T Waterfield (eds), *Global Warming of 1.5°C: An IPCC Special Report on the Impacts of Global Warming of 1.5°C above Pre-industrial Levels and Related Global Greenhouse Gas Emission Pathways, in the Context of Strengthening the Global Response to the Threat of Climate Change, Sustainable Development, and Efforts to Eradicate Poverty* (IPCC, 2019) at 549, <https://www.ipcc.ch/site/assets/uploads/sites/2/2019/06/SR15_AnnexI_Glossary.pdf> (hereafter IPCC, *Special Report 2018*).

[11] Ibid.

[12] Ibid at 550.

[13] Ibid.

[14] IPCC, H de Coninck, A Revi, M Babiker, P Bertoldi, M Buckeridge, A Cartwright, W Dong, J Ford, S Fuss, J C Hourcade, D Ley, R Mechler, P Newman, A Revokatova, S Schultz, L Steg, and T Sugiyama, 'Chapter 4: Strengthening and Implementing the Global Response' in IPCC, *Special Report 2018* (n 10) at 315, <https://www.ipcc.ch/site/assets/uploads/sites/2/2019/05/SR15_Chapter4_Low_Res.pdf> (hereafter IPCC, 'Global Response 2018').

support to build capacity in developing countries, and scaling-up finance.[15] The IPCC has suggested that an effective governance framework would include:

> accountable multilevel governance that includes nonstate actors, such as industry, civil society and scientific institutions; coordinated sectoral and cross-sectoral policies that enable collaborative multi-stakeholder partnerships; strengthened global-to-local financial architecture that enables greater access to finance and technology; addressing climate-related trade barriers; improved climate education and greater public awareness; arrangements to enable accelerated behaviour change; strengthened climate monitoring and evaluation systems; and reciprocal international agreements that are sensitive to equity and the Sustainable Development Goals.[16]

Beate Sjåfjell and Christopher Bruner suggest that corporate sustainability must ultimately involve corporate legal and governance structures promoting practices that contribute to and, at a minimum, do not undermine society's potential for achieving the overarching goal of sustainability.[17] They take as their normative starting point the natural sciences concept of planetary boundaries, within which all human activity must be positioned to ensure a safe operating space for humanity, recognizing that planetary boundaries are continuous work-in-progress precautionary boundaries.[18]

Sjåfjell and Bruner suggest that the notion of planetary boundaries can inform regulators globally in their decision-making on sustainability.[19] They define corporate sustainability as business and finance contributing to the overarching aim of securing the social foundation for people everywhere, while remaining within planetary boundaries.[20] They suggest that the minimum requirement intrinsic in securing the social foundation of humanity now and in the future is that of ensuring the realization of basic human rights, including the right to sufficient water, food, and medicine, the right to equality, and the right to work in just and favourable conditions. Sjåfjell and Bruner observe that social foundation is the minimum that we must seek to achieve for humanity while the planetary boundaries represent the limits for how much pressure we can put on our ecosystems to accomplish this foundation.[21]

We know that climate change is an urgent and existential threat to humanity and thus to economies and society. We also now know that there are planetary boundaries beyond which we cannot survive. We have very strong scientific evidence that the current climate mitigation plans of the vast majority of countries globally are not sufficient to reverse the trajectory of climate change and prevent the most devastating effects of global warming. We know that peoples in the global south and Indigenous

[15] Ibid.

[16] Ibid at 317.

[17] Beate Sjåfjell and Christopher Bruner, 'Corporations and sustainability' in Beate Sjåfjell and Christopher Bruner (eds), *Cambridge Handbook of Corporate Law, Corporate Governance and Sustainability* (CUP, 2019) at 2 (hereafter Sjåfjell and Bruner).

[18] Ibid at 3.

[19] Ibid at 6, also citing W Steffen et al, 'Planetary Boundaries: Guiding Human Development' (January 2015) 347 Science 746, <https://www.researchgate.net/publication/270898819_%27Planetary_Boundaries_Guiding_Human_Development_on_a_Changing_Planet%27>.

[20] Ibid.

[21] Ibid at 9.

communities are suffering the most from the current impacts of climate change, even though they are not responsible for most of the carbon emissions generated since the industrial revolution. Given these parameters, there is urgent need for regulatory design that sets bold requirements for carbon emissions, carbon pricing, and more equitable distribution of benefits arising from a more sustainable economy. These insights and principles regarding fairness, equity, social foundation, and planetary boundaries serve as a backdrop to assessing developments in regulatory oversight of climate change.

II. Challenges for International Regulatory Oversight

A significant challenge is how to seriously augment the governance capacity of organizations to develop, implement, and evaluate the mitigation and adaptation strategies needed to address climate change within diverse and highly interlinked global social, ecological, economic, and political systems.[22] There are tremendous challenges to garnering international co-operation on climate change that sets specific targets and takes into account equity, justice, poverty eradication, and multiple stakeholder perspectives in the decision-making process. Yet there is need to reach meaningful and equitable decisions between different governments and different levels of governments within countries on decarbonization and on achieving the United Nations Sustainable Development Goals. Such agreement, in turn, could enhance the capacity to raise financing and support for technological and human resource development.[23]

The initial UN PRI *Fiduciary Duty in the 21st Century* report recommended government action to modernize definitions and interpretations of fiduciary duty in a way that ensures these duties are relevant to current investors.[24] It suggested that regulators enact standards to clarify that fiduciaries must analyse and take account of ESG issues in their investment processes, active ownership activities, and public policy engagement; and that they specify that fiduciary duty requires that investors pay attention to long term investment value drivers, including ESG issues. It called on governments to require institutional investors to support public policy efforts promoting responsible investment, requiring investor transparency in all aspects of ESG investment practice and corporate governance.[25] It recommended regulation to heighten trustee competence and skill. It urged harmonization of national and regional responsible investment legislation and policy instruments, and the development of an international statement on the duties that fiduciaries owe to their beneficiaries. The report stressed the need for consideration of ESG issues as core to investment processes, investment beliefs, ownership activities, integrated reporting on performance, and public policy engagement.[26]

[22] IPCC, M Allen, O Dube, W Solecki, F Aragón-Durand, W Cramer, S Humphreys, M Kainuma, J Kala, N Mahowald, Y Mulugetta, R Perez, M Wairiu, and K Zickfeld, 'Chapter 1: Framing and Context' in IPCC, *Special Report 2018* (n 10) at 71, <https://www.ipcc.ch/site/assets/uploads/sites/2/2019/05/SR15_Chapter1_Low_Res.pdf> (hereafter IPCC, 'Framing').

[23] Ibid.

[24] UN PRI, *Fiduciary Duty in the 21st Century* (n 2) at 21.

[25] Ibid.

[26] Ibid at 10, 21.

Since that report, it is evident that the greatest regulatory advances are in the area of disclosure. However, disclosure of efforts to address climate change is not sufficient, and regulatory action on carbon pricing and specific targets for moving to net zero carbon economies are much slower to develop. Regulatory action that could have distributive consequences is still almost non-existent, such as poverty eradication and funds flowing to countries that have had the smallest carbon footprint but are suffering the greatest impacts.

It is also of note that even where national governments fail to regulate, municipal and regional governments may be effective in tackling lower carbon emissions. For example, in the United States, as a reaction to President Trump withdrawing from the Paris Agreement, a 'We are still in declaration' has been signed by 3,841 mayors, county executives, governors, tribal leaders, college and university leaders, businesses, faith groups, and investors declaring that they will continue to support climate action to meet the Paris Agreement.[27] They represent 158.6 million people across fifty US states. The declaration states:

> The Trump administration's announcement undermines a key pillar in the fight against climate change and damages the world's ability to avoid the most dangerous and costly effects of climate change. Importantly, it is also out of step with what is happening in the United States.
>
> In the US, it is local, tribal, and state governments, along with businesses, that are primarily responsible for the dramatic decrease in greenhouse gas emissions in recent years. Actions by each group will multiply and accelerate in the years ahead, no matter what policies Washington may adopt.
>
> In the absence of leadership from Washington, states, cities, counties, tribes, colleges and universities, healthcare organizations, businesses and investors, representing a sizeable percentage of the US economy will pursue ambitious climate goals, working together to take forceful action and to ensure that the US remains a global leader in reducing emissions.[28]

Inspired by this leadership in the US, in Japan over 100 companies, local governments, research institutions, and non-governmental organizations established the Japan Climate Initiative, a network committed to strengthening communication and exchange of strategies and solutions among all actors that are implementing climate actions in Japan.[29] Its declaration states: 'While the government of Japan's actions have been delayed, many local governments participating in the Japan Climate Initiative, such as Tokyo, Yokohama, and Kyoto, are taking initiative, aiming to be carbon neutral by 2050.'[30]

Neil Gunningham suggests that climate governance is an instrumental process of mandating changes in behaviour, an expressive and symbolic nurturing of new norms,

[27] 'We are still in declaration' (2017, updated 2019) <https://www.wearestillin.com/we-are-still-declaration>.

[28] Ibid.

[29] Japan Climate Initiative (2019), <https://japanclimate.org/english/>.

[30] Ibid.

and an institutionalizing a new set of moral principles.[31] The rest of this chapter highlights a number of notable regulatory developments in climate oversight as they relate to business.

III. The European Union Leadership on Investor Transparency and a Green Investment Taxonomy

The European Union ('EU') has demonstrated leadership in regulatory oversight of institutional investors and asset managers. In March 2019, the EU Parliament and Council agreed on a resolution to require financial market participants to integrate ESG factors, noting that clarifying the fiduciary duties of investors has been a priority for United Nations Environment Programme ('UNEP') Finance Initiative for many years.[32] The new regulation sets out how financial market participants and financial advisors must integrate ESG risks and opportunities in their processes, as part of their duty to act in the best interest of clients.[33] It sets uniform rules on how financial market participants should inform investors about their compliance with the integration of ESG risks and opportunities. It addresses information asymmetries on sustainability issues between end-investors and financial market participants and financial advisors. It requires integration of risks related to the impact of ESG events on the value of investments, such as assets located in flood-prone areas.[34] The regulation requires the disclosure of adverse impact on ESG matters, such as assets that pollute water or devastate biodiversity, to ensure the sustainability of investments.[35]

The new EU regulation is built around three main pillars. The first is elimination of 'greenwashing', i.e. making unsubstantiated or misleading claims about sustainability characteristics and benefits of an investment product. The second pillar is regulatory neutrality, meaning that the rules introduce a disclosure toolbox to be applied in the same manner by different financial market operators, directing the three European Supervisory Authorities and the Joint Committee of the Authorities to ensure further convergence and harmonization of disclosures in all concerned sectors.[36] The third pillar is a 'level playing field', in that the regulation covers investment funds, insurance-based investment products (life insurance products with investment components available as individual retail life policies, as well as group life policies), private and occupational pensions, individual portfolio management, and insurance and investment advice.[37]

[31] Neil Gunningham, 'Building Norms from the Grassroots Up: Divestment, Expressive Politics, and Climate Change' (2017) 39(4) Law & Policy 372 at 374–80.

[32] UNEP Finance Initiative (7 March 2019), <https://www.unepfi.org/news/industries/investment/eu-policy-makers-achieve-political-agreement-on-investor-disclosures-and-esg/>.

[33] European Commission, 'Capital Markets Union: Commission Welcomes Agreement on Sustainable Investment Disclosure Rules', European Commission Press Release (7 March 2019), <https://europa.eu/rapid/press-release_IP-19-1571_en.htm>.

[34] Ibid.

[35] Ibid.

[36] Ibid.

[37] Ibid.

The Commission has established a unified EU classification system ('EU Taxonomy') of sustainable economic activities.[38] It is setting uniform criteria for determining whether an economic activity is environmentally sustainable, with the aim of placing ESG considerations at the heart of the financial system, in order to support the transformation of Europe's economy into a greener, more resilient, and circular system.[39] It defines 'circular economy' as maintaining the value of products, materials, and resources in the economy for as long as possible, and minimizing waste, including through the application of the waste hierarchy.[40] The European Supervisory Authorities have had a key role in the development of the EU Sustainability Taxonomy, to ensure that it is usable by financial institutions, applicable to financial products, and compatible with EU financial legislation.[41]

The EU Taxonomy establishes the framework to set out uniform criteria for the purposes of determining the degree of sustainability of an investment.[42] Article 3 requires that the economic activity contributes substantially to one or more environmental objectives and does not significantly harm any others. Article 4 provides that Member States and the EU use the uniform criteria for environmentally sustainable economic activities when setting out the requirements for marketing financial products or corporate bonds as environmentally sustainable, in particular, in the context of labelling schemes for products such as green bonds.[43] In this respect, the taxonomy has benefitted from the rigorous standards developed by the Climate Bonds Initiative, which has garnered global support for its green bonds standards.[44] The Climate Bonds Initiative is focused on mobilizing the US $100 trillion bond market for climate change solutions. It reports that the 2020 green bond market is now US $134 billion in issued bonds that aligned with its climate bond and green standards.

Article 5 of the taxonomy regulation establishes that the environmental objectives of the regulation are climate change mitigation and adaptation, sustainable use and protection of water and marine resources, transition to a circular economy, waste prevention and recycling, pollution prevention and control, and protection of healthy ecosystems. Climate change mitigation in this context means the process of limiting the temperature increase to 1.5°C above pre-industrial levels.[45] The provisions related to each environmental objective will become applicable six months after the technical

[38] Ibid. The European Commission has proposed a 'Regulation on the establishment of a framework to facilitate sustainable investment' (Taxonomy Regulation, 2018), COM(2018) 353 final 2018/0178 (COD) (24 May 2018), <https://ec.europa.eu/info/law/better-regulation/initiatives/ares-2017-5524115_en#pe-2018-3333> (hereafter EU, 'Sustainable Investment Regulation').

[39] EU, 'Sustainable Investment Regulation', ibid at 2.

[40] Ibid, Article 2, at 5, as laid down in Article 4 of Directive 2008/98/EC of the European Parliament and of the Council.

[41] Ibid at 10.

[42] Proposal for a Regulation of the European Parliament and if the Council on the establishment of a framework to facilitate sustainable investment COM(2018) 353 final 2018/0178 (COD), (18 June 2019), Article 1, <https://ec.europa.eu/info/publications/sustainable-finance-teg-taxonomy_en> (hereafter Taxonomy Regulation).

[43] Ibid at 13.

[44] Climate Bonds Initiative, 'International Best Practice for Labeling Green Bonds', <https://www.climatebonds.net/>.

[45] Taxonomy Regulation (n 42), Article 2, to at least well below 2°C above pre-industrial levels.

screening criteria are established, in order to give market participants sufficient time to prepare.[46]

Article 6 specifies that an economic activity shall be considered to contribute substantially to climate change mitigation where that activity substantially contributes to the stabilization of GHG concentrations in the atmosphere at a level that prevents dangerous anthropogenic interference with the climate system by avoiding or reducing GHG emissions or enhancing GHG removals. It includes generating, storing, or using renewable energy or climate-neutral energy, including through the use of innovative technology; improving energy efficiency; increasing clean or climate-neutral mobility; switching to use of renewable materials; increasing carbon capture and storage use; phasing out anthropogenic GHG emissions, including from fossil fuels; establishing energy infrastructure required for enabling decarbonization of energy systems; and producing clean and efficient fuels from renewable or carbon-neutral sources.[47]

Article 7 of the regulation defines what a substantial contribution to climate change adaptation is: where that activity contributes substantially to reducing the negative effects of the current and expected future climate change or preventing an increase or shifting of negative effects of climate change.[48] Preventing or reducing the location- and context-specific negative effects of climate change on economic activity and preventing or reducing the negative effects that climate change may pose to the natural and built environment within which the economic activity takes place must also be assessed and prioritized using available climate projections.[49] Article 8 defines a substantial contribution to sustainable use and protection of water and marine resources. Article 9 defines substantial contribution to the circular economy and waste prevention and recycling. Article 10 protects against Indigenous peoples being forcibly removed from their lands. Article 11 defines substantial contribution to protection of healthy ecosystems. The EU Taxonomy Regulation considerably advances the policy discussion on how institutional investors and financial institutions can determine and disclose their investment activities in respect of climate mitigation and adaptation.[50]

The EU Taxonomy initially addressed only green finance, but the EU decided in December 2019 to develop a taxonomy for 'transition finance'.[51] The EU Taxonomy specifies that in establishing thresholds for screening criteria, climate change mitigation objectives mean net zero emissions by 2050 and a 50–55 per cent reduction by 2030 consistent with the EU Green Deal.[52] To reach these goals, it recognizes that sectors already at near-zero carbon levels must be expanded, and heavily emitting sectors must rapidly decarbonize. The EU Taxonomy recognizes that there may be economic activities for which there is no technologically and economically feasible

[46] Ibid at 15.
[47] Ibid, Article 6.
[48] Ibid, Article 7.
[49] Ibid.
[50] Ibid at 7.
[51] European Union Technical Expert Group on Sustainable Finance, 'Taxonomy: Final Report of the Technical Expert Group on Sustainable Finance' (March 2020), <https://ec.europa.eu/knowledge4policy/publication/sustainable-finance-teg-final-report-eu-taxonomy_en>.
[52] Ibid.

low carbon alternative, but has determined that they can support the transition to a climate-neutral economy where that activity has GHG emission levels that 'correspond to the best performance in the sector or industry; does not hamper the development and deployment of low-carbon alternatives; and does not lead to a lock-in in carbon-intensive assets considering the economic lifetime of those assets'.[53] The EU Taxonomy has the potential to be adopted by other national governments outside the EU, given its innovative features and its linking of the transition to net zero carbon to the circular economy.

In 2020, the European Commission launched a consultation on a proposed obligation for investment firms to advise clients on social and environmental aspects of financial products.[54] Specifically, it is proposing to amend EU Directive 3014/95 to integrate sustainability in fiduciary duty and suitability tests.[55]

IV. Regulation of Climate Governance

Disclosure can make a tremendous contribution to advancing climate governance as often companies, asset owners, and asset managers will manage what they are required to measure and disclose. The legislative reforms below illustrate how jurisdictions are approaching these issues.

i. Regulation of Corporate Disclosure and Duty to Act on Climate Change

France

France led the world in terms of regulatory change that makes visible how publicly held companies and financial institutions are addressing a move to a low carbon economy. The French National Assembly enacted *La Loi de transition énergetique pour la croissance verte* ('Law for Energy Transition and Green Growth') in 2015.[56] The law addresses carbon budgets and a national low carbon strategy, regulating the quantity of GHG of certain types of large-scale operations, converting energy consumed or waste processed into corresponding emission factors.[57] *La Loi de transition énergetique* is aimed at reducing GHG emissions, capping fossil fuel production, and increasing renewable energy usage. Article 173 strengthens mandatory climate

[53] Ibid.

[54] European Commission, 'Have Your Say on the European Path towards Sustainable Finance' (2020), <http://www.eurosif.org/have-your-say-on-the-european-path-towards-sustainable-finance-july-oct-2020/>.

[55] Ibid.

[56] French National Assembly, *Law for Energy Transition and Green Growth* (22 July 2015). On 18 November 2015, modifications were made to the *Code de l'environnement*—L222-1 in response to Article 173 of the *Law for Energy Transition and Green Growth* (hereafter *Transition énergétique*). On 19 August 2016, modifications were made to the *Code de commerce*—Art R225-105-1(M) in response to Articles 70 and 173 of the *Transition énergétique.*

[57] Ibid.

disclosure requirements for listed companies and financial institutions, introducing the first mandatory requirements for institutional investors.

Listed companies must disclose annually 'the financial risks related to the effects of climate change and the company's measures to reduce them', including how they are implementing a low carbon strategy in every component of their activities. They must disclose 'the consequences on climate change of the company's activities and of the use of goods and services it produces'.[58] Institutional investors, including mutual funds and pension funds, as well as investment companies with variable share capital, must disclose how their investment decision-making takes ESG criteria into consideration, and disclose how they are contributing to the energy and ecological transition to limit global warming.[59]

Institutional investors such as mutual funds must also report on how their investment decision-making is directed at moving towards low carbon emissions and increased sustainability. *La Loi de transition énergetique pour la croissance verte* was an important advance in transparency regarding climate-related financial risk, both in the extensive reporting required and the obligation to disclose the governance strategies being deployed to mitigate climate change issues. It helped inform the EU regulation discussed above.

Then in 2018, France introduced its multiannual energy programme, with the express objectives of reducing fossil fuel consumption and ensuring 'clear, fair and sustainable transition for all'.[60] It focuses on the building and transport sectors, as they account for more than half of energy consumption and GHG emissions in France. The programme will shut all coal plants, compensating and retraining workers, and massively developing a new offshore wind energy sector, tripling onshore wind energy, and increasing by fivefold photovoltaic energy by 2030.[61]

France's Commercial Code now requires environmental assessments, including disclosure of significant emissions from the use or development of the company's product; undertakings on steps being taken to prevent environmental risks and pollution, including measures to reduce or repair damage, waste management, including recycling, reuse, use of sustainable resources, minimization of energy consumption, and protection of biodiversity. It specifies societal commitments to sustainable development, including a commitment to use resources sustainably and to adapt to the consequences of climate change.[62]

Catherine Malecki observes that France's Commercial Code provisions mark a turning point in governance, in that companies need to disclose how they hold discussions with different stakeholder groups on their climate governance, and while the provisions are 'comply or explain', they require a clear, reasoned explanation justifying

[58] Ibid.

[59] As well as how they exert the voting rights attached to the financial instruments resulting from those choices. 'Environmental' includes the exposure to climate-related risks, including GHG emissions associated with assets owned, ibid.

[60] Government of France, 'Multiannual Energy Programme' (November 2018), <https://www.gouvernement.fr/en/multiannual-energy-programme-what-are-its-aims>.

[61] Ibid.

[62] Ibid.

the lack of a company policy.[63] Pursuant to Article 225-102-1, funds must now disclose specific information relating to the consequences for climate change of the company's activities and the use of the goods and services that it produces.[64] They must disclose societal commitments in favour of sustainable development, the circular economy, the fight against food waste, the collective agreements made within the company and their impact on economic performance, the working conditions of their employees, and actions aiming to fight discrimination and promote diversity.[65]

In 2019, the French government introduced new legislation that has the express goal of achieving net zero GHG emissions by 2050.[66] It has increased targets for decarbonization, speeding up reduction of fossil fuel energy consumption, cutting it by 40 per cent in 2030, rather than 30 per cent as provided for in the 2015 law. It will end all coal-based electricity generation in France by 2022.

United Kingdom

In the United Kingdom ('UK'), the government has also regulated aspects of climate governance. The UK Companies Act 2006 specifies that directors are to exercise care and skill in the best interests of the company; and s 172 provides for a specific duty to have regard to a number of factors, including environmental impact, in discharging the general duty to promote the success of the company.[67] The Act requires larger companies to report on the implementation of the s 172 duty, specifically, a strategic report to include, to the extent necessary for an understanding of the development, performance or position of the company's business, information about environmental matters, and the impact of the company's business on the environment.[68] Effective January 2019, directors must describe how they have regard to the matters set out in s 172(1), including climate impact.[69] The Companies (Miscellaneous Reporting) Regulations requires directors to explain how they have performed their s 172 duty.[70]

Lord Sales has observed that the:

> close nexus between financial detriment and environmental impact would also seem to apply on a plain reading of the general section 172 duty to promote the company's success in England, independent of the specific duty to have regard to environmental impact under section 172(1)(d). In short, there is growing recognition of the fact that good environmental practices will often be financially prudent, at least in the

[63] Catherine Malecki, 'French Implementation of the EU CSR Directive: Sustainable Corporate Governance has Begun', Law and Financial Markets Review (2018) at 5, <https://doi.org/10.1080/17521440.2018.1467816>.

[64] Ibid.

[65] Ibid.

[66] Government of France, 'France Wants to Be the First Country in Europe to Put the Carbon Neutrality Goal on a Statutory Footing', Statement (3 May 2019), <https://www.gouvernement.fr/en/france-wants-to-be-the-first-country-in-europe-to-put-the-carbon-neutrality-goal-on-a-statutory>.

[67] UK, Companies Act 2006, ss 170–174.

[68] Ibid, s 414C(7)(b)(i).

[69] Ibid, s 414CZA, strategic reports to include a 'section 172(1) statement'. Section 426B requires a 'section 172(1) statement' to be made available on a website maintained by or on behalf of the company and which identifies the company. This requirement operates if s 414CZA applies and the company is an unquoted company.

[70] See also Regulation 40(3)(o) of the Charities (Accounts and Reports) Regulations 2008.

long term, on top of being laudable from a corporate social responsibility or ethical perspective.[71]

It will not be sufficient to pay lip service to the factors, and, in many cases, the directors will need to take action to comply with this aspect of the duty.[72]

The 2018 UK Corporate Governance Code prepared by the Financial Reporting Council, the competent authority for auditing, refers to the necessity of boards carrying out 'a robust assessment of the company's emerging and principal risks, including events or circumstances that might threaten the company's business model, future performance, solvency or liquidity, and reputation'.[73] The GC100 guidance notes that the s 172 duty requires directors to weigh all the relevant factors and decide what best leads to the success of the company.[74] Directors are held to the objective standard of a reasonably diligent person in their position *and* to a subjective standard based on the director's own abilities, of care, skill, and diligence.[75]

UK quoted companies (publicly traded companies) are now required to report on their GHG emissions as part of their annual directors' report and account publicly for their contributions to climate change on an annual basis.[76] The requirement affects all UK incorporated companies listed on the main market of the London Stock Exchange, a European Economic Area market, or whose shares are listed on the New York Stock Exchange or NASDAQ.[77] Directors and officers must make every reasonable effort to acquire all material data to comply with the regulations.[78] They are also required to report on environmental matters to the extent it is necessary for an understanding of the company's business in their annual report, including where appropriate, the use of key performance indicators.[79] In circumstances where directors and officers find it difficult to compile all necessary data in a timely manner to comply with reporting requirements, they are to state what is omitted and explain why in the directors' report.[80]

The UK Financial Conduct Authority is developing new rules to improve climate-related disclosures for entities over which it has regulatory oversight and to clarify existing obligations. It is finalizing rule changes that will require independent governance committees to oversee and report on firms' ESG and stewardship policies, as

[71] Lord Sales, Justice of UK Supreme Court, 'Directors' Duties and Climate Change: Keeping Pace with Environmental Challenges' (27 August 2019) at 5, <https://www.supremecourt.uk/docs/speech-190827.pdf>.

[72] Explanatory notes to s 172 of the Companies Act 2006 at paras 325–8.

[73] Financing Reporting Council, *The UK Corporate Governance Code* (July 2018).

[74] GC100, *Guidance on Directors' Duties: Section 172 and Stakeholder Considerations* (October 2018).

[75] Ibid.

[76] UK, Companies Act 2006, 'Strategic Report and Directors' Report Regulations 2013' (hereafter 'Strategic Report and Directors' Report Regulations 2013'). See also Climate Change Act 2008 and UK Government, 'Environmental Reporting Guidelines: Including Mandatory Greenhouse Gas Emissions Reporting Guidance' (June 2013), <https://www.gov.uk/government/publications/environmental-reporting-guidelines-including-mandatory-greenhouse-gas-emissions-reporting-guidance> (hereafter UK, 'Guidance').

[77] 'Strategic Report and Directors' Report Regulations 2013', ibid.

[78] UK, 'Guidance' (n 76) at 28.

[79] Environmental key performance indicators are quantifiable measures that reflect the environmental performance of an organization in the context of achieving its wider goals and objectives, focusing on relevance, transparency, accurateness, and comparability.

[80] Ibid.

well as separate rule changes to facilitate investment in patient capital opportunities.[81] In March 2020, the Financial Conduct Authority proposed introduction of a new rule for commercial companies with a UK premium listing, requiring them to state whether they comply with the recommendations of the TCFD and to explain any non-compliance.[82] The new rule requires affected companies to include a statement in their annual financial report setting out whether they have made disclosure consistent with TCFD in their annual financial report; to explain why they have not done so if they have not disclosed to these standards or have disclosed but in a document other than their financial report; and to specify where their TCFD disclosure can be found within their disclosure documents.[83] It has stated that the new rule is a first step towards wide adoption of TCFD disclosure for listed companies and financial services companies.

The Bank of England has published its supervisory expectations that set out how banks and insurance companies under its oversight need to develop an enhanced approach to managing the financial risks from climate change.[84] It covers governance, risk management, scenario analysis, and disclosure, with a view to boards of financial institutions being both strategic and accountable.[85] It has endorsed the TCFD disclosure framework, particularly emphasizing the need for forward-looking disclosure regarding emissions, future risks, and opportunities. The Bank of England also established the Climate Financial Risk Forum ('CFRF'), bringing together regulators, financial institutions, the London Stock Exchange, and asset managers.[86]

In April 2019, then Bank of England Governor Mark Carney proposed that regulators and finance businesses should integrate the monitoring of climate-related financial risks into day-to-day supervisory work and risk management by company boards; lead by example, with central banks and financial institutions integrating sustainability into their own portfolio management. They are to collaborate to bridge data gaps in relation to climate risks, and build in-house capacity and share knowledge about climate-related financial risks.

Sweden

Sweden enacted legislation effective 2018, aimed at reaching net zero GHG emissions by 2045, and after that period, to achieve negative net emissions.[87] The Swedish Climate Act states that the government must present a climate report in its budget bill each year; draw up a climate policy action plan every fourth year to describe how the

[81] Financial Conduct Authority, 'FS19/6: Climate Change and Green Finance' (18 October 2019), <https://www.fca.org.uk/publications/feedback-statements/fs19-6-climate-change-and-green-finance> (hereafter FCA, 'Climate Change').

[82] UK Financial Conduct Authority, 'CP20/3: Proposals to Enhance Climate-Related Disclosures by Listed Issuers and Clarification of Existing Disclosure Obligations' (March 2020), <https://www.fca.org.uk/publications/consultation-papers/cp20-3-proposals-enhance-climate-related-disclosures-listed-issuers-and-clarification-existing>.

[83] Ibid at 6.

[84] Sarah Breeden, 'Avoiding the Storm: Climate Change and the Financial System', Bank of England (15 April 2019) (hereafter Breeden).

[85] FCA, 'Climate Change' (n 81).

[86] Ibid.

[87] Swedish Environmental Protection Agency, 'Sweden's Climate Act and Climate Policy Framework' (December 2019), <http://www.swedishepa.se/Environmental-objectives-and-cooperation/Swedish-environmental-work/Work-areas/Climate/Climate-Act-and-Climate-policy-framework-/>.

climate targets are to be achieved; and make sure that climate policy goals and budget policy goals work together. The emissions from domestic transport, with the exception of domestic flights, are to be reduced by at least 70 per cent by 2030, compared to 2010.[88]

The legislation establishes an independent Climate Policy Council, an interdisciplinary expert body tasked with providing independent assessments of how the overall government policy is compatible with the national climate targets. The Council consists of members that have scientific competence in the fields of climate, climate policy, economics, social sciences, and behavioural sciences.[89]

Hong Kong

The Hong Kong government has enacted regulation to reduce green-washing. There are a number of Hong Kong Securities and Futures Commission ('SFC') authorized funds with investment focus on climate, green, environmental, or sustainable development.[90] The SFC found that many funds name green or ESG factors in their investment strategy, but a majority of these funds do not specifically disclose how the management companies incorporate such green or ESG factors in their investment selection process. It issued a circular in 2019 setting out the Commission's expectations on enhanced transparency and comparability between similar types of SFC-authorized green or ESG funds, in order to facilitate investors' informed investment decisions.[91] The circular applies to SFC-authorized funds that incorporate one or more of the globally recognized green or ESG criteria or principles as their key investment focus.

The Hong Kong SFC circular requires, at a minimum, a description of the key investment focus, such as climate change, green, low carbon footprint, or sustainability financing. It requires disclosure of targeted objectives, such as financial return; mitigating climate change or environmental damage of the green or ESG fund; a description of the investment strategies adopted by the green or ESG fund, including the relevant green or ESG criteria or principles considered; and the expected exposure to the securities or other investments that reflect the stated green or ESG investment focus. The SFC also requires disclosure of the investment selection process and criteria adopted by the green or ESG fund, such as the carbon footprint and environmental impact associated with companies, the proportion of revenue or profits generated from the relevant green or ESG activities of the issuer companies; any reference ESG benchmark being tracked and the characteristics and general composition of the benchmark. The SFC also requires a description of whether an exclusion policy is adopted by the green or ESG fund; a description of risks associated with green or ESG fund's investment theme.[92] It also directs the manager of the green or ESG fund to regularly monitor and evaluate the underlying investments to ensure the green or

[88] Ibid.

[89] Ibid.

[90] Hong Kong Securities and Futures Commission ('HKSC'), 'Circular to Management Companies of SFC-Authorized Unit Trusts and Mutual Funds—Green or ESG funds' (13 April 2019), <https://www.sfc.hk/edistributionWeb/gateway/EN/circular/doc?refNo=19EC18>.

[91] Ibid.

[92] Ibid.

ESG fund continues to meet the stated investment objective and requirements set out in the circular.[93]

Canada

The Bank of Canada is now building climate-related risks into its financial system review process and is developing a multiyear research plan focused on climate-related risks to the macroeconomy and the financial system. In addition to its domestic efforts to develop climate scenario testing and financial oversight of the banking sector and Canadian monetary system, as a member of the Central Banks and Supervisors Network for Greening the Financial System ('NGFS'), the Bank of Canada has helped developed tools aimed at improving global understanding of the impact of climate change on the global financial system, specifically, a Guide on Climate Scenario Analysis for Central Banks and Supervisor; Research Priorities for Macroeconomic and Financial Stability Impacts of Climate Change; and Climate Change and Monetary Policy.

Securities law in Canada is provincially regulated, but securities regulators adopt national instruments and guidance aimed at consistency across the country. In 2019, the Canadian Securities Administrators ('CSA') published 'Staff Notice 51-358 Reporting of Climate Change-related Risks', aimed at assisting companies in identifying and improving their disclosure of material risks posed by climate change, clarifying existing legal requirements.[94] The CSA observes that:

> Climate change-related risks are a mainstream business issue. Issuers should consider these risks as part of their ongoing risk management and disclosure processes and they must disclose any such risks that are material to their business. Like other business risks, the materiality of climate change-related risks varies among industry sectors and issuers within those sectors.[95]

The guidance was issued after complaints by institutional investors that they are receiving insufficient disclosure of these risks from companies. The guidance is primarily focused on companies' disclosure obligations as they relate to the management disclosure and analysis ('MD&A') and annual information forms.[96] The CSA observed that securities legislation imposes a different test for materiality in certain other contexts, and issuers should consider the applicable test when preparing disclosure in respect of climate change-related information or other information.

Canada has been slower than many countries in terms of regulatory oversight of climate change. The *Pan-Canadian Framework on Clean Growth and Climate Change* provides a comprehensive overview of the major steps Canada must take to meet its 2030 emissions reduction target, requiring large capital investments in major sectors of the economy. Some of this progress has been stalled by disagreements between the

[93] Ibid.

[94] CSA, 'Staff Notice 51-358 Reporting of Climate Change-related Risks' (1 August 2019) at 1, <https://www.osc.gov.on.ca/en/SecuritiesLaw_csa_20190801_51-358_reporting-of-climate-change-related-risks.htm>. See also CSA Staff Notice 51-333 Environmental Reporting Guidance.

[95] Ibid at 2.

[96] Ibid at 1.

liberal federal government and a couple of conservative provincial governments regarding what level of government has the regulatory authority to act and the degree to which regulation is needed.

Australia

In 2018, the Australian Securities and Investment Commission published a report indicating that directors and officers of listed companies need to understand and continually reassess existing and emerging risks, including climate risk, that may affect the company's business. This assessment extends to both short and long term risks.[97] In 2019, the Australian Securities Exchange ('ASX') Corporate Governance Council published new guidance for listed companies; they should disclose whether they have any material exposure to environmental risks, including climate change risks, and report on how they manage or intend to manage those risks, encouraging disclosure recommended by the TCFD.[98] The Australian Accounting Standards Board and the Auditing and Assurance Standards Board issued a joint guidance statement on the relevance of climate-related risks for financial statement accounting estimates, and while the guidance is voluntary, it carries some normative weight for accountant and auditor practice.[99] It offers a benchmark for materiality assessments relating to climate risk. The guidance states that entities engaged in both financial and non-financial sectors should consider how climate risk affects their impairment assessments and other decisions made in relation to the recognition or measurement of items in the financial statements, including fair valuation of assets, onerous contracts, and changes in expected credit losses for loans and other financial assets.

Based on the Australian accounting standards initiative, the International Accounting Standards Board issued an advisory on how the international financial reporting standards ('IFRS') directly apply to climate-related risk, even though the words 'climate change' do not appear in the standard.[100] It points out that as part of making judgments about materiality in financial reporting under IFRS, companies should determine whether investors would reasonably expect that climate-related risks could affect amounts and disclosures in the financial statements. Financial implications may include impairment of assets such as property, plant, and equipment, changes in the useful life of assets, changes in fair valuation of assets, effects on impairment calculations because of increased costs or reduced demand, changes in contingent liabilities

[97] Australian Securities and Investments Commission ('ASIC'), 'Climate Risk Disclosure by Australia's Listed Companies: REP 593' (20 September 2018) at 3, <https://asic.gov.au/regulatory-resources/find-adocument/reports/rep-593-climate-risk-disclosure-by-australia-s-listed-companies>. See also ASIC Commissioner John Price, 'Climate Change', Speech delivered at Centre for Policy Development, Sydney (18 June 2018) <https://asic.gov.au/about-asic/news-centre/speeches/climate-change/>.

[98] ASX Corporate Governance Council, 'Corporate Governance Principles and Recommendations' (4th edn, February 2019) at 28, <https://www.asx.com.au/documents/asx-compliance/cgc-principles-andrecommendations-fourth-edn.pdf>.

[99] Australian Accounting Standard's Board, *Climate-Related and Other Emerging Risks Disclosures: Assessing Financial Statement Materiality Using AASB Practice Statement 2* (December 2018) at 6–7, <https://www.aasb.gov.au/admin/file/content102/c3/AASB_AUASB_Joint_Bulletin_13122018_final.pdf>.

[100] International Accounting Standards Board, 'IFRS Standards and Climate-Related Disclosures (November 2019), <https://cdn.ifrs.org/-/media/feature/news/2019/november/in-brief-climate-change-nick-anderson.pdf?la=en>.

arising from fines and penalties, changes in expected credit losses for loans and other financial assets, and other climate-related risks. Even where the company concludes there is no material impact on the financials, it may have to disclose how it considered climate-related risks in terms of its financials and why it determined that disclosure was not needed pursuant to IFRS.

Other Regulatory Initiatives

The China Securities and Regulatory Commission issued guidelines requiring listed companies that are heavy polluters to give specific information on emissions, with all listed firms to disclose environmental impact information by the end of 2020.[101]

Singapore has pledged to reduce emissions intensity by 36 per cent between 2005 and 2030, the year it expects its emissions to peak.[102] Sixty per cent of emissions are generated by industry and three-quarters of that comes from oil refining and petrochemicals.[103] One third of Singapore, including its central business district, is less than five metres above mean sea level, at high risk of sea level rise. The Singapore government's plan is to spend billions of dollars to encircle the country in protective dykes or connecting a chain of offshore islands with barrages to create a giant reservoir. Singapore has also created Southeast Asia's first carbon tax, levied at S $5 per tonne on facilities that produce 25,000 tonnes of CO_2 or more per year, expected to rise to S $15 a tonne by 2030.[104] The government plans to install solar energy panels on the rooftops of its 10,000 public housing buildings in order to reduce demand for carbon-intensive energy. Currently, Singapore imports 90 per cent of its food, and the Singapore Food Agency is targeting 30 per cent locally produced food by 2030.[105] The government is offering funding for companies to introduce water-saving technologies such as on-site recycling systems.[106]

V. Regulation of Investor Transparency Obligations Will Assist in Climate Governance

A European Commission report on the fiduciary duties of investors observed that another challenge is the pursuit of financial returns in situations of a market failure, often leading fiduciaries to take action that avoids weaker short term returns while ignoring the long term consequences.[107] It observed that climate change and its related risks have become a crucial issue in fiduciaries' decision-making process, and the

101 Climate Disclosure Standards Board, 'Climate Disclosure in China' (2018), <https://www.cdsb.net/sites/default/files/ciff_policy_briefing_china.pdf>.

102 Bloomberg News, 'Singapore Has a S$100 Billion Plan to Survive in a Far Hotter World Than Experts Predicted' (25 February 2020), <https://www.bloomberg.com/news/features/2020-02-25/singapore-has-a-100-billion-plan-for-adapting-to-climate-change>.

103 Ibid.

104 Ibid.

105 Ibid.

106 Ibid.

107 European Commission DG ENV, 'Resource Efficiency and Fiduciary Duties of Investors' (2014), <http://ec.europa.eu/environment/enveco/resource_efficiency/pdf/FiduciaryDuties.pdf> (hereafter EC, 'Fiduciary Duties').

liability or litigation risk places an obligation on fiduciaries to consider climate-related risks as part of their fiduciary duty.[108] The European Commission report stated that failure to do so could potentially lead to claims for damages by beneficiaries and clients of financial institutions who may allege that the fiduciaries have not acted in their best interests.[109] It suggests extending the definition of the prudent person principle, namely that:

> Fiduciaries should throughout their decision-making process consider the broad range of long term interests of their beneficiaries. In doing so, it should be made clear to financial actors that the long term interests of beneficiaries include not despoiling the planet and exploiting their fellow human beings.[110]

The EU also leads on regulation to advance engagement strategies. In addition to the transparency requirements discussed above, it has introduced a suite of regulations to enhance climate governance. The EU Shareholder Rights Directive requires mandatory disclosure of stewardship policies by investor fiduciaries, requiring asset owners to report publicly and to their clients on how their investment strategy and stewardship approach contribute to the long term performance of their assets.[111] The Directive notes that shares of listed companies are often held through complex chains of intermediaries that are an obstacle to shareholder engagement, and that data should be available in a form that companies can identify existing shareholders in order to communicate directly with them, with a view to facilitating the exercise of shareholder rights within the company.[112] The EU Shareholder Rights Directive requires institutional investors and asset managers to develop and publicly disclose a policy on shareholder engagement or explain why they have chosen not to do so. The policy should describe how institutional investors and asset managers integrate shareholder engagement in their investment strategy; which different engagement activities they carry out; their policies to manage actual or potential conflicts of interests; and how they make this information publicly available online.[113] Its premise is that facilitating shareholder engagement will enhance climate governance.

The Directive also specifies that institutional investors and asset managers should publicly disclose how they have exercised their voting rights.[114] In order to enhance responsible stewardship of assets, the Directive specifies that institutional investors should disclose, annually, information explaining how the main elements of their equity investment strategy are consistent with the profile and duration of their liabilities and how those elements contribute to the medium to long term performance of their assets.[115] Where the pension fund or other institutional investor uses asset managers,

[108] UN PRI, *Fiduciary Duty in the 21st Century* (n 2) at 25.
[109] EC, 'Fiduciary Duties' (n 107).
[110] Ibid.
[111] Directive (EU) 2017/828 of the European Parliament and of the Council of 17 May 2017, amending Directive 2007/36/EC as regards the encouragement of long-term shareholder engagement, <https://eur-lex.europa.eu/legal-content/EN/TXT/?uri=CELEX%3A32017L0828> (hereafter EU Shareholder Rights Directive).
[112] Ibid, Preamble.
[113] Ibid at para 17.
[114] Ibid at para 18.
[115] Ibid at para 19.

they are to disclose how they incentivize the asset manager to align its investment strategy and decisions with the profile and duration of the liabilities of the institutional investor, in particular, long term liabilities. The institutional investor must disclose how it evaluates the asset manager's performance, including its remuneration, how it monitors portfolio turnover costs incurred by the asset manager, and how it incentivizes the asset manager to engage in the best medium to long term interest of the institutional investor.[116] For purposes of the Directive, 'institutional investor' means pension funds, life insurance companies, and reinsurance companies; and institutions for occupational retirement.[117] 'Asset manager' means an investment firm that provides portfolio management services to investors, an alternative investment fund manager, or a management company or investment company.[118]

Pursuant to the Directive, asset managers are to give information to the institutional investor that is sufficient to allow the investor to assess whether and how the manager acts in the best long term interests of the investor.[119] That disclosure should cover reporting on the key material medium to long term risks associated with the portfolio investments, including climate change, more effectively integrating those matters into investment processes.[120] The asset manager should also inform the institutional investor of how the asset manager adopts a long term oriented and active approach to asset management, taking ESG matters into account.[121]

Proxy advisors are also subject to transparency requirements, including disclosing certain key information relating to the preparation of their research, advice, and voting recommendations, and any actual or potential conflicts of interests or business relationships that may influence the preparation of the research, advice, and voting recommendations.[122] 'Proxy advisor' is defined as a legal person that analyses, on a professional and commercial basis, the corporate disclosure and, where relevant, other information of listed companies, with a view to informing investors' voting decisions by providing research, advice, or voting recommendations related to the exercise of voting rights.[123] Here again, transparency requirements should allow investors to press proxy advisors to embed climate considerations as material factors in their research, advice, and proxy voting services.

i. Regulation Specific to Pension Funds

The 'European Union Directive on the activities and supervision of institutions for occupational retirement provision' (Directive 2016/2341) specifies that ESG factors, as referred to in the UN PRI, are important for the investment policy and risk management systems of institutions for occupational retirement provision

[116] Ibid at para 19 and Article 2.
[117] Ibid.
[118] Ibid, authorized in accordance with EU Directive 2009/65/EC.
[119] Ibid at para 20.
[120] Ibid at para 20.
[121] Ibid at para 22.
[122] Ibid at para 26.
[123] Ibid, Article 2.

('IORP') and Member States should require IORP to explicitly disclose where such factors are considered in investment decisions and how they form part of their risk management system.[124] They are now required to disclose the relevance and materiality of ESG factors to a pension scheme's investments.[125] Where ESG factors are considered in investment decisions, they are to disclose an assessment of new or emerging risks, including risks related to climate change, use of resources and the environment, social risks, and risks related to the depreciation of assets due to regulatory change.[126] Member States are directed to require IORP to ensure that prospective plan members are given information on whether and how ESG factors, expressly including climate governance factors, are considered in the investment approach.[127]

Amendment to Directive 2016/2341 specifies that financial market participants shall include descriptions of the following in precontractual disclosures: the procedures and conditions applied for integrating sustainability risks in investment decisions; the extent to which sustainability risks are expected to have a relevant impact on the returns of the financial products made available; and how the remuneration policies of financial market participants are consistent with the integration of sustainability risks and are in line, where relevant, with the sustainable investment target of the financial product.[128]

In the UK, the Pension Protection Fund (Pensionable Service) and Occupational Pension Schemes (Investment and Disclosure) Regulations, effective 2019,[129] specify that financially material considerations include, but are not limited to, ESG considerations, including climate change, which the trustees of the trust scheme consider financially material. The appropriate time horizon is the length of time that the trustees consider necessary for the funding of future benefits by the investments of the scheme.[130] Pursuant to the UK Occupational Pension Schemes (Investment) Regulations, the trustees' statements of investment policy must include a statement of the extent to which social, environmental, or ethical considerations are taken into account in the selection, retention, and realization of investments.[131]

[124] Directive (EU) 2016/2341 of the European Parliament and of the Council of 14 December 2016 on the activities and supervision of institutions for occupational retirement provision (14 December 2016), <https://eur-lex.europa.eu/legal-content/EN/TXT/?uri=CELEX:32016L2341> (hereafter IORP Directive). See also UK Department for Work and Pensions, 'Clarifying and Strengthening Trustees' Investment Duties' (2018), <https://assets.publishing.service.gov.uk/government/uploads/system/uploads/attachment_data/file/739331/response-clarifying-andstrengthening-trustees-investment-duties.pdf>.

[125] IORP Directive, Preamble, ibid at para 58.

[126] Ibid, Article 28(2)(h).

[127] Ibid, Article 41.

[128] EU, Directive (EU) 2016/2341 of the European Parliament and of the Council of 14 December 2016 on the activities and supervision of institutions for occupational retirement provision. See also EU Parliament, 'Proposal for a Regulation of the European Parliament and of the Council on disclosures relating to sustainable investments and sustainability risks and amending Directive (EU) 2016/2341 (2019) (hereafter EU, 'Disclosure').

[129] UK, Pension Protection Fund (Pensionable Service) and Occupational Pension Schemes (Investment and Disclosure) (Amendment and Modification) Regulations 2018 (SI 2018/988), <http://www.legislation.gov.uk/uksi/2018/988/contents/made>.

[130] UN PRI, *Fiduciary Duty in the 21st Century* (n 2) at 14.

[131] Occupational Pension Schemes (Investment) Regulations 2005 (SI 2005/3378), reg 2(3)(b)(vi).

The South Africa Pension Fund Act codifies fiduciary duty and states that it applies to trustees of pension funds; its Regulation 28 now requires funds to consider all factors, including ESG, which may be relevant to its long term success.[132]

In Brazil, Resolution n 4661/2018 states that pension funds shall consider ESG aspects in their risk analysis processes, whenever possible, in addition to an economic sustainability analysis, enhanced by 'Instrução Previc n 6/2018', which states that pension funds' investment policies must include guidelines for complying with ESG, preferably by economic sector.[133]

In Canada, pensions are provincially regulated, except for employees in the federal sector, which are federally regulated. The legislation varies slightly across the country, but in all cases, imposes a duty of loyalty and a prudential duty on pension fiduciaries. For example, the Ontario Pension Benefits Act specifies 'the administrator of a pension plan shall exercise the care, diligence and skill in the administration and investment of the pension fund that a person of ordinary prudence would exercise in dealing with the property of another person'.[134] The administrator of a pension plan must, in its administration of the pension plan and in the administration and investment of the pension fund, use all relevant knowledge and skill that the administrator possesses or, by reason of the administrator's profession, business or calling, ought to possess.[135] This obligation, as well as provisions of Canadian trust legislation and the common law duties to exercise care, diligence, and skill, would seem to indicate that climate change risk is a necessary consideration for all pension administrators in Canada, particularly since many pension funds are invested in fossil fuels and other carbon-intensive assets at risk.

The Ontario Pension Benefits Act requires pension funds to disclose information about whether ESG factors are incorporated into the plan's investment policies and procedures and, if so, how those factors are incorporated.[136] It is a 'disclose and/or explain' approach.[137] Pursuant to Regulation 909 under the Pension Benefits Act, the administrator of a pension plan is required to establish a statement of investment policies and procedures ('SIPP').[138] Plan administrators are required to file their SIPP and any amendments with the Financial Services Commission of Ontario ('FSCO').[139] The FSCO observes that reporting how ESG factors are incorporated into the plan's broader investment policies and procedures requires action by the administrator

[132] UN PRI, *Fiduciary Duty in the 21st Century* (n 2) at 14.

[133] Ibid.

[134] Canada: Ontario Pensions Benefits Act, RSO 1990, c P 8, s 22, as amended (hereafter Ontario Pension Benefits Act).

[135] Ibid, s 22(2). Section 22(3) states that: 'Subsection (2) applies with necessary modifications to a member of a pension committee or board of trustees that is the administrator of a pension plan and to a member of a board, agency or commission made responsible by an Act of the Legislature for the administration of a pension plan.'

[136] O Reg 235/14, s 8 of Regulation 909 under the Pension Benefits Act, RRO 1990, Reg 909, 40, 78.

[137] Section 78(1) of Regulation 909 under the Pension Benefits Act, ibid. The Statement of Investment Policies and Procedures must meet the requirements of the federal investment regulations, as modified in sections 47.8 and 79 of the Regulation: Financial Services Commission for Ontario, 'Statement of Investment Policies and Procedures' ('SIPP'), <http://www.fsco.gov.on.ca/en/pensions/legislative/Pages/sipp.aspx#ESG> (hereafter SIPP).

[138] Ontario Pension Benefits Act (n 134).

[139] Ibid.

beyond a broad delegation. Some examples of actions that administrators may take include: summarizing policies where the managers incorporate ESG factors into their investment policies; describing how the administrator incorporates ESG factors as part of the manager search, selection, and review process; and describing how the administrator incorporates ESG in the choice of investment fund options.[140] The FSCO has observed that administrators have a fiduciary duty to supervise their investment managers, including ensuring that the managers are complying with the Pension Benefits Act and with the SIPP. This supervision requirement extends to the incorporation of ESG factors, including climate change, where the SIPP contains them.[141]

The Ontario legislative provisions have been important in stimulating boards of trustees to explicitly discuss ESG issues and to seek advice on how responsible investment is consistent with their fiduciary obligation.[142] Pension plans across Canada should be required to incorporate ESG factors, including climate change risk, into the plan's investment policies and procedures; but to date, this regulation had not been adopted in other provinces.

VI. Carbon Pricing as an Effective Policy and Regulatory Tool

A significant issue for regulatory oversight is carbon pricing. Any business or individual that uses fossil fuels emits CO_2 in the atmosphere, but since they do not pay for the environmental and social costs of the emissions, the emissions are an externality. A key consideration for regulatory options in respect of carbon pricing is to design a policy that recognizes that companies and their investors have profited considerably from the externalities of their activities. For many decades they have externalized the costs of harms created by GHG emissions. It makes sense to try to internalize some of these costs in regulatory design. The European Commission has reported that internalizing the external costs of transport emissions is a prerequisite for making the most efficient choices in terms of technology and transport mode.[143] A carbon price creates incentives to reduce carbon emissions. As of 2019, over 70 jurisdictions, representing approximately 20 per cent of global GHG emissions, have put a price on carbon.[144]

[140] SIPP (n 137).

[141] Ibid.

[142] UN PRI, *Fiduciary Duty in the 21st Century* (n 2) at 15. See also SIPP, ibid. The Financial Services Commission for Ontario reports that Ontario is saving approximately Cdn $4.4 billion annually in health, environmental and financial costs since it eliminated coal-fired energy generation. Ontario Government Green Ontario Fund, 'Climate Changes Everything' (2017), <https://www.ontario.ca/page/climate-change>.

[143] European Commission, *A Clean Planet for all, A European strategic long-term vision for a prosperous, modern, competitive and climate neutral economy* COM/2018/773 final (28 November 2018), Communication from the Commission to the European Parliament, the European Council, the European Economic and Social Committee, the Committee of the Regions and the European Investment Bank at 11, <https://ec.europa.eu/clima/policies/strategies/2050_en> (hereafter EC, *Clean Planet*).

[144] British Columbia Government, 'British Columbia's Carbon Tax' (2019), <https://www2.gov.bc.ca/gov/content/environment/climate-change/planning-and-action/carbon-tax> (hereafter 'British Columbia's Carbon Tax').

William Nordhaus observes that emissions are driven by population, GDP per capita, and the carbon intensity of GDP.[145] He suggests that damage caused by climate change is a global externality, highly challenging because the economic and political mechanisms for dealing with them effectively are weak or absent.[146] He notes that unregulated markets cannot efficiently deal with harmful externalities, and absent regulation, there will be excessive amounts of GHG emissions because there is a zero price on the external damages.[147] He and other economists have pointed out that for any policy to be effective, there must be a price on CO_2 and other GHG emissions that corrects for the underpricing of the externality in the marketplace.[148] That price can be through a direct carbon tax or by putting regulatory tradable limits on the amount of emissions ('cap and trade'), but that either strategy must price carbon sufficiently high to act as an effective incentive.[149] Nordhaus observes that negotiating a single minimum carbon price globally would be much easier than negotiating emissions quotas.[150]

Nordhaus also notes that a carbon price provides signals to consumers about what goods and services have high carbon content and should therefore be consumed less.[151] It provides signals to producers regarding which inputs use more carbon, encouraging them to move to low carbon technologies; and he observes that it will give market incentives to innovators to develop and market low carbon products and processes to replace current carbon-intensive technologies.[152]

Economists price carbon using two general approaches. One is to estimate the required price of carbon that would achieve different climate objectives using IAM.[153] The other is to calculate the 'social cost of carbon', i.e. the economic damage caused by each additional tonne of carbon emissions or their equivalent; in other words, monetizing the incremental unit of carbon emission in order to assess climate policies.[154] There are numerous estimates of the social cost of carbon that aid governments in setting pricing policies.[155]

Nordhaus observes that business investment in low carbon innovation is inhibited by a double externality: innovators capture only a small fraction of the social returns on innovation and the environmental externality of global warming in the absence of a price on carbon, as returns on innovation are depressed because

[145] W D Nordhaus, *The Climate Casino: Risk, Uncertainty, and Economics for a Warming World* (Yale University Press, 2013) at 30 (hereafter Nordhaus, *Climate Casino*).

[146] Ibid at 244.

[147] Ibid at 6, 18.

[148] Ibid.

[149] Ibid.

[150] Ibid at 251.

[151] Ibid at 224–5.

[152] Ibid at 225.

[153] Ibid at 227. See also US Government Interagency Working Group on Social Cost of Carbon, 'Technical Support Document—Technical Update of the Social Cost of Carbon for Regulatory Impact Analysis—Under Executive Order 12866' (2016), <https://www.epa.gov/sites/production/files/2016-12/documents/sc_co2_tsd_august_2016.pdf>; and Government of Canada, 'Technical Update to Environment and Climate Change Canada's Social Cost of Greenhouse Gas Estimates' (2016), <http://www.ec.gc.ca/CC/default.asp?lang=En&n=BE705779-1>.

[154] Ibid.

[155] See for example, Pei Wang, Xiangzheng Deng, Huimin Zhou, and Shangkun Yu, 'Estimates of the Social Cost of Carbon: A Review Based on Meta-Analysis' (2019) 209 Journal of Cleaner Production 1494.

the market price of carbon is below its true social cost.[156] He notes that the major trade-off in climate change policy involves trading off consumption today for consumption in the future.[157] He argues that discounting future benefits does not mean indifference to future impacts; rather, there is need to invest now in research and development of new low carbon energy technologies; in technologies that allow lower-income countries to thrive in a warmer world; and in workforce training that can respond to surprises that will inevitably arise as the Earth warms up.[158] Nordhaus notes that efficiency requires near-universal participation and cost effectiveness, requiring that countries have roughly equal marginal costs of emissions reductions.[159]

In receiving the Nobel Prize in 2018, Nordhaus observed that virtually all integrated assessment models have several key findings that can inform regulatory oversight of climate change:

- One major finding of integrated assessment models is that policies to slow emissions should be introduced *as soon as possible*.
- A second finding is *uniformity of price*—that the most effective policies are ones that equalize the incremental or marginal costs of reducing emissions. Equivalently, in a market context, that means that the carbon prices should be equalized in every sector and in every country.
- Effective policies should have the highest possible *participation*; that is, the maximum number of countries and sectors should be on board as soon as possible. Free-riding should be discouraged.
- Finally, an effective policy is one that *ramps up over time*—both to give people time to adapt to a high-carbon-price world and to tighten the screws increasingly on carbon emissions.
- Most experts agree on these central principles—universal participation, equalizing marginal costs or carbon prices in all uses in a given year, full participation, and increasing stringency over time.[160]

Nordhaus observes that for national public goods, the challenge is to make national political institutions responsive to the diffuse national public interest rather than concentrated national private interests—responsive to public health rather than private profits.[161]

The IPCC reports that governments need to implement a range of policy instruments that include reducing inefficient fossil fuel subsidy regimes, and using innovative price and non-price national and international policy instruments.[162] Policy needs to be complemented by de-risking financial instruments aimed at reducing

[156] Nordhaus, *Climate Casino* (n 145) at 286.
[157] Ibid at 186.
[158] Ibid at 191–2.
[159] Ibid at 194.
[160] William Nordhaus, 'Climate Change: The Ultimate Challenge for Economics' (2019) 109 American Economic Review 1991 at 2002, <https://doi.org/10.1257/aer.109.6.1991>.
[161] Ibid at 1992.
[162] IPCC, 'Global Response 2018' (n 14) at 317.

the demand for carbon-intensive services and shifting market preferences away from fossil fuel-based technology, also helping to develop long term low emission assets.[163]

The European Commission notes that environmental taxation and carbon pricing systems are important to steering transition, increasing energy efficiency, reducing GHG emissions, and enhancing the circular economy.[164] It also advocates consistent application of the 'polluter-pays' principle and the phasing out of existing fossil fuel subsidies in line with the EU's G20 commitments.[165]

i. Low Carbon Benchmarks, Carbon Budgets, and Statutory Requirements for Net Zero Carbon Emissions

United Kingdom

In 2019, the UK became the first major economy in the world to pass law to bring all GHG emissions in the UK to net zero by 2050, improving previous targets.[166] The UK Climate Change Act 2008 had established a legally binding target to reduce the UK's GHG emissions by at least 80 per cent below 1990 base year levels by 2050.[167] The Act introduced a system of carbon budgets that provide legally binding limits on the amount of emissions that may be produced in successive five-year periods, beginning in 2008: requiring emissions to be reduced by at least 34 per cent below 1990 levels in 2020; and then from 2023 to 2027, requiring emissions to be at a level equivalent to around 51 per cent below 1990 base year levels.[168] The fifth carbon budget was set in 2016, at a level of 1,725 $MtCO_2e8$ over the five year period from 2028 to 2032, equivalent to a reduction of around 57 per cent compared to 1990.[169] The UK Government also maintained a carbon price support of £18 per tonne of carbon dioxide on top of the EU Emissions Trading System, to encourage the transition to low carbon electricity generation by driving coal-to-gas switching.[170]

The revised UK Climate Change Act's express aim is 100 per cent reduction in the net UK carbon account for the year 2050 from the 1990 baseline; to provide for a system of carbon budgeting; to establish trading schemes for the purpose of limiting GHG emissions or encouraging activities that reduce or remove GHG from the atmosphere; to confer powers to make schemes that provide financial incentives to

[163] Ibid.

[164] EC, *Clean Planet* (n 143) at 18.

[165] Ibid.

[166] UK, 'UK Becomes First Major Economy to Pass Net Zero Emissions Law' (27 June 2019), <https://www.gov.uk/government/news/uk-becomes-first-major-economy-to-pass-net-zero-emissions-law>.

[167] The UK Government estimates that to be, in million tonnes of carbon dioxide equivalent (MtCO2e), around 165 MtCO2e in 2050, compared to 798 MtCO2e in the base year. See BEIS, 'Final UK greenhouse gas emissions national statistics: 1990–2016' (2018), <https://www.gov.uk/government/statistics/final-uk-greenhouse-gas-emissionsnational-statistics-1990-2016>. (This figure includes an allowance for international aviation.)

[168] Ibid.

[169] UK, The Carbon Budget Order 2016, <http://www.legislation.gov.uk/uksi/2016/785/made>.

[170] UK Government, 'Delivering Clean Growth Progress Against Meeting Our Carbon Budgets: The Government Response to the Committee on Climate Change' (October 2018) at 15, <https://assets.publishing.service.gov.uk/government/uploads/system/uploads/attachment_data/file/748296/delivering-clean-growth.pdf>.

produce less domestic waste and to recycle more; and to create carbon emissions reduction targets.[171] The UK Climate Change Act framework legislation is supported by subordinate legislation.[172]

The UK government has a duty to set, for each succeeding period of five years, an amount for the net UK carbon account ('carbon budget').[173] The matters to be taken into account in setting carbon budgets are: scientific knowledge about climate change; technology relevant to climate change; economic circumstances and the likely impact of the decision on the economy and the competitiveness of particular sectors; fiscal circumstances, including the likely impact of the decision on taxation, public spending, and public borrowing; social circumstances, including the likely impact of the decision on fuel poverty; energy policy, the likely impact of the decision on energy supplies, and the carbon and energy intensity of the economy. It is to take account of differences in circumstances between England, Wales, Scotland, and Northern Ireland; circumstances at the European and international levels; and the estimated amount of reportable emissions from international aviation and international shipping for the budgetary period or periods in question.[174] It has strong provisions for annual reporting of carbon emissions and reductions.

European Union

France is also a first mover on enshrining net zero GHG emissions by 2050 in statute.[175] In April 2019, the government enacted legislation on energy and the climate, aimed at achieving net zero GHG emissions by 2050, the first in continental Europe.[176] Building on France's adoption of an energy and climate strategy in 2018,[177] the legislation is aimed at accelerating reduction of fossil energy consumption, cutting it by 40 per cent in 2030, and ending coal-based electricity generation in France by 2022.[178] It extends the deadline for cutting nuclear power's share to 50 per cent to 2035 instead of 2025, to prevent building new gas-fired plants that would increase GHG emissions. It established *l'Haut Conseil pour le Climat* (High Council for the Climate), which is responsible for assessing compliance and facilitating development of renewable energies.[179] France's National Low Carbon Strategy will be revised every five years

[171] UK, Climate Change Act 2008, s 1 <http://www.legislation.gov.uk/ukpga/2008/27/contents>; Climate Change Act 2008 (Credit Limit) Order 2016 (SI 2016/786); Climate Change Act 2008 (2020 Target, Credit Limit and Definitions) Order 2009 (SI 2009/1258); and Climate Change and Sustainable Energy Act 2006 (Sources of Energy and Technologies) Order 2008 (SI 2008/1767).

[172] Ibid.

[173] Ibid, s 4.

[174] Ibid, s 10.

[175] Gouvernment de France, 'France Wants to Be the First Country in Europe to Put the Carbon Neutrality Goal on a Statutory Footing', *Communiqué* (3 May 2019), <https://www.gouvernement.fr/en/france-wants-to-be-the-first-country-in-europe-to-put-the-carbon-neutrality-goal-on-a-statutory> (hereafter Gouvernment de France 2019).

[176] Ibid.

[177] Gouvernment de France, *'Stratégie française pour l'énergie et le climat'* (2018), <https://www.ecologique-solidaire.gouv.fr/dossier-presse-strategie-francaise-lenergie-et-climat>.

[178] Gouvernment de France 2019 (n 175).

[179] L'Haut conseil pour le climat, *'Remise du rapport du Haut Conseil pour le Climat'* (25 June 2019), <https://www.gouvernement.fr/partage/11070-remise-du-rapport-du-haut-conseil-pour-le-climat> (hereafter Haut conseil).

to be responsive to evolution of France's emissions.[180] In 2019, l'Haut Conseil pour le Climat made its first report to the government, finding that actions to date need to be even more amplified because of the urgent need to combat climate change.

The Swedish government has set a target of being fossil-free by 2045 and moving to 100 per cent renewable energy.[181] Its goal is to transition to full sustainability and build a modern welfare state within nature's limits. Sweden has emphasized that green growth can drive transition through technical innovation.

In 2019, the European Parliament and Member States agreed on a new generation of low carbon benchmarks to boost investment in sustainable projects and assets.[182] It created two categories of low carbon benchmarks: a climate-transition benchmark and a specialized benchmark that brings investment portfolios in line with the Paris Agreement. The European Commission notes that benchmarks have an important impact on investment flows, as many investors rely on them for the creation and measurement of performance of investment products and for asset allocation strategies.[183] The categories are voluntary labels designed to orient the choice of investors that wish to adopt a climate-conscious investment strategy, aimed at avoiding misleading greenwashing or unsubstantiated claims about the environmental benefits of a benchmark. A technical expert group is advising the European Commission on how to select the companies eligible for inclusion in the new benchmarks.[184]

Canada

In Canada, the government of British Columbia successfully imposed the first carbon tax in North America in 2008.[185] The broad-based carbon tax applies to the purchase and use of fossil fuels and covers approximately 70 per cent of provincial GHG emissions.[186] Between 2007 and 2016, provincial real GDP grew by 19 per cent, while net emissions declined by 3.7 per cent. In April 2019, British Columbia's carbon tax rate rose from Cdn $35 to Cdn $40 per tonne of carbon dioxide equivalent emissions ('tCO_2e') and the tax rate will increase each year by Cdn $5 per tonne until it reaches Cdn $50 per tonne in 2021.[187] Revenues generated from the carbon tax are used to encourage new green initiatives and provide carbon tax relief and protect affordability, by increasing the Climate Action Tax Credit to Cdn $154.50 per adult and Cdn $45.50 per child as of July 2019.[188] The government also offers several carbon tax programmes for businesses and local governments. For example, the CleanBC Program for Industry directs an amount equal to the incremental carbon tax paid by industry

180 Gouvernment de France 2019 (n 175).

181 Government of Sweden, 'Saving the Climate', (2019), https://sweden.se/climate/#safeguarding-the-future.

182 European Commission Press Release, 'Sustainable Finance: Commission Welcomes Agreement on a New Generation of Low-Carbon Benchmarks' (25 February 2019), <https://europa.eu/rapid/press-release_IP-19-1418_en.htm>.

183 Ibid.

184 Ibid.

185 British Columbia Government, 'Revenue-neutral Carbon Tax Program', <http://www.fin.gov.bc.ca/tbs/tp/climate/carbon_tax.htm>.

186 'British Columbia's Carbon Tax' (n 144).

187 Ibid.

188 Ibid.

above Cdn $30 per tonne into incentives for cleaner operations, designed for regulated large industrial operations, such as pulp and paper mills, natural gas operations and refineries, and large mines.[189]

The Government of Canada announced a pan-Canadian framework that includes a national floor price on carbon.[190] Canadian provinces were given until 2018 to implement a carbon pricing policy. The federal government then implemented a coordinated nation-wide carbon price, beginning at Cdn $20 per tCO_2e in 2019 and rising to Cdn $50 per tonne. Yet carbon pricing has been hotly contested in Canada, bringing the federal government and some provincial governments into conflict. Two appellate judgments that held federal carbon pricing legislation to be constitutional[191] are under appeal at the Supreme Court of Canada, expected to be finally decided in 2020. Another from Alberta decided the constitutional question differently and is also under appeal.[192] Thus while governments and economists globally have agreed that carbon pricing is an important part of the transition to net zero, Canadians await the Supreme Court of Canada's ruling on the constitutionality of its national carbon pricing strategy. The Canadian Expert Panel on Sustainable Finance observed that an explicit carbon price is arguably the most efficient way to account for the externalized cost of emissions in markets, supporting the federal government's decision to implement a national carbon price.[193]

The Government of Canada's pan-Canadian framework is federal-provincial agreement to phase out the use of coal to produce electricity by 2030; reduce methane and hydrofluorocarbon emissions from the extraction of oil and gas by 40 to 45 per cent by 2025; create more rigorous vehicle emissions standards; and develop models for net zero energy building codes by 2030.[194] The Low Carbon Economy Fund, part of the Pan-Canadian Framework on Clean Growth and Climate Change, is directing Cdn $2 billion to leverage investments in projects that will generate clean growth, reduce GHG emissions, and help meet Canada's Paris Agreement commitments.[195]

The Canadian federal government invested more than Cdn $59.3 billion in the clean technology sector from 2010 to 2016.[196] Cleantech companies generated over Cdn $11.5 billion in revenues and employed over 274,000 people in 2016.[197] The Toronto Stock Exchange ('TSX') and TSX-Venture exchanges list ninety companies in

[189] Ibid.

[190] Government of Canada, 'Federal Actions for a Clean Growth Economy' (2017), <https://www.canada.ca/content/dam/themes/environment/documents/weather1/20170119-en.pdf>.

[191] *Reference re Greenhouse Gas Pollution Pricing Act*, 2019 ONCA 544 (Ont CA); and *Reference re Greenhouse Gas Pollution Pricing Act*, 2019 SKCA 40 (Sask CA).

[192] *Reference re Greenhouse Gas Pollution Pricing Act*, 2020 ABCA 74 (Alta CA).

[193] Government of Canada, Final Report of the Expert Panel on Sustainable Finance, *Mobilizing Finance for Sustainable Growth* (June 2019) at 10, <http://publications.gc.ca/collections/collection_2019/eccc/En4-350-2-2019-eng.pdf> (hereafter Canada Expert Panel).

[194] Ibid at 15.

[195] Government of Canada, 'Low Carbon Economy Fund' (2019), <https://www.canada.ca/en/environment-climate-change/services/climate-change/low-carbon-economy-fund.html>.

[196] Natural Resources Canada, 'Energy Factbook 2017–2018' at 20–22 (hereafter NRCan).

[197] The Toronto Stock Exchange Venture ('TSXV') defines Cleantech companies as companies whose operations fall under one of five environmental categories: Energy Efficiency; Low-Impact Material and Products; Renewable Energy Equipment Manufacturing and Technology; Renewable Energy Production and Distribution; and Waste Reduction and Water Management.

the cleantech sector, with a total market capitalization of Cdn $40.8 billion. Of those companies, seventy-seven are headquartered in Canada, with a total market capitalization of $37.1 billion.[198] Some provincial governments have legislatively addressed treatment of stranded fossil fuel assets, an issue increasingly important. In upholding the validity of the legislation, the courts have observed that the treatment of stranded assets is, at its foundation, a policy issue informed by public interest considerations. The costs of many stranded assets are likely to fall on taxpayers through the tax base as Canada transitions its economy, unless effective pricing mechanisms are created to internalize a significant portion of the remediation costs among the firms that have benefitted to date from externalising the costs of stranded assets.[199]

Significantly, the Office of the Auditor General of Canada in 2018 reported that, on the basis of current government policies and actions, Canada is not expected to meet its 2020 target for reducing GHG emissions, and that substantially more effort is needed.[200] A collaboration of eleven Auditors General across Canada, the report concludes that no government in Canada has met all its climate change commitments; many that have set GHG reduction targets are not on track to meet them, and none of them are fully prepared to adapt to the impacts of a changing climate.[201] Most provinces have developed high-level mitigation strategies that include actions to reduce emissions, but they lack detailed timelines, implementation plans, and cost estimates. The Auditors General conclude that meeting the 2030 target will require a joint and significant effort by all levels of government.[202]

Canada's 2019 federal election revealed that Canada's electorate was also concerned that not enough was being done to address climate change, hopefully offering the government a stronger mandate to be highly proactive in a net zero carbon strategy in 2020.

China

Looking across the Pacific Ocean, the Chinese government's regulatory activities in respect of climate change are very uneven and sometimes contradictory. David Sandalow of the Columbia Center on Global Energy Policy reports that, on the one hand, in 2018, China's CO_2 emissions rose 2.5 per cent; it added roughly 30 gigawatts ('GW') of new coal-fired power capacity; and its financial institutions continued to lead the world in financing new coal-fired power plants abroad.[203] In 2018, China's CO_2 emissions were approximately 28 per cent of the global total that year.[204] On the other hand, Sandalow reports that China led the world again in 2018 in renewable

[198] NRCan (n 196) at 21.

[199] Janis Sarra, 'The Anthropocene at the Time of Trump' (2018) 51 UBC Law Review 489–547 (hereafter Sarra, 'Anthropocene').

[200] Office of the Auditor General of Canada, *Perspectives on Climate Change Action in Canada: A Collaborative Report from Auditors General* (27 March 2018), <http://www.oag-bvg.gc.ca/internet/docs/osh_20180327_e_42964.pdf>.

[201] Ibid.

[202] Ibid at 9.

[203] David Sandalow, 'Guide to Chinese Climate Policy 2019', Columbia Center on Global Energy Policy (18 September 2019) at 3, <https://energypolicy.columbia.edu/sites/default/files/file-uploads/Guide%20to%20Chinese%20Climate%20Policy_2019.pdf>.

[204] Ibid at 11.

power and electric vehicle deployment, with 45 per cent of the electric cars in the world in China.[205] The Chinese government has announced four principal climate goals: to achieve peak CO_2 emissions around 2030; to lower emissions per unit of GDP by 60–65 per cent from the 2005 level by 2030; to increase the share of non-fossil fuels in primary energy to around 20 per cent by 2030; and to increase the forest stock volume by around 4.5 billion cubic meters from 2005 levels by 2030.[206]

China uses more coal than the rest of the world combined, with approximately 50 per cent of global consumption; and in 2018, 20 per cent of global CO_2 emissions were from Chinese combustion of coal.[207] Sandalow observes that the Chinese government's policies are aimed at reducing coal use, including a national cap on coal consumption, targets for reducing coal's share of energy, requirements to dramatically reduce urban area coal use, investments in coal-to-gas switching, CO_2 emissions standards for power plants, and ordering closure of tens of thousands inefficient coal-fired boilers.[208] At the same time, Sandalow argues that several Chinese government policies promote coal use, such as grid dispatch rules that favour coal over renewables, cheap shipping costs for coal on state-owned railroads, and cheap capital for coal power plants from state-owned banks.[209]

On the positive side, China is the largest producer of renewable energy. In 2018, 43 per cent of the renewable power capacity added globally was in China and renewables provide approximately 25 per cent of electricity generated in China, 18 per cent from hydropower, 5 per cent from wind, and 3 per cent from solar.[210] China leads the world in deployment of wind power, with roughly one-third of global capacity.[211] China leads the world in solar power, with more than one-third of global solar capacity. In 2018, China had roughly 175 GW of solar power.[212] China's energy plan is aimed at increasing renewable power capacity to 680 GW by 2020, promote offshore wind development, developing new renewable energy technology, scaling-up solar power, and regulating to reduce carbon emissions.[213]

These regulatory developments in jurisdictions around the world illustrate slow and uneven, but nonetheless forward moving, paths to regulatory oversight of climate change. The concern is whether the pathways are developing fast enough to shift the trajectory of global warming.

VII. Supervisory Oversight of Financial Institutions

Financial institutions play a pivotal role in financial systems. It makes sense that their active participation towards a net zero carbon economy is an important feature of the

[205] Ibid at 3.
[206] Ibid at 39.
[207] Ibid at 57.
[208] Ibid at 62.
[209] Ibid.
[210] Ibid at 66.
[211] Ibid at 70.
[212] Ibid at 72.
[213] Ibid at 67, citing Government of China, '13th Five-Year Plan for Renewable Energy'.

regulatory framework. The European Commission notes that supervisory authorities and central banks can play an active role in reorienting investments towards long term sustainable development.[214] The European Central Bank states that it is engaging with banks to raise awareness of risks emerging from climate change, with the objective of ensuring that banks are able to manage these risks properly.[215] It has observed that understanding exposures of financial institutions to climate-related risks is challenging in that while country-level data can be used for tracking the implementation of political commitments, monitoring financial exposures to the global effects of climate change requires reliable and comparable data at the level of euro area financial institution exposures.[216]

The UK's Prudential Regulation Authority ('PRA') has taken the global lead in directing financial institutions how to manage climate-related risks. In 2019, it published a Supervisory Statement for banks, insurers, and investment firms regarding managing risks from climate change.[217] This statement sets out the PRA's expectations regarding firms' approaches to managing the financial risks from climate change, including with respect to governance, where firms are expected to embed fully the consideration of climate risks into governance frameworks, including at board level, and assign responsibility for oversight of these risks to specific senior role holders..[218] The supervisory statement also sets out expectations with respect to risk management, whereby firms need to consider climate change in line with their board approved risk appetites; regularly use scenario analysis to test strategic resilience; and develop and maintain an appropriate disclosure of climate risks.

The PRA expects boards to understand and assess the financial risks from climate change that affect the firm, and to be able to address and oversee these risks within the firm's overall business strategy, including demonstrating an understanding of the distinctive elements of the financial risks from climate change and a sufficiently long term view of the financial risks that can arise beyond standard business planning horizons.[219] The PRA has stated that it expects to see evidence of how the firm monitors and manages the financial risks from climate change in line with its risk appetite statement, and that statement should include the risk exposure limits and thresholds for the financial risks that the firm is willing to bear. It should take into account factors such as long term financial interests of the firm, and how decisions today affect future financial risks; results of stress and scenario testing, for shorter and longer time horizons; uncertainty around the timing and the channels through which the financial risks from climate change may materialize; and sensitivity of the balance sheet to changes in key risk drivers and external conditions.[220]

214 EC, *Clean Planet* (n 143) at 18.

215 European Central Bank Statement, 'Climate Change and the ECB' (2019), <https://www.ecb.europa.eu/ecb/orga/climate/html/index.en.html>.

216 Ibid.

217 UK: Prudential Regulatory Authority, 'Enhancing Banks' and Insurers' Approaches to Managing the Financial Risks from Climate Change', Supervisory Statement 3/19 (15 April 2019), <https://www.bankofengland.co.uk/-/media/boe/files/prudential-regulation/supervisory-statement/2019/ss319.pdf?la=en&hash=7BA9824BAC5FB313F42C00889D4E3A6104881C44>.

218 Ibid at 4.

219 Ibid.

220 Ibid at 4–5.

The PRA has asked UK insurance companies, as part of a market-wide insurance stress test, to consider how their businesses will be affected in different climate-related physical and transition risks scenarios.[221] The banks are also required to conduct climate-change scenario stress tests. The PRA is assessing whether, across the financial system, financing flows are consistent with an orderly transition to the climate outcome set out in the Paris Agreement.[222] The other goal of this testing is to consider whether the financial system is resilient to shorter term shocks when climate risks materialize suddenly.[223] Carney observed that a system-wide stress test can help supervisors and climate policy-makers judge the adequacy of the current transition and whether further actions should be expected.[224]

VIII. The Governance Role of Debt Investors in the Transition to Net Zero Carbon

Banks and other lenders have an important governance role in keeping directors and officers accountable for decisions regarding climate-related financial risk.[225] Triantis and Daniels posited that, in the past, banks assisted in correcting governance problems of firms through their monitoring activities, superior access to information under loan covenants, and through direct intervention with corporate officers or exiting the relationship.[226] To the extent that the bank's monitoring deterred directors from shirking their obligations, it reduced the risk on the firm's debt, and both equity and debt investors benefited from the bank's governance role.[227] A fundamental assumption underlying this notion of interactive corporate governance was that all stakeholders shared the goal of firm-value maximization.[228] For companies relying on public debt markets, while an indenture trustee often had limited responsibility to monitor compliance, issuers frequently were required to back their commercial paper with lines of credit from banks, with the banks serving a similar governance role.[229]

Hence, the decision to lend and the subsequent screening and monitoring activities of a lender produced positive externalities that benefited numerous stakeholders with an interest in the company.[230] It signalled to potential and existing stakeholders the quality of the borrower. The imposition of fixed obligations under the loan agreement prevented managerial slack, through security rights that constrained the ability of

[221] Mark Carney, 'A New Horizon', Bank of England, Speech delivered to European Commission Conference: A Global Approach to Sustainable Finance (21 March 2019) at 7–8, <https://www.bankofengland.co.uk/-/media/boe/files/speech/2019/a-new-horizon-speech-by-mark-carney.pdf?la=en&hash=F63F8064E0408F038CABB1F29C58FB1A0CD0FE25>, (hereafter Carney, 'New Horizon').

[222] Ibid.

[223] Ibid.

[224] Ibid.

[225] Janis Sarra, 'Creating Fairness and Sustainability in the Credit Derivative Market Design' in C Williams and P Zumbansen (eds), *The Embedded Firm* (CUP, 2011) at 205–33 (hereafter Sarra, 'Credit Derivatives').

[226] George Triantis and Ronald Daniels, 'The Role of Debt in Interactive Corporate Governance' (1995) 83 University of California Law Review 1073–113 (hereafter Triantis and Daniels).

[227] Sarra, 'Credit Derivatives' (n 225).

[228] Triantis and Daniels (n 226) at 1081.

[229] Ibid at 1084, 1088, and 1089.

[230] Sarra, 'Credit Derivatives' (n 225).

managers to liquidate non-cash assets or unilaterally sell more debt; and through loan covenants and monitoring of specified prohibited types of behaviour.[231] Triantis and Daniels referred to this practice as 'interdependent screening' to describe positive externalities that flowed among creditors and from lenders to shareholders, employees, and other stakeholders.[232] Understanding this potential, there is a governance role for banks in ensuring that directors and officers are addressing climate change risk in an effective and timely manner by tailoring lending decisions to the debtor company's climate action plan.[233]

One example is the decision by the European Investment Bank ('EIB') in November 2019 to stop financing most fossil fuel projects by the end of 2021 to bring its business in line with the Paris Agreement.[234] EIB's new energy lending policy details principles that will govern its future engagement in the energy sector, prioritizing energy efficiency with a view to supporting new targets under the EU Energy Efficiency Directive. Its lending policy is aimed at enabling energy decarbonization through increased support for low or zero carbon technology, targeting a 32 per cent renewable energy share throughout the EU by 2030; financing decentralized energy production, innovative energy storage, and e-mobility, ensuring grid investment essential for new, intermittent energy sources like wind and solar; and increasing the impact of investment to support energy transformation outside the EU.[235] This decision sends a strong signal to the market and to consumers in respect of what businesses the EIB will invest in, and how these businesses are supporting the transition to a net zero carbon economy.

However, a shift in the nature of debt markets in recent years also acts as a barrier to addressing climate change. Many lending arrangements are now 'covenant light', meaning that contractual terms of debt securities or lending instruments are not as rigorous as previously, in terms of specifying or scoping the objectives for which the financing is to be used and monitoring of those uses during the period of the contract. The large number of lenders, through syndicated debt structures, as well as widely dispersed bondholders with equally widely dispersed interests, have created collective action challenges in terms of monitoring of use of the funds raised through green financial products. It creates challenges for engaging with the decision-makers such as the indenture trustee to shift investment priorities to address climate change risk. The trustees for bonds and other syndicated debt have little authority to impose attention to climate-related financial risk as a condition of financing. Any shift towards new requirements for bonds already in place requires the syndicated loan trustee or bond trustee to get unanimous approval of widely dispersed holders of the financial instrument in order to negotiate any changes in terms and conditions with the counterparty

231 Ibid.

232 Triantis and Daniels (n 226) at 1084.

233 See for example, RBC, <http://www.rbc.com/community-sustainability/index.html>.

234 Isabella Kaminski, 'EU Bank Announces It Will Phase Out Funding Most Fossil Fuel Projects' *Climate Liability News* (15 November 2019) <https://www.climateliabilitynews.org/2019/11/15/eu-bank-eib-fossil-fuel-funding-climate/>.

235 European Investment Bank ('EIB') Press Statement, 'EU Bank Launches Ambitious New Climate Strategy and Energy Lending Policy' (14 November 2019), <https://www.eib.org/en/press/all/2019-313-eu-bank-launches-ambitious-new-climate-strategy-and-energy-lending-policy>.

company. Important will be bond issuances that specifically raise funds for green finance, measurable against a global standard such as the Climate Bonds Standard developed by the Climate Bonds Initiative.[236]

Michael Ohlrogge points to how legal rules that impact recovery for firms' creditors can work to shape the positive or negative externalities those firms generate in respect of environmental harms.[237] Analysing the US Court of Appeals for the Seventh Circuit ruling in *US v Apex Oil Co*,[238] which restricted the ability of corporations to discharge obligations to clean up toxic chemical contamination that they caused prior to bankruptcy, he conducted an empirical study of lenders post this judgment. He found evidence that some lenders imposed stricter covenants at the time of lending regarding environmental protection and toxic chemical disposal, so that they would not be disadvantaged in terms of their claims if the firm subsequently failed, resulting in low-cost but meaningful impact on reducing pollution harms and improving net social efficiency.[239] These findings may be relevant for the role of debt in addressing climate change, in that lenders could impose covenants in respect of climate mitigation and adaptation, including penalties for the debtor failing to comply, as a condition of extending credit.

The continual introduction of new structured financial products and the shift to non-bank debt financing, including syndication, securitization, and collateralization, have profoundly altered the nature of debt in the past two decades.[240] The result has been a fundamental shift in credit relationships. For many years, lending was 'relational'. The bank as operating lender had an ongoing relationship with the business and often the community in which the business was located. That relationship meant that lender and borrower shared goals of sustaining economic activity in the community. However, lending has radically changed. Domestic and foreign creditors often now have little interest or direct connection with companies, their stakeholders, and the communities in which they operate.[241] Their focus is on short term returns on their debt investment. In turn, there has been a loss in governance oversight of the debt by senior lenders, as they have fully hedged their risk by bundling the loans and selling them in tranches in the market as securities.[242] While there are early indications that banks are beginning to think about climate change risk in terms of their lending portfolio priorities, many of these new types of debt have only a short term time horizon and place pressure on corporate officers to deliver short term returns or repayment as a condition of financing.[243]

[236] Climate Bonds Initiative, 'Climate Bonds Standard and Certification Scheme', <https://www.climatebonds.net/standard>.

[237] Michael Ohlrogge, 'Bankruptcy Claim Dischargeability and Public Externalities: Evidence from a Natural Experiment' (19 April 2019), <https://papers.ssrn.com/sol3/papers.cfm?abstract_id=3273486&download=yes>, (hereafter Ohlrogge).

[238] *United States v Apex Oil Co*, 579 F 3d 734 (7th Cir. 2009), leave to appeal to US Supreme Court refused.

[239] Ohlrogge (n 237) at 4, 29, and 59.

[240] Sarra, 'Credit Derivatives' (n 225).

[241] See the discussion in Janis Sarra, 'The Oscillating Pendulum: Canada's Sesquicentennial and Finding the Equilibrium for Insolvency Law' in J Sarra and B Romaine (eds), *Annual Review of Insolvency Law 2016* (Carswell, 2017).

[242] Ibid.

[243] Sarra, 'Credit Derivatives' (n 225).

Products currently being developed, such as catastrophe bonds and climate derivatives, have potential to advance or to hinder climate adaptation. For example, credit default swaps can help companies manage transition risks by hedging against failed strategies to move to low carbon technologies. However, speculative credit default swaps can also hedge against development of green technologies, creating incentives to cause the failure of an alternative energy initiative or company, as the payout is higher if the business fails.[244] Unlike insurance, which requires the purchaser to have an insurable interest in the asset or business, the incentives in respect of numerous derivatives are skewed towards immediate profit, not long term investment. The opaqueness, speed, and sophistication of these markets makes them problematic for addressing climate change.[245] There is need for new principles that link transactions in the climate finance market with sustainability goals.

IX. Additional Regulatory Challenges

i. Financial Advisors and Other Financial Intermediaries

In addition to asset managers who are fiduciaries by virtue of managing the investment portfolios of pension and other fiduciaries, there are a host of other intermediaries in financial markets that give advice or are integral players in financial markets. They should also have an obligation to consider climate change and the need for sustainability.

The *Fiduciary Duty in the 21st Century* report contains a list of recommendations for intermediaries, such as legal advisors, actuaries, investment consultants, stock exchanges, brokers, and data providers.[246] The 2019 report points out that they should report to their fiduciary clients on how climate commitments have been implemented (or not) and the implications for the research and advice provided. Intermediaries should advise fiduciaries that, as an integral part of their duties, they are to analyse and account for long term value drivers, including climate change risk, in their investment practices and processes.[247] Intermediaries should support research on the relationship between ESG issues and investment performance, and on the relationship between engagement and corporate performance. They should make ESG issues an integral part of professional training and codes of professional ethics; and raise market awareness of the investment case for ESG integration.[248]

These recommendations are very important. If pension fiduciaries are relying on these intermediaries for expert advice and the intermediaries fail to develop the knowledge and skills to give that advice, the current pattern of investor risk from climate change will be reinforced, rather than reduced. Moreover, the failure of intermediaries

244 For a discussion of the incentive effects, see ibid.

245 Janis Sarra, *Fiduciary Obligations in Business and Investment: Implications of Climate Change* (CCLI, 2018), <https://law-ccli-2019.sites.olt.ubc.ca/files/2019/08/Janis-Sarra-Fiduciary-Obligation-in-Business-and-Investment.pdf> (hereafter Sarra, *Fiduciary Obligations*).

246 UN PRI, *Fiduciary Duty in the 21st Century* (n 2) at 21.

247 Ibid

248 Ibid.

to be informed of climate-related developments, and to give timely and relevant advice, could lead to erosion of the due diligence defence if a court determines that it was not reasonable to rely on their advice.[249]

There need to be fairness measures for smaller retail investors in their relationship with financial advisors. With the diminution of pension funds, individuals in many countries are increasingly forced to turn to capital markets to generate some return on their earnings savings in preparation for retirement, yet they are not being given investment options appropriate to their risk-bearing capacity.[250] There needs to be regulatory oversight of the financial products that will transition the economy, to ensure that retail investors do not unnecessarily suffer losses. For example, a very important step for Canada would be to follow most of the world and impose a fiduciary obligation on investment advisors to consider the best interests of their clients when giving investment advice.[251] That advice should pay attention to climate risk, as well as other financial risks, to the retail investor.

As is required in the EU, mutual funds in other countries should be required to make their proxy voting records public in an accessible form. Given that such disclosures are currently available only to unitholders, prospective purchasers are unable to evaluate the degree to which such funds are aligning their voting in support of climate change mitigation and adaptation.

Estimates by the French investment management firm Mirova found that many of the index benchmarks most commonly used to assess asset management performance are compatible with 3.5°C to 5.5°C global warming scenarios.[252] Similar analysis by Blackrock found that the MSCI Canada Index has higher carbon intensity than most parallel indices, due in part to the prevalence of energy and resource sector firms in the Canadian fund.[253] Canada's Expert Panel observed that Canada's retail investment space is dominated by index-based and mutual funds that are generally absent of emissions or climate considerations; nor do they provide transparency into forward-looking climate impacts or emissions exposure.[254] Yet retail investors are being directed to indexes as safe investments in planning for their retirement.

The Canadian Expert Panel found that inconsistent awareness of the failure of funds and indexes to embed climate factors among individual investors and their investment advisors has limited demand for climate-conscious products.[255] It recommended measures to enable and encourage Canadians to contribute to sustainable outcomes through their retail investments by motivating retail investment advisors to understand the sustainability-related preferences of their clients, and increase their expertise in relevant market themes and products; increasing education about sustainability principles and climate-related opportunities to a more significant segment of the Canadian population and becoming integrated into mainstream investment markets. In turn, it would create demand for new 'best-in-class' financial products,

[249] Ibid.
[250] Sarra, 'Anthropocene' (n 199).
[251] On all matters, including climate financial risk, ibid.
[252] Canada Expert Panel (n 193) at 29.
[253] Ibid.
[254] Ibid at 30.
[255] Ibid at 11.

which will incent supply and mobilize more capital toward low-emissions, climate-smart investments.[256]

ii. Credit Rating Organizations

Credit rating agencies can influence the transition, or not, to a net zero economy. Yet credit rating agencies are compensated by the companies selling the financial products and thus they have been slow to act when it comes to building climate-related risk into their ratings.[257]

In 2016, one hundred UN PRI signatories representing US $16 trillion of assets and six credit rating agencies signed the 'Statement on ESG in credit risk and ratings'.[258] The objective of the statement is to develop more systemic, practical, and transparent incorporation of ESG into credit ratings and analysis, recognizing that ESG factors can affect borrowers' cash flows and likelihood of default of debt obligations.[259] The statement specified:

> We, the undersigned, recognise that environmental, social and governance (ESG) factors can affect borrowers' cash flows and the likelihood that they will default on their debt obligations. ESG factors are therefore important elements in assessing the creditworthiness of borrowers. For corporates, concerns such as stranded assets linked to climate change, labour relations challenges or lack of transparency around accounting practices can cause unexpected losses, expenditure, inefficiencies, litigation, regulatory pressure and reputational impacts.
>
> At a sovereign level, risks related to, *inter alia,* natural resource management, public health standards and corruption can all affect tax revenues, trade balance and foreign investment. The same is true for local governments and special purpose vehicles issuing project bonds. Such events can result in bond price volatility, and increase the risk of defaults.
>
> In order to more fully address major market and idiosyncratic risk in debt capital markets, underwriters, credit rating agencies and investors should consider the potential financial materiality of ESG factors in a strategic and systematic way. Transparency on which ESG factors are considered, how these are integrated, and the extent to which they are deemed material in credit assessments will enable better alignment of key stakeholders.[260]

The UN PRI suggests that a framework for embedding ESG and thus climate-related risks into credit ratings includes profiling the different types of ESG factors, such as

[256] Ibid at 11–12.

[257] Janis Sarra, 'Embedding Fairness as a Fundamental Norm in Financial Markets' in J Sarra, ed, An *Exploration of Fairness, Interdisciplinary Inquiries in Law, Science and the Humanities* (Toronto, Carswell, 2013) at 207.

[258] UN PRI, 'Statement on ESG in Credit Risk and Ratings' (2016), <https://www.unpri.org/credit-ratings/statement-on-esg-in-credit-risk-and-ratings-also-available-in-chinese/77.article>.

[259] Ibid.

[260] Ibid.

event driven, trend driven, or policy driven, to establish if they are relevant to credit and over what time horizon.[261] In terms of credit-relevant time horizons, it means establishing how visible the ESG factors are, how likely they are to materialize and how often, and, finally, their impact on creditworthiness, including the company's balance sheet strength and whether they have been mitigated.[262] It also recommends that once credit-relevant ESG factors and time horizons have been identified, it is important to rank them in order of importance or urgency by linking an estimate of their severity to the probability of them materializing, suggesting that 'heat maps' can be a useful synthetic indicator to prioritize material ESG factors and provide a relative assessment of their potential impact.[263] Credit rating agencies need to assess a company's awareness of ESG factors, including climate change, that may affect its credit quality and its ability and willingness to address them, including looking at how management has addressed the credit implications of ESG factors, conducting scenario analysis and stress tests.[264]

By early 2020, the UN PRI statement was being supported by 160 investors with more than US $30 trillion in assets under management and twenty-three credit rating agencies.[265] While this commitment in principle is important, ripe for further research inquiry are the deficiencies and biases currently in credit rating systems, and the need for intermediaries and others to correct them before ESG credit ratings, including climate related ratings, become more accurate and thus helpful to addressing climate-related financial risk.

X. Regulating Climate-Resilient Pathways

There are challenges for transitioning from climate change mitigation and adaptation planning to practical policy implementation. They include access to scaled-up financing, reducing information asymmetries, increasing use of new technologies, protecting social values and practices, and building institutional capacity to deploy available knowledge and resources.[266] In order to clear some of these barriers to transition, regulatory intervention is necessary. Eric Posner recently observed that the only way to force corporations to act in the public interest is to subject them to legal regulation.[267]

The IPCC has advocated a 'climate-resilient pathway approach' to transition. Companies and investors need to be aware of this pathway approach, as it is a much

[261] UN PRI, 'Credit ratings' (2019), <https://www.unpri.org/credit-ratings/statement-on-esg-in-credit-risk-and-ratings-also-available-in-chinese/77.article>.

[262] Ibid.

[263] Ibid.

[264] UN PRI, *Shifting Perceptions: ESG, Credit Risk and Ratings*, (January 2019), <https://www.unpri.org/download?ac=5819>.

[265] UN PRI, 'Statement on ESG in Credit Risk and Ratings' (January 2020), <https://www.unpri.org/credit-ratings/statement-on-esg-in-credit-risk-and-ratings-available-in-different-languages/77.article>.

[266] IPCC, 'Framing' (n 22) at 71.

[267] Eric Posner, 'Milton Friedman Was Wrong, the Famed Economist's "Shareholder Theory" Provides Corporations with Too Much Room to Violate Consumers' Rights and Trust', *The Atlantic* (22 August 2019), <https://www.theatlantic.com/ideas/archive/2019/08/milton-friedman-shareholder-wrong/596545/>.

broader conception of transition than confined to the sustainability of businesses. There is live policy debate as to the extent to which corporations and institutional investors have a responsibility to advance social development goals in the transition to net zero carbon. Should governments consider it part of corporations' social licence to operate, and to what extent do former externalities need to be internalized in the transition? 'Social license' has been defined by a group of Canadian scholars as the permission to operate granted by the local community through conditional acceptance, or revoked by public protest or boycott, which must be continually earned and not assumed, notwithstanding permission granted by government to operate.[268]

The IPCC discusses pathways that could limit global warming and align with the goals of sustainable development and poverty eradication.[269] The notion of a pathway has multiple meanings. It can describe the temporal evolution of a set of scenario features, such as reducing GHG emissions, or it can mean a solution-oriented trajectory describing a pathway from today's world to achieving a set of future goals.[270] The IPCC *Fifth Assessment Report* suggested that climate-resilient pathways combine the goals of adaptation, mitigation, and sustainable development, in order to reduce disruptions and enhance opportunities associated with climate change.[271] These pathways require a series of choices that involve trade-offs between short and long term goals and values.[272]

The IPCC observes that effective governance of climate change recognizes the contributions of all levels of government and the contributing role of the private sector, of non-governmental actors, and of civil society, in managing mitigation and adaptation.[273] In order for governance to be truly deliberative, decision-making must be made through inclusive public conversation that increases opportunities for developing policy options. This conception of climate resilient pathways prioritizes the use of citizen involvement, social learning, and rapid feedback mechanisms in policy-making and iterative management processes.[274] The IPCC has observed that the large regional diversity between highly carbon-invested economies and emerging economies are important considerations for sustainable development and equity in pursuing efforts to limit warming to 1.5°C.[275] The IPCC *Fifth Assessment Report* found that equity, sustainable development, and poverty eradication are best understood as mutually supportive and co-achievable within the context of climate action, and are underpinned by various other international hard and soft law instruments.[276]

The Paris Agreement refers to the principle of equity, within the context of broader international goals of sustainable development and poverty eradication, as a longstanding principle of climate change law.[277] It expressly recognizes that effective

268 Sustainable Canada Dialogues, *Acting on Climate Change, Solutions from Canadian Scholars* (UNESCO, 2015) at 22.
269 IPCC, 'Framing' (n 22) at 59 and 63.
270 Ibid at 63.
271 Ibid.
272 Ibid.
273 IPCC, 'Glossary' (n 10) at 550.
274 Ibid.
275 IPCC, 'Framing' (n 22) at 71.
276 IPCC, *Fifth Assessment Report* (IPCC 2014), <https://www.ipcc.ch/site/assets/uploads/2018/05/SYR_AR5_FINAL_full_wcover.pdf> (hereafter IPCC, Fifth Assessment Report).
277 Ibid at 55.

responses to climate change require a global collective effort that should be guided by the UN Sustainable Development Goals.[278] Very ambitious mitigation actions are indispensable to limit warming, which requires fairness in burden sharing both between generations and between and within nations.[279]

An important point to remember is that global economic growth has been accompanied by increased life expectancy and income in much of the world. However, many regions of the world have significant poverty and severe inequality in income distribution and access to resources, amplifying vulnerability to climate change.[280] The spread of fossil-fuel-based material consumption is a major driver of global resource use, and the main contributor to rising GHG emissions.[281]

The IPCC describes three dimensions of equity: intergenerational, which is fairness between generations; international equity, which is fairness between states; and national equity, which is fairness between individuals.[282] The principle of equity involves both procedural justice, including the right to participate in decision-making, and distributive justice in terms of the distribution of the economic and social benefits of new technologies and advances in climate mitigation.[283] The IPCC observes that different levels of warming due to climate change can be understood in terms of 'their different implications for equity—that is, in the comparative distribution of benefits and burdens for specific states, persons, or generations, and in terms of their likely impacts on sustainable development and poverty'.[284] Another challenge is to ensure capacity building now and in the future, given the current asymmetry in capacity to shape economic and policy solutions and response strategies to transition to a net zero carbon economy, because the worst-affected states, groups, and individuals are not always well represented.[285]

The United Nation's Multidimensional Poverty Index estimates that about 1.5 billion people globally live in multidimensional poverty, especially in rural areas of South Asia and Sub-Saharan Africa, with an additional billion people at risk of falling into poverty.[286] The IPCC *Fifth Assessment Report* noted that climate change-driven impacts often act as a threat multiplier by compounding other drivers of poverty.[287] 'Extreme events, such as floods, droughts, and heat waves, especially when they occur

[278] United Nations ('UN') Framework Convention on Climate Change ('FCCC') (COP21), 'Paris Agreement' (12 December 2015) FCCC/CP/2015/10/Add.1, <https://unfccc.int/resource/docs/2015/cop21/eng/10a01.pdf>.

[279] IPCC, 'Framing' (n 22) at 51.

[280] Ibid at 53. See also J S Dryzek, 'Institutions for the Anthropocene: Governance in a Changing Earth System' (2016) 46(4) British Journal of Political Science 937–56; Lövbrand et al (n 9).

[281] IPCC, 'Framing' (n 22) at 53.

[282] Ibid.

[283] Ibid.

[284] Ibid at 55. The IPCC *Fifth Assessment Report* discussed 'poverty' in terms of its multidimensionality, referring to 'material circumstances' (e.g. needs, patterns of deprivation, or limited resources), as well as to economic conditions (e.g. standard of living, inequality, or economic position), and/or social relationships (e.g. social class, dependency, lack of basic security, exclusion, or lack of entitlement: see IPCC, *Fifth Assessment Report* (n 276). See also C F Schleussner, P Pfleiderer, and E M Fischer, 'In the Observational Record Half a Degree Matters' (2017) 7 Nature Climate Change 460–2.

[285] IPCC, 'Framing', ibid at 55.

[286] UN Development Programme, 'The 2019 Global Multidimensional Poverty Index' (2019), <http://hdr.undp.org/en/2019-MPI>.

[287] IPCC, 'Framing' (n 22) at 55.

in series, can significantly erode poor people's assets and further undermine their livelihoods in terms of labour productivity, housing, infrastructure, and social networks'.[288] It concluded that equity is an integral dimension of sustainable development and that 'mitigation and adaptation measures can strongly affect broader sustainable development and equity objectives'.[289]

The Intergovernmental Science-Policy Platform on Biodiversity and Ecosystem Services ('ISPPBES') has reported that societal goals related to food, water, energy, health, and the achievement of human well-being for all can be achieved in sustainable pathways through the rapid deployment of existing policy instruments and new initiatives that more effectively enlist individual and collective action for transformative change.[290] It notes that current structures often inhibit sustainable development. It reports that five main interventions have the potential to generate transformative change by tackling the underlying indirect drivers of the deterioration of nature: incentives and capacity-building; cross-sectoral co-operation; pre-emptive action; decision-making in the context of resilience and uncertainty; and environmental law and implementation.

To use these tools effectively requires developing incentives and widespread capacity for environmental responsibility.[291] The ISPPBES advocates taking pre-emptive and precautionary actions in regulatory institutions and businesses to avoid, mitigate, and remedy the deterioration of nature, monitoring their outcomes; and managing for resilient social and ecological systems.[292] Strengthening climate mitigation and environmental laws and their implementation, and promoting sustainable agricultural and agro-ecological practices, such as multifunctional landscape planning and cross-sectoral integrated management, are pathways that support the conservation of genetic diversity and the agricultural biodiversity.[293]

The IPCC notes that the global transformation needed to limit warming to 1.5°C requires enabling conditions that involve recognizing the global interconnectivity of human-environmental relations, assessed across many dimensions of feasibility—geophysical, environmental, ecological, technological, economic, socio-cultural, and institutional. The unifying lens of the Anthropocene acknowledges profound, differential, but increasingly geologically significant, human influences on the entire Earth system.[294] The move to net zero carbon requires substantial societal and technological transformations through global and regional sustainable development pathways. These pathways need to address multiple dimensions of feasibility, as well as identifying technology and policy levers to accelerate the pace of transformation.[295]

[288] Ibid.

[289] Ibid at 56. See also M Fleurbaey et al, 'Sustainable Development and Equity' in O Edenhofer et al (eds), 'Climate Change 2014: Mitigation of Climate Change—Contribution of Working Group III to the Fifth Assessment Report of the Intergovernmental Panel on Climate Change' (CUP, 2014) at 283–350.

[290] S Diaz et al, *The Global Assessment Report on Biodiversity and Ecosystem Services*, Intergovernmental Science-Policy Platform on Biodiversity and Ecosystem Services (May 2019), <https://ipbes.net/system/tdf/inline/files/ipbes_global_assessment_report_summary_for_policymakers.pdf?file=1&type=node&id=36213>.

[291] Ibid at 17.

[292] Ibid.

[293] Ibid at 18.

[294] IPCC, 'Framing' (n 22) at 52.

[295] Ibid at 56.

XI. Capacity Building of Women's Role in Policy-Making

No discussion of regulatory oversight is complete without noting that women are only infrequently at the national and international decision-making table. Racialized women are even more excluded from policy-making. It means that regulatory policy-making in respect of companies, institutional investors, and these broader climate resilient pathways often exclude 50 per cent of the world's population in the decision-making process.

As noted in Chapter 3, climate change impacts women and men differently, and these inequitable impacts are more pronounced in developing countries and for some local communities and Indigenous peoples. This differentiation is based on historical and existing inequalities.[296] The UN underlines the importance of considering intersectional factors such as gender, age, ethnicity, disability, poverty, and socioeconomic status, when considering or assessing the vulnerability of individuals, groups, or communities to climate impacts.[297] The IPCC *Fifth Assessment Report* observes:

> Differences in vulnerability and exposure arise from non-climatic factors and from multidimensional inequalities often produced by uneven development processes ... These differences shape differential risks from climate change. People who are socially, economically, culturally, politically, institutionally or otherwise marginalized are especially vulnerable to climate change and also to some adaptation and mitigation responses ... This heightened vulnerability is rarely due to a single cause. Rather, it is the product of intersecting social processes that result in inequalities in socio-economic status and income, as well as in exposure. Such social processes include, for example, discrimination on the basis of gender, class, ethnicity, age and (dis)ability.[298]

The United Nations ('UN') has also recognized that:

> Climate change has a greater impact on those sections of the population, in all countries, that are most reliant on natural resources for their livelihoods and/or who have the least capacity to respond to natural hazards, such as droughts, landslides, floods and hurricanes. Women commonly face higher risks and greater burdens from the impacts of climate change in situations of poverty, and the majority of the world's poor are women. Women's unequal participation in decision-making processes and labour markets compound inequalities and often prevent women from fully contributing to climate-related planning, policy-making and implementation.

[296] UN FCCC, 'Differentiated Impacts of Climate Change on Women and Men; the Integration of Gender Considerations in Climate Policies, Plans and Actions; and Progress in Enhancing Gender Balance in National Climate Delegations, Synthesis Report by the Secretariat' (12 June 2019) at para 8, <https://unfccc.int/sites/default/files/resource/sbi2019_inf8.pdf> (hereafter UN, 'Differentiated Impacts').

[297] Ibid at para 19.

[298] IPCC, *Climate Change 2014: Synthesis Report. Contribution of Working Groups I, II, and III to the Fifth Assessment Report of the Intergovernmental Panel on Climate Change* (IPCC, 2014) at 54, <https://www.ipcc.ch/report/ar5/syr/>.

> Yet, women can (and do) play a critical role in response to climate change due to their local knowledge of and leadership in e.g. sustainable resource management and/or leading sustainable practices at the household and community level. Women's participation at the political level has resulted in greater responsiveness to citizen's needs, often increasing cooperation across party and ethnic lines and delivering more sustainable peace. At the local level, women's inclusion at the leadership level has led to improved outcomes of climate related projects and policies. On the contrary, if policies or projects are implemented without women's meaningful participation, it can increase existing inequalities and decrease effectiveness.[299]

Karin Bäckstrand and Eva Lövbrand utilize Michel Foucault's concept of political rationalities to capture how forms of reasoning and justification of particular ways of governing necessitate women's involvement in climate governance decision-making.[300] Their discursive framework draws attention to characteristic ways of knowing and articulating the problems to which climate governance is directed, seeking to capture the ethos of climate governance and asking which moral or normative principles need to be invoked to justify particular forms of political intervention, such as economic efficiency, justice, and sustainability.[301] They note that the main subjects of governance are the poor, the vulnerable, and marginalized communities of farmers, fishers, and Indigenous peoples that are suffering from the worst impacts of climate change.[302] They advocate that these individuals 'should assert democratic control over natural, intellectual, and financial resources, and reorient them towards serving social needs rather than increasing profits and corporative growth', observing that the climate justice discourse has called for an equitable and democratic representation of vulnerable communities in official bodies for national and international climate action.[303]

The United Nations Entity for Gender Equality and the Empowerment of Women has called for gender mainstreaming in climate change policies and plans, gender-responsive budgeting, and development of gender-responsive project proposals, climate-smart agriculture, climate-smart urban development, and climate finance mechanisms, all designed to ensure that climate governance takes account of the special circumstances of women.[304] It suggests that there is need to create a community of practice and networks to share lessons, train advocates in gender and climate change, and create the capacity to find solutions to business and societal challenges by various stakeholders on gender-responsive climate policies and actions.

The United Nations' Gender Action Plan, approved at the UN Climate Change Convention COP23, is aimed at supporting women's participation in climate

[299] UN Climate Change, 'Introduction to Gender and Climate Change' (2019), <https://unfccc.int/gender>.

[300] Karin Bäckstrand and Eva Lövbrand 'The Road to Paris: Contending Climate Governance Discourses in the Post-Copenhagen Era' (2019) 21 Journal of Environmental Policy & Planning 5.

[301] Ibid at 9.

[302] Ibid.

[303] Ibid at 12.

[304] United Nations Entity for Gender Equality and the Empowerment of Women, 'Implementation of UNFCCC's Gender Action Plan 1.0: Capacity Building for Gender-Responsive Climate Policies and Plans' (COP25 2019), <https://unfccc.int/documents?search2=&search3=women>.

negotiations, strengthening gender-responsive policy development, and raising awareness of gender and climate change issues.[305] It acknowledges that gender-responsive climate policy requires further strengthening in all decision-making and implementation of mitigation and adaptation, including, finance, technology development and transfer, and capacity-building.[306] It recognizes the need for women to be represented in all aspects of the United Nations Framework Convention on Climate Change ('UN FCCC') process and the need for gender mainstreaming through all relevant targets and goals in activities under the Convention as an important contribution to increasing their effectiveness.[307]

The World Economic Forum has observed that, globally, climate change can be solved if women are included as corporate decision-makers.[308] It recommends scaling-up the knowledge and capability of women, in order to find sustainable solutions, recognizing the important contributions of women as decision-makers, caretakers, stakeholders, experts, and educators across all sectors.[309] The Women's Environment and Development Organization and countries such as Canada and France are engaged in training new female climate change negotiators to support negotiation training for women from African countries and other emerging nations.[310]

XII. Observing Legal Requirements for Consultation with, Accommodation of, and Partnership with Indigenous Communities

Many countries have recognized and enshrined Indigenous rights in their constitutions or other foundational human rights legislation. While land claims in many jurisdictions are not yet resolved, there has emerged a very clear legal duty to consult and to accommodate when companies are seeking to develop projects that impact the land on which Indigenous peoples have an historical claim or on land or waters in relation to which they conduct their traditional activities.

The United Nations Declaration on the Rights of Indigenous Peoples ('UN DRIP') recognizes that Indigenous peoples have suffered from historic injustices as a result of their colonization and dispossession of their lands, territories, and resources, thus preventing them from exercising their right to development in accordance with their own needs and interests.[311] It recognizes the urgent need to respect and promote the

305 UN, Gender Action Plan, 'Decision 3/CP.23: Establishment of a Gender Action Plan', FCCC/CP/2017/11/Add.1 (2019), <https://unfccc.int/resource/docs/2017/cop23/eng/11a01.pdf#page=13>.

306 Ibid.

307 Ibid at para 3.

308 World Economic Forum, 'We Can Solve Climate Change—If We Involve Women' (16 September 2019), <https://www.weforum.org/agenda/2019/09/why-women-cannot-be-spectators-in-the-climate-change-battle/>.

309 Ibid.

310 See for example, Women's Environment and Development Organization and Canada-France Climate and Environment Partnership.

311 United Nations, 'Declaration on the Rights of Indigenous Peoples', UN Doc. A/RES/61/295 (13 September 2007) at 3, <https://www.un.org/development/desa/indigenouspeoples/wp-content/uploads/sites/19/2018/11/UNDRIP_E_web.pdf> (hereafter UN DRIP).

inherent rights of Indigenous peoples, which derive from their political, economic, and social structures, and from their cultures, spiritual traditions, histories, and philosophies, especially their rights to their lands, territories, and resources.[312] The UN DRIP was adopted by the United Nations General Assembly in 2007, by a majority of 144 states in favour, with four votes against. Those four countries have subsequently changed their vote and officially endorsed the declaration.[313]

The UN DRIP recognizes that Indigenous peoples are free and equal to all other peoples and have the right to be free from discrimination in the exercise of their rights based on their origin or identity, including the right to full enjoyment of all human rights and fundamental freedoms as recognized in the Charter of the United Nations, the Universal Declaration of Human Rights, and international human rights law.[314] It states that Indigenous peoples have the right to self-determination, to freely determine their political status, freely pursue their economic, social, and cultural development, and to belong to an Indigenous community or nation in accordance with the traditions and customs of the community or nation concerned.[315] Indigenous peoples are not to be forcibly removed from their lands or territories, and no relocation is to take place without the free, prior, and informed consent, and agreement on just and fair compensation.[316] Indigenous peoples have the right to practice their cultural traditions and customs, and the right to participate in decision-making in matters that affect their rights, through representatives chosen by themselves.[317] Indigenous peoples have the right to maintain and develop their political, economic, and social institutions, and to be secure in the enjoyment of their own means of subsistence and development.[318] Indigenous people have the right to autonomy or self-government, including the ways and means for financing their autonomous functions.[319]

Companies and institutional investors ought to be aware of specific provisions of the declaration that directly affect development of commercial projects. Article 25 of the UN DRIP specifies that Indigenous peoples have the right to maintain and strengthen their distinctive spiritual relationship with their traditionally owned or otherwise occupied and used lands, territories, waters, coastal seas, and other resources, and to uphold their responsibilities to future generations in this regard. Indigenous peoples have the right to own, use, develop, and control the lands, territories, and resources that they possess by reason of traditional ownership or other traditional occupation or use, as well as those lands that they have otherwise acquired. States are to give legal recognition and protection to these lands and resources, with due respect to their customs, traditions, and land tenure systems.[320]

312 Ibid.

313 UN Department of Economic and Social Affairs Indigenous People, 'UN Declaration on the Rights of Indigenous Peoples' (2019), <https://www.un.org/development/desa/indigenouspeoples/declaration-on-the-rights-of-indigenous-peoples.html>.

314 UN DRIP (n 311), Articles 1 and 2.

315 Ibid, Articles 8 and 9.

316 Ibid, Article 10.

317 Ibid, Articles 11 and 18.

318 Ibid, Article 20.1.

319 Ibid, Articles 3 and 4.

320 Ibid, Articles 26 and 27. Article 27 specifies that 'states shall establish and implement, in conjunction with Indigenous peoples concerned, a fair, independent, impartial, open and transparent process, giving due recognition to Indigenous peoples' laws, traditions, customs and land tenure systems, to recognize and

Indigenous peoples have the right to the conservation and protection of the environment and the productive capacity of their lands or territories and resources. The UN DRIP specifies that states must take effective measures to ensure that no storage or disposal of hazardous materials take place on the lands or territories of Indigenous peoples without their free, prior, and informed consent.[321] Article 32 specifies that Indigenous peoples have the right to determine and develop priorities and strategies for the development or use of their lands or territories and other resources, and states must consult and co-operate in good faith with the Indigenous peoples in order to obtain their free and informed consent prior to the approval of any project affecting their lands and resources, particularly in connection with the development, utilization, or exploitation of mineral, water, or other resources. States must provide effective mechanisms for just and fair redress for any such activities, and appropriate measures must be taken to mitigate adverse environmental, economic, social, cultural, or spiritual impact.[322]

The endorsement of these principles by 148 countries means that development of lands and resources that impact Indigenous communities are subject to many obligations of the state. Since development of resources, whether carbon intensive or renewable, requires government approval for permits, licences, and sometimes financing, these rights to consultation and agreement are important for corporations and their investors to understand and fulfil if they want regulatory permission to extract and develop resources. These issues are becoming even more important as countries move towards circular economic thinking that includes new approaches to mineral extraction, forestry, and other economic activity that impacts the Earth.

Some of these obligations have been enshrined in national constitutions. For example, Canada's Constitution specifies that the 'existing aboriginal and treaty rights of the aboriginal peoples of Canada are hereby recognized and affirmed',[323] and its Charter of Rights and Freedoms, includes 'any rights or freedoms that now exist by way of land claims agreements or may be so acquired'.[324] Canadian appellate courts have recently rendered three significant judgments in respect of the duty to consult Indigenous peoples regarding proposed economic activities that may impact them: *Chippewas of the Thames First Nation v Enbridge Pipelines Inc*,[325] *Clyde River (Hamlet) v Petroleum Geo-Services Inc*,[326] both judgments of the Supreme Court of

adjudicate the rights of Indigenous peoples pertaining to their lands, territories and resources, including those that were traditionally owned or otherwise occupied or used'.

[321] Ibid, Article 29.

[322] Ibid, Article 32.

[323] Canada, Constitution Act 1982, Schedule B to the Canada Act 1982 (UK), 1982, c 11, s 35(1) (hereafter Constitution Act). Section 35(3) specifies: 'For greater certainty, in subsection (1) 'treaty rights' includes rights that now exist by way of land claims agreements or may be so acquired'.

[324] Canada, Charter of Rights and Freedoms, s 25, Constitution Act, ibid. Section 25 specifies: 'The guarantee in this Charter of certain rights and freedoms shall not be construed so as to abrogate or derogate from any aboriginal, treaty or other rights or freedoms that pertain to the aboriginal peoples of Canada including (a) any rights or freedoms that have been recognized by the Royal Proclamation of October 7, 1763; and (b) any rights or freedoms that now exist by way of land claims agreements or may be so acquired.'

[325] *Chippewas of the Thames First Nation v Enbridge Pipelines Inc*, 2017 SCC 41, [2017] 1 SCR 1099 (hereafter *Enbridge Pipelines*).

[326] *Clyde River (Hamlet) v Petroleum Geo-Services Inc*, 2017 SCC 40 (hereafter *Clyde River v Petroleum Geo-Services*).

Canada, and the *Tsleil-Waututh Nation v Canada and Trans Mountain Pipeline*,[327] a judgment of the Federal Court of Appeal. The courts have held that the duty to consult seeks to protect Aboriginal and treaty rights while furthering reconciliation between Indigenous people and the Crown.[328] It has both a constitutional and a legal dimension.[329] The Supreme Court of Canada held that its constitutional dimension is grounded in the honour of the Crown; this principle is in turn enshrined in s 35(1) of the Constitution Act 1982, which recognizes and affirms existing Aboriginal and treaty rights.[330]

In Canada, the duty to consult entails the Crown's (i.e. 'the government') obligation to act honourably in all dealings with Aboriginal peoples.[331] The duty to consult is an obligation owed by the Crown to Indigenous peoples and not directly owed by corporations that are project proponents. As a result, there is no direct cause of action against corporations should they fail to adequately consult.[332] However, there are a number of instances in which the government relies on the companies that are seeking to develop projects to fulfil the duty, a form of delegation of the duty.[333] Realistically, if a project proponent neglects to carry out consultation and accommodation required of it by governments or their regulatory tribunals, it may undermine the company's reputation and increase its risk profile, which should be disclosed to investors. The Supreme Court of Canada has held that the duty to consult requires an informed and meaningful opportunity for dialogue with Indigenous groups whose rights may be impacted.[334] The government has an obligation to ensure the adequacy of consultation.[335]

A step further would be to require that companies partner with Indigenous communities at the very outset of a project conceptualization. Rather than expending huge amounts of resources litigating issues regarding the scope of the duty to consult and accommodate, companies could better use resources to engage in project planning with Indigenous communities at the outset of any proposed economic activity that impacts their traditional lands or waters. They would benefit from local and Indigenous knowledge, which is then more likely to result in co-benefits in the sustainable use of resources, while also protecting and enhancing biodiversity and natural capital.

[327] *Tsleil-Waututh Nation v Canada (Attorney General)* [2018] FCA 153. Another appellant judgment, *Coldwater First Nation v Canada (Attorney General)* [2020] FCA 34, was rendered as this book goes to print, in which the Federal Court of Appeal held that that there was no basis for interfering with the Governor in Council's second authorization of the Trans Mountain Pipeline Project.

[328] *Clyde River v Petroleum Geo-Services* (n 328) at para 15. See also *Rio Tinto Alcan Inc v Carrier Sekani Tribal Council*, 2010 SCC 43, [2010] 2 SCR 650 at para 34.

[329] *Clyde River v Petroleum Geo-Services* (n 328) at para 19. See also *R v Kapp*, 2008 SCC 41, [2008] 2 SCR 483 at para 6 (hereafter *R v Kapp*).

[330] *Clyde River v Petroleum Geo-Services* (n 326) at para 19. See also *Taku River Tlingit First Nation v British Columbia (Project Assessment Director)*, 2004 SCC 74, [2004] 3 SCR 550 at para 24. The Court observed that, as a legal obligation, it is based in the Crown's assumption of sovereignty over lands and resources formerly held by Indigenous peoples, *Clyde River v Petroleum Geo-Services* (n 326) at para 19. See also *Haida Nation v British Columbia (Minister of Forests)*, 2004 SCC 73, [2004] 3 SCR 511 (hereafter *Haida Nation v British Columbia (Minister of Forests)*); *R v Kapp*, ibid at para 53.

[331] *Haida Nation v British Columbia (Minister of Forests)*, ibid at para 16.

[332] Ibid at para 56.

[333] Ibid.

[334] Ibid at para 2.

[335] *Clyde River v Petroleum Geo-Services* (n 326) at para 30.

In Canada, another issue is that title to the traditional lands of most Indigenous peoples has never been resolved, notwithstanding extensive negotiations for decades and an extensive national truth and reconciliation process. These important issues need resolution if Canada is to encourage meaningful partnerships with Indigenous communities in the transition to net zero emissions and if it is to meet its obligations under the UN DRIP.

In New Zealand, the idea of a bicultural partnership between Māori and the Crown is well-established—each must act towards the other in good faith.[336] While decisions by the courts are mixed with respect to the extent of consent required,[337] the rights have received a high degree of recognition.

An example of the exact opposite, a failure to consult and accommodate has occurred in respect of the proposed expansion of the Dakota Access Pipeline in the US. The Standing Rock Sioux Nation has peacefully protested and is now legally fighting expansion of the pipeline through their ancestral homelands and their main source of water. The Tribe had been shut out of discussions even though it had technical expertise and evidence showing that oil spill risks were gravely underestimated.[338] Its peaceful demonstration was met by police using water cannons fired directly on them, stinger rounds, tear gas grenades, pepper spray, mace, tasers, and a sound weapon, resulting in 300 injured during the conflict and more than two dozen hospitalized.[339] The Obama administration had denied Dakota Access Pipeline operators a permit to cross the Missouri River, just upstream of the Standing Rock Sioux Tribe Indian reservation; but the Trump Administration reversed that decision.[340] A federal judge ordered the US Army Corps of Engineers, the regulatory agency in charge of the project, to redo an environmental review because the corps' permits fell short of legal standards.[341] The Corps redid its environmental analysis, but did not include the Tribe in the review process and concluded that its previous analysis had been sufficient. In response, the Tribe, represented by Earthjustice, went back to court. In the meantime, Energy Transfer and Sunoco, the companies that own the pipeline, applied to double the capacity of the pipeline from 570,000 to 1.1 million barrels a day.[342] In 2020, the

[336] Dominic O'Sullivan, 'Lessons from New Zealand on the "Duty to Consult" First Nation', *The Conversation* (29 November 2018), <https://theconversation.com/lessons-from-new-zealand-on-the-duty-to-consult-first-nations-106245> citing the Treaty of Waitangi and the Court of Appeal of New Zealand's judgment in *New Zealand Māori Council v Attorney General* [1987] 1 NZLR 641.

[337] See for example, the judgment of the New Zealand Supreme Court in *New Zealand Māori Council v Attorney-General* [2013] NZSC 6, in which the Court held that partial privatisation of Mighty River Power would not impair to a material extent the Crown's ability to remedy any Treaty breach in respect of Māori interests in the river, but that proposed sale of shares in the power generating company is reviewable for consistency with the principles of the Treaty of Waitangi.

[338] 'Standing Rock Sioux Tribe Seeks Court Ruling to Halt Pipeline Operations, as Dakota Access LLC Pushes for Expansion' (16 August 2019), <https://www.standingrock.org/content/standing-rock-sioux-tribe-seeks-court-ruling-halt-pipeline-operations-dakota-access-llc>.

[339] Julia Carrie Wong and Sam Levin, 'Standing Rock Protesters Hold Out against Extraordinary Police Violence', *The Guardian* (29 November 2016), <https://www.theguardian.com/us-news/2016/nov/29/standing-rock-protest-north-dakota-shutdown-evacuation> (hereafter Wong and Levin).

[340] Mike Faith, 'Our Fight against the Dakota Access Pipeline is Far from Over', *The Guardian* (15 November 2019), <https://www.theguardian.com/commentisfree/2019/nov/15/dakota-access-pipeline-standing-rock>.

[341] Wong and Levin (n 341).

[342] Ibid.

Court concluded that the Corps had violated the National Environmental Policy Act when it granted an easement to Dakota Access, LLC to construct and operate a segment of the crude-oil pipeline running beneath the lake because it failed to produce an Environmental Impact Statement despite conditions that triggered such a requirement.[343] The Court held that owners of the Dakota Access Pipeline must halt operations while the government conducts a full analysis examining the risk the pipeline poses to the Standing Rock Sioux Tribe.[344] Although mindful of the disruption a shutdown would cause, the Court concluded that the seriousness of the Corps' deficiencies outweighed the negative effects of halting the oil flow for the thirteen months that the Corps estimated an Environmental Impact Statement will take.[345]

The duty to consult and accommodate Indigenous peoples is therefore in need of greater attention if the aspirational goals of the UN DRIP are to be met. The duty needs to be fair and meaningful. Absent clarity in expectations and understanding of all parties, there are bound to be conflicts between Indigenous communities and corporate entities that have different visions of deployment of resources in the transition to net zero carbon and sustainability of the planet. A truly progressive approach would be to consider Indigenous peoples full partners in any strategy to develop resources on their traditional lands. As will be discussed in Chapter 8 on sustainable finance, this notion of partnership has led to some innovative financing collaborations between Indigenous peoples, companies, and institutional investors.

XIII. A New Green Deal?

In December 2019, the EU released its European Green Deal to enshrine the 2050 climate neutrality target into law.[346] The idea of a new deal comes from the US depression New Deal in the US, enacted by President Franklin D Roosevelt in the 1930s to help the country recover from the Great Depression; it was based on recovery of the economy, reform of the financial system to prevent another crisis, and relief for the poor.[347]

EU President Ursula von der Leyen has made climate change a top priority, promising a new European Green Deal that will work to aggressively reallocate investment and labour in key economic sectors, ramping up carbon pricing, developing mechanisms to encourage sustainable finance, while supporting the most vulnerable segments of society throughout the decarbonization process.[348] The European Green Deal provides a roadmap to scale-up efficient use of resources by moving to a clean, circular economy, halt biodiversity loss, and cut emissions. It sets out investments

[343] *Standing Rock* VI, 2020 WL 1441923.

[344] *Standing Rock Sioux Tribe et al v US Army Corps of Engineers and Dakota Access LLC*, (2020) Civil Action No 16-1534 (US District Court for the District of Columbia).

[345] Ibid.

[346] European Union, 'The European Green Deal' (11 December 2019), <https://ec.europa.eu/commission/presscorner/detail/e%20n/ip_19_6691> (hereafter European Green Deal). See also Ursula von der Leyen, 'A Union that Strives for More', <https://ec.europa.eu/commission/sites/beta-political/files/political-guidelines-next-commission_en.pdf> (hereafter von der Leyen).

[347] Michael Hiltzik, *The New Deal: A Modern History* (Free Press, 2011).

[348] Von der Leyen (n 346) at 7.

needed and financing tools available.[349] The European Green Deal requires that every person and every sector will have to contribute in terms of paying a price for carbon; and there will be a carbon border tax to avoid carbon leakage, and a strategy to become a circular economy, using the European Investment Bank as a 'climate bank'. It will direct €1 trillion of investment over the next decade towards climate mitigation and adaptation.[350]

Another pillar of the European Green Deal is the Just Transition Mechanism, focusing on the regions, industries, and workers who will face the greatest challenges in transition. It will mobilize €150 billion to help with the socio-economic impact of the transition, aimed at 'leaving no one behind'.[351] It includes facilitating employment opportunities in new sectors and sectors in transition; offering re-skilling opportunities; improving energy-efficient housing; investing to fight energy poverty; and facilitating access to clean, affordable, and secure energy. For companies, the Just Transition Mechanism is to support the transition to low-carbon technologies and economic diversification based on climate-resilient investments and jobs; providing easier access to loans and financial support; and investing in the creation of new firms, research, and innovation activities.[352]

The EU is also developing a biodiversity strategy for 2030 as part of the European Green Deal, to preserve biodiversity, work with farmers on a 'farm to fork strategy' on sustainable food along the whole value chain, to implement a ban on single use plastics, to set an aspirational goal of zero pollution, and to develop a new circular economy action plan focusing on sustainable resource use, especially in resource-intensive and high impact sectors such as textiles and construction.[353]

The World Economic Forum has observed that the European Green New Deal would enable the European Investment Bank to issue green investment bonds, and that their value, in turn, would be backed by the European Central Bank and secondary markets.[354] It envisions a public works agency with a democratic mandate that would involve citizen assemblies in municipalities and regions across Europe, which would determine where the investments are most needed.[355]

In the US, two democrats have proposed a new Green Deal for the US that proposes to reach net zero carbon emissions over the next decade, upgrading green infrastructure, and creating millions of jobs through a combination of taxation and deficit spending.[356] The resolution, 'Recognizing the duty of the Federal Government to create a Green New Deal', tabled by House Representative Alexandria Ocasio-Cortez, states:

[349] European Green Deal (n 346).

[350] Ibid at 6.

[351] European Union, 'Just Transition Mechanism' (March 2020), <https://ec.europa.eu/info/strategy/priorities-2019-2024/european-green-deal/actions-being-taken-eu/just-transition-mechanism_en>.

[352] Ibid.

[353] Von der Leyen (n 346) at 7.

[354] Kate Whiting, 'This Is What a Green New Deal for Europe Could Look Like', World Economic Forum (21 May 2019), <https://www.weforum.org/agenda/2019/05/this-is-what-a-green-new-deal-for-europe-could-look-like/>.

[355] Ibid.

[356] US Green New Deal, proposed in February in a resolution by Rep Alexandria Ocasio-Cortez (D-NY) and Sen Ed Markey (D-MA).

(1) it is the duty of the Federal Government to create a Green New Deal—
  (A) to achieve net-zero greenhouse gas emissions through a fair and just transition for all communities and workers;
  (B) to create millions of good, high-wage jobs and ensure prosperity and economic security for all people of the United States;
  (C) to invest in the infrastructure and industry of the United States to sustainably meet the challenges of the 21st century;
  (D) to secure for all people of the United States for generations to come—(i) clean air and water; (ii) climate and community resiliency; (iii) healthy food; (iv) access to nature; and (v) a sustainable environment; and
  (E) to promote justice and equity by stopping current, preventing future, and repairing historic oppression of indigenous communities, communities of color, migrant communities, deindustrialized communities, depopulated rural communities, the poor, low-income workers, women, the elderly, the unhoused, people with disabilities, and youth (referred to in this resolution as 'frontline and vulnerable communities'.[357]

The Green New Deal mobilization would require the following goals and projects:
  (A) building resiliency against climate change-related disasters, such as extreme weather, including by leveraging funding and providing investments for community-defined projects and strategies;
  (B) repairing and upgrading the infra-structure in the United States, including—(i) by eliminating pollution and greenhouse gas emissions as much as technologically feasible; (ii) by guaranteeing universal access to clean water; (iii) by reducing the risks posed by flooding and other climate impacts; and (iv) by ensuring that any infrastructure bill considered by Congress addresses climate change;
  (C) meeting 100 per cent of the power demand in the United States through clean, renewable, and zero-emission energy sources, including—(i) by dramatically expanding and up-grading existing renewable power sources; (ii) by deploying new capacity;
  (D) building or upgrading to energy-efficient, distributed, and 'smart' power grids, and working to ensure affordable access to electricity;
  (E) upgrading all existing buildings in the United States and building new buildings to achieve maximal energy efficiency, water efficiency, safety, affordability, comfort, and durability, including through electrification;
  (F) spurring massive growth in clean manufacturing in the United States and removing pollution and greenhouse gas emissions from manufacturing and industry as much as is technologically feasible, including by expanding renewable energy manufacturing and investing in existing manufacturing and industry;

[357] Resolution, Recognizing the duty of the Federal Government to create a Green New Deal (February 2019), <https://assets.documentcloud.org/documents/5729033/Green-New-Deal-FINAL.pdf> (hereafter US New Green Deal).

(G) working collaboratively with farmers and ranchers in the United States to eliminate pollution and greenhouse gas emissions from the agricultural sector as much as is technologically feasible, including—(i) by supporting family farming; (ii) by investing in sustainable farming and land use practices that increase soil health; and (iii) by building a more sustainable food system that ensures universal access to healthy food;
(H) overhauling transportation systems in the United States to eliminate pollution and greenhouse gas emissions from the transportation sector as much as is technologically feasible, including through investment in—(i) zero-emission vehicle infrastructure and manufacturing; (ii) clean, affordable, and accessible public transportation; and (iii) high-speed rail; mitigating and managing the long term adverse health, economic, and other effects of pollution and climate change, including by providing funding for community-defined projects and strategies;
(J) removing greenhouse gases from the atmosphere and reducing pollution, including by restoring natural ecosystems through proven low-tech solutions that increase soil carbon storage, such as preservation and afforestation;
(K) restoring and protecting threatened, endangered, and fragile ecosystems through locally appropriate and science-based projects that enhance biodiversity and support climate resiliency;
(L) cleaning up existing hazardous waste and abandoned sites to promote economic development and sustainability;
(M) identifying other emission and pollution sources and creating solutions to eliminate them; and
(N) promoting the international exchange of technology, expertise, products, funding, and services, with the aim of making the United States the international leader on climate action, and to help other countries achieve a Green New Deal; a Green New Deal must be developed through transparent and inclusive consultation, collaboration, and partnership with frontline and vulnerable communities, labor unions, worker cooperatives, civil society groups, academia, and businesses.[358]

As is evident, the aspirational goals of the proposed US New Green Deal are substantial. The goals are to mobilize capital over a ten-year period to build resiliency against climate change-related disasters, upgrade infrastructure, meet power demand with zero emission energy sources, and overhaul the farming and transportation sectors.[359] Another objective is to ensure that public lands, waters, and oceans are protected and that eminent domain is not abused.[360] It calls for a just and fair transition, but while it acknowledges the need to consider racialized communities, it is still thin on concrete

[358] Ibid.
[359] Emily Houlden, 'What Is the Green New Deal and How Would It Benefit Society?', *The Guardian* (11 February 2019), <https://www.theguardian.com/us-news/2019/feb/11/green-new-deal-alexandria-ocasio-cortez-ed-markey>.
[360] US New Green Deal (n 357).

recommendations. It requires the participation and assistance of those communities to articulate and implement green economic policies that address longstanding racial discrimination in the United States and the disproportionate impact of climate change on those communities. With 2020 an election year in the US, it will be interesting to see if the proposed US New Green Deal receives the support of the US electorate, and if so, whether it can kickstart a much needed shift in US regulatory policy in respect of climate change.

In addition to regulatory oversight of corporate activities to move to net zero carbon emissions, there are a number of engagement strategies being deployed by investors and other stakeholders, the subject of the next chapter.

7
Effective Engagement and Current Litigation on Climate Governance

There are a number of different ways to engage with companies regarding their carbon footprint and the need to address climate-related financial risks and opportunities. This chapter gives an overview of corporate engagement relating to climate change, including direct engagement with boards by investors and other stakeholders, shareholder proposals and proxy-voting, divestment, policy engagement, and litigation as five strategies being deployed to shift companies' and institutional investors' activities towards achieving net zero carbon emissions. If one thinks about climate change as the most serious 'symptom' of failure to sustainably develop,[1] various strategies of investors and other stakeholders to engage with companies can help them enhance their governance, shift trajectory to take meaningful climate mitigation and adaption measures, and chart a course towards sustainability.

Large institutional investors are considered 'universal investors' in the sense that they cannot easily diversify away from climate-related risk, given that it exists across most subsectors, and thus, they own risk that they cannot easily hedge purely from choice of investments. Thus engagement becomes very important. While a range of engagement strategies offers an alternative to simply divesting, lack of response by companies to engagement often leads to divestment.

I. Direct Engagement with the Board of Directors, Chief Executive Officers, and Chief Financial Officers

Engagement allows pension fiduciaries and their asset managers, as well as other institutional investors, to directly support companies on the path to competitive advantage in transitioning their economic activities.[2] Engagement offers an opportunity to hold constructive dialogue with companies particularly exposed to transition or other climate risks. That engagement can be with the chief executive officer, chief financial officer, or the entire corporate board.

One example is Climate Action 100+, mentioned in Chapter 3. More than 450 investors with over US $40 trillion in assets are directly engaging with corporate boards, advising them to curb emissions, improve governance, and strengthen climate-related

[1] Sustainable Canada Dialogues, *Acting on Climate Change: Solutions from Canadian Scholars* (UNESCO, 2015) at 15.

[2] Government of Canada, 'Final Report of the Expert Panel on Sustainable Finance: Mobilizing Finance for Sustainable Growth' (June 2019) at 29, <http://publications.gc.ca/collections/collection_2019/eccc/En4-350-2-2019-eng.pdf> (hereafter Canada Expert Panel).

From Ideas to Action. *Janis Sarra*, Oxford University Press (2020). © Janis Sarra. DOI: 10.1093/oso/9780198852308.003.0007.

financial disclosures.[3] Targeted companies include 100 systemically important emitters that account for two-thirds of annual global industrial emissions.[4] For example, following discussions with investors as part of Climate Action 100+, Swiss mining company Glencore has disclosed that it will move to limit the amount of coal that it will extract from the Earth to current levels (c 145 million tons).[5] Climate Action 100+ investors' dialogue with energy companies Total and Royal Dutch Shell plc led to recent announcements that the business plan of both companies is to become net zero on all emissions from manufacture of all their products by 2050 at the latest.[6] Canadian institutional investors are in the early stages of a Canadian-specific Climate Action 100+ initiative that will target Canada's largest carbon emitters. Other engagement efforts include the Portfolio Decarbonization Project, the Global Investor Coalition on Climate Change, and CDP, the latter of which is a non-governmental organization that collects data on how publicly held firms manage climate risks.

The Canadian Expert Panel on Sustainable Finance observed that company engagements are a valuable tool for investors to learn new information and best practices; to understand how companies are managing key risks and opportunities; to influence corporate behaviours; and to constructively address issues in portfolio companies.[7]

For example, the Ontario Teachers' Pension Plan ('OTPP'), Canada's largest single-profession pension plan with Cdn $207.4 billion in net assets, engages with boards and management to encourage climate-positive actions by portfolio companies, with a focus on compelling companies to provide information on their resource use, greenhouse gas ('GHG') emissions, and management of these emissions.[8] In its private company investments, it has regular discussions with management, and frequently has one board seat. It asks at-risk companies to engage in board-level oversight of climate change, and include material climate change considerations in their corporate strategy. OTPP seeks clear and specific information about climate risk management practices and asks its investee companies to provide metrics and targets on climate-related factors, including emissions.[9]

In 2018, OTPP examined forty-five large and mid-cap North American exploration and production ('E&P') companies with a total enterprise value of over US $600 billion in terms of their performance and incentive structures through the most recent

[3] Climate Action 100+, 'About Us', <http://www.climateaction100.org/>.

[4] Ibid.

[5] See Glencore, 'Furthering our commitment to the transition to a low-carbon economy' Press Release (20 February 2019) https://www.glencore.com/media-and-insights/news/Furthering-our-commitment-to-the-transition-to-a-low-carbon-economy Nassim Khadem, 'Glencore Moves to Cap Global Coal Output after Investor Pressure on Climate Change', *ABC News* (20 February 2019), <https://www.abc.net.au/news/2019-02-20/glencore-moves-to-capglobal-coal-output-post-investor-pressure/10831154>.

[6] See Joint Statement Total and Institutional Investors as Participants in Climate Action 100+, 'Total to Achieve Net Zero Emissions by 2050 or Sooner' (2020), <https://new-publications.total.com/05052020/pr/original-joint-statement-total-climate-action-100-plus.pdf>; and Royal Dutch Shell plc, 'Responsible Investment Annual Briefing Update (April 2020), <https://www.shell.com/media/news-and-media-releases/2020/responsible-investment-annual-briefing-updates.html>.

[7] Canada Expert Panel (n 2) at 30.

[8] OTPP, 'Climate Change Report 2018' (2019) at 11, <https://www.otpp.com/documents/10179/859251/2018+Climate+Change+Report/152d6724-3d35-4f69-8971-641ec13ed737>.

[9] Ibid at 14.

energy business cycle over a five-year period.[10] It found that during both high and low oil prices, E&P companies have earned below market returns. It attributed this underperformance to the fact that management pay incentive structures and company performance often diverge, executive compensation often tied to absolute growth targets in the short term.[11] It is therefore engaging with investee companies to urge corporate boards to change short term growth incentives to include production and reserve metrics that are per share and debt adjusted, to set compensation around long term targets and include GHG or closely related emission targets.[12]

CalPERS, a US pension fund with US $400 billion in total assets, assessed its public assets' carbon footprint in 2015, and found that out of more than 10,000 companies in its portfolio, eighty companies were responsible for 50 per cent of the portfolio's GHG emissions.[13] It has led the Climate Action 100+ initiative and directly engages with boards and senior management of companies to urge them to implement a strong governance framework that clearly articulates the board's accountability and oversight of climate change risk and opportunities. It presses investee companies to take action to reduce GHG emissions across their value chain, consistent with the Paris Agreement's goals, and to provide enhanced corporate disclosure in line with the TCFD recommendations, to enable it to assess the robustness of companies' business plans against a range of climate scenarios.[14]

ABP pension fund (*Pensioenfonds voor overheid en onderwijs*) is also very engaged with companies in which it invests. For example, ABP carried out an intensive dialogue with Shell, urging the company to formulate concrete targets for emissions reductions in the short and medium term and to link the targets to the management's remuneration. In December 2018, Shell announced, in a joint statement with Climate Action 100+, that the remuneration of senior executives will be linked to the company's carbon dioxide ('CO_2') targets.[15] ABP's goal is to reduce the carbon footprint of its equity portfolio by 25 per cent in 2020, by focusing on the best performing companies in the sector where the reduction of CO_2 is needed and by shifting towards renewable energy, to date investing €4.96 billion in renewable energy.[16]

In Canada, the Shareholder Association for Research and Education ('SHARE') assists institutional investors in engagement by facilitating constructive shareholder dialogues with companies on key ESG issues, including climate change, amplifying the voices of small and medium sized investors.[17] In 2019, it engaged in outcome-oriented dialogues with more than eighty-five Canadian and international companies, asking

[10] OTPP, '*Oil & Gas Exploration & Production, Is Management Compensation Rewarding the Right Behaviour*' (March 2018), <https://www.otpp.com/documents/10179/785362/Ontario+Teachers+-+Is+Management+Compensation+Rewarding+the+Right+Behaviour_March+2018/91fd60b3-2dba-412d-aea9-0a30e5057a75>.

[11] Ibid at 3.

[12] Ibid at 4.

[13] CalPERS, 'Climate Engagement' (2019), <https://www.calpers.ca.gov/page/investments/sustainable-investments-program/climate-change>.

[14] Ibid. See also Global Investor Coalition on Climate Change, 'Investor Expectations on Climate Change'.

[15] ABP, 'Sustainable and responsible investment 2018' (2019) at 35, <https://www.abp.nl/images/responsible-investment-report-2018.pdf>.

[16] Ibid at 36.

[17] SHARE, '*Canadian and Global Equities Shareholder Engagement Plan 2019: Snapshot*' (2019), <https://share.ca/wp-content/uploads/2019/02/SHARE-EngagementPlanSnapshot-01-019.pdf>.

them to reduce their environmental impact by setting and meeting ambitious GHG reduction targets, and to reduce their risks by testing the resilience of the company's business strategy and financial planning under different climate change scenarios.[18]

Direct engagement with corporate boards can also make them aware of the upside potential in shifting production towards activities that support the transition to net zero carbon. For example, mineral resourcing and climate change are inextricably linked, not only because of the need to reduce carbon emissions in extraction, but because new raw materials will be needed to manufacture clean technologies in a net zero carbon economy.[19]

In 2017, the World Bank, in collaboration with the International Council on Mining and Metals, analysed the role of minerals and metals in a future low carbon world, finding that there is likely increased demand for aluminium, cobalt, copper, iron ore, lead, lithium, nickel, manganese, the platinum group of metals, rare earth metals, silver, steel, titanium, and zinc.[20] For example, it observed that demand for copper will increase substantially with greater adoption of renewables and growing markets for electric vehicles and electronics, as copper is durable, antibacterial, corrosion resistant, and 100 per cent recyclable. The World Bank study found that Chile, Brazil, Peru, and Argentina are in an excellent position to supply the global climate-friendly energy transition because of their abundance of copper, iron ore, silver, lithium, aluminium, nickel, manganese, and zinc; and that Africa is well placed with its reserves in platinum, manganese, bauxite, and chromium.[21] China dominates in both base and rare Earth metals required to supply new low carbon technologies and India is dominant in iron and steel and titanium.[22]

Ceres has published a 'Blueprint for Responsible Policy Engagement on Climate Change', which offers specific recommendations on how companies can establish systems that address climate change as a systemic risk and integrate this understanding into their direct and indirect lobbying on climate policies and engagement with companies.[23]

SHARE and the National Aboriginal Trust Officers Association, as part of the Reconciliation and Responsible Investment Initiative, have published a guide for Indigenous institutional investors.[24] The Guide recommends that Indigenous investors consider their community's interests and values in engaging with companies in their portfolio about issues of concern. It observes that 'the Seventh Generation Principle is an important basis for decision making in some Anishinaabe and Haudenosaunee

[18] Ibid.

[19] Saleem Ali et al, 'Mineral Supply for Sustainable Development Requires Resource Governance' (2017) 543 Nature 367.

[20] World Bank Group, *The Growing Role of Minerals and Metals for a Low Carbon Future* (World Bank, 2017) at vii, <https://documents.worldbank.org/en/publication/documents-reports/documentdetail/207371500386458722/the-growing-role-of-minerals-and-metals-for-a-low-carbon-future>.

[21] Ibid at 8.

[22] Ibid at 27.

[23] CERES, 'Blueprint for Responsible Policy Engagement on Climate Change' (2020), <https://www.ceres.org/resources/reports/blueprint-responsible-policy-engagement-climate-change>.

[24] SHARE Reconciliation and Responsible Investment Initiative, 'Investing for Today, Tomorrow, and Future Generations: A Guide for Indigenous Investors', <https://reconciliationandinvestment.ca/portfolio-item/investing-for-today-tomorrow-and-future-generations-a-guide-a-guide-for-indigenous-investors/>.

nations ... the decisions we make today should work for the benefit of the seventh generation into the future'.[25] The Guide notes, for example, that the 'Investment Policy Statement for the Chippewas of the Thames First Nation's Thunderbird Trust sets forth that investment decisions must be made in keeping with the Nation's values, and requires that investment managers restrict asset allocation to companies that are socially responsible'.[26] The Guide recommends that stewardship helps align investments with Indigenous values, suggesting that effective engagement is based on constructive dialogue with the aim of building more successful companies and ultimately creating better outcomes for investors, communities, workers, the environment, and for future generations.[27] It notes that among the issues that investors should consider engaging with investee companies are human and Indigenous rights policies, remediation of environmental impacts, and reduction of emissions.[28] Investors should ask their asset managers about their approach to engagement and regularly review their voting record.[29]

Investor engagement can encourage investee companies to consider new product lines, energy efficiency, water efficiency, and shifting manufacturing and supply chains in a way that will reduce GHG emissions and reorient their production processes towards circular economic activity.

There is also a growing movement of citizen engagement with high-carbon-emitting companies, a topic beyond the scope of this book. As more research is undertaken with respect to the relationship between climate change and systemic racial and gender discrimination, there is likely to be more direct engagement with companies, as well as boycotts, public demonstrations, or climate strikes that bring public attention to their failure to decarbonize.

II. Shareholder Proposals and Proxy Voting on Climate Governance

Climate change considerations should be incorporated into proxy voting principles and priorities. Institutional shareholders have the ability to influence companies by exercising their rights to vote for directors. If directors have a poor record on climate risk management and action, they can be replaced if a sufficient number of shareholders vote not to re-elect them. For example, BNP Paribas Asset Management has adopted an engagement policy that uses its voting rights to vote against selected boards that do not report Scope 1 and 2 emissions.[30]

Placing shareholder resolutions on the agenda of the company's annual general meeting is another form of engagement. Voting on shareholder proposals offers investors a mechanism to advise directors of actions they should be taking on climate

[25] Ibid at 18.
[26] Ibid at 20.
[27] Ibid at 23.
[28] Ibid.
[29] Ibid at 16.
[30] BNP Paribas Asset Management, 'Global Sustainability Strategy' (2018) at 27, <https://docfinder.bnpparibas-am.com/api/files/1FC9FC6C-0DA8-468E-90B3-016DDB5CD270>.

change or express disapproval of their failure to act. While a majority vote on a shareholder proposal does not require the directors to implement the proposed action, such as setting decarbonization targets, it does send a strong message to directors that investors are unhappy with their governance. It can also signal an intention to vote against those directors' re-election the next time they are seeking to be renewed. Often, when faced with a shareholder resolution, the company will agree to the action before it goes to the shareholders' annual general meeting and thus the proposal can be an effective tool of engagement even where a formal vote does not take place.
For example, during the 2020 proxy season, BlackRock Inc voted against management at fifty-three companies worldwide, most of them energy companies, for lack of progress on climate concerns, and warned another 191 companies to take faster action.[31] This voting included BlackRock voting against the re-election of one or more directors of a company's board; voting for climate-related shareholder proposals; and 'voting against the discharge of directors' or the entire board, which is a practice in certain European markets where investors have concern about a board's performance over the year.[32]

The International Corporate Governance Network ('ICGN') suggests that there should be development and use of bespoke proxy voting guidelines and corporate governance principles, and the investor fiduciary should take care to ensure votes are cast in the interests of beneficiaries or clients.[33] It calls for engagement on climate-related issues as a priority, including collaboration with like-minded investors on proxy-voting and other company engagement initiatives, and climate and other ESG factors need to be incorporated into assessing engagement results.[34]

One study found ninety shareholder resolutions about climate change in Europe and the United States ('US') in 2018.[35] A growing number of shareholder resolutions call for enhanced disclosure regarding climate-related risk and its management.[36] Horster and Papadopoulos report that proposals focusing on the environment, including climate change, ranked first among the various categories of environmental and social proposals filed in 2018, reporting a total of 121 proposals filed at US companies.[37]

[31] Ross Kerber, 'BlackRock Cast Tougher Climate Votes, Environmentalists Want More', *Reuters Sustainable Business* (2020), <https://www.reuters.com/article/us-climate-blackrock/blackrock-cast-tougher-climate-votes-environmentalists-want-more-idUSKCN24F1UP>; BlackRock, 'Our Approach to Sustainability', <<https://www.blackrock.com/corporate/literature/publication/our-commitment-to-sustainability-full-report.pdf> (hereafter BlackRock).

[32] BlackRock, ibid at 9–10.

[33] ICGN, *Global Stewardship Principles* (2016), <https://www.icgn.org/sites/default/files/ICGNGlobalStewardshipPrinciples.pdf> (hereafter *Global Stewardship Principles*).

[34] Ibid.

[35] M Horster and K Papadopoulos, 'Climate Change and Proxy Voting in the US and Europe' (7 January 2019), <https://corpgov.law.harvard.edu/2019/01/07/climate-change-and-proxy-voting-in-the-u-s-and-europe/> (hereafter Horster and Papadopoulos).

[36] One hundred and sixty-seven resolutions in 2015 in North America. See CERES, 'Letter to SEC' at 12, citing Investor Network on Climate Risk, 'Shareholders Spur Action on Climate Change: Company Commitments from 2014 & 2015 Proxy Seasons 3, 4 (Ceres)' (2015), <http://www.ceres.org/resources/reports/shareholdersspur-action-on-climate-change-company-commitments-from-the-2014-2015-proxy-seasons>; Press Release, 'Record Number of Climate and Corporate Political Spending Resolutions Dominate 2016', Shareholder Votes: Proxy Preview (8 March 2016), <http://www.proxypreview.org/wpcontent/>.

[37] Horster and Papadopoulos (n 35).

Climate-related proposals reached a record-high of ninety filed proposals. They observe that, following exceptionally high support levels in 2017, including majority support levels at the high-profile meetings of Exxon Mobil Corporation and Occidental Petroleum Corporation, in 2018 companies were more willing to address proponent requests prior to the general meeting.[38] As a result, the majority of climate-related proposals were withdrawn from ballots, indicating a successful engagement with the company. They also observe that while traditionally, the focus has been disclosure, in recent years, shareholder proposals have been pushing companies to establish reduction targets, including goals of net zero emissions.[39]

A report by SHARE, *Climate Voting by Large Canadian Investors 2016–2017*, revealed that climate change is high on the agenda of significant investors. Investors are asking companies to develop a climate strategy or risk report related to the impact of meeting the Paris Agreement targets. A significant number of resolutions related to improving climate risk management, initiatives in renewable energy and energy efficient technology, and a call for targeted GHG emissions reductions.[40]

In Australia, there are a growing number of shareholder resolutions on climate-related risk seeking better disclosure of climate risks and targets, and scrutinizing memberships in industry or lobbying associations. Shareholder resolutions at QBE Insurance Group, Origin Energy, and Whitehaven Coal are illustrative.[41]

Horster and Papadopoulos observe that European investors are generally more engaged regarding climate change, in line with the more advanced regulatory developments, but that the topic of climate change rarely appears as a voting item in European shareholder meetings.[42] In 2018, there were only two climate change proposals, both of which received low support rates. They observe that there are barriers in Europe to this type of engagement. In the US, they note that shareholders need only have US $2,000 in shares to be able to file a shareholder proposal, while, in most European countries, shareholders are required to own between 0.5 per cent and 5 per cent of a company in order to be able to file a proposal, and in some countries, the proposal process gives managers broad discretion to exclude a resolution from the ballot.[43] They also observe that from a cultural standpoint, European markets, including businesses, are closer to reaching a broader consensus around climate change risks, and that consensus building through engagement is an approach preferred to the more public avenue of shareholder resolutions.[44]

[38] Ibid.

[39] Ibid.

[40] SHARE, 'Annual Report 2018' at 20, <https://share.ca/wp-content/uploads/2019/03/19-03-15-SHARE_2018_Annual_Report_ENG_Final.pdf>.

[41] Ruth Williams, 'Shareholders Target QBE over Climate Change "Failure"', *Sydney Morning Herald* (1 March 2018), <https://www.smh.com.au/business/companies/shareholders-target-qbe-over-climate-changefailure-20180301-p4z2e0.html>. See also Cole Latimer, 'Activist Shareholders Make History in Anti-Lobby Resolution at Origin AGM', *Sydney Morning Herald* (17 October 2018), <https://www.smh.com.au/business/companies/activist-shareholdersmake-history-in-anti-lobby-resolution-at-origin-agm-20181017-p50a4u.html>.

[42] Horster and Papadopoulos (n 35).

[43] Ibid.

[44] Ibid.

III. Divestment as a Form of Engagement or Disengagement

Divestment is another strategy to move the world to net zero carbon economic activity. It can be a form of engagement in the sense that the threat of divesting can force an investee company to radically shift its commitment to reducing its carbon footprint and to redirect its resources towards renewable energy, reduction of waste, and other sustainability measures. If investee companies fail to respond to dialogic exchanges about the need for new strategies, investors will divest their holdings. This disengagement by investors has a governance impact, in that companies are likely to respond to large amounts of capital exiting the company. Equally important is that a sizeable amount of capital will necessarily be redirected towards investment in net zero productive activities if there is to be any hope of meaningfully remedying the harmful effects of climate change. That means divestment to redirect that investment to sustainable activities.

As reported by Former Bank of England Governor Mark Carney in Chapter 3, to hold global warming to even 2°C means that 80 per cent of coal assets, 50 per cent of gas assets, and one-third of oil assets are completely un-burnable and will be stranded. To achieve net zero will require even more fossil fuels to be left in the ground. Divestment offers a route to protect pension and other financial assets, in turn protecting pension beneficiaries and individuals with savings, while at the same time creating pressure on companies to decarbonize and work towards circular economy goals.

The early divestment movement was named 350.org, taking the idea from NASA's James Hansen and his colleagues, who argued that 350 parts per million of CO_2 is the safe upper limit for atmospheric CO_2 and beyond that level, the world risks dangerous climate change.[45] Richard Heede of the Climate Accountability Institute points out that nearly two-thirds of CO_2 emitted between 1751 and 2010 are traceable to the ninety largest fossil fuel and cement producers ('carbon majors') and half those emissions have been emitted since 1986; hence he argues that these corporations have an ethical obligation to keep their carbon in the ground or undertake aggressive programmes to prevent or offset further emissions.[46]

Increasingly, institutional investors are shifting their investment priorities towards renewable energy, energy efficiency, and the circular economy. The Rockefeller Brothers Fund, with US $86 million in assets, committed to divestment, stating: 'You start with the symbolic gesture because you have to lead with your morals and your principles, and then you also build the financial case for doing it ... it is increasingly

[45] Julie Ayling and Neil Gunningham, 'Non-State Governance and Climate Policy: The Fossil Fuel Divestment Movement' (2017) 17(2) Climate Policy 131–49 at 134 (hereafter Ayling and Gunningham). See also J Hansen, M Sato, P Kharecha, D Beerling, R Berner, V Masson-Delmotte, M Pagani, M Raymo, D L Royer, and J C Zachos, 'Target Atmospheric CO2: Where Should Humanity Aim?' (2018) 2 Open Atmospheric Science Journal 217–31. See also <http://350.org>.

[46] Richard Heede, 'Tracing Anthropogenic Carbon Dioxide and Methane Emissions to Fossil Fuel and Cement Producers: 1854–2010' (2014) 122 Climatic Change 229, <https://www.researchgate.net/publication/259634408_Tracing_anthropogenic_carbon_dioxide_and_methane_emissions_to_fossil_fuel_and_cement_producers_1854-2010>.

risky not to be willing to make this sort of important gesture for our future'.[47] Five years later, the Rockefeller Brothers Fund reports that its investments have outperformed market benchmarks, and despite the potential risks associated with a loss of portfolio diversification, it has found that divestment from fossil fuels contributed to less volatility in the portfolio over time.[48]

The Calouste Gulbenkian Foundation, built on one of the world's first oil fortunes, has sold its stake in Partex Oil and Gas in 2019, and is reinvesting the generated US $622 million into renewable energy projects.[49] The Foundation's decision to divest holds much symbolic value, it recognizes that it has generated significant profits from the fossil fuel industry, but stated that reconfiguration of the Foundation's financial portfolio and investments will reinforce its diversification, social and environmental impact, and alignment with the philanthropic nature of the Foundation's activities.[50]

As noted in Chapter 6, the European Investment Bank ('EIB') has committed to stop financing most fossil fuel projects by the end of 2021, to bring its business in line with the Paris Agreement.[51] Since 2013, the bank has loaned over US $14 billion to fossil fuel projects, mainly gas. Oil and gas production and traditional fossil fuel-based heating infrastructure will be excluded under EIB's divestment strategy, although projects that it will still consider are projects that use carbon capture and storage, combined heat and power generation, or mix renewable gases with fossil gas.[52] BNP Paribas Asset Management recently announced divestment in 2020 from all companies that derive more than 10 per cent of their revenue from mining thermal coal and/or account for 1 per cent or more of total global production, a divestment of US $1 billion in coal assets.[53]

A 2019 report by the Croatan Institute concluded that philanthropic foundations that have divested from fossil fuels experienced positive impacts on their financial performance.[54] It surveyed all philanthropies that had signed the Divest-Invest pledge since 2014, and among sixty foundations that participated in the survey, 94 per cent report that dropping the conventional carbon-intensive energy sector resulted in a positive or neutral impact on returns. Since the launch of Divest Invest Philanthropy in 2014, more than 1,246 foundations, faith-based organizations, and family offices

[47] Rockefeller Brothers Fund, 'Why the Fund Decided to Divest from Fossil Fuels', Statement (April 2015), <https://www.rbf.org/news/why-fund-decided-divest-fossil-fuels>.

[48] Rockefeller Brothers Fund, 'New Report Shows Divesting Foundations Can Build Value Without Sacrificing Values' (31 October 2019), <https://www.rbf.org/news/new-report-shows-divesting-foundations-can-build-value-without-sacrificing-values>.

[49] Calouste Gulbenkian Foundation, 'The Calouste Gulbenkian Foundation Announces the Sale of Partex', Press statement (17 June 2019), <https://gulbenkian.pt/en/news/the-calouste-gulbenkian-foundation-announces-the-sale-of-partex/>.

[50] Ibid.

[51] Isabella Kaminski, 'EU Bank Announces It Will Phase Out Funding Most Fossil Fuel Projects', *Climate Liability News* (15 November 2019), <https://www.climateliabilitynews.org/2019/11/15/eu-bank-eib-fossil-fuel-funding-climate/>.

[52] Ibid.

[53] J Hill, 'BNP Paribas Announces Plans to Hasten Divestment from Coal', *CleanTechnica* (15 March 2019), <https://cleantechnica.com/2019/03/15/bnp-paribas-announces-plans-to-hasten-divestment-from-coal/>.

[54] Christi Electris, Kristin Lang, and Olive Watkins, *Divest Invest Philanthropy Five Years After Launch* (Croatan Institute, October 2019), <http://croataninstitute.org/total-portfolio/publication/divest-invest-philanthropy-2>.

have pledged to divest their assets, collectively worth US $14 trillion, from the largest oil, gas, and coal companies.[55]

Neil Gunningham suggests that the divestment movement identifies three core frames: the incompatibility of the fossil fuel industry with a just and sustainable future; social, racial, and economic justice; and the social and moral responsibility as institutions to advance the greater good.[56] With Julie Ayling, he examined the evolution of the divestment movement, describing it as a transnational advocacy network that uses a range of strategies to pressure institutional investors to divest their holdings in fossil fuel companies in favour of climate-friendly alternatives.[57] They suggest that it is the failure of efforts by governments and intergovernmental initiatives to deliver on credible mitigation that has driven non-governmental organizations ('NGO') to engage directly with the private sector.[58] They argue that the divestment movement represents a novel form of private investor-targeted climate governance, operating as a norm entrepreneur persuading institutional investors to modify their portfolios.[59] They also suggest that the divestment movement, which primarily rests its arguments on morality, is still evolving, and that one can see its growing capacity to catalyse public discourse and motivate investors to consider divestment, including institutions firmly wed to market liberalism.[60] Holley, Gunningham, and Shearing argue that 'new environmental governance' emphasizes participation, collaboration, deliberation, learning, and adaptation, and is a new form of accountability emerging globally, with potential to overcome limitations of national governments and markets.[61]

Ben Caldecott observes that the divestment movement seeks to pressure fossil fuel companies to leave oil, gas, and coal reserves in the ground and to switch energy production as a strategy to radically reduce carbon emissions.[62] Bulkeley et al note that transnational governance networks are also being used to advocate for climate mitigation, as well as greater transparency regarding emissions by companies and their supply chains.[63]

Benjamin Richardson observes that the primary arguments for divestment are an emerging sense of a legal duty to divest; investors' moral responsibility to avoid complicity in the fossil fuel economy and to use their leverage against climate polluters; and the power of financial sanctions to create a business case for abandoning fossil fuels.[64] He suggests that each of these rationales have limitations, but in combination,

[55] Ibid. See also DivestInvest, https://www.divestinvest.org/.

[56] Neil Gunningham, 'Building Norms from the Grassroots Up: Divestment, Expressive Politics, and Climate Change' (2017) 39(4) Law & Policy 372 at 380 (hereafter Gunningham, 'Building Norms').

[57] Ayling and Gunningham (n 45) at 132.

[58] Ibid at 131.

[59] Ibid at 132.

[60] Ibid at 133.

[61] Cameron Holley, Neil Gunningham, and Clifford Shearing, *The New Environmental Governance* (Routledge, 2012).

[62] Ben Caldecott, *Stranded Assets and the Environment: Risk, Resilience, and Opportunity* (Routledge, 2018).

[63] H Bulkeley, L B Andonova, M M Betsill, D H Compagnon, T Hale, M J Hoffmann, and S D Vandever, *Transnational Climate Change Governance* (CUP, 2014) at 3. See also Carbon Tracker, *Unburnable Carbon 2013: Wasted Capital and Stranded Assets* (2013), <https://www.carbontracker.org/reports/>.

[64] Benjamin J Richardson, 'Divesting from Climate Change: The Road to Influence' (2017) 39 Law & Policy 4.

they may be effective. However, he also observes that the divestment movement does not engage sufficiently with the systemic qualities of finance capitalism that must also be addressed to shift patterns of environmental unsustainability.[65]

Ayling and Gunningham have found that the divestment movement is directing its attention to investing institutions designed to serve the public good, such as pension funds and university endowments, because they have social roles that leave them open to shaming if they do not approach investment ethically.[66] They suggest that another goal of the movement is to breed uncertainty among investors about the future stability of the fossil fuel industry and its reliability as a continuing source of profitable investment, based on the Carbon Tracker Initiative's view that there is a 'carbon bubble'.[67] Carbon Tracker suggests that 80 per cent of reserves must stay the ground in order to avoid catastrophic warming, which will result in substantial stranded assets.[68] Ayling and Gunningham suggest that the value of fossil fuel shares is inflated because it is based on a false assumption that all reserves will be consumed and on an unwillingness to factor in the true costs of fossil fuel carbon emissions.[69] They argue that divestment advocates are fully aware that the divestment of holdings in fossil fuels is unlikely to have much direct effect on the valuations of fossil fuel companies, because a number are not publicly held and are not vulnerable to divestment pressures.[70] They note that the indirect effect of divestment could be significant, removing fuel companies' social license to operate through a process of reputational damage and stigmatization.[71]

When scholars at Oxford University urged the university to divest from fossil fuels, they argued that the university has 'a responsibility to show leadership in tackling one of the greatest challenges we as a society currently face'.[72] When Stanford University announced that it would divest its endowment of coal shares and make no new direct investments in companies for which coal extraction is the primary business, President John Hennessy stated that 'Stanford has a responsibility as a global citizen to promote sustainability for our planet, ... Moving away from coal in the investment context is a small, but constructive, step while work continues, at Stanford and elsewhere, to develop broadly viable sustainable energy solutions for the future'.[73]

By the end of 2016, the divestment movement had persuaded 688 institutions, such as banks, insurers, and investment funds, and 58,399 individuals across seventy-six countries to commit to divesting from fossil fuel companies based on climate change concerns.[74] Gunningham suggests that the movement's growth has been dramatic, and it has become a significant climate change actor on the global stage, along with

[65] Ibid.

[66] Ayling and Gunningham (n 45) at 135.

[67] Ibid.

[68] Ibid.

[69] Ibid.

[70] See R Thamotheram, 'What Impact Could Divestment Have on Share Price and the Energy Sector?', *Responsible Investor* (23 April 2014), <https://www.responsible-investor.com/home/article/rt_ff/>.

[71] Ayling and Gunningham (n 45) at 135.

[72] Ibid, citing <https://oxfordacademicsfordivestment.wordpress.com/signatories/>.

[73] Stanford University, 'Stanford to Divest from Coal Companies', *Stanford Report* (6 May 2014), <http://news.stanford.edu/news/2014/may/divest-coal-trustees-050714.html>.

[74] Gunningham, 'Building Norms' (n 56) at 373.

climate strikes, online petitions, and consumer boycotts.[75] Gunningham attributes the trajectory of the divestment movement to its capacity for 'naming, shaming, and framing', taking the moral high ground.[76] He observes that the fossil fuel industry has substantial instrumental and structural power, particularly in states such as Australia, whose economies rely heavily on the extraction of fossil fuels. Gunningham considers whether the divestment movement should be located within the broader framework of 'nonstate climate governance', given its interactions with and impact on a range of other climate actors.[77] He suggests that individuals who work within the conceptual framework of network governance believe the influence of nonstate actors tends to be greatest when they work through policy and reform networks, observing that while top-down climate initiatives orchestrated through international co-operation and international agreements play crucial roles in shaping our climate future, ground-up approaches are also important.[78] Behavioural change through groundswell of popular support can stimulate changes in norms, Gunningham noting that the divestment movement's naming and shaming is now at the forefront of civil society initiatives to raise public consciousness about the need for a fossil-free future.[79]

Ayling and Gunningham observe that the divestment movement eschews engagement because of the need for far more fundamental change to the global economy to bring about climate change mitigation.[80] They argue that publicity for the movement is necessary to its success, using its high profile to exert pressure on investors.[81] Yet they further observe that divestment action is unlikely to alter directly the fundamental economics of fossil fuel production or 'keep carbon in the ground', although it can be symbolic.[82] They suggest that if enough investors redirect investment away from fossil fuels and towards renewables, and markets continue to respond by providing more low carbon investment options, governments may have little choice but to follow with economically responsive regulation that removes current barriers that make it difficult for investment professionals to include climate change imperatives in their investment priorities.[83]

A 2018 study reports that nearly 1,000 institutional investors with $6.24 trillion in assets have committed to divest from fossil fuels, up from $52 billion four years prior.[84] It also reports that faith-based organizations are divesting in higher numbers, with an additional 138 institutions committing since 2016.[85]

[75] Ibid at 375–6.

[76] Ibid at 379, citing B Jarvis, 'Can a Divestment Campaign Move the Fossil Fuel Industry' (2013) Yale 360, <http://e360.yale.edu/feature/can_a_divestment_campaign_move_the_fossil_fuel_industry/2629/>; and G Seidman, 'Divestment Dynamics: Mobilizing, Shaming, and Changing the Rules' (2015) 82 Social Research 1015–37.

[77] Neil Gunningham, 'Review Essay: Divestment, Nonstate Governance, and Climate Change' (2017) 39 Law & Policy 309–24 at 385.

[78] Ibid at 386.

[79] Ibid at 387.

[80] Ayling and Gunningham (n 45) at 140.

[81] Ibid at 140.

[82] Ibid at 142.

[83] Ibid.

[84] Arabella Advisors, *The Global Fossil Fuel Divestment and Clean Energy Investment Movement* (2018), <https://www.arabellaadvisors.com/wp-content/uploads/2018/09/Global-Divestment-Report-2018.pdf>.

[85] Ibid at 8.

IV. Policy Engagement

It is important that companies and institutional investors engage with policy-makers and regulators in their advocacy for an effective transition to a net zero carbon economy. A priority is to encourage adoption of policy measures to require companies and investors to internalize externalities, for example, through the adoption of carbon pricing, as an integral part of their license to operation and the fiduciary duties of their directors.[86] Many investors want rules that ensure greater transparency in securities law disclosures, as discussed in Chapter 5. Many companies and institutional investors want certainty on carbon pricing and legal obligations so that the 'playing field' is level. They need to engage with decision-makers so that legislators make meaningful choices in enacting laws and engaging in regulatory oversight. In any such engagement, directors and officers need to consider the best interests of the company. Pension trustees and other pension fiduciaries must consider the intergenerational interests of their beneficiaries.

However, as much as capital markets participants can lobby governments to act boldly to regulate with an objective of a net zero carbon economy, there continue to be economic interests that strongly lobby for the opposite from their legislators. The coal, oil, and gas sectors have poured millions of dollars into lobbying decision-makers to have 'business as usual' in the face of clear climate change risk and its growing impacts. Thus policy engagement has to involve a much broader set of perspectives than parties with deep pockets. In particular, policy-makers need to hear from racialized and Indigenous people as to the particularly negative impacts of climate change experienced by their communities, and listen to and incorporate their ideas for more effective stewardship of ecosystems through regulatory oversight and enforcement.

Thus, a key question is how law-makers can hear the voices of the entire population (aside from infrequent elections), and not just the interests of capital markets participants as they make climate policy. There is a vast literature on deliberative democracy and how better policy decisions are made when a broad number of perspectives are included. Dialogic exchange can assist large numbers of people to understand, and then make decisions on, urgent and complex challenges such as climate change. They can offer 'other-regarding' perspectives, as discussed in Chapter 6, and can mediate against the very short time horizons of elected officials. If done well, there is potential for such deliberations to advance the public interest and the public good. If information on the challenges, costs, and potential opportunities of climate change is made sufficiently accessible and transparent, the discussions on policy options can be informed and innovative. In turn, policy decisions are likely to reflect the principles of fairness and equity discussed earlier.

While it takes time to build citizen capacity to participate in democracy, the recent global climate strikes reveal that people can ramp up their understanding of the issues

[86] ICGN, *Guidance on Investor Fiduciary Duties* (2018) at 18, <http://icgn.flpbks.com/icgn-fiduciary_duties/files/extfile/DownloadURL.pdf>.

and send clear messages to their elected officials. More than four million people in 4,500 locations in 150 countries participated in the September 2019 climate strike.[87]

In 2019, a citizens' assembly on climate action in Ireland showed that, given the time and the evidence, diverse citizens can agree on courageous proposals, including the national roll-out of low carbon public vehicles, state support for community energy generation, and huge buy-in on carbon taxes.[88] The Irish citizens' assembly consisted of a chairperson and ninety-nine citizens, randomly selected to be representative of the Irish electorate in age, gender, social class, and regional spread.[89] They met on weekends to deliberate on five public policy topics, of which two weekends were devoted to climate change. Ultimately, they voted by 80 per cent or more in favour of thirteen recommendations on climate change, including proposals to ensure climate change is at the centre of policy-making through a new governance architecture, increasing Ireland's carbon tax, and taxing GHG emissions from agriculture, which is Ireland's biggest carbon emitter.[90] While the process had limitations, it did result in a more participatory type of democratic discussion.

The United Kingdom ('UK') is undertaking something even bolder in respect of citizen democracy. Thousands of Britons were invited to the climate crisis citizens' assembly over four weekends in Birmingham in early 2020.[91] In July 2019, six select committees of the UK parliament announced plans to hold a citizens' assembly on 'combating climate change and achieving the pathway to net zero carbon emissions', which the government has committed to achieving by 2050.[92] Of 30,000 invitations, 2,000 people responded that they wanted to be involved and 110 people were selected by computer to participate in 'Climate Assembly UK'.[93] They deliberated over six weekends in early 2020 on how the UK can move to net zero emissions and their recommendations will be presented to six UK House of Commons Select Committees: Business, Energy, and Industrial Strategy; Environmental Audit; Treasury; Housing, Communities, and Local Government; Science and Technology; and Transport. *The Guardian* quoted Rachel Reeves, the chair of the Business, Energy, and Industrial Strategy Select Committee, who said:

> Adopting the net-zero target was a major milestone for the UK, reflecting the strong cross-party support for action on climate change. We now need to set out a clear

[87] Eliza Barclay and Brian Resnick, 'How Big was the Global Climate Strike? 4 million People, Activists Estimate', *Vox* (22 September 2019), <https://www.vox.com/energy-and-environment/2019/9/20/20876143/climate-strike-2019-september-20-crowd-estimate>.

[88] Riley Thorold, 'Democracy versus the Climate?', *Resilience* (10 July 2019) <https://www.resilience.org/stories/2019-07-10/democracy-versus-the-climate/>.

[89] M Coleman et al, 'Ireland's World-Leading Citizens' Climate Assembly: What Worked? What Didn't?', *Climate Home News* (27 June 2019), <https://www.climatechangenews.com/2019/06/27/irelands-world-leading-citizens-climate-assembly-worked-didnt/>.

[90] Ibid.

[91] Fiona Harvey, 'Thousands of Britons Invited to Climate Crisis Citizens' Assembly' *The Guardian* (2 November 2019), <https://www.theguardian.com/environment/2019/nov/02/thousands-britons-invited-take-part-climate-crisis-citizens-assembly> (hereafter Harvey).

[92] Ibid.

[93] Ibid. She reports that the £520,000 cost of Climate Assembly UK is being met partly by the House of Commons—providing £120,000—with the rest split between two philanthropic foundations: the Esmée Fairbairn Foundation and the European Climate Foundation.

roadmap, and finding solutions which are equitable and have public support will be crucial. Parliament needs to work with the people and with government to address the issue of climate change.[94]

Corporations and institutional investors may be able to learn something from these initiatives. Broader consultation with the communities in which they operate could reveal new insights in how to reduce waste, increase energy efficiency, and reduce their carbon footprints. Opening up discussions in the community to discuss potential pathways to net zero carbon could have multiple benefits.

V. Emerging Litigation on Climate Governance

One of the transition risks identified in Chapter 3 is litigation risk. There are lawsuits against governments for failure to act, against companies for failure to disclose or for misleading disclosure, and against companies for breach of fiduciary obligations.[95] Investors are among some of the stakeholder groups commencing litigation. This part provides an overview of the types of lawsuits being brought and the potential implications for climate governance.

For corporations and pension funds, a decade ago the question would have been, can directors and officers consider climate-related risk in the exercise of their duties, given its long time horizon?[96] Today, the appropriate question is whether directors, officers, and pension trustees understand that ignoring climate-related risk in the exercise of their fiduciary duties, including their duty of care, may leave their company or pension fund open to liability, and themselves open to personal liability.

As of May 2020, 1,587 cases of climate litigation have been identified, including 1,213 cases in the US and 374 cases in thirty-six other countries and eight regional or international jurisdictions.[97] Outside the US, the majority of lawsuits filed in the past year have been brought in Australia (ninety-eight cases), the UK (sixty-two cases), and the EU bodies and courts (fifty-seven cases).[98]

[94] Ibid.

[95] Climate Change Laws of the World database maintained by the Grantham Research Institute on Climate Change and the Environment, at the London School of Economics and Political Science, jointly with the Sabin Center, 'Climate Change Laws of the World Database' (2017), <www.lse.ac.uk/GranthamInstitute/climate-change-laws-of-the-world>. US cases are listed in the Climate Litigation Database maintained by the Sabin Center, <http://climatecasechart.com/us-climate-changelitigation>.

[96] Janis Sarra, *Fiduciary Obligations in Business and Investment: Implications of Climate Change* (CCLI, 2018), <https://law-ccli-2019.sites.olt.ubc.ca/files/2019/08/Janis-Sarra-Fiduciary-Obligation-in-Business-and-Investment.pdf> (hereafter Sarra, *Fiduciary Obligations*).

[97] Joana Setzer and Rebecca Byrnes, 'Global Trends in Climate Change Litigation: 2020 Snapshot', <https://www.lse.ac.uk/granthaminstitute/wp-content/uploads/2020/07/Global-trends-in-climate-change-litigation_2020-snapshot.pdf> (hereafter 'Global Trends 2020'). These data were produced mainly by the Sabin Center for Climate Change Law at Columbia University, with inputs from the Grantham Research Institute.

[98] Joana Setzer and Rebecca Byrnes, 'Global Trends in Climate Change Litigation: 2019 snapshot', Grantham Research Institute on Climate Change and the Environment ('GRI') July 2019, <http://www.lse.ac.uk/GranthamInstitute/wp-content/uploads/2019/07/GRI_Global-trends-in-climate-change-litigation-2019-snapshot-2.pdf> (hereafter 'Global Trends 2019').

The UN Environment Programme ('UN EP'), in co-operation with the Sabin Center for Climate Change Law at Columbia University, has reported that climate change litigation is proliferating and growing in effectiveness.[99] Cases filed in the US, Australia, the UK, the European Union ('EU'), New Zealand, Brazil, Spain, and India allege that governments and corporations have taken insufficient action to mitigate or adapt to climate threats.[100]

Former Nasa climate scientist James Hansen calls for a 'litigate-to-mitigate' campaign; his view is that 'judges are less likely than politicians to be in the pocket of oil, coal and gas companies'.[101] He advocates making the carbon majors, the 100 companies responsible for approximately 70 per cent of GHG emissions, pay for the transition to cleaner energy, and argues that until governments are prepared to make them pay, lawsuits are the best mechanism.[102] He is involved in a lawsuit brought in 2015 by his granddaughter and twenty others under twenty-one years of age against the US federal government, alleging that its failure to curb CO_2 emissions violated their constitutional rights to life, liberty, and property.[103]

The Grantham Institute found that outside the US, 43 per cent of the 305 cases brought between 1994 and 2019 led to an outcome that is considered favourable to advancing climate change efforts, while 27 per cent of the cases analysed have hindered climate change efforts. From May 2019 to May 2020, for non-US cases, 58 per cent of cases had outcomes favourable to climate change action, 33 per cent had unfavourable outcomes, and 9 per cent had no discernible likely impact on climate policy.[104] Grantham Institute has also reviewed whether climate law and/or policies were amended after a judgment to include more stringent requirements to respond to climate change, or if climate change obligations were weakened or not amended at all.[105]

i. Litigation against Governments

While not the focus of this book, it is helpful to briefly mention the types of litigation being brought against governments. The section following will discuss litigation against companies and their directors and officers. There are ongoing legal

[99] Sabin Center for Climate Change Law, Columbia Law School, 'US Climate Change Litigation in the Age of Trump: Year Two' (June 2019), <http://columbiaclimatelaw.com/files/2019/06/Adler-2019-06-US-Climate-Change-Litigation-in-Age-of-Trump-Year-2-Report.pdf>; UN Environment Programme, 'The Status of Climate Change Litigation: A Global Review' (2017), <http://wedocs.unep.org/bitstream/handle/20.500.11822/20767/climate-changelitigation.pdf?sequence1&isAllowedy>.

[100] Canada Expert Panel (n 2).

[101] Johnathan Watts, 'We Should Be on the Offensive: James Hansen Calls for Wave of Climate Lawsuits', *The Guardian* (17 November 2017), <https://www.theguardian.com/environment/2017/nov/17/we-should-be-on-the-offensive-james-hansen-calls-for-wave-of-climate-lawsuits> (hereafter Watts). See also Oliver Milman, 'Ex-Nasa Scientist: 30 Years On, World Is Failing 'Miserably' to Address Climate Change', *The Guardian* (19 June 2018), <https://www.theguardian.com/environment/2018/jun/19/james-hansen-nasa-scientist-climate-change-warning>.

[102] Watts, ibid.

[103] Ibid. See the discussion below on the *Juliana* case.

[104] Global Trends 2020 (n 97) at 11.

[105] Watts (n 101) at 4.

proceedings regarding states' human rights obligations to mitigate climate change in Ireland, France, Belgium, Sweden, Switzerland, Germany, the US, Canada, Peru, and South Korea.[106]

In *Urgenda Foundation v The Netherlands*, Urgenda Foundation and a group of 900 Dutch citizens sued the Netherlands government, seeking an order compelling the State to reduce GHG emissions more aggressively.[107] At first instance, the Court held that the State breached its duty of care under the Dutch Civil Code, which requires parties to take precautionary measures to mitigate a hazardous situation. The Court declared that implementation of adaptation measures alone would not satisfy the State's duty of care and that mitigation is the only effective remedy; thus the Netherlands government 'has a duty of care to mitigate as quickly and as much as possible'.[108] On appeal, the Hague Court of Appeals upheld the District Court's decision that the Netherlands was breaching its duty of care by 'failing to pursue a more ambitious reduction' of GHG emissions, and held that the State should reduce its emissions by at least 25 per cent by the end of 2020.[109] The Court of Appeals held that:

> the Court believes that it is appropriate to speak of a real threat of dangerous climate change, resulting in the serious risk that the current generation of citizens will be confronted with loss of life and/or a disruption of family life. As has been considered above by the Court, it follows from Articles 2 and 8 ECHR (European Convention on Human Rights) that the State has a duty to protect against this real threat.
>
> ...
>
> The State's defence of the lack of a causal link also fails. First, these proceedings concern a claim for imposing an order and not a claim for damages, so that causality only plays a limited role. In order to give an order, it suffices (in brief) that there is a real risk of the danger for which the measures have to be taken. It has been established that this is the case. Moreover, if we were to follow the State's interpretation, an effective legal remedy for a global problem as complex as this one would be lacking. After all, each state held accountable would then be able to argue that it does not have to take measures if other states do not do so either. That is a consequence that cannot be accepted, also because Urgenda does not have the option to summon all eligible states to appear in a Dutch court.[110]

On 20 December 2019, the Dutch Supreme Court, the highest court in the Netherlands, upheld the previous decisions in *Urgenda*, finding that the Dutch government has obligations to urgently and significantly reduce emissions in line with its human rights

[106] Global Trends 2020 (n 97) at 15.

[107] See *Urgenda Foundation v The Netherlands* (2015) HAZA C/09/00456689 (24 June 2015) (District Court of the Hague) (hereafter District Court judgment), affirmed (9 October 2018), The Hague Court of Appeal (on appeal), ECLI:NL:GHDHA:2018:2610; and *Stichting Urgenda v Government of the Netherlands (Ministry of Infrastructure and the Environment)* ECLI:NL:RBDHA:2015:7145, Rechtbank Den Haag, C/09/456689/HA ZA 13-1396 (hereafter Court of Appeals judgment).

[108] District Court judgment, ibid at paras 4.54, 4.73–4.75.

[109] Court of Appeals judgment (n 107) at para 76.

[110] Ibid at paras 45, 64.

obligations.[111] The Supreme Court directed the State to reduce GHG by the end of 2020 by at least 25 per cent compared to 1990.[112] The Court held that:

> An inadequate climate policy will, in the second half of this century, result in hundreds of thousands of victims in Western Europe alone. It is not just the consequences that become more severe as global warming progresses. The accumulation of CO_2 in the atmosphere may cause the climate change process to reach a tipping point, which may result in abrupt climate change, for which neither mankind nor nature can properly prepare. The risk of reaching such a tipping point increases at a steepening rate upon a rise in temperature of between 1°C and 2°C.
>
> ...
>
> The protection afforded by Articles 2 and 8 ECHR [European Convention on the Protection of Human Rights and Fundamental Freedoms] is not limited to specific persons, but to society or the population as a whole. The latter is for instance the case with environmental hazards. In the case of environmental hazards that endanger an entire region, Articles 2 and 8 ECHR offer protection to the residents of that region.
>
> ...
>
> In addition, the courts can assess whether the State, with regard to the threat of a dangerous climate change, is complying with its duty mentioned above in 5.5.3 under Articles 2 and 8 ECHR to observe due diligence and pursue good governance. Under certain circumstances, the obligation to take measures of a certain scope or quality may arise from this duty. Furthermore, this duty implies that, under certain circumstances, the State must properly substantiate that the policy it pursues meets the requirements to be imposed, i.e. that it pursues a policy through which it remains above the lower limit of its fair share.[113]

The Dutch Supreme Court also based its judgment on the Dutch State's legal duties to protect the life and well-being of citizens in the Netherlands, finding that the Dutch Constitution requires the courts to apply the provisions of the ECHR. The role of the courts is to offer legal protection, which is a fundamental rule of constitutional democracy.[114]

Litigation has commenced in other jurisdictions to press governments to step up their climate actions. In *Lho'imggin et al v Her Majesty the Queen*, two houses of the Wet'suwet'en Indigenous group filed a legal challenge on February 2020 alleging that the Canadian government's approach to climate change has violated their constitutional and human rights.[115] The plaintiffs allege that they have experienced significant

[111] Dutch Supreme Court Press Release, 'Dutch State to reduce greenhouse gas emissions by 25% by the end of 2020' (20 December 2019), <https://www.rechtspraak.nl/Organisatie-en-contact/Organisatie/Hoge-Raad-der-Nederlanden/Nieuws/Paginas/Dutch-State-to-reduce-greenhouse-gas-emissions-by-25-by-the-end-of-2020.aspx>.

[112] *The State of Netherlands v Stichting Urgenda*, (20 December 2019), No 19/00135, ECLI:NL:HR:2019:2007 (Supreme Court of the Netherlands), <<<https://www.urgenda.nl/wp-content/uploads/ENG-Dutch-Supreme-Court-Urgenda-v-Netherlands-20-12-2019.pdf>.

[113] Ibid at 2.1, 5.3.1, and 6.5.

[114] Ibid at 8.2.1.

[115] *Lho'imggin et al v Her Majesty the Queen* (February 2020), <<<<http://climatecasechart.com/non-us-case/gagnon-et-al-v-her-majesty-the-queen/>.

warming effects on their territories and expect to experience negative health impacts due to climate change, and assert that Canada's historical and ongoing racial discrimination of Indigenous peoples exacerbate the psychological and social trauma caused by climate change.[116] They are seeking declaratory relief; an order requiring the government to amend each of its environmental assessment statutes that apply to extant high GHG emitting projects to allow project approval to be cancelled if Canada will be unable to keep its Paris Agreement commitments or considers climate change to be a national emergency; and an order requiring the government to complete an annual account of its cumulative GHG emissions in a format that allows comparison to Canada's carbon budget.[117]

In the United States, *Juliana v US*—heard in 2019 by the US Ninth Circuit Court of Appeals in Portland, Oregon—involves youth plaintiffs who assert that the government's actions that cause climate change violate their constitutional rights to life, liberty, and property, as well as fail to protect essential public trust resources. The plaintiffs are seeking declaratory relief and an injunction ordering the government to implement a plan to phase out fossil fuel emissions and draw down excess atmospheric CO_2.[118] The case has survived multiple challenges by the Trump administration over several years. The intricacies of the case are important, but beyond the scope of this book. Of note, however, are two opinions. First is the opinion of US District Judge Ann Aitken in 2016, in rejecting one of many applications to throw the case out, who observed 'I have no doubt that the right to a climate system capable of sustaining human life is fundamental to a free and ordered society.'[119] Also of note is that in January 2020, the US Court of Appeals for the Ninth Circuit, by majority, dismissed the case, although opinion was sharply divided.[120] The majority of the judges did observe that 'the federal government has long promoted fossil fuel use despite knowing that it can cause catastrophic climate change, and that failure to change existing policy may hasten an environmental apocalypse'.[121] The majority held that the climate change 'is approaching "the point of no return". Absent some action, the destabilizing climate will bury cities, spawn life-threatening natural disasters, and jeopardize critical food and water supplies.'[122] The Court noted that the US government contributes to climate change not only through inaction, but affirmatively, by promoting fossil fuel use. However, the majority of the Court ultimately found against the plaintiffs on the basis of institutional competence and non-justiciability, concluding that the relief was a matter for the legislature. Importantly, the Court upheld the district court's finding that the causation requirement was satisfied and that the plaintiffs' injuries were caused by carbon emissions from fossil fuel production, extraction, and

[116] Ibid.

[117] Ibid.

[118] Our Children's Trust, <https://www.ourchildrenstrust.org/juliana-v-us> (hereafter Our Children's Trust).

[119] *Kelsey Cascadia Rose Juliana et al v USA et al*, Opinion and Order of US District Judge Ann Aiken, US District Court, Oregon, Case No 6:15-cv-01517-TC at 32. Our Children's Trust, ibid.

[120] *Juliana v United States*, US Court of Appeals for the Ninth Circuit, <http://blogs2.law.columbia.edu/climate-change-litigation/wp-content/uploads/sites/16/case-documents/2020/20200117_docket-18-36082_opinion.pdf> (hereafter *Juliana v United States*).

[121] Ibid at 11.

[122] Ibid at 15.

transportation.[123] In a strong dissent, Judge Staton wrote: 'It is as if an asteroid were barreling toward Earth and the government decided to shut down our only defenses. Seeking to quash this suit, the government bluntly insists that it has the absolute and unreviewable power to destroy the Nation.'[124] He held that 'the mere fact that this suit cannot alone halt climate change does not mean that it presents no claim suitable for judicial resolution.'[125]

In March 2020, attorneys for the youth plaintiffs in the Juliana case filed a petition for 'rehearing en banc' with the Ninth Circuit Court of Appeals, asking the court to convene a new panel of eleven circuit court judges to review the court's sharply divided opinion. The petition submits that this case about children's rights is of 'unparalleled gravity' and that while these children cannot vote to secure their fundamental rights, they can invoke the constitutional duty of the federal judiciary to protect them from government-inflicted harm.[126] The lawsuit is pending as this book goes to press.

In Canada, the Québec Superior Court refused to grant ENvironnement JEUnesse the authorization to institute a class action on behalf of all young Québec residents aged thirty-five years old or under against the Government of Canada seeking an order that government implement a target and the measures necessary to respect the fundamental rights of Québec young people, and to pay an amount equivalent to Cdn $100 per member of the class action to take measures to address the climate crisis.[127] That judgment was appealed in August 2019 and is pending.[128]

Another youth lawsuit was filed in Canada in October 2019 on behalf of fifteen youths aged between ten and nineteen years of age, seeking an order from the Federal Court that the government be required to develop and implement an enforceable plan, consistent with Canada's fair share of the global carbon budget necessary to achieve GHG emissions reductions, in order to protect public trust resources and the plaintiffs' constitutional rights.[129] The notice in part addresses the barriers to

[123] Ibid at 5, 16.

[124] Ibid at 32.

[125] Ibid at 33.

[126] *Juliana v United States*, Petition for rehearing en banc filed by plaintiffs-appellees, <http://climatecasechart.com/case/juliana-v-united-states/>.

[127] *Environnement Jeunesse c Procureur Général du Canada*, 2019 QCCS 2885 (C s Q) (11 July 2019) at para 87: « Le Tribunal estime que la doctrine de justiciabilité ne représente pas, en l'espèce, un obstacle à l'autorisation de l'action collective que Jeunesse cherche à exercer. . . . (136) Même si la mission et les objectifs de Jeunesse sont admirables sur le plan sociopolitique, ils sont trop subjectifs et limitatifs, de par leur nature, pour constituer en l'espèce la base d'un groupe approprié aux fins d'exercer une action collective. Jeunesse peut donner la « parole » aux jeunes, mais elle n'a pas l'autorité de changer le statut légal et les pouvoirs des mineurs ». Unofficial English translation: "The Court finds that the doctrine of justiciability does not, in this case, constitute an obstacle to the authorization of the class action that Jeunesse seeks to exercise... (136) Although the mission and objectives of the youth are admirable from a socio-political point of view, they are too subjective and limiting, by their nature, to constitute, in this case, the basis of an appropriate group for the purpose of collective action. Jeunesse can give a "voice" to youth, but it does not have the authority to change the legal status and powers of minors."

[128] See <https://enjeu.qc.ca/justice-eng/> (12 November 2019).

[129] La Rose v Her Majesty the Queen Statement of Claim, Federal Court of Canada, BC, Court File No 1750-19, <http://blogs2.law.columbia.edu/climate-change-litigation/wp-content/uploads/sites/16/non-us-case-documents/2019/20191025_T-1750-19_complaint.pdf>. See also Rhianna Schmunk, 'Young Canadians File Lawsuit against Government over Climate Change', *CBC News* (25 October 2019), <https://www.cbc.ca/news/canada/british-columbia/canadian-teens-lawsuit-federal-government-over-climate-change-1.5335349>.

recognition found in the earlier Québec lawsuit. In February 2020, the government filed a statement of defense acknowledging that climate change is real and that stating that it recognizes that, to the greatest extent possible, present generations must take responsibility for reducing the repercussions of climate change for the benefit of all future generations. However, it is arguing that the plaintiffs lack 'public interest' standing and their claims are not justiciable.[130] This lawsuit is pending as this book goes to press.

In the US, the Trump administration has undertaken an extensive programme of climate change deregulation, and over twenty lawsuits have defended the federal climate policies of the previous administration. The Grantham Institute reports that as of May 2019, no rollback of a climate regulation initiated by President Trump's administration brought before the courts has survived a legal challenge.[131] However, industry has brought lawsuits to support climate change deregulation and to challenge the novel efforts of states such as California, Illinois, New York, and Connecticut, which are trying to lower their carbon footprint, claiming they are overstepping their legal authority.[132]

Geetanjali Ganguly, Joana Setzer, and Veerle Heyvaert have observed that 148 countries have enshrined some form of environmental rights in their constitutions, and that countries such as Brazil, Colombia, Kenya, and Mexico have constitutional provisions that recognize the right to a healthy environment.[133] They suggest that the role of the public prosecutor's office in the enforcement of this right against corporations, combined with the growing body of robust climate change legislation, provides an increasingly solid basis for climate litigation. For example, the Brazilian Superior Court of Justice relied on Brazil's federal legislation providing for the 'polluter pays' principle and strict liability for environmental offences to ban the use of fires in sugarcane harvesting because of the GHG emissions generated by this activity.[134] There have also been cases brought to the Court of Justice of the European Union, the Inter-American Court on Human Rights, the Inter-American Commission on Human Rights, and the UN Human Rights Committee.[135] Ganguly et al suggest that strategic public climate litigation has the objective of influencing public policy on climate change, primarily through the attainment of injunctive relief.[136]

130 La Rose v Her Majesty the Queen Statement of Claim, Federal Court of Canada, BC, Court File No 1750-19, Attorney-General of Canada, Statement of Defence, (February 2020).

131 Ibid at 6, citing Sabin's climate deregulation tracker: <http://columbiaclimatelaw.com/resources/climate-deregulation-tracker>. In 2019, the Philippines Commission on Human Rights convenes a 'carbon majors inquiry', aimed at determining the impact of climate change on human rights in the Philippines and the responsibility of large fossil fuel producers, framing the investigation as dialogic hearings in the Philippines, New York and London; 'Global Trends 2019' (n 98) at 8.

132 Ibid.

133 Geetanjali Ganguly, Joana Setzer, and Veerle Heyvaert, 'If at First You Don't Succeed: Suing Corporations for Climate Change' (2018) 38(4) Oxford Journal of Legal Studies at 841–86, <https://academic.oup.com/ojls/article/38/4/841/5140101> (hereafter Ganguly et al). See also Roderic O'Gorman, 'Environmental Constitutionalism: A Comparative Study' (2017) 6 TEL 435 at 436, 461.

134 Ganguly et al, ibid, citing Recurso Especial No 1.000.731—RO, 25 August 2009, Braulino Basílio Maia Filho v Instituto Brasileiro do Meio Ambiente e dos Recursos Naturais Renova´veis—IBAMA.

135 'Global Trends 2019' (n 98) at 3.

136 Ganguly et al (n 133) at 843, 844.

ii. Investor Actions against Companies

In the private sector, litigation on climate-related risk is most likely to arise in the context of securities disclosure obligations or alleged breach of fiduciary duty and duty of care obligations. Since corporations act through directors and officers, it is their actions or inaction that will determine the liability of the corporation.[137] As courts determine the scope of the duty to disclose in relation to climate risk, they may look to how directors and officers have devised processes to identify material risk, and what programmes, processes, and strategies they have adopted to address the risks identified, even where securities law has not been amended to expressly require directors and officers to identify and disclose climate-related financial risk.[138]

Early lawsuits against US companies were dismissed based on challenges to standing or causation; however, development of attribution science has meant that the tide could be shifting on finding liability. Developments in science can now attribute proportional harms caused by the specific activities of GHG emitting firms.[139] Climate change litigation is increasing in the Americas, Europe, Asia, and the Pacific region, with several cases brought in low and middle income countries.[140]

Ganguly et al have observed that the first wave of cases against corporations in respect of climate change began in the early 2000s, framed largely as public nuisance claims, and largely unsuccessful, usually dismissed on the grounds of non-justiciability of a political question or failure to establish causation and redressability.[141] They observe that the rapidly evolving scientific, discursive, and constitutional context generates new opportunities for judges to rethink the interpretation of existing legal and evidentiary thresholds for enhancing the accountability of private GHG emitters.[142] They suggest that the increase in private litigation targeting corporations is consistent with the transnationalization of climate change governance in response to inadequate international regulation by states.[143] Douglas Kysar has observed that US tort law is currently ill-equipped to respond to climate change; however, increasing private climate litigation will ultimately compel the tort system to adapt and shift into alignment with the administrative state's regulatory role in relation to climate change.[144]

[137] Sarra, *Fiduciary Obligations* (n 96).

[138] Ibid.

[139] Sophie Marjanac and Lindene Patton, 'Extreme Weather Event Attribution Science and Climate Change Litigation: An Essential Step in the Causal Chain?' (2018) 36(3) Journal of Energy and Natural Resources Law at 265–98 (hereafter Marjanac and Patton); Centre for Policy Development and ClimateWorks, *Climate Horizons Scenarios and Strategies for Managing Climate Risk* (June 2018) at 39, <https://cpd.org.au/2018/06/climate-horizons-2/> (hereafter CPDC).

[140] CPDC, ibid at 2.

[141] Marjanac and Patton (n 139) at 846, citing *People of the State of California v General Motors Corp*, No C06-05755 (ND Cal) (17 September 2007); *American Electrical Power Co (AEP) v Connecticut*, 564 US 410; *Kivalina v ExxonMobil Corporation et al*, 696 F 3d 849, 2012 WL 4215921 (9th Cir 2012); *Comer v Murphy Oil USA Inc*, 607 F.3d 1049 (5th Cir 2010); *Native Village of Kivalina v ExxonMobil Corp*, 696 F 3d 849, 858 (9th Cir 2012), cert denied, 133 S Ct 2390 (2013).

[142] Ganguly et al (n 133) at 842.

[143] Ibid at 845.

[144] Douglas A Kysar, 'What Climate Change Can Do about Tort Law' (2011) 41 Environmental Law 1, 5.

Climate change-related claims are also being pursued by investors, activist shareholders, cities, and states.[145] Plaintiffs have made claims against investment funds and companies for failing to incorporate climate risk into their decision-making, and for failing to disclose climate risk. As of May 2019, there were 1,023 climate-related cases in the US.[146] This number is not counting the 750 lawsuits in the PG&E climate-related Chapter 11 US *Bankruptcy Code* proceedings.

In *Abrahams v Bank of Australia*, shareholders of the Commonwealth Bank of Australia ('CBA') sued the bank, alleging that it violated the Corporations Act of 2001 in failing to disclose climate change-related business risks, including possible investment in a coal mine.[147] The shareholders alleged that CBA knew, or ought to have known, that its climate change business risks might have a material or major impact on its operations, and financial position; that CBA ought to have had business strategies to manage its climate change business risks; and that CBA's members (shareholders) reasonably require a summary of CBA's climate-related risks and business strategies, if any, employed to manage those risks.[148] The action in Australia came on the heels of the Australian Prudential Regulation Authority observing that entities can no longer treat climate change as non-financial and that risks associated with climate change extend far beyond the ecological realm to economic transition risks that 'are actionable now by Australian banks, insurers, asset owners and asset managers'.[149] The shareholders subsequently dropped their lawsuit when CBA agreed to start reporting climate risks, and in CBA's 2017 annual report, the directors acknowledged that climate change posed a significant operational risk and promised to undertake risk scenario analysis; it also undertook not to lend to a coal mine to which it had planned to lend.[150]

In a US lawsuit, purchasers of Exxon Mobil Corporation ('Exxon') common stock during the period between 19 February 2016 and 27 October 2016 commenced a class action.[151] The complaint alleged that Exxon and its directors and officers

[145] 'Global Trends 2019' (n 98), citing <www.lse.ac.uk/GranthamInstitute/climate-change-laws-of-the-world/>.

[146] Sabin Center for Climate Change Law, 'Climate Change Laws of the World database', <http://climatecasechart.com/us-climate-change-litigation/>.

[147] London School of Economics and Political Science ('LSE'), 'Summary: *Abrahams*' (2019), <http://www.lse.ac.uk/GranthamInstitute/litigation/abrahams-v-commonwealth-bank-of-australia/>, citing *Abrahams v Commonwealth Bank of Australia*, No VID/879 (2017), <https://envirojustice.org.au/sites/default/files/files/170807%20Concise%20Statement%20(as%20filed).pdf>. See also 'Commonwealth Bank Shareholders Sue over "Inadequate" Disclosure of Climate Change Risks', *The Guardian* (8 August 2017), <https://www.theguardian.com/australia-news/2017/aug/08/commonwealth-bank-shareholders-sue-over-inadequate-disclosure-of-climate-change-risks>.

[148] Notice of Filing, *Guy Abrahams v Commonwealth Bank of Australia*, Victoria Registry, Federal Court of Australia (8 August 2017), <http://envirojustice.org.au/sites/default/files/files/170807%20Concise%20Statement%20(as%20filed).pdf>.

[149] Geoff Summerhayes (Australian Prudential Regulation Authority), 'Australia's New Horizon: Climate Change Challenges & Prudential Risk', Speech to the Insurance Council of Australia (17 February 2017).

[150] Gareth Hutchens, 'Commonwealth Bank Shareholders Drop Suit over Nondisclosure of Climate Risks', *The Guardian* (21 September 2017), <https://www.theguardian.com/australia-news/2017/sep/21/commonwealth-bank-shareholders-drop-suit-over-non-disclosure-of-climate-risks>, referencing the CBA, 'Annual Report' (2017) at 10–11, 24, 44–47, and 151, <https://www.commbank.com.au/content/dam/commbank/about-us/shareholders/pdfs/annual-reports/annual_report_2017_14_aug_2017.pdf>.

[151] Robbins Geller Rudman & Dowd LLP, 'Robbins Geller Rudman & Dowd LLP Files Class Action Suit Against Exxon Mobil Corporation', Press statement (7 November 2016), <http://www.rgrdlaw.com/cases/exxon/>; *Ramirez v Exxon Mobil Corporation et al*, No 16-cv-3111, Northern District of Texas, <http://

violated the US Securities Exchange Act of 1934 in making materially false and misleading public statements; that they failed to disclose that Exxon's own internally generated reports concerning climate change recognized the risks associated with global warming and climate change, the inability of the company to extract existing hydrocarbon reserves and, therefore, a material portion of Exxon's reserves were stranded and should have been written down; and that Exxon had employed an inaccurate price of carbon in evaluating the value of its future oil and gas prospects, materially overstating the value of its reserves.[152] In September 2016, the market learned that federal regulators were actively scrutinizing Exxon's reserve accounting related to climate change and its refusal to write down any of its oil and gas reserves in the face of declining global oil prices.[153] On these disclosures, the price of Exxon common stock fell more than 13 per cent, erasing billions of dollars of market capitalization.[154]

This lawsuit continues. Judge Ed Kinkeade denied Exxon's motion to dismiss the class action.[155] The Court found that 'accounting violations are sufficient to plead material misstatements', rejecting Exxon's arguments that its statements were protected by the Private Securities Litigation Reform Act safe harbour and the 'bespeaks caution' doctrine.[156] The Court also found that the plaintiff had adequately alleged the misrepresentations were made with scienter as to the company and three of its senior officers: the CEO and Chair; the Senior VP and Principal Financial Officer; and the VP Controller and Principal Accounting Officer.[157] The Court found that the plaintiff sufficiently pleaded loss causation and control person liability under s 20(a) of the Exchange Act.[158]

The Attorney General of the State of New York also filed a complaint against Exxon, seeking redress for fraud against investors. A Judge of the State New York Court held that the Attorney General failed to establish by a preponderance of the evidence that ExxonMobil violated the NY Martin Act or Executive Law s 63(12) in connection with its public disclosure of how ExxonMobil accounted for past, present, and future climate change risks.[159] The *Martin Act* gives the state authority to pursue actions for misrepresentation or fraud in the sale of securities and the Executive law prohibits repeated fraudulent acts in conducting business.[160] The Court held that:

www.prnewswire.com/news-releases/robbins-geller-rudman--dowd-llp-files-class-action-suit-against-exxon-mobil-corporation-300358768.html>.

[152] *Ramirez v Exxon Mobil Corporation et al*, No 16-cv-3111, ibid.

[153] Through a series of partial disclosures issued by different news sources between mid-August 2016 and late September 2016, ibid.

[154] It fell to US $82.54 per share on 20 September 2016, ibid.

[155] Robbins Geller Rudman & Dowd LLP, 'Robbins Geller Prevails Over Exxon Mobil's Motion to Dismiss', Press statement (15 August 2018), <https://www.rgrdlaw.com/news-item-Robbins-Geller-Prevails-Over-Exxon-Mobils-Motion-to-Dismiss.html>.

[156] *Ramirez v Exxon Mobil Corp*, No 3:16-cv-03111-K, Memorandum Opinion and Order (ND Tex) (14 August 2018) at 21, 26, and 27, <https://www.rgrdlaw.com/assets/htmldocuments/Exxon%20order.pdf>.

[157] Ibid at 42.

[158] Ibid at 45–6.

[159] *State of New York v Exxon Mobil Corporation*, SC State NY, Judge Ostrager, NYSCEF Doc No 567 (10 December 2019) at 1.

[160] Ibid at 6, 7.

> Nothing in this opinion is intended to absolve ExxonMobil from responsibility for contributing to climate change through the emission of greenhouse gases in the production of its fossil fuel products ... [but] this is a securities fraud case, not a climate change case. Applying the applicable legal standards, the Court finds that the Office of the Attorney General failed to prove by a preponderance of the evidence that ExxonMobil made any material misrepresentation that would have been viewed by a reasonable investor as having significantly altered the 'total mix' of information made available.[161]

The Court held that it must determine whether there is a substantial likelihood that the misrepresentation or disclosure would have been viewed by the reasonable investor as having significantly altered the 'total mix' of information made available', the Court finding that Exxon's publication of *Managing the Risks* had no market impact and was, as far as the evidence adduced at trial reflected, essentially ignored by the investment community.[162] Other lawsuits are pending against Exxon in the states of Massachusetts, Texas, and New Jersey.[163]

A verified shareholder derivative action has also been commenced against Exxon, alleging breach of fiduciary duty, violations of federal securities laws, waste of corporate assets, and unjust enrichment.[164] The action alleges that Exxon intentionally misled the public concerning global climate change and its connection to fossil fuel usage, as well as the impact climate change will have on Exxon's reserve values and long-term business prospects.

As noted above, investors have also initiated a wildfire-related securities class action lawsuit and another shareholder derivative lawsuit in federal court against the CEO, CFO, and other officers of Pacific Gas & Electric ('PG&E'), relating to their role in the Camp fire.[165] PG&E has self-identified as one of the first climate-related bankruptcy proceedings in the US. One lawsuit in respect of the 2017 wildfires alleges that the company and its directors and officers made false and/or misleading statements and/or failed to disclose that PG&E had failed to maintain electricity transmission and distribution networks in compliance with state safety regulations; knew that PG&E's electricity networks would cause numerous wildfires in California; and as a result, the defendants' statements about the company's business and operations were materially false and misleading at all relevant times.[166]

161 Ibid at 3.

162 Ibid at 6, 54.

163 Nate Raymond, 'Massachusetts Accuses Exxon in Lawsuit of Climate Change Deceit', Reuters (24 October 2019), <https://www.reuters.com/article/us-exxon-mobil-lawsuit-massachusetts/massachusetts-accuses-exxon-in-lawsuit-of-climate-change-deceit-idUSKBN1X32GA>. The Massachusetts Attorney General's lawsuit claims that Exxon failed to disclose its climate change-related business risks, see *Commonwealth v Exxon Mobil Corp*.

164 Sarah von Colditz, Derivatively on Behalf of Exxon Mobil Corp v Woods et al, 3:19-cv-01067 US District Court Northern District of Texas, Demand for Jury Trial (ND Tex 2 May 2019) at para 1.

165 Kevin LaCroix, 'Further Wildfire-Related Management Liability Litigation: Harbinger of Things to Come?', *The D&O Diary* (26 November 2018), <https://www.dandodiary.com/2018/11/articles/director-and-officer-liability/wildfire-related-management-liability-litigation-harbinger-things-come/>.

166 David C Weston et al v PG&E Corp et al, Class Action complaint for violation of federal securities law (12 June 2018), <http://securities.stanford.edu/filings-documents/1066/PEC00_02/2018612_f01c_18CV03509.pdf>, a federal securities class action on behalf of all investors who purchased or otherwise acquired PG&E common stock between 29 April 2015 and 8 June 2018.

The derivative action alleges that the company violated state safety requirements and regulations and failed to maintain its transmission and distribution networks; the company had made less progress on wildlife safety and vegetation management enhancements than directors had represented; its electricity transmission and distribution networks could foreseeably, and ultimately did, cause a number of wildfires; the company's dividend was not as secure as the directors and officers led the market to believe; the company failed to maintain internal controls; and due to the foregoing, defendants' statements regarding the company's business, operations, regulatory compliance, and prospects were materially false, misleading, and lacked a reasonable basis in fact.[167] The complaint further alleges that directors and officers breached their fiduciary duties by failing to maintain internal controls to address climate risk and in failing to correct the company's misleading statements, rendering them personally liable. It alleges that the misleading statements inflated the company's share price, and while the share price was inflated, five individual defendants (officers of PG&E) traded in their own shares of company stock. The complaint seeks damages under § 14(a) of the Securities and Exchange Act of 1934 for alleged proxy statement misrepresentations; damages from the individual defendants for alleged breaches of fiduciary duty; and damages from the individual defendants for alleged unjust enrichment.[168] Five additional derivative actions were subsequently filed for directors' breach of fiduciary duty, unjust enrichment, corporate waste, and other allegations.[169]

Bond purchasers also commenced a securities class action against PG&E alleging that PG&E failed to take proper fire mitigation measures, and in failing to do so, directly contradicted representations made in offering documents for US $4 billion worth of bonds.[170] The lawsuit alleges that PG&E stated in offering documents that it had taken precautions to address climate change risks, but failed to disclose the heightened risk caused by PG&E's own conduct and failure to comply with applicable regulations governing the maintenance of electrical lines. These lawsuits are pending as this book goes to press. The company is exiting from bankruptcy with a reorganization plan; however, claims pursuant to alleged breaches of securities law and directors' alleged breach of fiduciary obligation have not been resolved by the plan of reorganization and are proceeding.[171]

Another example of litigation risk is a recent judgment out of Poland in which shareholders successfully challenged a decision to proceed with Ostrołęka C coal plant. A shareholder alleged that directors had breached their fiduciary duty to the company in that their decision to proceed with the new plant posed unjustifiable financial risk

[167] Ron Williams et al v PG&E Corporation and named directors and officers, Verified Shareholder Derivative and Double Directive Complaint, US District Court Northern District of California (15 November 2018), Part 1, <https://www.dandodiary.com/wp-content/uploads/sites/265/2018/11/PGE-complaint-part-1.pdf> and Part 2, <https://www.dandodiary.com/wp-content/uploads/sites/265/2018/11/PGE-complaint-part-2.pdf>.

[168] Ibid.

[169] PG&E Corp and Pacific Gas and Electric Co., Form 10-Q, US SEC, Quarterly report pursuant to s 13/15(d) of the Securities Exchange Act of 1934, <<https://www.sec.gov/ix?doc=/Archives/edgar/data/75488/000100498020000048/pcg-20200630.htm#ic851b9069d4b4f518af0ffc6d06d6b20_64> (hereafter PG&E Form 10-Q SEC).

[170] York County v Rambo (2019) 3:19-cv-00994 US District Court for the Northern District of California.

[171] PG&E Form 10-Q SEC (n 169).

to shareholders as it was a stranded asset in the making.[172] The Court found in favour of the shareholder on the ground that the resolution consenting to the construction of the plant was legally invalid.

A lawsuit by New York City pension funds alleged that TransDigm Group Inc unlawfully excluded from its proxy materials their shareholder proposal requesting that the company adopt a management plan for GHG emissions in violation of § 14(a) of the Securities Exchange Act of 1934 and Rule 14a-8, 17 CFR14a-8.[173] It sought to compel the aerospace company to include its shareholder proposal for a GHG management plan in its proxy materials. In 2019, the federal lawsuit was resolved by a stipulation of settlement, including inclusion of the shareholder proposal for consideration at the shareholders' meeting.

These developments suggest that it is only a matter of time before some legal action is taken in a number of jurisdictions. Directors and officers should therefore be proactive in addressing climate-related risk, rather than be reactive to lawsuits under corporations law, securities law, environmental law, civil codes, or the common law. There are defences to such litigation if directors have acted on climate-related financial risk. If directors and officers are duly diligent in identifying whether there are climate-related risks and the scope of those risks, and if identified, in developing strategies to address the risk, including accurate disclosure to their investors, they are unlikely to be held personally liable.[174] Such diligence is also likely to help protect the corporation from losses due to climate-related civil actions. Thus, good governance would suggest directors and officers act now to meet their obligations.

iii. Litigation outside the United States against Corporations Based on Their Contribution to Harms Arising from Global Warming

Climate litigation is at a nascent stage and many cases are ongoing. Most are being aggressively fought. One study observes that assessing the impact of climate change litigation cases depends on a number of variables, including time scales, type of impact being considered, and risk associated with lengthy and expensive proceedings.[175] The Grantham Institute reports that climate change litigation continues to expand across jurisdictions as a tool to strengthen climate action; and cases against major emitters are seeking compensation for loss and damage.[176]

In 2019, the environmental group Milieudefensie/Friends of the Earth Netherlands and co-plaintiffs, NGO, and 17,000 citizens, filed a proceeding in the Hague Court of Appeals alleging that Royal Dutch Shell's contributions to climate change violated

[172] Client Earth, News Release, (1 August 2019); Client Earth, 'Ostrołęka C: Energa's and Enea's Board Members' Fiduciary Duties to the Companies and Shareholders' (20 September 2018), <https://www.documents.clientearth.org/library/download-info/ostroleka-c-energas-and-eneas-board-members-fiduciary-duties-to-the-companies-and-shareholders/>.

[173] New York City Employees' Retirement System v TransDigm Group Inc, 2018 Southern District of New York, <http://climatecasechart.com/case/new-york-city-employees-retirement-system-v-transdigm-group-inc/>.

[174] For a discussion, see Sarra, *Fiduciary Obligations* (n 96).

[175] 'Global Trends 2019' (n 98) at 10.

[176] Ibid.

its duty of care under Dutch law and human rights obligations by failing to take adequate action to curb contributions to climate change.[177] The plaintiffs seek a court ruling that Royal Dutch Shell must reduce its CO_2 emissions by 45 per cent by 2030 compared to 2010 levels and to zero by 2050, in line with the Paris Agreement.[178] The lawsuit alleges that, for at least thirty years, Royal Dutch Shell knew of the catastrophic danger that was likely to manifest itself in the future if the use of fossil fuels continued, has done everything since to produce and sell as many fossil fuels as possible, and has lobbied and engaged in other practices to oppose legislation to protect the climate and reduce the use of fossil fuels.[179] It argues that Royal Dutch Shell's long knowledge of climate change harms, misleading statements on climate change, and inadequate action to mitigate climate change, all support a finding of its unlawful endangerment of Dutch citizens, constituting hazardous negligence.[180] The case is pending as this book goes to press.

The lawsuit against Royal Dutch Shell seeks to extend the reasoning in *Urgenda* to corporations, arguing that the Paris Agreement, scientific evidence regarding climate change, and articles of the Dutch Civil Code and the European Convention on Human Rights make clear that Shell has a duty of care to take action to reduce its GHG emissions.[181] It alleges that a party that has, for a long time, been well aware of the great risks of climate change, is a substantial contributor to global emissions, and is able to exert control over the emissions in question, plays an important role in the transition to a sustainable society and should take effective mitigating and precautionary measures.[182] It claims that Royal Dutch Shell is well aware that it has a duty of care, and it publicly acknowledges that it has an obligation to respect human rights in the pursuit of its business. The lawsuit alleges that Shell's present actions have serious consequences for the human living environment in the second half of this century and beyond.[183] The litigation was launched after shareholder resolutions were brought to the company in 2017 and 2018.[184] The claimants argue that due care, especially when one person or legal entity creates a danger to another, is about balancing the right interests, and that Royal Dutch Shell is failing to look after the legitimate interests of the plaintiffs in its failure to prevent dangerous climate change with its catastrophic consequences.[185]

[177] *Milieudefensie et al v Royal Dutch Shell plc* (2019), <http://www.lse.ac.uk/GranthamInstitute/litigation/milieudefensie-et-al-v-royal-dutch-shell-plc/> (hereafter *Milieudefensie v Royal Dutch Shell).* See also unofficial translation of the Dutch summons in LSE, 'Summary: *Milieudefensie*' (2019), citing *Milieudefensie et al v Royal Dutch Shell plc*, (2019) Hague DC No 90046903 at 2, <http://blogs2.law.columbia.edu/climate-change-litigation/wp-content/uploads/sites/16/non-us-case-documents/2019/20190405_8918_summons.pdf> (hereafter *Milieudefensie* summons). The plaintiff non-governmental organizations are ActionAid NL, Both ENDS, Fossielvrij NL, Greenpeace NL, Young Friends of the Earth NL, and Waddenvereniging. *Milieudefensie v Royal Dutch Shell*, ibid.

[178] *Milieudefensie v Royal Dutch Shell*, ibid.

[179] Ibid at 13.

[180] Ibid.

[181] Ibid at 16.

[182] Ibid.

[183] Ibid at para 286.

[184] Ibid at para 305.

[185] Ibid at para 507.

In *Lliuya v RWE*, Germany's Appeals Court in 2017 overturned a lower court decision dismissing the lawsuit of a Peruvian farmer, Saúl Luciano Lliuya, seeking a declaratory judgment and damages in a German court against RWE, Germany's largest electricity producer.[186] Lliuya's suit alleges that RWE, having knowingly contributed to climate change by emitting substantial volumes of GHG, bears some of the responsibility for the melting mountain glaciers near his town of Huaraz, which has given rise to an acute threat from the nearby glacial lake experiencing a substantial volumetric increase, accelerated since 2003.[187] Lliuya asked the court to order RWE to reimburse him for a portion of the costs that he and town authorities have incurred to establish flood protections, 0.47 per cent of the total cost, the estimate of RWE's annual contribution to global GHG emissions.[188] In overturning the court at first instance, the Court of Appeals allowed the case to move forward into the evidentiary phase to determine whether Lliuya's home is threatened by flooding or mudslide as a result of the recent increase in the volume of the glacial lake, and how RWE's emissions contribute to that risk.[189] As this book goes to press, the case against RWE is still in the evidentiary phase.. The Grantham Institute observes that under German procedural law, it means that the Hamm court has accepted that the case is plausible, and its decision will depend on the scientific evidence provided.[190] While the facts of this case are still to be adjudicated, the Grantham Research Institute observes that the court's recognition that a private company could potentially be held liable for the climate change related damages of its GHG emissions marks a significant development in law.[191]

Ganguly et al observe that recent developments in climate science and research allow for new types of evidence on causal links between climate change-related harm and a private company's behaviour, including the IPCC's research on climate science, better and up-to-date localized data on climatic changes, the increased possibility of quantifying the proportional contribution of the world's largest emitters to climate change, and developments in attribution science.[192] They suggest that enhanced prospects for establishing causal connections between climate change harm and the behaviour of an identifiable group of corporate defendants could, in turn, augment the precedential value of successful tobacco and asbestos litigation. They examine the changing environmental constitutional context and the jurisdictions in which climate-based claims are more likely to be successfully private litigated.[193]

[186] LSE, 'Summary: *Lliuya*' (2019), <http://www.lse.ac.uk/GranthamInstitute/litigation/lliuya-v-rwe/>, citing *Lliuya v RWE AG*, (2015) No 2-O-285/15 Essen Regional Court, <http://climatecasechart.com/non-us-case/lliuya-v-rwe-ag/> (hereafter *Lliuya v RWE*); *Saul Luciano Lliuya v RWE* (2018) Az 5 U 15/17 OLG Hamm. Judgment (in German), Rechtsstreit Lliuya/RWE—Beweisaufnahme angeordnet (30 November 2017), <http://blogs2.law.columbia.edu/climate-change-litigation/wp-content/uploads/sites/16/non-us-case-documents/2017/20171130_Case-No.-2-O-28515-Essen-Regional-Court_press-release.pdf>.

[187] Ibid.

[188] Ibid.

[189] Ibid.

[190] 'Global Trends 2020' (n 97) at 20.

[191] *Lliuya v RWE* (n 186).

[192] Ganguly et al (n 133) at 851.

[193] Ibid at 850.

They cite Richard Heede's study, which was the first to map and quantify the cumulative emissions of the ninety largest carbon producers from 1854–2010, calculating a percentage of contribution of each 'carbon major entity', and finding that the ninety carbon majors released more than half of their total contribution of carbon emissions after 1988, which means the emissions are easier to trace than previously assumed.[194]

The Grantham Institute reports that there are currently at least forty ongoing climate cases worldwide against the 'carbon major' companies, including thirty-three lawsuits in the US, two in France, and one in each of Argentina, Germany, Netherlands, Nigeria, and the UK, seeking damages for claims that companies defrauded shareholders and misrepresented the impacts of climate change on their business, claims alleging disclosure greenwashing, claims related to inadequate environmental assessment of projects, and claims dealing with the violation of human rights obligations.[195]

Although there are many lawsuits against big tobacco companies, potential climate-related class action plaintiffs could learn from the recent judgment of the Québec Court of Appeal in Canada, which in 2019 upheld a class action award of Cdn $15 billion to smokers in Québec because the companies knew since the 1950s that their product was causing cancer and other illnesses and failed to warn consumers adequately.[196] The judgment, at over 400 pages, is too long to analyse here. On note, however, is that the Court of Appeal held that information provided by the manufacturer must be accurate and complete; the warnings must be sufficient in order for the user to fully understand the danger and risk associated with the use of the product.[197] The Court held that if the manufacturer does not provide users with sufficient information as to the risks and dangers of the product and as to the means to avoid them, it causes a safety defect, which, if harm is caused, triggers liability.[198] The manufacturer's obligation to inform is not limited to the dangers that could not have been known at the time of the initial putting onto the market of the product, but extends to when it knows of the danger.[199] The plaintiff must prove that the injury constitutes the materialization of the risk associated with the danger inherent in the thing, but nothing more is required in terms of proof of causation, and proof of a safety defect does not require the plaintiff to establish the source of the safety defect.[200] While enforcement of the judgment is temporarily stayed under Canadian insolvency proceedings pending development of a plan of arrangement, the court's reasoning deserves careful reading in respect of how large companies that failed to disclose danger can be held liable for significant monetary damages.

[194] Ibid at 852–3, citing Richard Heede, 'Tracing Anthropogenic Carbon Dioxide and Methane Emissions to Fossil Fuel and Cement Producers, 1854–2010' (2014) 122 Climatic Change 229.

[195] Global Trends 2020 (n 97) at 19.

[196] *Imperial Tobacco Canada ltée c Conseil québécois sur le tabac et la santé*, 2019 QCCA 358.

[197] Ibid at para 283.

[198] Ibid at para 289.

[199] Ibid at para 298.

[200] Ibid at para 401.

iv. Litigation in the United States against Corporations Based on Their Contribution to Harms Arising from Global Warming

In the first cases brought in the US against corporations for their proportional contribution to the negative effects of carbon emissions, corporate defendants prevented the lawsuits from proceeding to the merits stage by challenging the court's jurisdiction through the invocation of standing issues, the doctrine of 'no tort cause of action where legislation has been enacted', and the 'political question doctrine' as a first line of defence.[201] US courts have accepted 'injuries' such as damage claims for rising sea levels and loss of recreational value from changing landscapes, but cases were dismissed on the basis of failure to establish causation and failure to establish that the injury is capable of being redressed by the court, two requirements under the US doctrine of standing in federal court.[202] Under American constitutional law, the political question doctrine prescribes that courts can exclusively adjudicate on questions of law, which are deemed justiciable; thus, courts will generally refrain from adjudicating questions that are inherently political.[203]

The current lawsuits in the US are making use of new attribution science that links emissions of specific companies to acute events that are climate-related. Brenda Ekwurzel et al use a simple climate model to quantify the contribution of historical (1880–2010) and recent (1980–2010) emissions traced to major carbon producers to the historical rise in global atmospheric CO_2, surface temperature, and sea level.[204] They use a global energy-balance coupled climate-carbon-cycle model to assess change in atmospheric CO_2 that are directly relevant to impacts such as ocean acidification, while global mean surface temperature ('GMST') correlates closely with many terrestrial and ocean impacts.[205] Emissions traced to these ninety carbon producers

[201] See for example, *Native Village of Kivalina v ExxonMobil Corp*, No 4:08-cv-01138-SBA, Complaint (ND Cal, (26 February 2008) (9th Cir 2012), <http://climatecasechart.com/case/native-village-of-kivalina-v-exxonmobil-corp/>; *Native Village of Kivalina v ExxonMobil Corp*, No 4:08-cv-01138-SBA, Complaint (ND Cal, 26 February 2008) (9th Cir 2012), <http://climatecasechart.com/case/native-village-of-kivalina-v-exxonmobil-corp/>; *Native Village of Kivalina v ExxonMobil Corp*, 09-17490, Opinion (9th Cir 2012) (21 September 2012); *Native Village of Kivalina v ExxonMobil Corp*, No 12-1072 US (2013). In *Native Village of Kivalina v ExxonMobil Corp*, an action by native Alaskans seeking damages from oil and power companies for impacts of climate change on their village, the Federal Court dismissed the lawsuit brought against twenty-four oil, energy, and utility companies by Inupiat Eskimos from Kivalina, Alaska. In dismissing the case for 'lack of subject matter jurisdiction', the Court held that the question of how best to address climate change was a political question and the plaintiffs could not demonstrate that the companies had caused them injury, and the appeal was also dismissed on the basis that a tort for public nuisance had been displaced by the Clean Air Act; petition for rehearing denied, and the Supreme Court denied the village's petition for a writ of *certiorari* without comment.

[202] Niran Somasundram, 'State Court Solutions: Finding Standing for Private Climate Change Plaintiffs in the Wake of Washington Environmental Council v Bellon' (2015) 42 Ecology LQ 1, under Article III of the US Constitution.

[203] Ganguly et al (n 133) at 848, citing *Massachusetts v Environmental Protection Agency (EPA)*, 549 US 497 (2007); US Supreme Court's decision in *Marbury v Madison*, 5 US (1 Cranch) 137; and *Baker v Carr*, 369 US 186.

[204] B Ekwurzel, J Boneham, M W Dalton, R Heede, R J Mera, M R Allen, and P C Frumhof, 'The Rise in Global Atmospheric CO_2, Surface Temperature, and Sea Level from Emissions Traced to Major Carbon Producers' (2017) 144(4) Climatic Change 579–90, <https://link.springer.com/article/10.1007/s10584-017-1978-0>.

[205] Ibid, s 2.2.

contributed approximately ('~')57 per cent of the observed rise in atmospheric CO_2, ~42–50 per cent of the rise in GMST, and ~26–32 per cent of global sea level ('GSL') rise over the historical period and ~43 per cent (atmospheric CO_2), ~29–35 per cent (GMST), and ~11–14 per cent (GSL) since 1980.[206] Ekwurzel et al write:

> A benefit of the simple climate model approach is the ability to explore the emissions traced to major carbon producers in a way that is consistent with major climate- and impact-relevant Earth processes. Since annual carbon emissions partition between the main carbon reservoirs—ocean, terrestrial, and atmosphere—a climate model can assess the fraction of CO_2 remaining in the atmosphere while keeping track of the CH_4 lifetime in the atmosphere and the resulting change in GMST.[207]
>
> ...
>
> The attribution of climate responsibility among non-state actors such as investor-owned fossil fuel companies might also take account of the timing by which companies should have reasonably been expected to respond to evidence of the climate risks of their products by, for example, investing in low carbon energy technologies, supporting climate policies and legislation, or communicating these risks with consumers and shareholders. Strikingly, more than half of all emissions traced to carbon producers over the 1880–2010 period were produced since 1986, the period in which the climate risks of fossil fuel combustion were well established. Consistent with this, our results show that bounding consideration of cumulative emissions to recent decades (1980–2010) only modestly reduces the global climate impact of major carbon producer-traced emissions with regard to global mean surface temperature. Global sea level rise response to climate forcing operates on slower times scales, so emissions from 1980 to 2010 have less of a relative contribution for GSL compared with GMST.
>
> ...
>
> To explore the potential climate responsibilities of non-state actors, it is of particular interest to understand the contribution of emissions traced to major carbon producers that are fully or partially investor-owned. Consider, for example, the contributions of emissions traced to the top 20 investor and majority state-owned companies to the increase in atmospheric CO_2. Emissions traced to the top 20 investor and majority state-owned companies from 1880 to 2010 contributed ~27.2 (±1.4)% of increase in atmospheric CO_2 over the historical period, using best estimate parameters and full historical forcing. Combustion of products from the top 20 companies from 1980 to 2010 contributed 19.6 (±0.6)% of the historical rise in atmospheric CO_2.[208]

These studies and others are providing evidence of both the timeframe and quantification of CO_2 emissions generated by the activities of major carbon emitters.

In *Pacific Coast Federation of Fishermen's Associations v Chevron Corp*, a private industry group seeks to hold thirty fossil fuel companies responsible for major losses

206 Ibid, s 1, based on best-estimate parameters and accounting for uncertainty arising from the lack of data on aerosol forcings traced to producers.

207 Ibid, s 1.

208 Ibid, s 3.1. References omitted.

suffered by crabbers in California and Oregon as a result of algae blooms attributed to global warming poisoning shellfish.[209] The plaintiff seeks an order that petroleum interests finance the changes needed to sustain the crab-fishing industry in the future. The plaintiff alleges that the companies have known for decades that use of their products could be 'catastrophic' and that 'only a narrow window existed' for action before consequences would be irreversible.[210] The plaintiff asserts that the companies took action to obscure the harms and avoid regulation, and that the companies' actions prevented the development of alternatives that could have eased the transition to a less fossil fuel-dependent economy.[211] The complaint contains five causes of action: nuisance, strict liability for failure to warn, strict liability for design defect, negligence, and negligent failure to warn. The plaintiff seeks compensatory damages, equitable relief including abatement of the nuisance, punitive damages, disgorgement of profits, and attorneys' fees and costs.[212] The case is pending.[213]

In the US, local governments and states have filed lawsuits against major fossil fuel companies, alleging that they have continued to produce fossil fuels while knowingly concealing the climate risks.[214] In 2018, the Federal District Court for the Northern District of California acknowledged that fossil fuels have led to global warming and sea level rise, but dismissed a lawsuit due to the legal challenges in establishing liability for climate change, a decision that is being appealed.[215]

There are numerous recent examples of litigation in which attribution science is being used to bring tort and nuisance claims against fossil fuel companies, claiming damages based on their specific contributions to harms.[216] In the past two years, cities and counties in more than ten US states have filed separate lawsuits against major fossil fuel companies, alleging that they continued to produce fossil fuels while knowingly concealing their clear scientific evidence of the harms being caused to the

209 *Pacific Coast Federation of Fishermen's Associations Inc v Chevron Corp*, CGC-18-571285, Complaint (Cal Super Ct) (14 November 2018), <http://blogs2.law.columbia.edu/climate-change-litigation/wp-content/uploads/sites/16/case-documents/2018/20181114_docket-CGC-18-571285_complaint.pdf>. See also *Pacific Coast Federation of Fishermen's Associations Inc v Chevron Corp*, Docket 3:18-cv-07477, <http://climatecasechart.com/case/pacific-coast-federation-of-fishermens-associations-inc-v-chevron-corp/>.

210 Ibid at paras 2, 103–7.

211 Ibid at paras 6–16, 149–62.

212 Ibid at paras 179–239. The defendants Chevron Corporation and Chevron USA, Inc filed a notice of removal to federal court in December 2018, and the Federal Court ordered that the case be reassigned to the San Francisco division for further proceedings; see *Pacific Coast Federation of Fishermen's Associations v Chevron Corp*, Docket 3:18-cv-07477, Notice of Removal (ND Cal) (12 December 2018), <http://blogs2.law.columbia.edu/climate-change-litigation/wp-content/uploads/sites/16/case-documents/2018/20181212_docket-318-cv-07477_notice.pdf>; *Pacific Coast Federation of Fishermen's Associations v Chevron Corp*, Docket 3:18-cv-07477, Order reassigning case (24 December 2018), <http://blogs2.law.columbia.edu/climate-change-litigation/wp-content/uploads/sites/16/case-documents/2018/20181224_docket-318-cv-07477_order.pdf>; Erik Larson, 'Exxon's Climate Trial is Over in New York. But the Legal War is Just Beginning', *Bloomberg News* (15 November 2019), <https://www.latimes.com/business/story/2019-11-15/exxons-climate-change-trial>.

213 Three cases are stayed pending the appeal in the City of Oakland case: *Pacific Coast Federation of Fishermen's Associations, Inc v Chevron Corp*, Docket 3:18-cv-7477 (ND Cal); *King County v BP PLC*, No 18-cv-758 (WD Wash); and *City and County of Honolulu v Sunoco LP*, No 20-cv-163 (D Haw).

214 'Global Trends 2019' (n 98) at 6.

215 Ibid at 8.

216 Janis Sarra, 'Bad Moon Rising: New Dawn Ahead? Climate Change and Solvency Risk' in J Corraini and B Nixon (eds), *Annual Review of Insolvency Law 2019* (Carswell, 2020) (hereafter Sarra, 'Bad Moon Rising').

climate. Complainants are seeking compensation for the portion of companies' GHG emissions that have caused climate change and resulting damages from sea level rise, flooding, and other catastrophes.[217] All of these lawsuits are still pending, a number are currently at the appellate court level in terms of legal challenges to dismiss or to remand to state or federal courts. While jurisdiction is an issue, a number of courts at first instance have accepted the growing climate science.

For example, in 2018, the US State of Rhode Island brought a lawsuit in state court seeking to hold twenty-one fossil fuel companies liable for causing climate change impacts that adversely affect Rhode Island and jeopardize state-owned or state-operated facilities, real property, and other assets.[218] The lawsuit asserts that the companies should be held liable for climate change impacts that the State has experienced and will experience in the future. Alleged harms include substantial sea level rise, more frequent and severe flooding, extreme precipitation events, and a warmer and more acidic ocean.[219] Rhode Island asserted that the defendants were directly responsible for 182.9 gigatonnes of CO_2 emissions between 1965 and 2015, representing 14.81 per cent of total emissions during that time period. The complaint alleges that the defendants' production, promotion, and marketing of fossil fuel products, along with their 'simultaneous concealment of the known hazards of these products, and their championing of anti-science campaigns' actually and proximately caused Rhode Island's injuries.

The complaint asserts claims of public nuisance, strict liability for failure to warn, strict liability for design defect, negligent design defect, negligent failure to warn, trespass, impairment of public trust resources, and violations of the State Environmental Rights Act. Rhode Island seeks compensatory damages, equitable relief including abatement of nuisances, punitive damages, disgorgement of profits, and attorneys' fees and costs. Rhode Island alleges that the defendants have known for nearly fifty years that their oil, gas, and coal products create GHG pollution that warms the oceans, changes the climate, and causes sea levels to rise; and that they were so certain of this conclusion that they took steps to protect their own assets from rising seas and more extreme storms.[220] Despite this knowledge, Rhode Island alleges that the companies engaged for decades in a co-ordinated, multifront effort to conceal and contradict their own knowledge, to discredit the growing body of publicly available science, and to persistently create doubt in the minds of customers, consumers, regulators, and the media, even though their own scientists warned in the 1970s that a narrowing window of time remained before hard decisions regarding changes in energy strategy might become critical.[221]

[217] See for example, *County of Marin v Chevron Corp*, CIV-1702586, Complaint (Cal Super Ct) (17 July 2017); *County of San Mateo v Chevron Corp*, 17-CIV-03222, Complaint (Cal Super Ct) (17 July 2017); and *Mayor & City Council of Baltimore v BP plc* (31 July 2019), <http://blogs2.law.columbia.edu/climate-change-litigation/wp-content/uploads/sites/16/case-documents/2019/20190731_docket-118-cv-02357_memorandum.pdf>.

[218] *Rhode Island v Chevron Corp*, PC-2018-4716, Complaint (RI Super Ct) (2 July 2018), <http://climatecasechart.com/case/rhode-island-v-chevron-corp/>.

[219] Ibid.

[220] Motion to remand to state court at 4, ibid.

[221] Ibid.

In July 2018, one of the defendants, Shell Oil Products Company LLC, sought removal of the action to federal court, arguing that Rhode Island's claims should be governed by federal common law since they 'implicate uniquely federal interests' such as nationwide economic development, international relations, and national security, and that federal law completely pre-empts Rhode Island's claims.[222] In *Rhode Island v Chevron Corp,* Chief Judge William Smith of the US District Court for the District of Rhode Island remanded Rhode Island's lawsuit.[223] Judge Smith noted that climate change is expensive, and the State wants help paying for it from the defendant companies that together extracted, advertised, and sold a substantial percentage of the fossil fuels burned globally since the 1960s, activity that released an immense amount of GHG into the Earth's atmosphere.[224] The State brought the action under law and equity to relieve the damage defendants have inflicted and will inflict on all the non-federal property and natural resources in Rhode Island.[225] Judge Smith wrote:

> [T]he defendants understood the consequences of their activity decades ago, when transitioning from fossil fuels to renewable sources of energy would have saved a world of trouble. But instead of sounding the alarm, Defendants went out of their way to becloud the emerging scientific consensus and further delay changes—however existentially necessary—that would in any way interfere with their multibillion-dollar profits.[226]

Judge Smith noted that two district courts recently held that a state's public-nuisance claim premised on the effects of climate change is governed by federal common law.[227] Judge Smith observed that the linchpin of a 'complete pre-emption' analysis is whether Congress intended that federal law provide the exclusive cause of action for the claims asserted by the plaintiff and held that environmental federal common law does not—absent congressional say-so—completely pre-empt the state's public nuisance claim, and therefore, provides no basis for removal to federal jurisdiction.[228] With respect to the Clean Air Act, the Court held that a 'statute that goes so far out of its way to preserve state prerogatives cannot be said to be an expression of Congress's 'extraordinary pre-emptive power' to convert state-law into federal-law claims.'[229] The Court held that the state's claims are thoroughly state-law claims, and the rights, duties, and rules of decision implicated by the complaint are all supplied by state law, without reference to anything federal.[230] The significance of the decision is that the Court recognized

[222] *Rhode Island v Chevron Corp,* No 1:18-cv-00395, Notice (DRI, 13 July 2018).

[223] *State of Rhode Island v Chevron Corp et al,* US District Court for the District of Rhode Island (22 July 2019), CA No 18-395 WES, <http://blogs2.law.columbia.edu/climate-change-litigation/wp-content/uploads/sites/16/case-documents/2019/20190722_docket-118-cv-00395_opinion-and-order.pdf> (hereafter Opinion and Order). Federal judges in Northern California and Baltimore has also ruled that these cases belong in state court.

[224] Opinion and Order, ibid at 1–2.

[225] Ibid at 2.

[226] Ibid.

[227] Ibid at 5, citing *California v BP PLC,* Nos. C 17-06011 WHA, C 17-06012 WHA, 2018 WL 1064293 at 2, (ND Cal 27 February 2018); and *City of New York v BP PLC,* 325 F Supp 3d 466, 471–2 (SDNY 2018).

[228] Ibid at 8–9.

[229] Ibid at 11.

[230] Ibid at 12.

that the defendants had known for years that their emissions were harmful to the climate and did not act, and that the Judge deftly addressed all of the alleged obstacles to the lawsuit proceeding that the companies claimed as a means of avoiding a hearing on the merits. The case is now before the Court of Appeals for the First Circuit.

To give the particulars of each of the thirteen recent lawsuits would require hundreds of pages of text. However, the grounds for the lawsuits brought by state, regional and local governments in the US are very similar to the Rhode Island lawsuit, discussed at length above. A partial list of the lawsuits follows, with a few highlights that distinguish them a bit from the Rhode Island lawsuit.

A lawsuit was commenced by King County in Washington State against the world's five largest investor-owned fossil fuel companies;[231] and three Colorado local government entities filed a lawsuit against fossil fuel companies seeking damages and other relief for the companies' role in causing climate change.[232] Three separate lawsuits by California counties and cities were filed in the California Superior Court seeking damages and other relief from fossil fuel companies for sea level rise.[233]

The City of Oakland and City of San Francisco have brought public nuisance actions against five oil and gas companies, asking the state court to fund their climate adaptation programme.[234] The cities allege that the energy companies' production and promotion of massive quantities of fossil fuels caused or contributed to global warming-induced sea level rise, leading to coastal flooding of low-lying shorelines, increased shoreline erosion, salt-water impacts on the cities' wastewater treatment systems, and interference with stormwater infrastructure, among other injuries.[235] The cities further allege that they are incurring significant costs to abate these harms and expect the injuries will become more severe over the next eighty years.[236] Accordingly,

[231] *King County v BP plc*, 18-2-11859, Complaint (Wash Super Ct) (9 May 2018), <http://climatecasechart.com/case/king-county-v-bp-plc/> (hereafter *King County v BP plc* Complaint). See also City of New York, Plaintiff v BP plc, Chevron Corp, ConocoPhillips, Exxon Mobil and Royal Dutch Shell PC, Opinion and Order of Judge John Keenan, No 18 Civ 182 (JFK), (19 July 2018) at 3, where he held that the City's claims were ultimately based on the transboundary emission of GHG and thus arise under federal common law and require a uniform standard of decision, <http://blogs2.law.columbia.edu/climate-change-litigation/wp-content/uploads/sites/16/case-documents/2018/20180719_docket-118-cv-00182_opinion-and-order-1.pdf>, in which the court accepted the motion to dismiss.

[232] *Board of County Commissioners of Boulder County v Suncor Energy (USA) Inc*, 2018-cv-030349, Complaint (Colo Dist Ct) (17 April 2018), <http://blogs2.law.columbia.edu/climate-change-litigation/wp-content/uploads/sites/16/case-documents/2018/20180417_docket-2018CV030349_complaint.pdf> (hereafter *Board of County Commissioners of Boulder County v Suncor Energy (USA) Inc*). The entities were: the City of Boulder and the Boards of County Commissioners of Boulder and San Miguel Counties. Docket Link: <http://climatecasechart.com/case/board-of-county-commissioners-of-boulder-county-v-suncor-energy-usa-inc/>.

[233] *City of Imperial Beach v Chevron Corp*, C17-01227, Complaint (Cal Super Ct) (17 July 2017); *County of Marin v Chevron Corp*, CIV-1702586, Complaint (Cal Super Ct, 17 July 2017); *County of San Mateo v Chevron Corp*, 17-CIV-03222, Complaint (Cal Super Ct) (17 July 2017). As of 31 July 2019, parties still exchanging submissions on the removal issue. Docket: <http://climatecasechart.com/case/county-san-mateo-v-chevron-corp/>, (hereafter California lawsuits).

[234] *People of State of California v BP plc (San Francisco)*, CGC-17-561370, Complaint (Cal Super Ct) (19 September 2017); *City of Oakland v BP plc*, RG-17875889, Complaint (Cal Super Ct) (19 September 2017). Docket: <http://climatecasechart.com/case/people-state-california-v-bp-plc-oakland/> (hereafter City of Oakland Claim).

[235] *City of Oakland v BP plc et al*, No 18-16663, Opinion, US Court of Appeals for the Ninth Circuit (26 May 2020) at 10.

[236] Ibid.

they are seeking an order of abatement requiring the companies to fund a 'climate change adaptation programme' for Oakland and San Francisco that would consist of building sea walls, raising the elevation of low-lying property and buildings, and building other infrastructure necessary for the cities to adapt to climate change.[237] The cities contend their injuries are caused by climate change that is the result of GHG emitted, and that the five fossil fuel companies, by producing fossil fuels and promoting their use, have broken the common law, and that production and promotion of fossil fuels constitutes a public nuisance such that courts may impose on this group of defendants the costs of remedying all the cities' alleged injuries.[238]

The District Court denied the plaintiffs cities' motion to remand, holding that the nuisance claims addressed national and international geophysical phenomenon of global warming and thus are governed by federal common law.[239] In May 2020, the US Court of Appeals for the Ninth Circuit vacated the decisions in California/City of Oakland, holding that the District Court erred in concluding that there was subject-matter jurisdiction supporting federal removal on the ground that the plaintiffs' state-law nuisance claims were necessarily governed by federal common law.[240] The Ninth Circuit remanded for the District Court to determine whether there was an alternative basis for jurisdiction.[241] The Ninth Circuit held that because neither exception to the 'well-pleaded complaint' rule applies to the cities' original complaints, the District Court erred in holding that it had jurisdiction at the time of removal.[242] The Ninth Circuit found that the cities' nuisance claim did not raise a substantial federal question.[243] The companies claimed that the nuisance claim implicated federal interests such as energy policy, national security, and foreign policy, but the Court held that it was not sufficient to establish federal question jurisdiction even though the question of whether the companies should be held liable and be compelled to abate harms was 'no doubt an important policy question'.[244] The Ninth Circuit also rejected the companies' argument that the Clean Air Act completely preempted the cities' public nuisance claim.[245] The Ninth Circuit concluded that dismissal for failure to state a claim at the pleading stage did not warrant departure from the general rule that a case must be fit for federal adjudication at the time of removal.[246] As this book goes to press, the companies are seeking a rehearing at the Court of Appeals.[247]

[237] Ibid.

[238] Ibid.

[239] *City of Oakland v BP*, District Court Fed R Civ P 12(b)(6).

[240] *City of Oakland v BP plc et al*, No 18-16663, Opinion, US Court of Appeals for the Ninth Circuit (26 May 2020).

[241] Ibid at 9.

[242] Ibid at 23.

[243] Ibid at 19.

[244] Ibid at 20.

[245] Ibid at 21–2. The Ninth Circuit rejected the companies' argument that the cities waived their arguments in favour of remand by amending their complaint to add a federal common law claim; the Ninth Circuit said the cities' reservation of rights was sufficient.

[246] Ibid at 24–5. The Ninth Circuit also rejected the companies' contention that improper removal could be excused based on 'considerations of finality, efficiency, and economy', ibid at 25.

[247] Petition for Rehearing (2020), <http://climatecasechart.com/case/people-state-california-v-bp-plc-oakland/>.

The City and County of Santa Cruz filed lawsuits in California Superior Court against 29 fossil fuel companies, alleging that GHG pollution from production and use of the defendants' products has played a direct and substantial role in the unprecedented rise in emissions of GHG pollution and increased atmospheric CO_2 concentrations, causing injuries to the City and County.[248]

A citizen lawsuit in *Conservation Law Foundation Inc v Shell Oil Products US*, alleges that the company failed to incorporate climate risks in its investment decisions, specifically, a bulk storage and fuel terminal in Rhode Island.[249]

The City of Baltimore's lawsuit in 2018 is representative of all these lawsuits. The City of Baltimore is seeking to hold twenty-six fossil fuel companies liable for injuries resulting from climate change.[250] Baltimore alleges that the defendants' production, promotion, and marketing of fossil fuel products—while at the same time concealing the products' known hazards and championing anti-science campaigns—directly and proximately caused adverse climate change impacts such as more frequent and severe storms and flooding in the city; and substantial increases in average sea level, as well as heatwaves, disruptions of the hydrologic cycle including extreme precipitation and associated public health impacts.[251] In June 2019, the Federal District Court for the District of Maryland remanded the City of Baltimore's climate change lawsuit against oil and gas companies to state court, concluding that federal question jurisdiction did not exist; and the defendants had not demonstrated that jurisdiction existed under the Outer Continental Shelf Lands Act, or that the claims were removable to federal jurisdiction.[252] In March 2020, the defendant companies filed a *certiorari* petition seeking review of the Fourth Circuit's affirmance of a remand order in the US Supreme Court and the City of Baltimore filed a brief arguing that the court should deny the oil and gas companies' petition for writ of *certiorari*.[253] The lawsuit is continuing.

[248] *City of Santa Cruz v Chevron Corp*, 17-cv-03243, Complaint (Cal Super Ct) (20 December 2017); *County of Santa Cruz v Chevron Corp*, 17-cv-03242, Complaint (Cal Super Ct) (20 December 2017). Docket: <http://climatecasechart.com/case/county-santa-cruz-v-chevron-corp/> (hereafter Santa Cruz Complaints). In July 2018, the Federal District Court for the Northern District of California granted motions by the County of Santa Cruz, City of Santa Cruz, and City of Richmond to remand to state court their lawsuits seeking to hold fossil fuel companies liable for climate change harms; Order Granting Motions to Remand, US District Court Northern District of California (10 July 2018), <http://blogs2.law.columbia.edu/climate-change-litigation/wp-content/uploads/sites/16/case-documents/2018/20180710_docket-518-cv-00450_order-1.pdf>.

[249] 'Global Trends 2020' (n 97) at 9.

[250] *Mayor & City Council of Baltimore v BP plc*, 24-C-18-004219, Complaint (Md Cir Ct) (20 July 2018), <http://climatecasechart.com/case/mayor-city-council-of-baltimore-v-bp-plc/>. Pleading available online at <http://blogs2.law.columbia.edu/climate-change-litigation/wp-content/uploads/sites/16/case-documents/2018/20180720_docket-24-C-18-004219_complaint.pdf>.

[251] Ibid at paras 1, 8, 52–68, 75–83, and 141–70.

[252] Ibid at paras 18–20. On 31 July 2019, the Federal District Court for the District of Maryland denied oil and gas companies' motion for a stay of the remand order returning the Mayor and City Council of Baltimore's climate change lawsuit to state court. See *Mayor & City Council of Baltimore v BP plc* (31 July 2019), <http://blogs2.law.columbia.edu/climate-change-litigation/wp-content/uploads/sites/16/case-documents/2019/20190731_docket-118-cv-02357_memorandum.pdf>.

[253] *BP plc v Mayor & City Council of Baltimore*, Brief filed by Mayor & City Council of Baltimore in opposition to petition for writ of *certiorari* (2020), <http://climatecasechart.com/case/mayor-city-council-of-baltimore-v-bp-plc/>; *BP plc v Mayor & City Council of Baltimore*, Order in Pending Case (22 October 2019), <http://blogs2.law.columbia.edu/climate-change-litigation/wp-content/uploads/sites/16/case-documents/2019/20191022_docket-19A368_order.pdf>.

The City of New York brought suit against five companies, alleging that they are collectively responsible, through their production, marketing, and sale of fossil fuels, for over 11 per cent of all the carbon and methane pollution from industrial sources that has accumulated in the atmosphere since the Industrial Revolution.[254] The defendants successfully brought a motion to dismiss the action on the grounds of federal jurisdiction.[255] The Federal District Court for the Southern District of New York held that federal common law governed the City's claims because the claims were ultimately based on the 'transboundary' emission of GHG emissions, and require a uniform standard of decision.[256] The Court further concluded that the Clean Air Act displaced any federal common law claims for nuisance and trespass; that control of interstate pollution is primarily a matter of federal law; Congress had expressly delegated to the Environmental Protection Agency the determination as to what constitutes a reasonable amount of GHG emissions under the Clean Air Act; and to litigate an action for injuries from foreign GHG emissions in federal court would severely infringe upon the foreign-policy decisions that are squarely within the purview of the political branches of the US government. In filing for appeal, New York City argued that long-established common law causes of action under New York law provides a means of reallocating the costs imposed by the companies' lawful economic activity.[257] Five *amicus* briefs were filed in support of New York City. The matter was argued in late 2019 before the Second Circuit Court of Appeals and judgment is still pending in as this book goes to press in 2020.[258] As with other cases in progress, the lawsuit seeks a remedy that recognizes the precise percentage contribution of each company from the harms caused by their conduct.[259]

The first ground in all these lawsuits is that of nuisance, specifically, that the companies' 'production and promotion of massive quantities of fossil fuels, and their promotion of those fossil fuels' pervasive use' created a public nuisance of 'global warming-induced sea level rise and other climate change hazards'.[260] The lawsuits allege that the companies individually and collectively have substantially contributed to global warming, while promoting the use of fossil fuels despite knowing 'for many years that global warming threatened severe and even catastrophic harms to coastal areas'.[261] The lawsuits allege that the fossil fuel companies' production, marketing,

[254] *City of New York v BP plc*, No 1:18-cv-00182, Complaint (SDNY) (9 January 2018). Docket: <http://climatecasechart.com/case/city-new-york-v-bp-plc/>.

[255] Ibid.

[256] *City of New York v BP plc, Chevron*, No 18 Civ 182 (JFK), opinion and order of US District Judge Keenan (19 July 2018).

[257] Ibid at 12.

[258] See <http://climatecasechart.com/case/city-new-york-v-bp-plc/>.

[259] For example, the City and County of Santa Cruz alleged that the defendants were directly responsible for 17.5 per cent of total global emissions of CO_2 between 1965 and 2015, and that during the past fifty years the defendants had taken steps to protect their own assets from climate change effects while simultaneously promoting use of their products and working to undermine support for GHG regulation; see Santa Cruz Complaints (n 249).

[260] See for example, *King County v BP plc* Complaint (n 232); and *King County v BP plc*, No 2:18-cv-00758, Notice (WD Wash, 25 May 2018); *Board of County Commissioners of Boulder County v Suncor Energy (USA) Inc* (n 233).

[261] See for example, *Board of County Commissioners of Boulder County v Suncor Energy (USA) Inc*, ibid; California lawsuits (n 233).

and use of fossil fuel products, while concealing the known hazards of those products, caused injuries to the plaintiffs, including more frequent and more severe flooding and sea level rise that has jeopardized infrastructure, beaches, schools, and communities. Their complaints include claims for public nuisance, strict liability for failure to warn, strict liability for design defect, private nuisance, negligence, negligent failure to warn, and trespass.[262] They document the hundreds of millions of dollars needed to build infrastructure to protect residents, seeking compensatory damages for the costs the municipalities and counties have already incurred.[263] The lawsuits seek compensatory damages, equitable relief, including abatement of the nuisance, punitive damages, and disgorgement of profits, as well as attorneys' fees and other costs.[264]

There have been many *amicus* briefs filed in all these lawsuits, by scientists, and by NGO such as the Center for Climate Integrity. The briefs submit that the defendant companies had information fifty years ago, from their own internal research, that the unabated extraction, production, promotion, and sale of their fossil fuel products would result in material dangers to the public.[265] The companies failed to disclose this information or take steps to protect the public, their internal documents revealing that they acted affirmatively to conceal their knowledge and discredit climate science through marketing campaigns in direct contradiction to their own research.[266] The briefs submit that during the 1970s and 1980s the defendants amassed considerable data on climate change, their own research and data confirming their earlier knowledge that continuing to expand fossil fuel use would lead to irreversible and catastrophic climate change, citing almost twenty internal reports and studies that were written or commissioned by the defendants.[267]

The fossil fuel companies have been using the same defensive strategies in all the pending cases, primarily seeking removal of the lawsuits to federal court, arguing federal jurisdiction, asserting that the claims implicate 'uniquely federal interests' and alleging that they are governed by federal common law or statutory law.[268] It is clear

[262] See for example, California Complaints, ibid; Santa Cruz Complaints (n 249).

[263] See for example, *King County v BP plc* Complaint (n 232).

[264] See for example, *City of Richmond v Chevron Corp,* C18-00055, Complaint (Cal Super Ct, 22 January 2018).

[265] See for example, *amicus* brief filed by Robert Brule, Center for Climate Integrity, Justin Farrell, Benjamin Franta, Stephan Lewandowsky, Naomi Oreskes, and Geoffrey Supran in support of appellees and affirmance (29 January 2019), <http://blogs2.law.columbia.edu/climate-change-litigation/wp-content/uploads/sites/16/case-documents/2019/20190129_docket-18-15499-18-15502-18-15503_amicus-brief.pdf>. See <http://climatecasechart.com/case/county-san-mateo-v-chevron-corp/> for copies of the other *amici* briefs.

[266] Ibid at 1–3. See also City of Oakland Claim (n 235).

[267] Ibid at 16.

[268] Including the Clean Air Act and Outer Continental Shelf Lands Act. See for example, *Mayor & City Council of Baltimore v BP plc,* No 1:18-cv-02357, Notice (D Md) (31 July 2018), <http://blogs2.law.columbia.edu/climate-change-litigation/wp-content/uploads/sites/16/case-documents/2018/20180731_docket-118-cv-02357_notice-1.pdf>; Motion to remand filed, <http://blogs2.law.columbia.edu/climate-change-litigation/wp-content/uploads/sites/16/case-documents/2018/20180911_docket-118-cv-02357_motion.pdf>; *Mayor & City Council of Baltimore v BP plc* (10 June 2019), <http://blogs2.law.columbia.edu/climate-change-litigation/wp-content/uploads/sites/16/case-documents/2019/20190610_docket-118-cv-02357_memorandum-opinion-1.pdf>. See also *City of Imperial Beach v Chevron Corp,* No 4:17-cv-04934, Notice (ND Cal) (24 August 2017); *County of Marin v Chevron Corp,* No 3:17-cv-04935, Notice (ND Cal) (24 August 2017); *County of San Mateo v Chevron Corp,* No 3:17-cv-04929-MEJ, Notice (ND Cal) (24 August 2017), <http://blogs2.law.columbia.edu/climate-change-litigation/wp-content/uploads/sites/16/case-documents/2019/20190717_docket-18-16663_order.pdf>; *City of Richmond v Chevron Corp* (n 265);

that their strategy is to litigate as long and hard as possible, creating procedural hurdles, perhaps hoping to deplete the resources of the plaintiffs. Every opinion or decision made by the courts is appealed, and there are often motions seeking extensions or delays. While none of these cases are finally resolved before this book is published, of note for climate governance is the scope and breadth of allegations against companies believed to have failed in effective climate governance. There is a clear message that investors, consumers, and the public intend to hold corporate directors and officers accountable for their actions or inaction in respect of climate change.

v. Actions against a Pension Board

In the Australian case of *McVeigh v Retail Employees Superannuation Trust*, Mark McVeigh—a twenty-four-year-old Australian pension fund member employed as an environmental scientist for a local authority—filed a lawsuit against the Retail Employees Superannuation Trust ('REST') in the Federal Court of Australia, alleging that the fund violated the Corporations Act 2001 by failing to provide information related to climate change business risks and any plans to address those risks.[269] REST has AUS $57 billion in assets under management.[270] Pursuant to the Corporations Act 2001, 'super fund' beneficiaries are entitled to request information that they need to make an informed decision about the management and financial condition of the fund.[271] The plaintiff requested information from REST regarding the knowledge of REST's climate change business risks; its opinion of climate change, the physical risks, the transition risks, and REST's climate change business risks; its actions responding to those risks; and its compliance with its obligations under the Corporations Act and other laws with respect to REST's climate change business risks.[272]

The pleadings argue that the board of directors ('trustee directors') have a duty to: exercise their powers and discharge their duties with care and diligence; exercise their powers and discharge their duties in good faith in the best interests of REST; act in the best interest of the beneficiaries; exercise due care, skill, and diligence in relation

City of Santa Cruz v Chevron Corp, No 5:18-cv-00458, Notice (ND Cal) (19 January 2018); and *County of Santa Cruz v Chevron Corp*, No 5:18-cv-00450, Notice (ND Cal) (19 January 2018), <http://blogs2.law.columbia.edu/climate-change-litigation/wp-content/uploads/sites/16/case-documents/2018/20180119_docket-518-cv-00450_notice-1.pdf>.

269 Notice of Filing, *Mark McVeigh v Retail Employees Superannuation Pty Ltd*, Federal Court of Australia, File No NSD1333/2018; see also *Mark McVeigh v Retail Employees Superannuation Pty Ltd*, NSD/1333, ACN 001-987-739 (2018), <http://climatecasechart.com/non-us-case/mcveigh-v-retail-employees-superannuation-trust/?cn-reloaded=1> (hereafter McVeigh Notice of Filing).

270 Bloomberg, 'A 24-year-old Is Suing Rest Super for Not Being Green Enough', *Bloomberg* (15 November 2019), <https://www.pionline.com/courts/24-year-old-suing-rest-super-not-being-green-enough>.

271 The McVeigh Notice of Filing (n 270) specifies: '3. At all material times REST was, and remains, bound by duties, including to: (a) act honestly in relation to all matters concerning REST: s 52A(2)(a) of the Superannuation Industry (Supervision) Act 1993 (Cth) (hereafter SISA); (b) exercise the requisite degree of care, skill and diligence on behalf of the beneficiaries: s 52(2)(b) SISA; (c) perform its duties and exercise its powers in the best interests of the beneficiaries: s 52(2)(c) SISA; (d) promote the financial interests of beneficiaries of REST MySuper: s 29VN(a) SISA.'

272 McVeigh Notice of Filing, ibid.

to all matters affecting the 'RSE REST'; exercise care and diligence to ensure that REST promotes the financial interests of REST MySuper beneficiaries; exercise care and diligence to ensure that REST carries out its legal duties to exercise the requisite degree of care, skill, and diligence in relation to ensuring compliance with the RSE licensing regime and the Superannuation Industry (Supervision) Act ('SISA') .[273] The pleadings argue that s 1017C of the Corporations Act requires REST to give to a REST member or a beneficiary, within a reasonable time, information requested by that person if the person reasonably required that information for the purposes of making an informed judgment about the management and financial condition of the superannuation entity and the relevant sub-plan.[274] The plaintiff alleges that at all material times, each of REST and the trustee directors knew, or ought to have known, about climate change business risks to the REST.[275] The plaintiff alleges that the information provided by REST did not fulfil its obligations, and he therefore seeks declaratory relief that REST violated the Corporations Act by failing to disclose the requested information. He seeks an injunction requiring REST to provide that information, and in the alternative, he seeks a declaration and injunction in equitable jurisdiction.

Subsequently, the applicant amended his case also to allege that the pension fund breached its duties as a trustee by not having a more developed climate change policy, alleging breaches of its duties as trustee and breaches of the SISA.[276] Trial on the merits is scheduled for November 2020.

While the lawsuit is still pending as this book goes to press, the Federal Court of Australia did render a judgment denying an application for a maximum costs order.[277] The Court acknowledged that the public interest nature of a suit is relevant to the issue of whether a maximum costs order should be made. The Court held that 'the case appears to raise a socially significant issue about the role of superannuation trusts and trustees in the current public controversy about climate change. It is legitimate to describe the applicant's litigation as being of a public interest nature.'[278] However, the Court concluded that it was not sufficiently informed about capacity to pay, at this stage, to make a maximum costs order.[279]

vi. Judgments Denying Licenses and Other Economic Activities Harmful to Climate Mitigation and Adaptation

There is also litigation associated with companies seeking licenses and permits to commence or expand operations, in some cases being denied because of climate-related risks. Recall the discussion in Chapter 6 in which a US federal judge held that a government agency failed to produce an environmental impact statement on a pipeline

[273] McVeigh Notice of Filing, ibid at 2, citing ss 180(1) and 181 of the Corporations Act; SISA (n 272), ss 52 and 52A(2).
[274] Ibid at 4.
[275] Ibid at 3.
[276] *McVeigh v Retail Employees Superannuation Pty Ltd* [2019] FCA 14 at para 7 (hereafter *McVeigh*).
[277] Ibid.
[278] Ibid at para 9.
[279] Ibid at para 17. The Court reserved on the issue of costs at this stage, ibid at para 20.

expansion and the owners of the Dakota Access Pipeline were ordered to halt operations while the government conducts a full analysis examining the risk the pipeline poses to the Standing Rock Sioux Tribe.[280] The Court concluded that the seriousness of the deficiencies in the assessment process outweighed the negative effects of halting the oil flow.[281]

The New Zealand Court of Appeal refused an application by Warkworth for extension of an open-cut coal mine, including mining in parts of the designated non-disturbance areas and habitat management.[282] The existing consent to operate the mine was subject to numerous conditions, including conservation of areas of native vegetation and landforms to the North, West, and South-West of the mine that were designated as non-disturbance areas and habitat management areas. The Court held that the expansion would likely have significant and unacceptable adverse impacts on biological diversity, including on four endangered ecological communities, and that these impacts were not able to be avoided, mitigated, or compensated.[283] The Court linked some of its reasons to evidence on the projected impacts of climate change.[284] Balancing significant adverse environmental and social impacts against the material economic benefits, the Court held that the company had not established that the expansion was justified on environmental, social, and economic grounds. The appeal was allowed and the expansion refused.[285]

In Australia, the Land and Environment Court of New South Wales in *Gloucester Resources Ltd v Minister for Planning* rejected an application for development consent for an open-cut coal mine in New South Wales, in part because 'construction and operation of the mine, and the transportation and combustion of the coal from the mine, will result in the emission of greenhouse gases, which will contribute to climate change'.[286] The Court held that 'the project will emit greenhouse gases and contribute to climate change, the consequences of which will burden future generations'.[287] It concluded that the environmental impact statement must address the content requirements in environmental regulation, including an assessment of the likely impact on the environment of the development, and the reasons justifying carrying out the development, having regard to biophysical, economic, and social considerations; the principles of ecologically sustainable development, such as the precautionary principle, intergenerational equity, conservation of biological diversity, and ecological

280 *Standing Rock Sioux Tribe et al v US Army Corps of Engineers and Dakota Access LLC*, (2020) Civil Action No 16-1534 US District Court for the District of Columbia.

281 Ibid.

282 *Bulga Milbrodale Progress Association Inc v Minister for Planning and Infrastructure and Warkworth Mining Ltd* [2013] NSWLEC 48, Land and Environment Court, New South Wales, (15 April 2013) at paras 3, 14, <https://www.caselaw.nsw.gov.au/decision/54a639943004de94513da836>.

283 Ibid at para 15.

284 Ibid at paras 127, 128, and 135.

285 Ibid at para 20. See also LSE, 'Summary: *Bulga Milbrodale*' (2019), <http://www.lse.ac.uk/GranthamInstitute/litigation/bulga-milbrodale-progress-association-inc-v-minister-for-planning-infrastructure-and-warkworth-mining-ltd-new-south-wales-land-and-environment-court-2013/>, citing *Bulga Milbrodale Progress Association Inc v Minister for Planning and Infrastructure and Warkworth Mining Ltd* [2013] NSWLEC 48, <https://www.caselaw.nsw.gov.au/decision/54a639943004de94513da836>.

286 *Gloucester Resources Ltd v Minister for Planning* [2019] NSWLEC 7.

287 Ibid at para 415.

integrity; and improved valuation, pricing, and incentive mechanisms.[288] The Court held that:

> The direct and indirect GHG emissions of the Rocky Hill Coal Project will contribute cumulatively to the global total GHG emissions. In aggregate, the Scope 1, 2 and 3 emissions over the life of the Project will be at least 37.8Mt CO_2-e, a sizeable individual source of GHG emissions. It matters not that this aggregate of the Project's GHG emissions may represent a small fraction of the global total of GHG emissions. The global problem of climate change needs to be addressed by multiple local actions to mitigate emissions by sources and remove GHGs by sinks.
>
> ...
>
> There is a causal link between the Project's cumulative GHG emissions and climate change and its consequences. The Project's cumulative GHG emissions will contribute to the global total of GHG concentrations in the atmosphere. The global total of GHG concentrations will affect the climate system and cause climate change impacts. The Project's cumulative GHG emissions are therefore likely to contribute to the future changes to the climate system and the impacts of climate change. In this way, the Project is likely to have indirect impacts on the environment, including the climate system, the oceanic and terrestrial environment, and people.
>
> The approval of the Project (which will be a new source of GHG emissions) is also likely to run counter to the actions that are required to achieve peaking of global GHG emissions as soon as possible and to undertake rapid reductions thereafter in order to achieve net zero emissions (a balance between anthropogenic emissions by sources and removals by sinks) in the second half of this century.
>
> ...
>
> I find that the negative impacts of the Project, including the planning impacts on the existing, approved and likely preferred land uses, the visual impacts, the amenity impacts of noise and dust that cause social impacts, other social impacts, and climate change impacts, outweigh the economic and other public benefits of the Project. Balancing all relevant matters, I find that the Project is contrary to the public interest and that the development application for the Project should be determined by refusal of consent to the application.[289]

Hutley and Hartford Davis note that this judgment is significant for its emphatic rejection of what is sometimes called the 'market substitution assumption', namely that GHG emissions relating to the project will occur regardless of whether it is approved or not because of market substitution and carbon leakage.[290]

In *Public Prosecutor's Office v H Carlos Schneider S/A Comércio e Indústria*, the Brazilian trial court granted a civil proceeding against a group responsible for draining and clearing a mangrove forest and placing a landfill and various structures in its place, the Court relying on the Forest Code of 1965 and Art 225 of the Federal Constitution

[288] Ibid at para 488.

[289] Ibid at paras 515, 524, 525, and 688.

[290] Noel Hutley SC and Sebastian Hartford Davis, 'Climate Change and Directors' Duties, Supplementary memorandum of Opinion' (26 March 2019), Australia Centre for Policy Development at 8.

of 1988.[291] Before ordering the defendants to restore the forest, the Court noted that mangroves serve a variety of ecological, social, and economic functions, and that sea level rise makes it especially important to preserve them. The trial court's decision was upheld by the Regional Federal Court of the Fourth Region and the Superior Court of Justice.[292]

In 2019, the Kenya National Environmental Tribunal set aside the issuance of a license by the National Environmental Management Authority to Amu Power Company for the construction of the Lamu coal-fired power plant, which would be the first coal-fired power plant in Kenya.[293] The Tribunal found that the company's environmental and social impact assessment was incomplete and in violation of the regulations.[294] Applying the precautionary principle, the Tribunal found a significant insufficiency of the assessment was the inadequate consideration of climate change.[295] The Tribunal ordered the company—if it should choose to pursue the project—to conduct a new study in compliance with the Environmental Impact Assessment and Audit Regulations. The Tribunal further instructed the company that the new study must include 'all approved and legible detailed architectural and engineering plans for the plant and its ancillary facilities such as the coal storage and handling facility and the ash pit with its location in relation to the sea shore; and consideration of the Climate Change Act 2016, the Energy Act 2019 and the Natural Resources (Classes of Transactions subject to Ratification) Act 2016'.[296] The Tribunal did observe in its reasons for judgment that a coal-fired power plant project will not necessarily always be rejected in Kenya, but the projects must meet the required standards of the law and abide by conditions imposed to mitigate potential impacts to remain an acceptable mode of power generation.[297]

In *Gbemre v Shell Petroleum Development Co of Nigeria Ltd et al*, the Federal Court of Nigeria ruled that oil companies must stop flaring gas in the Niger Delta.[298]

[291] LSE, 'Summary: *Schneider*' (2019), <http://www.lse.ac.uk/GranthamInstitute/litigation/public-prosecutors-office-v-h-carlos-schneider-sa-comercio-e-industria-others/>, citing *Public Prosecutor's Office v H Carlos Schneider S/A Comércio e Indústria* (2007) Superior Tribunal de Justiça (Brazil) Special Appeal No 650.728.

[292] Ibid.

[293] *Save Lamu et al v National Environmental Management Authority and Amu Power Co Ltd*, Republic of Kenya National Environmental Tribunal, Appeal No Net 196 of 2016, judgment (26 June 2019), <http://blogs2.law.columbia.edu/climate-change-litigation/wp-content/uploads/sites/16/non-us-case-documents/2019/20190626_Tribunal-Appeal-No.-Net-196-of-2016_decision.pdf> (hereafter Lamu Tribunal decision). See also LSE, 'Summary: *Save Lamu*' (2019), <http://www.lse.ac.uk/GranthamInstitute/litigation/save-lamu-et-al-v-national-environmental-management-authority-and-amu-power-co-ltd/>, citing *Save Lamu et al v National Environmental Management Authority and Amu Power Co Ltd*, Tribunal Appeal No 196 (2016) (hereafter LSE, Lamu).

[294] LSE, Lamu, ibid the Tribunal finding that the National Environmental Management Authority violated the Environmental Impact Assessment and Audit Regulations by granting an Environmental Impact Assessment License without proper and meaningful public participation in the process.

[295] Lamu Tribunal decision (n 294) at paras 138 and 139.

[296] Ibid at para 155. The Amu Power Company had thirty days to appeal the decision.

[297] Ibid at para 17.

[298] *Gbemre v Shell Petroleum Development Co of Nigeria Ltd et al* (Federal Court of Nigeria, 2005) (2005) AHRLR 151 (NgHC 2005), <https://www.globalhealthrights.org/wp-content/uploads/2013/02/HC-2005-Gbemre-v.-Shell-Petroleum-Development-Company-and-Ors.pdf> (hereafter *Gbemre v Shell*). For a summary, see LSE, 'Summary: *Gbemre*' (2019), <http://www.lse.ac.uk/GranthamInstitute/litigation/gbemre-v-shell-petroleum-development-company-of-nigeria-ltd-et-al-federal-court-of-nigeria-2005/>.

Jonah Gbemre—representative plaintiff for the lwherekan community in the Niger Delta—filed the suit against both Shell and the Nigerian government. The Federal Court held that the company's practice of gas flaring in the course of its oil exploration and production activities was unconstitutional as it violates the guaranteed fundamental rights of life and dignity of human persons provided by ss 33 and 34 of the Constitution of the Federal Republic of Nigeria and the African Charter on Human and Peoples Rights.[299] The Court held that fundamental rights to life and dignity include the right to a clean, healthy, poison-free, and pollution-free environment.[300] It also held that failure of the company to carry out environmental impact assessment in the applicants' community concerning the effects of its gas flaring activities was a clear violation of the Environmental Impact Assessment Act, which contributed to a further violation of these fundamental rights.[301] The Court ordered the respondents to take immediate steps to stop the further flaring of gas in the community.[302]

The UK Court of Appeal in *Plan B Earth v Secretary of State for Transport* held that the government needed to consider its own policy commitments on climate change under the Paris Agreement in its policy framework for the expansion of Heathrow Airport, concluding that its failure to undertake such an analysis rendered the process invalid. Thus, the Court rejected expansion of the airport, finding the policy framework for the expansion had to be redone.[303] The Court held that the UK's Airports National Policy Statement must 'include an explanation of how the policy set out in the statement takes account of Government policy relating to the mitigation of, and adaptation to, climate change'.[304]

These and many other lawsuits reveal that stakeholders are willing to use a variety of claims under statutes, licensing processes, common law, and civil codes to challenge the decisions of corporations to exploit resources in a manner that exacerbates climate change. The courts are increasingly willing to consider climate impact and government commitments to the Paris Agreement as reasons to decline the approval of projects or to order government authorities and project proponents to undertake much more extensive environmental assessment before the court is willing to consider approval of licenses or projects.

vii. Consumer Protection Litigation against Companies

Another possible source of litigation are the consumer protection statutes in place in some countries. While not a claim for breach of fiduciary obligation, they may be a tool to hold companies accountable for failing to adequately disclose risks associated with climate change. If a consumer product being sold by a corporation carries a risk of negative impact on the environment, class action litigation risk associated with such

299 *Gbemre v Shell* (n 299) at para 5.
300 Ibid.
301 Ibid.
302 Ibid at para 6.
303 *Plan B Earth v Secretary of State for Transport* [2020] EWCA Civ 214 at paras 23–28.
304 Ibid at para 38.

matters should prompt directors and officers to diligently investigate their company's compliance and marketing practices.

In *Australian Competition & Consumer Commission v Prime Carbon Pty (2010)*, the Australian Federal Court ruled that a company, Prime Carbon Pty Ltd, had misrepresented its services and affiliations, violating s 53 of the Trade Practices Act 1974.[305] Prime Carbon Pty sold carbon credits and was found guilty of falsely claiming that it was certified by the National Stock Exchange of Australia and that the National Environment Registry, a company through which Prime Carbon supplied some of its credits, was regulated by the Australian government. Prime Carbon Pty was ordered to publicize the court's orders to its customers and the sole director of the company was ordered to undertake a course of compliance training.[306]

The Federal Court of Australia granted a lawsuit against a corporation, GM Holden Ltd, for false green advertising that Saab vehicles provided carbon-neutral motoring.[307] GM Holden had claimed that Saab would plant seventeen native trees for every Saab vehicle purchased to offset the carbon emissions. The Australian Competition and Consumer Commission filed its claim on the basis that GM Holden had not shown any change in the way it manufactured Saab vehicles subsequent to its carbon neutral campaign and that GM Holden's claim regarding the planting of seventeen native trees in an attempt to offset the carbon emissions was not proven and misleading.[308] The Federal Court declared that GM Holden had breached ss 52 and 53(c) of the Trade Practices Act 1974. GM Holden agreed to advise its marketing staff to avoid misleading and deceptive marketing tactics and to plant 12,500 native trees to offset all the carbon emissions that would occur by Saab vehicles sold during the marketing campaign.[309]

See also *Australian Competition & Consumer Commission v Goodyear Tyres*, in which the Federal Court of Australia held that Goodyear Tyres was falsely labelling its LS200 tyres as 'environmentally-friendly' because its production process emitted less CO_2 and its new BioTRED technology increased the life of the tyre and improved fuel economy. The Australian Competition and Consumer Commission charged that Goodyear Tyres was misleading consumers about the environmental benefits of its tyres, thereby breaching ss 52 and 53(c) of the Trade Practices Act 1974. Goodyear Tyres gave a court-enforceable undertaking that it would halt its false advertising and partially refund all customers who had relied on the representations over a specified two-year period.[310]

305 LSE, 'Summary: *Prime Carbon Pty*' (2019), <http://www.lse.ac.uk/GranthamInstitute/litigation/australian-competition-consumer-commission-v-prime-carbon-pty-ltd-federal-court-of-australia-2010/>.

306 Ibid.

307 *Australian Competition and Consumer Commission v GM Holden Ltd* [2008] FCA 1428, cited in <http://www.lse.ac.uk/GranthamInstitute/litigation/australian-competition-consumer-commission-v-gm-holden-ltd-federal-court-of-australia-2008/>.

308 LSE, 'Summary: *GM Holden*' (2019), <http://www.lse.ac.uk/GranthamInstitute/litigation/australian-competition-consumer-commission-v-gm-holden-ltd-federal-court-of-australia-2008/>, citing *Australian Competition and Consumer Commission v GM Holden Ltd* ibid.

309 Ibid.

310 LSE, 'Summary: *Goodyear Tyres*' (2019), <http://www.lse.ac.uk/GranthamInstitute/litigation/australian-competition-consumer-commission-v-goodyear-tyres-2008/>, referencing Australian Competition and Consumer Commission ('ACCC'), 'Goodyear Tyres Apologizes, Offers Compensation for Unsubstantiated Environmental Claims' (26 June 2008), Media Release No 181/08, <https://www.accc.gov.

In 2017, a Canadian class-action lawsuit against Volkswagen for cheating on its emissions testing received Ontario court approval of a Cdn $2.1 billion settlement plan for the 105,000 purchasers and individuals that leased certain Volkswagen or Audi vehicles in Canada.[311] Similarly, in 2017, two class proceeding were commenced against Mercedes-Benz Canada Inc, Daimler AG, and other defendants, alleging that Mercedes BlueTEC vehicles were non-compliant with Canadian emissions laws: both in emitting significantly higher levels of pollutants than are permissible and emitting toxic chemicals at much higher levels when the temperature drops below 10°C.[312] In both cases, companies are alleged to have sold cars as being 'clean and green', when in fact their emissions fell far below legal standards. Canadian consumer protection legislation allows for class members to rescind their contracts and receive a full refund when there has been misrepresentation during sale of a product.[313] The lawsuit is pending as this book goes to print.

One NGO, Beyond Pesticides, filed a lawsuit against Exxon with the Washington DC Superior Court in May 2020 for alleged violations of the US Consumer Protection Act. It alleges that Exxon's disclosure is 'greenwashing', claiming that Exxon is using false and deceptive marketing representing that it engages in and has invested significantly in the production and use of 'clean' energy and environmentally beneficial technology.[314] It is seeking a jury trial.

Consumer misrepresentation class actions provide another tool to hold corporations accountable when the misrepresentations by their officers lead to negative environmental consequences and reduced utility of the product purchased by consumers. Directors and officers have a duty to diligently investigate their company's business and marketing practices to avoid the litigation risk of such massive consumer fraud/misrepresentation cases.

Ganguly et al have examined the future prospects of private climate litigation.[315] They suggest that because climate change litigation takes place in a rapidly evolving scientific, discursive, and constitutional context, it will generate new opportunities for judges to rethink the interpretation of existing legal and evidentiary requirements and apply them in a way that will enhance the accountability of major private carbon

au/media-release/goodyear-tyres-apologises-offers-compensation-for-unsubstantiated-environmental-claims>. See also LSE, 'Summary: *V8 Supercars*' (2019), <http://www.lse.ac.uk/GranthamInstitute/litigation/australian-competition-consumer-commission-v-v8-supercars-australia-pty-ltd-2008/>, referencing ACCC, 'V8 Supercars Corrects Carbon Emissions Claims' (18 September 2008), Media Release No 265/08, <https://www.accc.gov.au/media-release/v8-supercars-corrects-carbon-emissions-claims> concerning misrepresentation regarding offsetting carbon by planting native trees.

311 Aleksandra Sagan, 'Volkswagen Emissions Lawsuit in Canada Reaches $2.1B Settlement', *Toronto Star Newspaper* (27 April 2017), <https://www.thestar.com/business/2017/04/27/volkswagen-emissions-lawsuit-in-canada-reaches-21b-settlement.html>.

312 Koskie Minsky LLP, 'Mercedes BlueTEC Class Action' (2017), <https://kmlaw.ca/cases/mercedes-bluetec-class-action/>.

313 Furthermore, the legislation does not require any reliance on the misrepresentation, or causation in the traditional sense, meaning it is very easy to prosecute these claims on a class-wide basis, ibid.

314 *Beyond Pesticides v Exxon Mobil Corp Beyond Pesticides v Exxon Mobil Corp*, Complaint filed with the Superior Court of the District of Columbia Civil Division (March 2020) at 1, <http://blogs2.law.columbia.edu/climate-change-litigation/wp-content/uploads/sites/16/case-documents/2020/20200515_docket-2020-CA-002532-B_complaint.pdf>.

315 Ganguly et al (n 133) at 841–86.

producers. They also observe that even unsuccessful cases can contribute to articulating climate change as a legal and financial risk, which may help to guide climate change-responsive adjudication in the longer term.[316] They suggest that a renewed effort to litigate climate change after failures in the early 2000s relates to the notion that corporations are the appropriate parties to bear responsibility for climate change, and the potential effectiveness of targeted private climate litigation means that successful action against a relatively small group of corporations responsible for a substantial percentage of emissions could generate a considerable global impact.[317]

One issue that is at a nascent stage is the risk of climate-related lawsuits that allege human rights violations or racism in respect of companies' carbon emitting activities. Observations have been made throughout the book regarding the disproportionate impacts of climate change on racialized people in all countries. It is likely that companies that continue to generate emissions will be subject to lawsuits that link their carbon activities to violations of human rights. Thus, an effective governance strategy is to embed considerations of race and gender into climate action plans, including how the company is going to decarbonize in a manner that also addresses systemic discrimination and the impacts of the company' activities on the communities in which it operates.

This chapter illustrates the range of engagement strategies that stakeholders are using to encourage or press companies to decarbonize in an effort to move to net zero. Some have been effective but others are at a nascent stage. In combination, they have tremendous potential. It is also evident from the discussion above that litigation risk is real and presents a material risk to carbon-intensive companies, as there is potential for sizeable monetary damages if lawsuits succeed. Even where companies are successful in defending lawsuits, the resources necessary to defend litigation are costly and companies face growing reputational damage. All of which reinforces the important point that directors and company officers need to act now to address climate change, rather than wait for future litigation. The next chapter turns to the more positive issue of sustainable finance and the move to a circular economy.

[316] Ibid at 842.

[317] Ibid at 844. See also Shi-Ling Hsu, 'A Realistic Evaluation of Climate Change Litigation through the Lens of a Hypothetical Lawsuit' (2008) 79 U Colo L Rev 13; and Jutta Brunnée et al, *Climate Change Liability: Transnational Law and Practice* (CUP, 2012) at 29.

8
Sustainable Finance and the Move to a Circular Economy

In order to truly move to net zero carbon and a circular economy, there needs to be a serious scaling-up of sustainable finance. A massive amount of capital needs to be redirected immediately towards climate mitigation and adaptation, including investment in efficient energy technologies, rapid expansion of natural carbon sinks, and massive reduction of waste. Governments in the European Union ('EU'), United Kingdom ('UK'), China, and other countries have started to commit to moving to a circular economy, in which every aspect of economic activity is being revamped to reduce carbon emissions, to utilize renewable energy, to design building codes and retrofit buildings to be energy efficient and carbon neutral, to develop new transport and production technologies, and to use goods and services for as long as possible and then reduce waste by redeploying and reusing materials in different capacities.

Sustainable finance includes a range of investments by both private and public entities through a variety of debt and equity finance, policies, and products to advance these objectives. Both governments and the private sector need to act with some urgency to scale-up net zero carbon technological innovation and move in a meaningful way towards renewable energy sources and a serious reduction in greenhouse gas ('GHG') emissions in all sectors. Financing that transition is an essential requirement for this strategy. Even better would be a climate positive carbon economy that would begin to slowly reverse the negative effects of climate change discussed throughout this book.

We have made a start. Since 2012, investments in renewable energy capacity have exceeded investments in fossil fuel generation, with 2018 being the eighth year in a row that global investment in renewables exceeded US $200 billion annually.[1] Yet to date, it is not enough, and not fast enough.

Equally important is the need to begin to transform our economies, our businesses, and our personal lifestyles into a circular economy. A circular economy is one in which we eliminate waste through the superior design of materials, products, systems, and business models.[2] The United Nations ('UN') observes that the circular economy means minimizing waste and maximizing the use of natural resources, the antithesis of the traditional, linear economy, in which we extract great quantities of

[1] Frankfurt School-United Nations Environmental Programme Centre and Bloomberg New Energy Finance, *Global Trends in Renewable Energy Investment 2018* (2018) (hereafter *Global Trends*).

[2] World Economic Forum ('WEF'), 'From Linear to Circular: Accelerating a Proven Concept' (2019), <http://reports.weforum.org/toward-the-circular-economy-accelerating-the-scale-up-across-global-supply-chains/from-linear-to-circular-accelerating-a-proven-concept/> (hereafter WEF, 'Circular'). The report citing W McDonough and M Braungart, *Cradle to Cradle: Remaking the Way We Make Things*, (North Point Press, 2002).

From Ideas to Action. *Janis Sarra*, Oxford University Press (2020). © Janis Sarra. DOI: 10.1093/oso/9780198852308.003.0008.

natural resources to make products that we often just use once, only to discard them to landfill.[3] It means that decisions need to take account of how we protect biodiversity, how we enhance natural carbon sinks, and how we share the benefits of transition to peoples and communities that are currently suffering disproportionate harms from the impacts of global warming. The move towards a circular economy requires a meaningful shift towards elimination of use of toxic chemicals that impair reuse and return to the biosphere, focusing on development of products that can be restored or generated into new products instead of being relegated to waste disposal. The successful achievement of a circular economy requires efforts at every level of business and society. Finance has a pivotal role in that transition.

The World Economic Forum reports that the circular economy is based on a few simple principles:

> First, at its core, a circular economy aims to design out waste. Waste does not exist: products are designed and optimized for a cycle of disassembly and reuse. These tight component and product cycles define the circular economy and set it apart from disposal and even recycling, where large amounts of embedded energy and labour are lost.
>
> Second, circularity introduces a strict differentiation between consumable and durable components of a product. Unlike today, consumables in the circular economy are largely made of biological ingredients or 'nutrients' that are at least non-toxic and possibly even beneficial, and can safely be returned to the biosphere, either directly or in a cascade of consecutive uses. Durables such as engines or computers, on the other hand, are made of technical nutrients unsuitable for the biosphere, such as metals and most plastics. These are designed from the start for reuse, and products subject to rapid technological advance are designed for upgrade.
>
> Third, the energy required to fuel this cycle should be renewable by nature, again to decrease resource dependence and increase systems resilience (to oil shocks, for example).[4]

The World Economic Forum reports that resource extraction and processing cause over 90 per cent of global biodiversity loss and water stress.[5] From 1970 to 2017, annual global extraction of materials grew from 27 billion tonnes to 92 billion tonnes, the main driver being consumption patterns, not population growth.[6] About 20 per cent of GHG emissions are caused by the extraction and processing of metals and non-metallic minerals alone, and these emissions plus plastics can only partially be abated by energy technology solutions.[7] Without a serious shift in resource use, it is estimated

[3] UN Department of Economic and Social Affairs, '"Waste not, want not" – European Union goes circular' (17 June 2019), <https://www.un.org/development/desa/en/news/sustainable/good-practice-circular-economy.html>.

[4] WEF, 'Circular' (n 2) at 2.

[5] World Economic Forum, *The Next Frontier: Natural Resource Targets Shaping a Competitive Circular Economy within Planetary Boundaries* (WEC, 2019) at 6, <http://www3.weforum.org/docs/WEF_The_Next_Frontier_Natural_Resource_Targets_Report.pdf> (hereafter WEF, *Next Frontier*).

[6] Ibid at 8.

[7] Ibid at 8.

to more than double from current levels to 190 billion tonnes by 2060, exceeding planetary boundaries.[8] The World Economic Forum advocates decoupling growth from resource use and effects on the environment, based on a strategy that accounts for and completely rethinks the role of natural resources in the design and use of products and practices.[9]

Such a shift would benefit the global economy, individual sectors, companies, and if accomplished in an equitable manner, society more generally. The International Resource Panel has shown through modelling that strong resource productivity policies, combined with climate change policies, could reduce global extraction by up to 25 per cent, decrease global GHG emissions by 90 per cent and increase global gross domestic product ('GDP') by 8 per cent, as compared with a historical trends scenario, from 2030 to 2060.[10]

Thus, the link between transitioning to net zero carbon and the circular economy is clear. Not only are technologies needed to radically reduce carbon emissions such that total emissions are net zero and shortly thereafter, climate positive, but we need to fundamentally rethink how we produce, reuse, and redeploy goods in our society.

I. Scaling-Up Sustainable Finance

There are two ways to look at financing the transition to a circular economy and net zero carbon world. The first is to view the huge transition costs as a barrier to economic stability. The second is to consider the challenges as opportunities, not just for financing climate mitigation and adaptation, but to really transition global economies towards a path of sustainability, more equitable distribution of income, and decision-making that accounts for a broader set of interests than just capital investors. I advocate this latter view. While these goals are highly aspirational, they can serve as principles that guide how capital is directed. Just as the discussion on corporate governance in Chapter 4 considered the notion of fairness and equity, these principles can inform decisions regarding public and private financing of the transition to a net zero economy. Fairness can inform how we link strategies to reduce emissions with efforts to design, deploy, and redeploy materials used in every sector.

There are a number of definitions of sustainable finance. Canada's Expert Panel on Sustainable Finance defines it as capital flows, as reflected in lending and investment, risk management activities such as insurance and risk assessment, and financial processes, including valuation, disclosure, and oversight, which 'assimilate environmental and social factors as a means of promoting sustainable economic growth and the long term stability of the financial system. The conditions for sustainable economic growth are to meet the needs of the present without compromising the future.'[11]

[8] Ibid at 6.

[9] Ibid at 9, citing United Nations Environment Programme ('UNEP'), 'Assessing Global Resource Use: A Systems Approach to Resource Efficiency and Pollution Reduction' (UNEP, 2017) (hereafter 'Systems Approach').

[10] Ibid at 9, citing 'Systems Approach', ibid.

[11] Canada Expert Panel on Sustainable Finance, *Interim Report*, (October 2018) at 3, <http://publications.gc.ca/collections/collection_2018/eccc/En4-350-1-2018-eng.pdf>.

A key component of moving to a net zero carbon circular economy is to undertake strong concurrent efforts to scale-up sustainable finance. Just as climate change is a challenge that requires global co-operation, so too, the 'greening of finance' requires a coordinated effort to develop financial products and financing infrastructure that makes sustainable finance the norm, not the innovative outlier. Objectives include mitigation, adaptation, a shift to natural components for production where possible, and the development of products that can be repurposed and reused, thus lowering the emissions generated by single-use plastics and other products. There is particular need for transition financing to support development of innovative technologies to effect the transition, and then financing to scale them up for domestic and international markets.

Estimates vary as to the amount of infrastructure investment that is required. The Organization for Economic Co-operation and Development ('OECD') reports that US $6.9 trillion investment is needed annually until 2030 to meet country climate commitments.[12] The International Energy Agency ('IEA') estimates that the low carbon transition could require US $3.5 trillion in energy sector investments every year for decades—twice the rate at present. It reports that, in order for carbon to stabilize by 2050, nearly 95 per cent of electricity supply will need to be low carbon, 70 per cent of new cars electric, and the carbon dioxide ('CO_2') intensity of the building sector will need to fall by 80 per cent.[13] As countries advance towards their climate goals and new technologies emerge, estimates will require updating.

The Intergovernmental Panel on Climate Change ('IPCC') estimates that, in addition to climate-friendly allocation of public investments, a potential redirection of 5 to 10 per cent of the annual capital revenues is necessary for limiting warming to 1.5°C, roughly 2.5 per cent of world GDP for energy transition alone, and there need to be new incentives for consumption and redirection of investment to long term productive low emission assets and services.[14] The IPCC advocates a 'whole systems' approach, which means that all relevant companies, industries, and stakeholders need to be involved in wide deployment of low emission technology such as renewable energy projects, and bio-based chemical plants need to become large scale. The IPCC observes that it requires the capacity to mobilize investment and generate employment opportunities, recognizing that this transition is highly dependent on social and

[12] OECD, *Developing Robust Pipelines for Low-Carbon Infrastructure* (OECD Publishing, 2018) at 3, <http://www.oecd.org/publications/developing-robust-project-pipelines-for-low-carbon-infrastructure-9789264307827-en.htm>.

[13] International Energy Agency, 'Deep Energy Transformation Needed by 2050 to Limit Rise in Global Temperature' (20 March 2017), <https://www.iea.org/newsroom/news/2017/march/deep-energy-transformation-needed-by-2050-to-limit-rise-in-global-temperature.html> (hereafter IEA).

[14] IPCC, H de Coninck, A Revi, M Babiker, P Bertoldi, M Buckeridge, A Cartwright, W Dong, J Ford, S Fuss, J C Hourcade, D Ley, R Mechler, P Newman, A Revokatova, S Schultz, L Steg, and T Sugiyama, 'Chapter 4 Strengthening and Implementing the Global Response' (hereafter IPCC, 'Global Response 2018'), in V Masson-Delmotte, P Zhai, H O Pörtner, D Roberts, J Skea, P R Shukla, A Pirani, W Moufouma-Okia, C Péan, R Pidcock, S Connors, J B Matthews, Y Chen, X Zhou, M I Gomis, E Lonnoy, T Maycock, M Tignor, and T Waterfield (eds), *Global Warming of 1.5°C: An IPCC Special Report on the Impacts of Global Warming of 1.5°C above Pre-industrial Levels and Related Global Greenhouse Gas Emission Pathways, in the Context of Strengthening the Global Response to the Threat of Climate Change, Sustainable Development, and Efforts to Eradicate Poverty* (IPCC, 2019) at 317, <https://www.ipcc.ch/site/assets/uploads/sites/2/2019/05/SR15_Chapter4_Low_Res.pdf>

cultural conditions such as awareness and acceptability of the move to a net zero and circular economy and institutional and political support.[15] While some transition is underway, the IPCC reports that we require a rapid escalation in the scale and pace of transition, particularly in the next 10 to 20 years. It observes that pathways limiting global warming to 1.5°C require rapid and far-reaching transitions in energy, land, urban infrastructure, and industrial systems, unprecedented in terms of scale.[16]

The European Commission has estimated that investments of €520 billion to €575 billion annually are needed to achieve a net zero carbon circular economy, about 2.8 per cent of GDP; and, in the EU alone, an additional €175 billion to €290 billion a year is required.[17] All of these estimates indicate that there is pressing need for mainstreaming of climate finance within financial system regulation and market practice.[18]

The economic and technical feasibility of solar energy, wind energy, and electricity storage technologies has improved dramatically over the past few years, while CO_2 capture and storage in the electricity sector has not yet shown similar improvements.[19] The IPCC notes that electrification, bio-based feedstocks and substitution, and, in several cases, CO_2 capture, utilization, and storage, could lead to emissions reductions required in energy-intensive industries, but that these options are limited by institutional, economic, and technical constraints, with attendant financial risks to many incumbent firms.[20] A mix of mitigation and adaptation measures, adopted in a participatory and integrated manner, could enable rapid, systemic transition, but such transition requires co-operation of national, regional, and local governments.[21]

Former Bank of England Governor Carney has discussed the tremendous opportunities for sustainable finance, pointing to an estimated US $90 trillion of infrastructure investment expected between 2015 and 2030, with growing market demand for large companies to take environmental, social, and governance ('ESG') factors more seriously.[22] Carney and others suggest that millennials, keenly focused on company values and sustainability, are set to inherit US $24 trillion of wealth in the United States ('US') alone over the next fifteen years and will seek the investment opportunities to match.[23]

[15] IPCC, 'Frequently Asked Questions' (March 2019), <https://www.ipcc.ch/site/assets/uploads/sites/2/2018/12/SR15_FAQ_Low_Res.pdf>.

[16] Ibid at 16.

[17] European Commission, 'A Clean Planet for All, A European Strategic Long-Term Vision for a Prosperous, Modern, Competitive and Climate Neutral Economy' COM/2018/773 final (28 November 2018) (Communication from the Commission to the European Parliament, the European Council, the European Economic and Social Committee, the Committee of the Regions and the European Investment Bank) at 16, <https://ec.europa.eu/clima/policies/strategies/2050_en> (hereafter EC, *Clean Planet*).

[18] IPCC, 'Global Response 2018' (n 14) at 317.

[19] Ibid at 315.

[20] Ibid.

[21] Ibid at 316.

[22] Mark Carney, 'A New Horizon', European Commission Conference: A global approach to sustainable finance (21 March 2019) (hereafter Carney, 'New Horizon').

[23] Ibid at 10, citing Deloitte, 'The Future of Wealth in the United States Mapping trends in Generational Wealth' (2016), <https://www2.deloitte.com/content/dam/insights/us/articles/us-generational-wealth-trends/DUP_1371_Future-wealth-in-America_MASTER.pdf>.

A number of countries lag in developing a commitment to seriously scaling-up sustainable finance, viewing such finance as optional instead of core to the financial system. The Taskforce on Climate-related Financial Disclosures ('TCFD') noted that opportunities relating to climate resilience are particularly important for companies with long-lived fixed assets or extensive supply or distribution networks, and those companies that depend critically on utility and infrastructure networks or natural resources in their value chain.[24]

In contrast, some countries and economic regions have identified essential components to scaling-up sustainable finance to mainstream status, notably the EU, the UK, France, and China. Specifically, they are working to ensure decision-useful climate information, including a taxonomy of terms, so that investors, businesses, and regulators globally can compare products and services and commit funding to move to net zero.

In 2018, the UK government published its Clean Growth Strategy, setting out a blueprint for the UK's low carbon future.[25] It includes strategies for private and public financing of the transition, companies having effective governance of the physical and transition risks, being transparent, and accountable to investors and other stakeholders. It is aimed at delivering increased economic growth while cutting emissions. The UK reduced its carbon emissions by 40 per cent from 1990 to 2019, while growing its economy by over two-thirds.[26] The UK's 2019 Green Finance Strategy seeks to align private sector financial flows with clean, environmentally sustainable, and resilient growth, while strengthening the competitiveness of the UK financial services sector.

The UK government introduced the Climate Change Agreements scheme, which allows energy intensive participants to pay significantly reduced rates of its climate change levy, which is a tax on the supply of energy, in exchange for signing up to energy efficiency or carbon reduction targets agreed with the government.[27] It also implemented the Energy Savings Opportunity Scheme, a mandatory energy assessment scheme; as well as the Energy Efficiency Scheme, a mandatory emissions trading scheme covering 2,000 large users of energy across the business and public sectors.[28] The UK government has also funded a £9.2 million Industrial Energy Efficiency Accelerator, aimed at lowering the cost of near-market energy efficient technologies for a range of industrial sectors through demonstration projects.[29] Its

[24] Financial Stability Board, Task Force on Climate-related Financial Disclosures, *Final Report, Recommendations of the Task Force on Climate-related Financial Disclosures* (15 June 2017) at 7 <https://www.fsb-tcfd.org/publications/final-recommendations-report/> (hereafter TCFD, *Final Report*).

[25] UK Government, 'Clean Growth Strategy' (2017), <https://www.gov.uk/government/publications/clean-growth-strategy>.

[26] UK Government, 'Delivering Clean Growth Progress Against Meeting Our Carbon Budgets: The Government Response to the Committee on Climate Change' (October 2018) at 2, <https://assets.publishing.service.gov.uk/government/uploads/system/uploads/attachment_data/file/748296/delivering-clean-growth.pdf> (hereafter 'Delivering Clean Growth Progress'), citing BEIS, BEIS provisional UK emissions statistics 1990–2017 (2018), <https://www.gov.uk/government/statistics/provisional-uk-greenhouse-gas-emissions-nationalstatistics-2017> and ONS, Quarterly National Accounts Statistical bulletins (Series ABMI: Seasonally Adjusted Chained Volume Measures) (2018) <https://www.ons.gov.uk/economy/ grossdomesticproductgdp/timeseries/abmi>.

[27] 'Delivering Clean Growth Progress' (n 26) at 37.

[28] Ibid.

[29] Ibid.

£18 million Industrial Heat Recovery Support programme, launched in 2018, is aimed at increasing investment in technologies to recover heat from industrial processes.[30] These initiatives are all aimed at serious scaling-up of sustainable finance and moving to net zero emissions.

Canada's Expert Panel on Sustainable Finance reported that if Canada is to meet its long term objectives, sustainable finance must become business-as-usual in financial services, and embedded in everyday business decisions, products, and services.[31] It found that while the transition to a clean, climate-smart economy is underway, there is a general lack of appreciation for the magnitude and pace of investment required to realize Canada's Paris Agreement target commitments of a 30 per cent reduction in emissions or a mid-century scenario of 80 per cent reduction. There needs to be capital investment in virtually every sector of the economy, from retrofitting buildings to reducing energy consumption, to more effective land use, to massive expansion of forests and other natural carbon sinks. The Expert Panel made a series of recommendations aimed at aligning mainstream financial activities with the transition to a competitive low emissions, climate-smart economy, mapping a transition plan to an associated capital investment plan.[32]

The Expert Panel set out a number of principles that should underpin Canada's sustainable finance strategy.[33] One is that regulatory and financial systems should motivate and empower businesses and financial services to leverage innovation as a source of sustainable growth.[34] Leadership across both public and private sectors is essential to generating transformational change, and the costs and benefits of transition need to be considered holistically in terms of distribution across communities, regions, and sectors.[35] The Expert Panel also recommended providing Canadians the opportunity and incentive to connect their savings to climate objectives.[36]

In Canada, cleantech is a broad-based and rapidly growing field of products, technologies, and services that improve productivity or efficiency, reduce energy consumption, and lessen environmental pollution across almost every economic industry and geographic region.[37] However, the sector is nascent compared with global developments. Canadian clean technology exports totalled $7.8 billion in 2016, compared to China at $245.2 billion; Germany at $125.3 billion; and the US at $113.2 billion.[38]

Some institutional investors and asset managers are ahead of the market on these issues. For example, BNP Paribas Asset Management, with €400 billion assets under management in thirty-six countries, has stated that it is committed to integrating

[30] Ibid at 39.

[31] Government of Canada, Final Report of the Expert Panel on Sustainable Finance, *Mobilizing Finance for Sustainable Growth* (June 2019) at 2, <http://publications.gc.ca/collections/collection_2019/eccc/En4-350-2-2019-eng.pdf> (hereafter Canada Expert Panel).

[32] Ibid at 2.

[33] Ibid at 8.

[34] Ibid.

[35] Ibid.

[36] Ibid at 2.

[37] The New Climate Economy, 'Unlocking the inclusive Growth Story of the 21st Century' (2018), <https://newclimateeconomy.report/2018/wp-content/uploads/sites/6/2018/09/NCE_2018_FULL-REPORT.pdf>.

[38] Canada Expert Panel (n 31) at 31.

sustainable investment practices across its portfolios, in the financial interest of its clients and the economy at large.[39] Its investment strategies integrate the key elements of sustainable investment: comprehensive integration of ESG factors; responsible business conduct and product-based exclusions; and a focus on thematic areas to promote a sustainable future. It is adopting firm-wide targets for measuring and progressively aligning its investment portfolios with a sustainable future, supported by stewardship and engagement.[40] Its Sustainable Investment Roadmap 2019–2022 is aimed at following a path towards a low carbon, more sustainable and equitable economic growth model, the firm observing:

> It is our belief that the current economic, social and environmental system is failing, and must be transformed in order for financial institutions to deliver sustainable returns. We are deeply attuned to the major systemic sustainability issues facing the world—climate change, resource scarcity, inequality—and committed to understanding not just how the associated risks and opportunities can impact our portfolios, but also how we as investors can help to shape the future, and minimize these risks over the long term.[41]

Innovative financing mechanisms can align with sustainable development practices. The IPCC notes that adaptation finance has increased quantitatively, but significant further expansion is required, accompanied by effective monitoring.[42] Sustainable finance will require collaboration among corporations, governments, development banks, small-scale local entrepreneurs, and community groups in developed and emerging countries as they work to shift to a low carbon economy.[43]

II. Moving to Clean Growth and a Circular Economy

There is growing understanding that critically important to preventing further global warming will be to develop circular economies that include new technologies and energy efficiency, a massive reduction of waste, and development of products that can be redeployed once their current use is finished.

Companies need to reduce operating costs by improving efficiency across their production and distribution processes, buildings, machinery and appliances, transport, water usage, and waste management.[44] Technological innovations are developing efficient heating solutions. Examples include advances in LED lighting technology and industrial motor technology, retrofitting buildings, employing geothermal, solar, and wind power, offering water usage and treatment solutions, and developing electric vehicles.[45] Companies that innovate and develop new low emission products and

[39] BNP Paribas Asset Management, *Global Sustainability Strategy* (BNP 2019), <https://docfinder.bnpparibas-am.com/api/files/1FC9FC6C-0DA8-468E-90B3-016DDB5CD270>.
[40] Canada Expert Panel (n 31) at 3.
[41] Ibid.
[42] IPCC, 'Global Response 2018' (n 14) at 315.
[43] TCFD, *Final Report* (n 24) at 7.
[44] Ibid at 6.
[45] Ibid at 7.

services may improve their competitive position and capitalize on shifting consumer and investor preferences for goods and services that reduce carbon footprints.

The TCFD recommended greater emphasis on a product's carbon footprint in its marketing and labelling, and producer goods that place emphasis on reducing emissions, such as adoption of energy-efficiency measures along the supply chain.[46] It observed that companies and investors that pro-actively seek opportunities in new types of assets or markets may be able to diversify and better position themselves for the transition to a low carbon economy.[47]

The Ellen MacArthur Foundation has outlined pathways from the linear economy to a circular economy.[48] It suggests that municipalities embed circular economy principles design for greater proximity between where people live, work, and conduct leisure activities. Shared transit, zero-emission cars, and people able to walk and cycle to work, are all strategies that reduce congestion and pollution.[49] Land that would otherwise be zoned for roads and car parks is freed up for green spaces, commerce, housing, and recreation. Critically important to this design of cities is a system whereby materials are returned, sorted, and reused, instead of directed to landfill or incineration, a new distributed system of resource management.[50]

China's Circular Economy Promotion Law 2008 requires factories, particularly in resource-heavy sectors such as cement and aluminium, to embed themselves in a network to make further use of industrial by-products.[51] Its Rizhao Economic and Technology Development Area ('REDA') in Shandong province represents its first wave of eco-industrial parks, which share infrastructure and exchange of by-products, using tax incentives to reduce waste. REDA includes a beer brewery, which provides vinasse, a by-product of sugar, to a fertilizer factory in the park.[52] Excess CO_2 captured during the fermentation process is used by another beverage company to carbonate soft drinks and soda water.[53] A paper and pulp plant in REDA receives scrap wood from a lumber yard as an input, while providing sludge for fertilizer, green mud for building materials, white sludge for a citric acid factory and a cement plant, and wood chips for a charcoal producer, all located in the same eco-industrial park. In 2011 alone, 71,446 tonnes of white sludge from the pulp and paper plant were used as a substitute for calcium carbonate in the citric and cement factories.[54] The material flow management is such that the eco-industrial park does not need a waste treatment plant. Ninety-eight per cent of the industrial solid waste in REDA is reused.[55]

China's Five Year Plan 2016–2020 introduces binding targets for the circular economy, requiring 75 per cent of more than 500 national-level industrial parks

[46] Ibid.
[47] Ibid.
[48] Ellan MacArthur Foundation, 'Circular Economy in Cities: Project Guide' (March 2019), <https://www.ellenmacarthurfoundation.org/assets/downloads/CE-in-Cities-Project-Guide_Mar19.pdf>.
[49] Ibid at 6.
[50] Ibid.
[51] Charles Arthur, 'Another First for China' in United Nations Industrial Development Organization, 'Making It, Industry for Development' (2019) No 26 at 33.
[52] Ibid.
[53] Ibid at 34.
[54] Ibid.
[55] Ibid.

to undertake a circular transformation. The Chinese Ministry of Commerce and Ministry of Science and Technology issued *Measures for the Administration of National Demonstration Eco-Industrial Parks and the Standard for National Demonstration Eco-industrial Parks*. As of March 2018, development plans for ninety-three eco-industrial parks had been approved and fifty-one of these parks accredited.[56]

A large part of achieving a circular economy will depend on tackling the pervasive amount of single-use plastics in the world. Such plastics generate a huge amount of carbon both in their production and in their deterioration in landfill and oceans. Tom Dowdall suggests that by emphasizing recyclability and recycling over reduction and elimination of plastic waste, major companies are still avoiding their responsibility to tackle plastic pollution.[57] He observes that only 9 per cent of all plastic ever made has been recycled, and most of that is downcycling to low-grade plastics.[58] Dowdall argues that we require dramatic reduction in single-use packaging and changing business models to increase reuse. A circular economy approach requires companies to determine how much plastic packaging each company is responsible for, to set clear absolute reduction goals combined with regular progress reports, to redesign business models to promote reuse in terms of circular economy packaging, and to withdraw from industry groups that delay or undermine required regulation.[59]

The New Plastics Economy Global Commitment, spearheaded by the Ellen MacArthur Foundation, is working to get businesses and governments to commit to change how we produce, use, and reuse plastic—eliminating the plastic items we don't need, and redesigning plastic to be safely reused, recycled, or composted; circulating everything used to keep it in the economy and out of the environment.[60] One example is the British supermarket chain, Iceland, which has announced that it will ban all single-use plastics from its own branded products by 2023, replacing all plastic packaging with trays made of paper and pulp and paper bags, which are recyclable through domestic waste collections or its own in-store recycling facilities.[61]

IKEA is an example of a large company moving its governance to the circular economy. Operating 422 stores in fifty markets, IKEA sells more than 9,500 products.[62] Currently 60 per cent of its products are based on renewable materials and 10 per cent are recycled materials; its goal is 100 per cent renewable and recycled materials by 2030.[63] It has installed almost 20,000 solar panels in its production facilities, is sourcing cotton, wood, and other inputs from sustainable sources, working with organizations such as the World Wildlife Federation, and is now designing products

[56] Ibid at 35.

[57] Tom Dowdall, *'Solving the Plastic Pollution Crisis Requires Focus on Another "R"–Responsibility'* in *United Nations Industrial Development Organization, Making It, Industry for Development* (2019) No 26 at 10.

[58] Ibid, citing *#breakfreefromplastic* campaign, which does plastic audits.

[59] Ibid at 12.

[60] Ellen MacArthur Foundation, <https://www.newplasticseconomy.org/projects/global-commitment>.

[61] Nicola Slawson, 'Iceland Supermarket Vows to Eliminate Plastic on All Own-Branded Products', *The Guardian* (15 January 2018), <https://www.theguardian.com/business/2018/jan/15/iceland-vows-to-eliminate-plastic-on-all-own-branded-products>.

[62] IKEA, *People & Planet Positive, IKEA Sustainability Report FY19* (IKEA, 2019) at 4, <https://preview.thenewsmarket.com/Previews/IKEA/DocumentAssets/535135.pdf>.

[63] Ibid at 8.

from the very beginning to be repurposed, repaired, reused, resold, and recycled.[64] It measures its annual progress against the UN Sustainable Development Goals.[65] It is gearing products to reduce waste, such as tap fixtures that cut water use by 90 per cent, and 'home solar', which allows customers to generate and store renewable energy using the roof of their homes.[66]

IKEA has committed to designing 100 per cent of its products according to circular design principles by 2030.[67] These principles include designing for use renewable materials, longer lasting products, using materials that can be recovered easily and given second, third, and fourth lives. It has reduced waste in production, created products easy to maintain, and is extending the life of products through Ikea care and repair services, enabling customers to prolong the life of their products by offering spare parts and fittings for all products.[68] For example, IKEA Retail Japan offers a buy-back service for IKEA furniture that's still in good condition but no longer needed; the furniture is then refurbished and sold at a reduced rate to a new customers; more than 3,400 items were sold back to IKEA Retail Japan in financial year 2018.[69] It phased out all single-use plastic products by January 2020.[70] IKEA is committed to becoming climate positive by 2030, reducing more GHG emissions than its value chain emits.[71] Product transport accounts for 3.9 per cent of IKEA's total emissions and it is working to decarbonize its transportation by replacing fossil fuels with alternatives such as electric trucks and increasing use of transportation of goods in large containers, avoiding the need to handle goods when changing between modes, having saved 83,000 shipments in 2018, even though its market size grew.[72]

These examples illustrate that product design and delivery can be reconceptualized to advance net zero carbon, even where the nature of the business, global production and distribution, has a significant carbon footprint.

III. Linking Sustainable Finance with Sustainable Development

'Sustainable development' has been viewed as development that meets the needs of the present generation without compromising the ability of future generations to meet their own needs.[73] It means embedding our climate strategies in sustainable development that balances social well-being, economic prosperity, and environmental protection. The UN Sustainable Development Goals, adopted in 2015, provide a framework for assessing the links between global warming and development goals that include

64 Ibid at 5.
65 Ibid at 10.
66 Ibid at 12.
67 Ibid at 22.
68 Ibid at 16.
69 Ibid at 18.
70 Ibid at 23.
71 Ibid at 27.
72 Ibid at 35. It reports that avoiding the use of diesel trucks saves 650 tonnes of CO_2 per year.
73 DB Climate Change Advisors, 'Sustainable Investing, Establishing Long-Term Value and Performance' (June 2012), <https://www.db.com/cr/en/docs/Sustainable_Investing_2012.pdf>.

poverty eradication, reducing inequalities, and climate action.[74] A number of the goals touch directly on climate issues.[75] For example, Goal 6 calls for clean, safe, and affordable drinking water and sanitation, recognizing that global warming is exacerbating water scarcity for more than 40 per cent of people globally. Goal 7 calls for investment in solar, wind, and thermal power, and other clean energy, improving energy productivity, and ensuring energy for all. Goal 11 advocates for sustainable cities and communities, including safe and affordable housing, investment in public transport, creating green public spaces, reduction of urban heat islands, and improving urban planning and management in participatory and inclusive ways.

Goal 12 calls for responsible production and consumption of food, both to eliminate hunger and to reduce the 22 per cent of total GHG emissions that the food sector generates. Goal 13 directly addresses the need for climate action, seeking to mobilize US $100 billion annually to address the needs of developing countries to adapt to climate change and invest in low-carbon development and sustainable natural resource management in the move to net zero. Goals 14 and 15 make recommendations in respect of life below water and life on land, drawing the deep connection between the devastating effects of climate change and protection of biodiversity, marine, land, and avifunal species, and protection of the ocean, land, and forests as carbon sinks and as sources of millions of livelihoods.[76]

An entire book could be written on the relationship between the UN Sustainable Development Goals and the need to move boldly to net zero carbon emissions. For the purposes of this chapter, it is important to keep the goals in mind because they are good for business and good for the planet, and they are driving many of the policy initiatives of governments, central banks, and other organizations in creating opportunities for sustainable finance.

The IPCC has reported that limiting warming requires transformative systemic change, integrated with sustainable development, including scaling-up and acceleration of the implementation of multilevel and cross-sectoral climate mitigation, linked to transformational adaptation.[77]

The United Nations Environmental Programme ('UNEP') has been working with countries, financial regulators, and the finance sector to align financial systems to direct financial flows to support the delivery of the UN Sustainable Development Goals.[78] It notes that at the core of today's globalized economy are financial markets through which banks and investors allocate capital to different sectors, and that such allocation needs redirection because it will shape ecosystems and the production and consumption patterns of tomorrow.

The Intergovernmental Science-Policy Platform on Biodiversity and Ecosystem Services ('ISPPBES') reports that, with safeguards, nature-based solutions can provide an estimated 37 per cent of climate change mitigation needed prior to 2030, with

[74] IPCC, 'Global Response 2018' (n 14).

[75] UN Sustainable Development Goals (2015), <https://www.undp.org/content/undp/en/home/sustainable-development-goals/goal-15-life-on-land.html>.

[76] Ibid.

[77] IPCC, 'Global Response 2018' (n 14).

[78] UNEP, 'Green Financing' (2019), <https://www.unenvironment.org/regions/asia-and-pacific/regional-initiatives/supporting-resource-efficiency/green-financing>.

co-benefits for biodiversity.[79] It advocates large-scale deployment of intensive bioenergy plantations as a cost-effective plan to meet the sustainable development goals in cities. It suggests that urban key biodiversity areas should be safeguarded, including retrofitting green and blue infrastructure, such as creating and maintaining green spaces and biodiversity-friendly water bodies, urban agriculture, rooftop gardens, and expanded and accessible vegetation cover in existing urban areas and new developments.[80] In addition to controlling urban heat islands, there are significant health benefits to residents' increased interaction with nature. The ISPPBES suggests that green infrastructure in cities can complement large-scale 'grey' infrastructure such as flood protection, cleaning of air and water, treating wastewater, and the provision of energy.[81]

The UK provided £5.8 billion financing over a four-year period to 2020 and committed to £11.6 billion in financing by 2026 to help developing countries reduce their emissions and build local capacity to deal with the impacts of climate change.[82] One fund will give British scientists and innovators up to £1 billion of aid funding to create new technologies to help developing countries reduce their emissions and meet global climate change targets.

IV. The European Commission's Vision for a Sustainable and Climate Neutral Economy

The European Commission is also a global leader in developing a strategy for the circular economy and massively scaled-up sustainable finance. The EU is striving for a single market approach to tackling climate change. The European Parliament and the European Council called on the European Commission to create a vision for a climate-neutral future that covers nearly all EU policies and is in line with pursuing efforts to keep warming to 1.5°C above pre-industrial levels.[83] Its long term vision for a climate-neutral economy by 2050 includes investing in technological solutions and aligning action in industrial policy, finance, and research. The European Commission's policy strategy includes citizen empowerment and the substantive objective of 'social fairness for a just transition' through societal and environmental benefits for European citizens.[84]

To foster private investment, the EU and its Member States have agreed that they need to offer clear, long term signals to guide investors, to avoid stranded assets, to raise

[79] S Diaz et al, *The Global Assessment Report on Biodiversity and Ecosystem Services*, Intergovernmental Science-Policy Platform on Biodiversity and Ecosystem Services (May 2019) at 18, <https://ipbes.net/system/tdf/inline/files/ipbes_global_assessment_report_summary_for_polciymakers.pdf?file=1&type=node&id=36213>.

[80] Ibid.

[81] Ibid.

[82] 'Delivering Clean Growth Progress' (n 26) at 3; Reliefweb, 'UK Aid to Double Efforts to Tackle Climate Change', OCHA (September 2019), <https://reliefweb.int/report/world/uk-aid-double-efforts-tackle-climate-change>.

[83] EC, *Clean Planet* (n 17) at 1. See also European Commission Work Programme for 2019 (COM (2018) 800) 4 for 2030 targets.

[84] EC, *Clean Planet*, ibid at 3–4.

sustainable finance, and to direct finance to clean innovation efforts.[85] The European Commission's new Governance of the Energy Union integrates involvement of stakeholders in the preparation of the national energy and climate plans, which need to be consistent with long term strategies.[86] The EU's Investment Plan for Europe ('Juncker plan'), including the European Fund for Strategic Investment ('EFSI') and the EU's provision of €70 billion for implementation of the Energy Union Strategy, are focused on sustainable investments in all sectors, allocating 40 per cent of EFSI infrastructure and innovation projects to climate action.[87]

A Clean Planet for All—A European Strategic Long Term Vision for a Prosperous, Modern, Competitive, and Climate Neutral Economy is aimed at generating a broad-based policy discussion involving European decision-makers and citizens at large as to how Europe should prepare itself towards a 2050 horizon.[88] The EU is responsible for 10 per cent of global GHG emissions.[89] Its objective is to reduce emissions by 80 to 95 per cent by 2050. Between 1990 and 2016, energy use was reduced by almost 2 per cent and GHG emissions were reduced by 22 per cent, while GDP grew by 54 per cent.[90] The European Commission reports that 'green jobs' already represent 4 million jobs in the EU.[91]

The European Commission's focus for the past decade has been 'decoupling' GHG emissions from economic growth in Europe, reporting that energy efficiency, fuel switch policies, and the penetration of renewables all reduced emissions significantly, in turn spurring sustainable economic growth.[92] For example, the percentage of renewable energy in final energy consumption increased from 9 per cent in 2005 to 17 per cent in 2018.[93]

However, the European Commission observed in 2018 that while it was broadly on track to achieve its 2020 GHG emissions target and its renewable energy and energy efficiency targets, there was some recent stagnation of energy efficiency improvements and GHG reduction trends. Hence policy initiatives were needed to further advance its Energy Union Strategy and finalize an advanced and cost-effective regulatory framework to achieve its clean energy transition.[94] It observed that regulatory stability is an important element for public authorities and private operators to achieve full implementation of this framework.[95]

EU policies include a reformed EU emissions trading system to strengthen the price signal for CO_2, national GHG emission reduction targets, legislation established to maintain the EU land and forest sinks, and 2030 targets on energy efficiency and renewable energy.[96] Approved regulatory targets are aimed at increasing renewable

85 Ibid at 17.
86 Ibid.
87 Ibid.
88 Ibid at 3–4.
89 Ibid at 4.
90 Ibid.
91 Ibid at 19.
92 Ibid at 4.
93 Ibid.
94 Ibid at 4.
95 Ibid at 5.
96 Ibid at 5 and 7.

energy to at least 32 per cent of the EU's final energy consumption by 2030 and improving the EU's energy efficiency by at least 32.5 per cent.[97] The EU enacted regulation to improve the CO_2 efficiency of cars, vans, and trucks, aimed at transitioning the transportation sector.[98]

The cumulative effect of these measures is that the EU is exceeding its commitments under the Paris Agreement and will reduce emissions by 45 per cent by 2030 compared to 1990.[99] However, the *Clean Planet* report acknowledged that the legislation in place will not be sufficient, and in order to limit temperature increase to 1.5°C, net zero carbon emissions at a global level need to be achieved by 2050 and neutrality for all other GHG later in the century.[100]

The European Commission has developed eight additional pathways, five of which are technologies and actions. In combination with land use and forestry sinks that absorb more CO_2 than they emit, these scenarios could achieve around 85 per cent net GHG emissions reductions by 2050 compared to 1990.[101] It calls for additional action to explore how biomass can be supplied in a sustainable way, while enhancing natural sinks or in combination with carbon capture and storage that can lead to increased negative emissions.[102] It is setting standards and implementing labelling requirements for all EU appliances and electronics, as well as any imported into the EU or exported to foreign markets.[103]

The European Commission's clean planet strategy includes significant investment in electrification, hydrogen and e-fuels (i.e. power-to-X), high deployment of storage (six times today's level), as well as end user energy efficiency. Expansion of e-fuels is expected to result in 150 per cent more electricity production in 2050.[104] These actions are key to decarbonization. The European Commission is linking this strategy to the need to reduce energy waste in the circular economy. It is promoting zero carbon energy carriers, relying on negative emissions technology in the form of bioenergy combined with carbon capture and storage to balance remaining emissions. It is advocating low carbon consumer choices.[105]

The European Commission has proposed mainstreaming climate finance by deploying at least 25 per cent of its next financial framework plan to leverage sustainable private and public investment and channel EU financial support to the clean energy transition.[106] It has observed that the financial sector has a key role in the transition towards net zero carbon emissions by reorienting capital flows and investments towards net zero solutions.[107] The EU's action plan is aimed at connecting finance with

[97] Ibid at 5.

[98] European Parliament and the Council adopted Regulation (EU) 2019/631 setting CO_2 emission performance standards for new passenger cars and for new vans in the EU, effective January 2020, <https://ec.europa.eu/clima/policies/transport/vehicles/regulation_en>.

[99] EC, *Clean Planet* (n 17) at 5.

[100] Ibid.

[101] Ibid at 7.

[102] Ibid.

[103] Ibid at 8.

[104] Ibid at 7.

[105] Ibid.

[106] Ibid at 18.

[107] Ibid.

the EU's agenda for sustainable development. As discussed in Chapter 7, the move towards a unified taxonomy on sustainable economic activities, proposed rules for low carbon benchmarks, and improved disclosure requirements for investment products should encourage investors to focus on sustainable investments.[108]

Investment in research innovation is needed to make net zero carbon solutions economically viable and bring about new solutions not yet mature or even known to the market.[109] 'Horizon Europe' is the European Commission's new research and innovation programme, aimed at investing 35 per cent of a €100 billion budget in the development of innovative and cost-effective zero carbon solutions.[110] The EU's European Innovation Council will focus on breakthrough products and processes, and the European Institute of Innovation and Technology is supporting young innovators and start-ups across Europe.[111] The EU Innovation Fund under the EU Emission Trading System will support commercial-scale demonstration of breakthrough emissions reducing technologies.[112]

The European Commission reports that while the EU seeks to attract climate-friendly investment and trade, it should also defend its right to reciprocal, fair, and transparently governed access to partner countries' markets, infrastructure, and critical raw materials.[113] It seeks to further embed climate change objectives and considerations in political dialogues, including in the area of migration and development co-operation.[114] The European Commission suggests that fair and rules-based trade can contribute to the global uptake of climate-friendly technologies, facilitate the energy transition, and help secure supplies of the necessary raw materials for low carbon technologies.[115] As noted in Chapter 7, its regulatory agenda is advancing these objectives.

'Social fairness' is a major part of the European Commission's climate finance and transition policy, the idea that a well-managed and just transition should leave no region, no community, and no worker and citizen behind.[116] Its strategy involves sharing knowledge and experience in developing long term strategies and implementing efficient policies so that the objectives of the Paris Agreement are accomplished; preparing for geopolitical shifts, and providing investment support to third countries for low carbon resilient development.[117]

A lot of initiatives have commenced, yet globally, there continue to be information silos in respect of progress, dissemination of information on lessons learned, and avoidance of duplication of efforts to move to a circular and net zero economy. In order to be sustainable, these initiatives need public support for the necessary expenditure of resources, as well as strong global leadership that recognizes the need for the private sector to bear part of the costs of transition. There also need to be new and

[108] Ibid.
[109] Ibid.
[110] Ibid.
[111] Ibid.
[112] Ibid at 19.
[113] Ibid at 20.
[114] Ibid.
[115] Ibid.
[116] Ibid at 24.
[117] Ibid.

accessible portals of information for consumers, businesses, and others to readily access innovations and new developments, as they do not have the time or resources to search each national data base.

The next part briefly examines the burgeoning area of 'green finance', offering examples of innovative collaborations internationally that are aimed at heralding in a new generation of governance in relation to climate finance. The latter part of the chapter explores a less known area, conservation finance, and its potential.

V. Green Finance

The UNEP defines green finance as financing that increases the level of financial flows from banking, micro-credit, insurance, and investment from the public, private, and not-for-profit sectors to sustainable development priorities, including better management of environmental and social risks, creating opportunities that create a decent rate of return and environmental benefits, and that deliver greater accountability.[118] Its priorities for work on green financing are supporting the public sector in creating enabling environments, promoting public-private partnerships on financing mechanisms such as green bonds, and capacity building of community enterprises on micro-credit.[119]

There has been rapid growth in green bond markets. The green bond market and green loan issuance grew from US $45 billion in 2015 to an adjusted US $257.7 billion in 2019.[120] Bonds are the principal source of external financing for US-based companies.[121] Of the thirty countries issuing green bonds, the US, UK, China, France, and Canada rank as the largest and most active markets.[122] In 2018, there were also inaugural sovereign green bond issues from five countries.[123] For example, BlackRock has launched six new Exchange Traded Funds that combine ESG factors with a 30 per cent reduction in carbon emissions.[124]

Green bonds are frequently issued to finance environmental projects. Examples are solar and other forms of clean or renewable energy, pollution reduction and prevention technology, environmentally sustainable management of living natural resources, environmentally sustainable fishery and aquaculture, terrestrial and aquatic biodiversity conservation, and climate change adaptation.[125] There are subspecies of such bonds, such as 'landscape green bonds', aimed at environmental investment in entire

[118] UNEP, 'Green Financing' (2019), <https://www.unenvironment.org/regions/asia-and-pacific/regional-initiatives/supporting-resource-efficiency/green-financing>.

[119] Ibid.

[120] Climate Bonds Initiative ('CBI'), *Bonds and Climate Change, the State of the Market 2019*, <https://www.climatebonds.net/resources/reports/2019-green-bond-market-summary> (hereafter *Bonds and Climate Change*).

[121] Organization for Economic Co-operation and Development ('OECD'), *Mobilizing Bonds Markets for a Low carbon Transition* (29 April 2017), <https://www.oecd.org/env/mobilising-bond-markets-for-a-low-carbon-transition-9789264272323-en.htm>.

[122] *Bonds and Climate Change* (n 120).

[123] By Indonesia, Belgium, Lithuania, Ireland, and Seychelles; Carney, 'New Horizon' (n 22) at 8.

[124] BlackRock, <https://www.ishares.com/us/strategies/sustainable-investing#esg>.

[125] Green Bond Principles (June 2017), <https://www.icmagroup.org/assets/documents/Regulatory/Green-Bonds/GreenBondsBrochure-JUNE2017.pdf> (hereafter Green Bond Principles).

landscapes, including reducing deforestation and creating sustainable livelihoods on a scaled-up and much longer term timeline.[126] Green finance now includes green bonds and loans, sustainability bonds, climate bonds, blue bonds, and resilience bonds.

Blue bonds are aimed at raising capital to finance marine and ocean-based projects that have positive environmental, economic, and climate benefits.

The European Investment Bank was one of the first to issue green bonds by issuing a climate awareness bond ('CAB'), of which it has now issued €19 billion, the proceeds directed towards financing 160 renewable energy and energy efficiency projects and climate action initiatives all over the world.[127] It views green bonds as crucially important to accelerating support for climate-related investment. It has committed to financing that is aimed at unlocking €1 trillion of climate action and environmentally sustainable investment by 2030, align all financing activities with the goals of the Paris Agreement.[128]

The Demark climate investment fund, Dansk Vækstkapital, has made climate investments in eighty-five developing countries.[129] It has invested in wind and solar parks, bio-gas plants, energy efficiency projects, upgrading of power and industrial plants, irrigation systems, and climate-friendly agricultural.

i. Protecting Investors and Consumers through Clear Standards of What Qualifies as Green Finance

While green bonds and other green financial products are experiencing exponential growth, there is concern that some products are allowing companies and asset managers to cash in on a growing interest by investors in investing in sustainable businesses, while not directing the funds as promised. 'Greenwashing' is a term used when businesses and financial firms offering green bonds or other financial products benefit from the growing interest, but do not necessarily invest in economic activities that protect or enhance the environment or move us towards a net zero carbon footprint.[130] The financial services firms or investment banks that sell green bonds often do not verify that they meet their promise of advancing sustainability. There is an opaqueness concern, specifically, that once the funds have been raised, there is often no tracking of their use to verify whether the activities financed are carbon reducing

[126] Andrew Mitchell, 'Landscape Green Bonds: An Emerging New Asset Class?', *Global Canopy* (12 September 2017), <https://medium.com/global-canopy/landscape-green-bonds-an-emerging-new-asset-class-41fcc515f02f>.

[127] European Investment Bank, '10 years of Green Bonds' (4 July 2017), <https://www.eib.org/en/infocentre/ten-years-of-green-bonds.htm#>.

[128] European Investment Bank, 'EU Bank Launches Ambitious New Climate Strategy and Energy Lending Policy', Press Statement (14 November 2019), <https://www.eib.org/en/press/all/2019-313-eu-bank-launches-ambitious-new-climate-strategy-and-energy-lending-policy>.

[129] Demark Climate Investment Fund (*Dansk Vækstkapital*) (2019), <https://www.danskvaekstkapital.dk/dvk1/investeringer/en-2/danish-climate-investment-fund/>.

[130] Luca Morreale, 'The Coming Backlash to "Greenwashing" of Bonds' *Bloomberg News* (10 August 2017), <https://www.bloomberg.com/news/articles/2017-08-11/the-coming-backlash-to-greenwashing-of-bonds-quicktake-q-a. See for example, International Capital markets Associate, 'Sustainability Bond Guidelines' (June 2018), <https://www.icmagroup.org/green-social-and-sustainability-bonds/sustainability-bond-guidelines-sbg/>.

or environmentally sound. Moreover, given the highly dispersed nature of green bond holders, these creditors are unlikely to engage in monitoring to ensure that the investments promised actually do occur, and that there is not greenwashing involved.

Any standards that exist have been voluntary and unenforceable, and are largely financial industry created.[131] Sustainability-oriented taxonomies for green finance are being developed in China, Japan, the UK, France, the Netherlands, as well as by a number of private associations such as the Asia Pacific Loan Market Association. The OECD plans to release mapping and analysis of current and emerging global sustainable finance taxonomies in 2020.[132] Three major credit rating agencies state that they will integrate environmental risk and green certification into credit ratings.[133]

The Climate Bonds Initiative ('CBI') and the International Capital Markets Association ('ICMA') have developed definitional frameworks, certification, and validation methods for green financing.[134] In order for a green bond to be certified by the CBI, it must meet pre- and post-issuance requirements under the Climate Bonds Standard, including independent third-party verification in accordance with existing auditing standards.[135]

For example, the 'Green Bond Principles' are voluntary principles aimed at promoting integrity in the green bond market through guidelines that recommend transparency, disclosure, and reporting.[136] The Principles define green bonds as 'any type of bond instrument where the proceeds will be exclusively applied to finance or refinance, in part or in full, new and/or existing eligible green projects'.[137] The green bonds must be aligned with the four core components. The first is 'use of proceeds', i.e. transparency in how the green projects for which the bonds have raised capital disclose clear environmental benefits, which will be assessed, and, where feasible, quantified by the bond issuer.[138] They must contribute to environmental objectives such as climate change mitigation, natural resource or biodiversity conservation, and pollution prevention. The second core component is a 'process for project evaluation and selection', with the issuer of a green bond clearly communicating to investors the environmental sustainability objectives; the process by which the issuer determines how the projects fit within the eligible green projects categories; the related eligibility criteria, including, if applicable, exclusion criteria or any other process applied to identify and manage potentially material environmental and social risks associated with the projects.[139]

[131] See for example, the Green Bond Principles (n 125), which aim to increase transparency and integrity of the Green Bond market.

[132] Canada Expert Panel (n 31) at 26 and 54.

[133] Carney, 'New Horizon' (n 22) at 9.

[134] See CBI, <https://www.climatebonds.net/about; and ICMA <https://www.icmagroup.org/green-social-and-sustainability-bonds/greenbond-principles-gbp/>.

[135] CBI, 'Climate Bonds Standard and Certification' (CBI 2019), <https://www.climatebonds.net/standard>.

[136] Green Bond Principles, 'Green Bond Principles Voluntary Process Guidelines for Issuing Green Bonds (June 2018), <https://www.icmagroup.org/green-social-and-sustainability-bonds/green-bond-principles-gbp/>.

[137] Ibid.

[138] Ibid at 3.

[139] Ibid at 4.

The third core component of the Green Bond Principles is 'management of proceeds', in that the net proceeds of the green bond should be credited to a sub-account, sub-portfolio, or otherwise tracked by the bond issuer. As long as the green bond is outstanding, the balance of the tracked net proceeds should be periodically adjusted to match allocations to eligible green projects made during that period.[140] The fourth component is 'reporting', suggesting that bond issuers should maintain readily available up to date information on the use of proceeds, to be renewed annually until full allocation, and on a timely basis. The annual report should include a list of the projects to which green bond proceeds have been allocated, project descriptions and amounts allocated, and their expected impact. Where confidentiality agreements exist, information should be presented on an aggregated portfolio basis.[141] While voluntary, the Green Bond Principles are trying to promote increased transparency and integrity, which could assist with increasing capital allocation to green projects.[142]

Transparency and monitoring are particularly key to preventing greenwashing. But definitions are important because products labelled green finance have been used to finance high carbon-emitting activities. The People's Bank of China defines green finance as 'financial services provided for economic activities that are supportive of environmental improvement, climate change mitigation and more efficient resource utilization'.[143] It was the first central bank to promulgate Guidelines for Establishing the Green Financial System.[144] In 2018, Chinese green bond issuances were approximately RMB 283 billion (US $43 billion), second highest to the US.[145] About 28 per cent of China's green bond proceeds finance solar, wind, and other clean energy projects, and approximately 33 per cent finance low carbon transport, including urban mass transit.[146] However, Sandalow observes that roughly 26 per cent of China's green bond proceeds went to projects that did not meet international green bond standards, including for retrofits of coal power plants.[147] It speaks to the need for regulatory oversight of green finance markets to avoid misuse of funds raised for sustainability objectives.

ii. Green Finance Policy and Regulatory Oversight

The European Commission has developed standards to create some oversight and accountability regarding how to label green bonds and other green investment products.[148] The only accountability check previously was that investors decided, with

[140] Ibid at 5.

[141] Ibid.

[142] Green Bond Principles, 'Green Project Mapping' (June 2019), <https://www.icmagroup.org/assets/documents/Regulatory/Green-Bonds/June-2019/Green-Projects-Mapping-Document-100619.pdf>.

[143] David Sandalow, Guide to Chinese Climate Policy 2019, Columbia Center on Global Energy Policy (18 September 2019) at 109, <https://energypolicy.columbia.edu/sites/default/files/file-uploads/Guide%20to%20Chinese%20Climate%20Policy_2019.pdf>.

[144] Ibid.

[145] Ibid at 110.

[146] Ibid.

[147] Ibid at 111.

[148] European Commission, 'Communication: Action Plan: Financing Sustainable Growth', <http://eur-lex.europa.eu/legal-content/EN/TXT/?uri=CELEX:52018DC0097>.

imperfect information, whether a bond was sufficiently green to meet their own investment priorities. As institutional investors consider investments to address climate-related financial risk, part of their fiduciary obligations arguably include ensuring that the green financial products they are investing in truly meet their climate-related objectives. The European Commission's Sustainable Finance Action Plan has developed a classification system for sustainable economic activities, a harmonized green bond standard, and methodologies for low carbon indices.[149] The European Commission reports that standardization and labelling of green finance products could facilitate growth of stable, rated, and liquid investments with long duration, allowing companies to access more of the US $100 trillion pool of patient private capital managed by global institutional fixed-income investors.[150]

The European Green Bond Standard Technical Expert Group in 2019 recommended that the European Commission create a standard to enhance the transparency, comparability, and credibility of the green bond market, and encourage branding of 'EU green bonds'.[151] It reported that the small but growing green bond market has now spread into all debt capital market asset classes from corporate issuers (investment grade and high yield), sovereign issuers, asset-backed securities, projects bonds, emerging market bonds, and private placements.[152] It recommended that the standard specify clear and mandatory requirements, aligning green projects with the EU taxonomy and its environmental objectives, the 'do-no-significant harm' principle, social safeguards, and technical screening criteria.

The European Green Bond Standard Technical Expert Group recommended that bond issuers should be required to provide details on all key aspects of the proposed use-of-proceeds, their green bond strategy, periodic reporting on use-of-proceeds and environmental impacts, supported by quantitative metrics, verification of conformity with the standard, and related reporting on use-of-proceeds by accredited verifiers.[153] It recommended that institutional investors use the requirements of the EU green bond standards in their green fixed-income investment strategy and communicate their expectations actively in their investor dialogue with bond issuers.[154]

These recommendations could facilitate massive transfer of capital to green finance, however, the normative justification for the standards remaining voluntary, as opposed to mandatory remains unclear.

Catherine Malecki argues that in creating the new green bond standards, the European Commission should introduce a distinction between low carbon and positive carbon impacts of green bonds.[155] A low carbon benchmark is where the underlying assets are selected so that the resulting benchmark portfolio has less carbon

[149] European Commission, 'Sustainable Finance Plan' (2019), <https://ec.europa.eu/info/business-economy-euro/banking-andfinance/sustainable-finance_en>.

[150] Ibid.

[151] European Green Bond Standard Technical Expert Group, *Report on EU Green Bond Standard* (EU June 2019) at 9, <https://ec.europa.eu/info/sites/info/files/business_economy_euro/banking_and_finance/documents/190618-sustainable-finance-teg-report-green-bond-standard_en.pdf>.

[152] Ibid at 17.

[153] Ibid at 10.

[154] Ibid.

[155] Catherine Malecki, 'Climate Finance: The French and European Leadership', (forthcoming: on file with author, 2020) at 11.

emissions when compared to the assets that comprise a standard capital-weighted benchmark, and a positive carbon impact benchmark means a benchmark where the underlying assets are selected on the basis that their carbon emissions savings exceed the asset's carbon.[156] She suggests that firms should be required to publish their methodology used for such calculations and advocates for accreditation and supervision of EU green bonds standards, with independent external verification that the funds have been used as promised.[157]

Increasingly, we see governments developing and beginning to implement green finance policies. In part, governments are puzzling through what is the optimal combination of public and private financing, in the context of deciding who is going to bear the risks and who is going to benefit from the upside potential. In terms of public finance, one issue is the extent to which tax dollars are directed towards privately-owned assets and economic activity and what structural arrangements are made for a return on investment. Such arrangements can involve offering public guarantees on financing for innovative technologies. Public-private partnerships can allow countries to benefit from the financing of new technologies and infrastructure. The challenging policy question is how to unlock private capital, but not have the public assume all the risk; rather, there needs to be a sharing of both risk and benefits in the financing of the transition to net zero carbon.

One possible model, InvestEU, is part of the European Commission's economic policy mix of investment and structural reforms, bringing together the European Fund for Strategic Investments and thirteen current EU financial instruments.[158] InvestEU will run from 2021 to 2027, building on the success of the Juncker Plan's European Fund for Strategic Investments by providing an EU budget guarantee to support investment and access to finance in the EU. The programme aims to boost investment, innovation, and job creation in Europe by €650 billion. The InvestEU Fund will support sustainable infrastructure, research, innovation, and digitization, small and medium-sized businesses, and social investment and skills. It is aimed at being flexible, with the ability to react to market changes. The InvestEU Advisory Hub will provide technical advice on investment projects needing financing, with the InvestEU Portal offering an accessible database that matches projects with potential investors worldwide.[159]

The InvestEU Fund will mobilize public and private investment through an EU budget guarantee of €38 billion that will back the investment projects of financial partners such as the European Investment Bank, and increase their risk-bearing capacity.[160] The financial partners are expected to contribute at least €9.5 billion in risk-bearing capacity. The guarantee will be provisioned at 40 per cent, meaning that €15.2 billion of the EU budget is set aside in case calls are made on the guarantee.[161] Additional international financial institutions active in Europe will have

[156] Ibid at 12.
[157] Ibid.
[158] InvestEU (2019), <https://ec.europa.eu/commission/priorities/jobs-growth-and-investment/investment-plan-europe-juncker-plan/whats-next-investeu-programme-2021-2027_en>.
[159] Ibid.
[160] Ibid.
[161] Ibid.

direct access to the EU guarantee, including the European Bank for Reconstruction and Development ('EBRD'), the World Bank, the Council of Europe Development Bank, and national banks, working jointly in groups so that they can cover at least three Member States.[162]

Another arrangement, blended finance, refers to the strategic use of public funds or risk capacity to mobilize private capital flows, aimed at encouraging private capital to invest in promising early to late-stage technologies that fall outside of domestic lending or investment criteria. The Canadian Expert Panel on Sustainable Finance recommended that blended finance can be used to calibrate risk-reward profiles to the needs of private investors, including a credible co-backer from an adopting industry and structuring to crowd-in a minimum threshold of private capital. It recommended making capital available to larger, more established companies, on condition that recipients partner with smaller innovation firms facing capital access constraints.[163] It also advocated creating privately-managed pooled investment platforms for targeted 'hard to fund' opportunities, using blended finance to deliver more favourable risk and return characteristics.[164] Transition-linked covenants could help assure investors that their capital is contributing to carbon reduction, giving companies access to competitively priced capital.[165]

One policy strategy, the United Nations Sustainable Stock Exchanges Initiative, a joint initiative of the United Nations Conference on Trade and Development ('UNCTAD'), the UN Global Compact, the UNEP Finance Initiative, and the UN PRI, seeks to facilitate growth of green finance products as well as greening mainstream financial markets.[166] A green finance action plan is to guide stock exchanges in the implementation of green finance strategies. The promotion of green labelled products and services seeks to direct funding towards green projects and environmentally aligned publicly held companies, accompanied by more systematic and holistic changes to the economic impacts of climate change. The guidance also advocates strengthening the quality and availability of climate-related and other environmental disclosure among companies and investors, and contributing to the growth of dialogue and consensus building on green finance with other capital market participants. Accreditation standards are developing, to avoid greenwashing.[167]

Another policy choice would be to create capital pools that encourage green and transition-linked fixed income products that can offer institutional investors scaled access to assets that align with their internal business plans and goals regarding pricing, quality, and diversification.[168] In 2016, only 3 per cent of private venture funds invested in Canada went toward cleantech, most of which was in smaller 'capital lite' technology deals that aligned with traditional holding periods and return hurdles.[169]

162 EC, The InvestEU Programme (5 June 2018), <https://ec.europa.eu/commission/presscorner/detail/en/MEMO_18_4010>.

163 Canada Expert Panel (n 31) at 32.

164 Ibid at 32.

165 Ibid at 37.

166 Sustainable Stock Exchanges Initiative, *How Stock Exchanges Can Grow Green Finance, A Voluntary Action Plan* (2017), <https://sseinitiative.org/wp-content/uploads/2017/11/SSE-Green-Finance-Guidance-.pdf>.

167 Ibid.

168 Canada Expert Panel (n 31) at 30.

169 Final Report of the Working Group on Clean Technology, Innovation, and Jobs (2016).

Canada's Expert Panel observed that long term and capital heavy technology development projects tend to fall outside of the investment horizon and scale of early stage venture capitalists, as well as the risk mandate and minimum size threshold of institutional investors.[170] It recommended that the Canadian government establish tailored structures that provide venture capital providers the ability to invest in longer-cycle or capital-intense cleantech on terms that meet their required investment time horizons.[171] For fossil fuel intensive economies, transition finance is needed. Such finance will not meet criteria for 'green finance' designation but may be essential to financing the transition away from carbon intensive economic activity.

In China, the People's Bank of China, in collaboration with six other government agencies, has issued guidelines establishing the green financial system, which includes proposals on: developing green lending, enhancing the role of the securities market through improving the rules and regulations for green bonds and guiding international investors to invest in green assets; launching green development funds and public private partnerships; developing green insurance; and improving and extending environmental rights trading markets.[172] China had issued RMB 45 billion (US $6.9 billion) of green bonds as of 2018, virtually all issued to finance activities domestically.[173]

The UK Financial Conduct Authority recently introduced a green finance regulatory sandbox to allow financial firms to test new products and services with consumers in a controlled environment.[174] The programme aims to reduce time to market at potentially lower cost, identify necessary consumer protection safeguards, and enable better access to finance. It is challenging firms where it sees potential greenwashing, and taking appropriate action to prevent consumers being misled.[175]

All of these policies and initiatives show promise, with different applicability and relevance in different countries and regions around the globe. However, to the extent that public funds or resources are expended to increase private capital flows, their success will depend on perceptions of the necessity and benefits of sustainable finance, and public confidence that there is an appropriate balance of risk taking and reward, as well as transparency and accountability in terms of the use of assets in advancing a net zero circular economy.

VI. Indigenous Partnerships in Green Finance

The shift to a low carbon economy offers new opportunities to build stronger partnerships with Indigenous communities. There are examples of successful partnerships all

170 Canada Expert Panel (n 31) at 30.

171 Ibid at 32.

172 UN PRI, *Fiduciary Duty in the 21st Century Final Report* (October 2019) at 16, <https://www.unpri.org/download?ac=9593> (hereafter UN PRI, *Fiduciary Duty in the 21st Century*).

173 Climate Bonds Initiative, 'China Green Bond Market Newsletter (March 2019), <https://www.climatebonds.net/files/files/Q1%202019%20China%20Newsletter_EN.pdf>.

174 Financial Conduct Authority ('FCA'), 'FS19/6: Climate change and green finance' (18 October 2019), <https://www.fca.org.uk/publications/feedback-statements/fs19-6-climate-change-and-green-finance> (hereafter FCA, 'Climate change').

175 Ibid.

over the world. One very successful example is economic development of the Great Bear Rainforest, discussed immediately below in the Part VII discussion of conservation finance. Other initiatives are developing internationally.

For example, Zimbabwe's Communal Areas Management Programme for Indigenous Resources co-develops and collaboratively implements plans that promote sustainable development, facilitate markets, and deliver benefits to people without eroding natural capital.[176] Its purpose is to try to empower the Zimbabweans who live near land insufficient for agricultural use but with unmanaged wildlife, by encouraging tourism to the region and by providing funds for wildlife ecology research, giving full control of wildlife management to rural communities. The theory is that Indigenous communities will invest time and energy if they can exploit resources on a sustainable basis for their own benefit.[177] Although normatively, the idea of letting hunters pay a very high fee to kill one game animal seems repugnant, the goal of the initiative is to sacrifice some animals to secure the longevity of species by the funds received; and in addition, the hunted meat and profits are given to the local Indigenous communities to support food availability, development of schools, clinics, and wildlife research facilities.[178]

Indigenous peoples value Mother Earth, view themselves as stewards of the Earth, and many have taken on the role of social entrepreneurs to safeguard their values.[179] Indigenous peoples have provided leadership in proposing renewable energy projects that protect land, air, and water, while creating employment.[180] Canada offers illustrative examples across the country. In Nova Scotia, the Mi'kmaq Millbrook First Nation operates four wind farm projects, putting more energy into the grid than it collectively uses.[181] The Inuit community of Inukjuak, in northern Québec, Canada, is using a public private partnership to build a 7.5 megawatt dam upstream on the Inukjuak River, which will replace diesel as the source of power, bringing greener energy to the town of 1,800 on the eastern coast of Hudson Bay, and much-needed revenue to help with Indigenous community projects.[182]

In Ontario, the Mother Earth Renewable Energy Wind project on the traditional territory of the M'Chigeeng First Nation on Manitoulin Island became fully

[176] Amanda Rodewald, Peter Arcese, Janis Sarra, John Tobin-de la Puentee, Jeffrey Sayer, Frank Hawkins, Tara Martin, Brodie Guy, and Kelly Wachowiczi, 'Innovative Finance for Conservation: Roles for Ecologists and Practitioners' (2020) Ecological Society of America, Issues in Ecology (in press) at 4 (hereafter Rodewald et al).

[177] F Murindagomo, 'Wildlife management in Zimbabwe: The CAMPFIRE programme', FAO (1990, updated), <http://www.fao.org/3/u5200e/u5200e06.htm>.

[178] Sophia Callahan, 'CAMPFIRE Project Zimbabwe', Environment & Society Portal (2019), <http://www.environmentandsociety.org/tools/keywords/campfire-project-zimbabwe>.

[179] Sustainable Canada Dialogues, *Acting on Climate Change, Solutions from Canadian Scholars* (2015) at 49, <http://www.sustainablecanadadialogues.ca/en/scd/endorsement> (hereafter *Acting on Climate Change*).

[180] Ibid at at 49, citing C Henderson, 'Aboriginal Power: Clean Energy and the Future of Canada's First Peoples' (Rainforest Editions, 2013).

[181] Jon Tattrie, 'Mi'kmaq Energy Summit Gives Update on Wind Farm Projects', *CBC News* (27 September 2016), <https://www.cbc.ca/news/canada/nova-scotia/mi-kmaq-energy-and-innovation-summit-wind-farm-turbine-1.3781065>.

[182] Elias Abboud, 'Nunavik Community to Make the Jump from Diesel to Hydroelectricity', *CBC News* (27 May 2019), <https://www.cbc.ca/news/canada/montreal/inukjuak-hydroelectric-dam-agreement-1.5152005>.

operational in 2013. It is 100 per cent owned by the M'Chigeeng First Nation, which is managing and operating a turbine windmill project under a 20 year agreement with Ontario Power Authority.[183] In Manitoba, the Wuskwatim Hydro Project, a 200-megawatt, run-of-river hydroelectric generating station, produces clean, renewable energy that earns revenues from the export market and assists in supplying domestic load in Manitoba.[184] The generating station was developed by Wuskwatim Power Limited Partnership, a legal entity involving the provincial hydro authority and the Nisichawayasihk Cree Nation, which incorporated Nisichawayasihk Cree Nation traditional knowledge to minimize project impacts on the environment.[185]

In British Columbia ('BC'), Canada, Blueberry River Enterprises GP Ltd is 100 per cent Blueberry First Nation owned, with strong partnerships with other local Indigenous peoples, specializing in the construction, alteration, repair, and development of earthwork, development of well sites, plant sites, roads, clean-ups, and right–of-way and seismic clearing.[186] It partnered with financial investors to operate a camp site for drilling for eight years in a shared financing arrangement, enhancing returns to both the Indigenous communities and investors. By 2017, there were 152 medium to large renewable energy projects with Indigenous involvement in Canada, and 1,200 smaller projects built with Indigenous participation that generate electricity for local communities.[187]

However, this idea of Indigenous partnerships for sustainable finance is still at a very nascent stage globally. As the United Nations Declaration on the Rights of Indigenous Peoples indicates,, discussed in Chapter 6, while many countries support Indigenous rights to economic development and self-government, there are not yet many examples of well-functioning full partnership initiatives globally.

VII. Conservation Finance

'Biodiversity' includes all the parts of natural terrestrial, freshwater, and marine ecosystems, sometimes referred to as 'natural capital'. Conserving and restoring degraded ecosystems is essential for humans to survive on Earth. Yet due to climate change, biodiversity loss has become a systemic risk, both to a range of these ecosystems and to businesses and communities operating and living within them. More than half of the world's GDP (US $44 trillion) is dependent on nature and its services, such as the provision of food, medicine, fibre, and fuel.[188] The unprecedented loss of biodiversity

[183] M'Chigeeng First Nation, <https://www.fnmhf.ca/english/participating_fn/participating_fn_024.html>.

[184] Wuskwatim Generating Station, 'A Source of Clean, Renewable Energy' (2019), <http://www.wuskwatim.ca/project.html>.

[185] Ibid.

[186] Blueberry River First Nation, <https://blueberryfn.com/blueberry-river-enterprises-2/>.

[187] M McDiarnid, 'Indigenous Communities Embracing Clean Energy, Creating Thousands Of jobs', *CBC News* (11 October 2017), <https://www.cbc.ca/news/politics/first-nations-renewable-energy-projects-1.4348595>.

[188] Conservation International, 'Why is Biodiversity Important?' (2020), https://www.conservation.org/ ; PRI, "Investor Action on Biodiversity Discussion Paper" (2020), https://www.unpri.org/sustainability-issues/environmental-social-and-governance-issues/environmental-issues/biodiversity.

places this value at risk, yet financing to preserve biodiversity has been inadequate to date. At the same time, Conservation International estimates that nature can deliver at least 30 per cent of the emissions reductions needed by 2030 to prevent climate catastrophe.[189]

'Conservation finance' refers to an emerging set of tools that seek to develop environmentally sustainable investments designed to generate returns for investors, while enhancing the provision of beneficial environmental and ecosystem services and safeguarding natural capital.[190] Amanda Rodewald et al observe that global efforts to conserve biodiversity and maintain ecosystem services have shifted from a traditional emphasis on the establishment of protected areas to one that includes the design of conservation projects that deliver positive social, ecological, and economic outcomes for people and the environment.[191]

Conservation finance can offer co-benefits for people and the environment, especially within working landscapes. Co-benefits can include protecting water quality and quantity for people, improving soil productivity and health, restoring forests to sequester carbon, and diversifying croplands to support rural livelihoods.[192] Rodewald et al suggest that this socio-ecological lens has become a hallmark of participatory conservation. In order to scale-up conservation finance, there needs to be standardization of monitoring and evaluation frameworks and the development of reliable metrics and indicators of project outcomes, necessary to facilitating conservation investment at large enough scales to enhance socio-economic and biodiversity outcomes.[193] Rodewald et al suggest that such metrics will demonstrate the value of projects to investors and local communities, through monitoring to ensure accountability, transparency, and continuous improvement.

Rodewald et al observe that landscape bonds represent a relatively new financial instrument. When first issued by the Tropical Landscapes Finance Facility in 2017, its landscape bond provided US $95 million to finance the creation of a sustainable rubber plantation on heavily degraded land across two provinces in Indonesia. It is operated in partnership with World Wildlife Fund, the project incorporating extensive social and environmental objectives, as well as safeguards to protect Bukit Tiga Puluh National Park, which had been threatened by encroachment.[194]

In Canada, conservation finance has been very successful for one project. The Coastal First Nations Great Bear Initiative is a conservation/economic development plan for the coastal rainforest, which includes nearly 8.5 million hectares of ecosystem-based management, of which about 2 million hectares is under strict protection.[195] The conservation and development funding totals Cdn $120 million. The Great Bear Rainforest is one of the largest remaining temperate rainforests left on Earth, stretching from Bute Inlet to the Alaskan border and is 6.4 million hectares in extent, comprising about one-quarter of the world's remaining old growth coastal temperate.[196] In 2000,

[189] Conservation International, ibid.
[190] Rodewald et al (n 176) at 4.
[191] Ibid at 1.
[192] Ibid at 15.
[193] Ibid at 16.
[194] Ibid at 31.
[195] Coast Funds (2019), <https://coastfunds.ca/great-bear-rainforest/#about-the-region>.
[196] Ibid.

after years of political conflict, under the banner of the Coast Forest Conservation Initiative, a number of companies agreed to halt development in more than 100 intact watersheds in the Great Bear Rainforest, and in return, non-governmental organizations such as ForestEthics, Greenpeace, and Rainforest Action Network modified their boycott campaigns.[197] This mutual standstill created the conditions for a broad dialogue with First Nations, the BC government, labour groups, and local communities regarding land-use planning and decision-making processes.[198]

Indigenous peoples in the Great Bear Rainforest wanted to promote economic development on the coast, while protecting the environment and quality of life. The First Nations alliance included the Wuikinuxv Nation, Heiltsuk, Kitasoo/Xaixais, Gitga'at, Haisla, Metlakatla, Old Massett, Skidegate, and Council of the Haida Nation. In the southern region of the Central Coast, First Nations leaders established the Nanwakolas Council representing Namgis First Nation, Mamalilikulla-Qwe-Qwa Sot'Em First Nation, Tlowitsis First Nation, Da'naxda'xw First Nation, Gwa'sala Nakwaxda'xw First Nation, Kwiakah First Nation, and Comox First Nation.[199] The goal was to restore and implement responsible land, water, and resource management approaches on the central and north coast of British Columbia and Haida Gwaii that are ecologically, socially, and economically sustainable. Each First Nation was working within its community, gathering traditional knowledge from elders and hereditary chiefs, and combining this information with western science to develop land use plans for its traditional territories that would give communities the rights and responsibilities to make decisions about, and care for, the lands, water, and resources in their traditional territories.[200]

Under the Coastal First Nations Great Bear Initiative, First Nations in British Columbia Canada are partnering with government, industry, and other groups to develop non-traditional economic sectors such as renewable energy, carbon credits, eco-system-based forestry management, ecotourism, non-timber forest products, shellfish aquaculture, and commercial shipping.[201] The funds management entity is the Coast Opportunity Funds. Created in 2007, it consists of two separate but related funds: the Cdn $60 million Conservation Fund, which is a permanent endowment for the protection of the included rainforest areas, and the Cdn $60 million Economic Development Fund, a sinking fund focused on sustainable development among the area's Indigenous peoples.[202]

With an aim to invest venture capital to enhance human well-being in rainforest communities, Coast Funds has, as of 2019, approved Cdn $87.4 million in 372 stewardship and economic development projects.[203] For example, Coast Funds provided start-up and operational funds to the 'Gitga'at Guardian Watchman' programme

197 Merran Smith and Art Sterritt, 'From Conflict to Collaboration: The Story of the Great Bear Rainforest' (2016), <https://coastfunds.ca/wp-content/uploads/2016/02/StoryoftheGBR.pdf> (hereafter Smith and Sterritt).

198 Ibid at 3–4.

199 Coast Funds (n 195).

200 Ibid at 6.

201 Coastal First Nations Great Bear Initiative, 'Our Economy' (2019), <https://coastalfirstnations.ca/our-economy/>.

202 Coast Funds (n 195).

203 Ibid.

to steward the nation's territory. The guardians serve their community by applying Indigenous knowledge in resource management, implement land use plans, and monitor tanker traffic, sport fishers, and illegal activity.[204] Cdn $2.8 million in Coast Funds support leveraged an additional Cdn $7.7 million, leading to seven protected area plans, research on animal and plant species that provide an essential ecological function, training, jobs, and Cdn $3.7 million in supporting salaries.[205]

In 2000, the Kitasoo/Xai'xais Nation identified ecotourism as a non-extractive economic opportunity that could help protect their territory. Coast Funds invested over Cdn $1 million to facilitate community development of Kitasoo/Xai'xais Nation's Spirit Bear Lodge, serving global ecotourism coming to the region and linking economic development, conservation, and human well-being in Indigenous communities. Such activities have enabled the Kitasoo/Xai'xais Nation to expand its role in stewardship, protect visual corridors, educate visitors, and facilitate research. The economic outcomes of the lodge are substantial, employing almost 10 per cent of the community, including women and youth.[206]

Coastal First Nations' strategic approach to development includes: sustainable ecosystem-based management of marine and land resources; increased local control and management of forestry and fisheries operations; coordinated development through regional strategic planning in forestry, fisheries, and tourism with an emphasis on value added initiatives; partnerships and co-operative arrangements with governments, industry, environmental non-governmental organizations, and other stakeholder groups; government-to-government relationships; and stronger governance institutions.[207]

Also as part of the Coastal First Nations Great Bear Initiative, renewable energy initiatives are helping communities protect their land and water, produce renewable, clean energy in traditional territories for community use, and are aimed at selling power from community-owned hydro installations.[208] For example, in Klemtu, the Kitasoo/Xai Xais Nation owns and operates its own small storage hydro-electric plant that delivers clean electricity to the community year round and has one of the largest remote solar energy projects in British Columbia.[209]

In 2011, Coastal Shellfish was established, with a multimillion-dollar investment from Coastal First Nations Great Bear Initiative and other partners. It worked with a Chinese scallop aquaculture company to build a modern shellfish hatchery in Prince Rupert, Canada, and began commercial trials with sea scallops, followed by commercial success in 2013.[210] Since then, the company has been rapidly expanding its farming capacity. The Metlakatla Nation is a majority shareholder and operates a farm in its territory to grow the scallop seed. Coastal Shellfish has set a goal of increasing

[204] Rodewald et al (n 176) at 59.

[205] Coastal First Nations Great Bear Initiative, 'Community Clean Energy Projects' (2019), <https://coastalfirstnations.ca/our-economy/clean-energy/community-clean-energy-projects/> (hereafter Coastal First Nations).

[206] Ibid.

[207] Rodewald et al (n 176) at 6.

[208] Coastal First Nations (n 205).

[209] Ibid.

[210] Ibid.

production to 15 million scallops per year, the hatchery also capable of supplying seed to farms to support other First Nations' plans for shellfish aquaculture development.[211]

Coastal First Nations are now exploring ways to generate income from old growth forests without cutting more trees. In 2019, two Coastal First Nations communities partnered with a local aromatherapy company to create Great Bear Rainforest Essential Oils, ethically-produced, sustainable essential oils made from the steam-distilled needles of conifers in the Great Bear Rainforest.[212]

Coastal First Nations communities are also collaboratively managing 130 land conservancies in their Territories, giving Indigenous peoples the right to continue traditional practices, such as harvesting cedar, hunting and fishing, and allowing for conservation-based activities such as wildlife viewing and guided-fishing. Conservancies now protect village sites, mortuary poles, and burial sites, also safeguarding traditional practices by protecting places where they harvest seaweed, salmon, and roe-on-kelp.[213]

The breadth and scope of initiatives under the Great Bear Rainforest initiative is an excellent example of the potential of partnering with Indigenous peoples in sustainable finance.

The BC government announced a new Great Bear Rainforest land-use order in 2016, enhancing ecological integrity by increasing the amount of protected old-growth forest to 70 per cent; and creating eight new special forest management areas covering almost 295,000 hectares that will be off-limits to logging.[214] With the new measures, 85 per cent of the forest will be protected and 15 per cent will be available for logging, supporting local jobs.[215] The land-use order also addresses First Nations' cultural heritage resources, freshwater ecosystems, and wildlife habitat, with new required protections for the marbled murrelet, northern goshawk, grizzly bear, and mountain goat. The provincial government has signed reconciliation protocols with the Coastal First Nations and N̲anwak̲olas Council, and these government-to-government relationships have reached human well-being agreements to address issues of special concern to each group of First Nations.[216]

The forestry industry supports these initiatives through the Coast Forest Conservation Initiative, jointly involved in the implementation and development of conservation and management plans based on the ecosystem of the region.[217] Their operating principles are that: ecosystem-based management will provide the basis for forest conservation and timber harvesting in the region; the social and economic impacts of change must be equitably addressed and must respect the interests of all

[211] Ibid.

[212] Coastal First Nations Great Bear Initiative, 'Sustainable Forests' (2019), <https://coastalfirstnations.ca/our-economy/sustainable-forests/>.

[213] Coast Forest Conservation Initiative, 'Conservancies' (2019), <https://coastalfirstnations.ca/our-land/land-stewardship/conservancies/>.

[214] Government of British Columbia, 'Great Bear Rainforest: Coast Land Use Decision Update' (2016), <https://www2.gov.bc.ca/gov/content/industry/crown-land-water/land-use-planning/regions/west-coast/great-bear-rainforest>.

[215] Ibid.

[216] Ibid.

[217] Coast Forest Conservation Initiative (2019), <http://www.coastforestconservationinitiative.com/index.html>.

affected parties as well as the need for community well-being; new approaches to investment and economic opportunities for conservation and ecosystem-based management of coastal forests can help create benefits for everyone involved; and everyone who benefits from forests in the region needs to contribute to solutions.[218]

Another option for conservation finance is the recognition of ecosystems as legal persons, an increasingly common strategy for conservation, because, as legal persons, ecosystems may contract with private investors, potentially simplifying conservation investment projects and facilitating market-based transactions, with the priority being protection of biodiversity and its ecosystems.[219] For example, New Zealand Parliament has enacted two such bills creating legal personality. The Te Urewera Act (2014) converted a national park into a separate legal entity for whom board members act as trustees of the Te Urewera Board, comprised jointly of Tūhoe and Crown members. It also enacted the Te Awa Tupua (Whanganui River Claims Settlement) Bill in 2017, which provides for the Whanganui River's long term protection and restoration by making it a legal person. This legislation provided a settlement of NZ $80 million to redress actions and omissions of the Crown, and an additional NZ $1 million to establish a legal framework to economically support the Whanganui River.[220] The Board released its management plan in 2017, focused on the management of activities people in Te Urewera, such as ecotourism.[221]

Conservation finance presents important opportunities for protecting entire ecosystems, offering comprehensive and integrated approaches to advancing a net zero and circular economy that distributes the benefits more equitably.

VIII. Examples of Sustainable Finance

The examples of sustainable finance in this section are just a tiny snapshot of developments happening across the globe. They are meant to spark the reader's imagination as to what can be accomplished if we have the financial, political, and social will to move towards a net zero carbon circular economy.

i. Energy Efficiency and Renewable Energy

Electrification, end-use energy efficiency, and increased share of renewables initiatives are lowering energy use and decarbonizing energy supply in the built environment, especially in buildings.[222] Cities are beginning to increase decarbonized public transportation, expanding use of electric vehicles.[223] Initiatives in urban transport could include electrifying all public transit, facilitating car-sharing fleets, infrastructure

[218] Ibid.
[219] Rodewald et al (n 176) at 32.
[220] Ibid at 33.
[221] Te Urewera Board, 'Te Urewera management plan future of conservation' (19 May 2017), <https://www.ngaituhoe.iwi.nz/te-urewera-management-plan-future-of-conservation>.
[222] IPCC, 'Global Response 2018' (n 14) at 316.
[223] Ibid.

to encourage active transportation such as bicycle paths, wide sidewalks, bicycle parking, and bike-sharing programmes.[224] 'Smart city planning' reduces the need to travel long distances to work and leisure, and creates space for active mobility, essentially designing cities with high amenity and mixed land use, with water, waste, energy, transport, and buildings systems made clean, accessible, and sustainable using advanced technologies.[225] One study noted that 'replacing over the road shipping with intermodal transportation such as rail for shipments of more than 1,000 miles would reduce GHG by 65 per cent.'[226] High-speed trains offer low carbon alternatives to personal vehicle use.

Numerous strategies for energy efficiency include smart grid technology and distributed generation from micro-grids, batteries, storage solutions, and other behind-the-meter management technology; possible use of distributed ledger technology to enhance data transparency, control, and interoperability; and cybersecurity for key electrical systems in deploying large-scale intelligent technologies and control system architectures.[227]

Wind energy

The UK has scaled-up financing of wind energy as key to sustainability. The UK created Hywind, the first floating offshore wind farm in the world, off the eastern coast of Scotland. The UK government's financing strategy was to identify early stage investment barriers to development of offshore wind energy.[228] It created capacity auctions and established institutions to encourage offshore wind technologies, and currently has almost 40 per cent of global installed wind power capacity.[229] Using the capacity auctions, it will deliver between 1 and 2 gigawatts of offshore wind each year from 2020 to 2029, with support of up to £557 million.[230] The Hywind project has a 30 megawatt capacity to power up to 20,000 homes, as well as having a new battery storage pilot project.[231] Storing energy generated by offshore wind turbines in batteries has the potential to mitigate the variability of wind, improve efficiency, and lower the cost of offshore wind energy even further.[232] The UK also commenced construction of the Hornsea Wind Farm in the North Sea in 2018, which will be the largest wind farm in the world, with 1.2 gigawatts capacity to power over one million homes.[233]

The use of coal in the UK's electricity mix dropped 80 per cent from 34 per cent in 2007 to 7 per cent in 2017.[234] Low carbon electricity's share of generation increased

[224] *Acting on Climate Change* (n 179) at 35.
[225] Ibid at 36.
[226] Ibid at 35.
[227] Canada Expert Panel (n 31) at 46.
[228] OECD, Developing Robust Pipelines for Low-Carbon Infrastructure (12 November 2018), <http://www.oecd.org/publications/developing-robust-project-pipelines-for-low-carbon-infrastructure-9789264307827-en.htm>.
[229] Ibid.
[230] 'Delivering Clean Growth Progress' (n 26) at 2.
[231] Ibid at 18.
[232] Ibid.
[233] Ibid.
[234] Ibid at 17, citing BEIS, 'Energy Trends: Electricity' (2018), <https://www.gov.uk/government/statistics/electricity-section-5-energy-trends> and BEIS, UK Energy Statistics (2018), <https://www.gov.uk/government/statistics/electricity-chapter-5-digest-of-united-kingdom-energy-statistics-dukes>.

to 48 per cent in 2018, and renewables' share of electricity generation is now just over 30 per cent.[235] The UK brought new boiler standards into force that ensure household heating is more efficient and comfortable, introducing requirements for control devices to ensure systems use no more fuel and power than is reasonable.[236]

Germany has the next largest wind power capacity globally.[237] In 2000, the German government introduced a new system of financial aid for renewable energy sources. The Renewable Energies Act targeted a 12 per cent share for electricity produced from renewable energy by 2010.[238] Producers of wind, hydro, and solar energy were able to sell to the grid at a price guaranteed by the law. Citizen ownership of renewable energy projects is one of the pillars of Germany's energy transition, Energiewende, with households and farms accounting for more than 40 per cent of renewables investment.[239] By 2018, onshore wind turbines generated almost 15 per cent of Germany's power mix.[240] Greater power yields and more operating hours per turbine have also compensated declining financial support rates and made harnessing previously unattractive locations possible.[241] Biomass accounts for 7 per cent, solar power 7 per cent, and hydro 2.6 per cent, for a total of over 35 per cent of Germany's energy being supplied through renewables in 2018.[242]

In 2017, the German government announced a change from the predetermined feed-in tariffs to 'price finding' in auctions, aimed at increasing wind power's market exposure. There was concern about the wind turbines that were approaching their twenty year end-of-life and fixed prices.[243] However, investors such as the public utility of Munich and car manufacturer Daimler announced plans for older wind farms that were no longer eligible for support—to retrofit them and continue to generate a profit by operating them at market prices, using older wind turbines to fulfil decarbonization goals.[244] Daimler announced that production of all Mercedes-Benz cars in Germany will run on CO_2-free energy by 2022 and Mercedes-Benz is the first major industrial company to source electricity from German wind farms.[245] The green

[235] BEIS, UK Energy Statistics Q1 (2018), <https://assets.publishing.service.gov.uk/government/uploads/system/uploads/attachment_data/file/720182/Press_ Notice_June_18.pdf>.

[236] 'Delivering Clean Growth Progress' (n 26) at 23, 28.

[237] Ibid at 18.

[238] Germany, Renewable Energies Act, in effect 1 April 2000, <https://www.iea.org/policiesandmeasures/pams/germany/name-21295-en.php>.

[239] Ibid.

[240] Clean Energy Wire, 'German Onshore Wind Power: Output, Business and Perspectives', *CEW Facts* (31 January 2019), <https://www.cleanenergywire.org/factsheets/german-onshore-wind-power-output-business-and-perspectives>.

[241] Ibid.

[242] Ibid.

[243] Clean Energy Wire, citing Munich public utilities subsidiary, Hanse Windkraft, plans to repower wind farms once they lose their guaranteed feed-in tariffs after twenty years, Clean Energy Wire, 'New Company Buys Old Wind Farms to Operate without Support Payments' (4 April 2018) and Clean Energy Wire, 'Daimler Sources Electricity from Wind Farms No Longer Eligible for Feed-In Tariffs' (13 December 2018), <https://www.cleanenergywire.org/news/daimler-sources-electricity-wind-farms-no-longer-eligible-feed-tariffs>. See also <https://www.cleanenergywire.org/news/new-company-bets-old-wind-farms-top-10-ets-emitters-mainly-german/new-company-buys-old-wind-farms-operate-without-support-payments>.

[244] Clean Energy Wire, ibid.

[245] Daimler, 'New Era for Renewable Energies in Germany: Mercedes-Benz Cars and Statkraft Make an Important Contribution to the Energy Transition', <https://media.daimler.com/marsMediaSite/en/instance/ko/New-era-for-renewable-energies-in-Germany-Mercedes-Benz-Cars-and-Statkraft-make-an-important-contribution-to-the-energy-transition.xhtml?oid=42052688&ls=L2VuL2luc3RhbmNlL2tvLnh

energy from the wind farms is to be used for the production of the EQC electric car at the Mercedes-Benz Bremen Plant, as well as for the battery production at the location of Deutsche Accumotive.[246]

In 2018, pension fund ABP invested €360 million in a green bond issued by the Belgian State, the proceeds being used for the construction of wind farms and a system of fast rail connections in the Brussels region.[247] ABP has also invested in green bonds issued by international institutions, such as the World Bank and regional development banks such as the African Development Bank and the Asian Development Bank, to finance projects in the areas of renewable energy and sustainable infrastructure.[248]

Many companies are now working with conservationists to ensure that location of wind farms pays careful attention to protection of biodiversity, such as locating them away from sensitive habitats or bird migration flight paths. It is illustrative of how renewable energy initiatives can align with protection of ecosystems.

Solar Energy

Solar energy also has huge potential. The IPCC reports that solar energy is the most abundant renewable energy source, and although solar energy generation still only represents a small fraction of total energy consumption, markets for solar technologies are growing rapidly.[249] Solar technologies deliver heat, cooling, natural lighting, electricity, and fuels for a host of applications. Direct solar energy technologies harness the energy of solar irradiance to produce electricity using photovoltaics ('PV') and concentrating solar power ('CSP'), to produce heating or cooling through passive or active means ('thermal energy') such as a plan to produce high-temperature heat, which is then converted to electricity via a heat engine and generator.[250] The IPCC reports that both approaches are growing in use.[251]

Solar technology ranging from the development stage to mature applications of both passive and active solar heating, and wafer-based silicon PV, are often modular in nature, which the IPCC reports means that they can be used in both centralized and decentralized energy systems.[252] Thermal storage within thermal solar systems is a key component to ensure reliability and efficiency, with four main types of thermal energy storage technologies—sensible, latent, sorption, and thermochemical heat storage.[253]

odG1sP29pZD00ODM2MjU4JnJlbElkPTYwODI5JmZyb21PaWQ9NDgzNjI1OCZib3JkZXJzPXRydWU mcmVzdWx0SW5mb1R5cGVJZD00MDYyNiZ2aWV3VHlwZT10aHVtYnM%21&rs=0>.

[246] Ibid.

[247] ABP, 'Sustainable and Responsible Investment 2018' (ABP 2019) at 35, <https://www.abp.nl/images/responsible-investment-report-2018.pdf> (hereafter ABP, 'Sustainable Investment').

[248] Ibid at 28.

[249] Intergovernmental Panel on Climate Change ('IPCC'), D Arvizu, P Balaya, L Cabeza, T Hollands, A Jäger-Waldau, M Kondo, C Konseibo, V Meleshko, W Stein, Y Tamaura, H Xu, and R Zilles, 'Direct Solar Energy' in O Edenhofer, R Pichs-Madruga, Y Sokona, K Seyboth, P Matschoss, S Kadner, T Zwickel, P Eickemeier, G Hansen, S Schlömer, and C von Stechow (eds), *IPCC Special Report on Renewable Energy Sources and Climate Change Mitigation* (CUP, 2012) at 337 (hereafter 'Direct Solar Energy').

[250] IPCC, *Renewable Energy Sources and Climate Change Mitigation* (IPCC, 2012) at 8, <https://www.ipcc.ch/site/assets/uploads/2018/03/SRREN_Full_Report-1.pdf> (hereafter IPCC, *Renewable Energy*)

[251] 'Direct Solar Energy' (n 249) at 337.

[252] IPCC, *Renewable Energy* (n 250) at 8.

[253] 'Direct Solar Energy' (n 249) at 349.

Rooftop solar is the fastest growing form of distributed energy.[254] One goal is now to move to net zero energy solar buildings, using smart solar-building control strategies to manage the collection, storage, and distribution of locally produced solar electricity and heat to reduce and shift peak electricity demand from the grid.[255] In China, Greece, Cyprus, and Israel, solar water heaters now make a significant contribution to supplying residential energy demand.[256] India's National Solar Mission in 2010 set the target of goal of 20,000 megawatts of solar power by 2022 through a 20 million square solar thermal collector area.[257] In 2015, it revised that target of grid connected solar power to 100,000 megawatts by 2022.[258]

The IPCC observes that solar technologies can improve the health and livelihood opportunities for many of the world's poorest populations as they can potentially address part of the gap in availability of energy services for the roughly 1.4 billion people who do not have access to electricity and 2.7 billion people who rely on traditional biomass for home cooking and heating needs.[259] The discussion of Solar Sister in Chapter 9 highlights the health benefits and reduction of carbon emissions from moving to solar.

The IPCC observes that solar home systems and PV-powered community grids can provide economically favourable electricity to many areas for which connection to a main grid is impractical, such as in remote and mountainous regions.[260] There are new deployments of solar technologies that have the potential to combat prevalent causes of morbidity and mortality in poor areas, such as solar desalination and water purification technologies to combat disease from lack of access to potable water supplies.[261] PV systems for health clinics can provide refrigeration for vaccines and lights for performing medical procedures.[262]

As noted earlier, China deploys more than one third of global solar capacity. In 2018, China had roughly 175 gigawatts of solar power.[263] China's Five-Year Plan for Solar Energy Development contains specific goals for solar panel innovation, including commercialized monocrystalline silicon cells with an efficiency of at least 23 per cent, the Chinese government spending heavily on solar power research and development. The Chinese government also has a programme that rewards high-efficiency, low-cost solar panels with subsidies and construction quotas, with China Development Bank and other banks financing Chinese solar manufacturers and developers.[264]

[254] *Acting on Climate Change* (n 179) at 24.
[255] 'Direct Solar Energy' (n 249) at 355.
[256] Ibid at 367.
[257] Government of India, 'National Solar Mission' (2009), <https://mnre.gov.in/scheme-documents>.
[258] Ibid.
[259] Direct Solar Energy' (n 249) at 372.
[260] Ibid.
[261] Ibid.
[262] Ibid at 373.
[263] David Sandalow, Guide to Chinese Climate Policy 2019, Columbia Center on Global Energy Policy (18 September 2019) at 72, <https://energypolicy.columbia.edu/sites/default/files/file-uploads/Guide%20to%20Chinese%20Climate%20Policy_2019.pdf> (hereafter Sandalow).
[264] Ibid at 74.

Other Energy Innovations

Geothermal energy is also being increasingly used, extracting heat from the Earth's interior geothermal reservoirs using wells or other means.[265] The IPCC reports that geo-thermal energy is a renewable resource, as the tapped heat from an active reservoir is continuously restored by natural heat production, conduction, and convection from surrounding hotter regions, and any extracted geothermal fluids are replenished by natural recharge and by reinjection of the cooled fluids.[266] Hydrothermal power plants and thermal applications of geothermal energy are mature technologies; however, they are nascent in terms of scaling-up such applications. There has been some social protest to geothermal energy as the process of high-pressure injection of cold water into hot rock generates small seismic events, and while to date, the IPCC reports such events that have not been large enough to lead to human injury or significant property damage, this issue will need to be addressed if there is to be expansion of geothermal energy.[267]

Energy production and use is responsible for more than 75 per cent of the EU's GHG emissions.[268] Moving to net zero carbon necessitates a sustainable energy supply, integrating electricity, gas, heating and cooling, and mobility systems and markets, with smart networks. The European Commission has emphasized the need to further scale-up technological innovations in energy, in terms of efficiency for buildings, transport, industry, and agriculture sectors.[269] Innovations in digitalization, artificial intelligence, and biotechnology are needed. The EU is fostering co-operation among Member States to maximize synergies by pooling resources and knowledge of low carbon energy technologies, the European Commission reporting that unco-ordinated action increases the risks of lock-in to carbon-intensive infrastructure and stranded assets, making transition costlier.[270] Circular economy goals require new business models that encourage a range of energy efficiency solutions.[271] The EU currently hosts six of the twenty-five largest renewable energy businesses, employing 1.5 million people.[272]

The EU anticipates that all mid-century scenarios involve large-scale electrification of the energy system that creates jobs and reduces Europe's energy import dependence.[273] By 2018, more than half of Europe's electricity supply was renewable and free from GHG emissions.[274] The European Commission is seeking to reduce fossil fuel import expenditures, at €266 billion in 2018, by 70 per cent, aiming for a reduced import bill of over €2 trillion over the period 2031–2050.[275] The EU is also examining how to harness ocean energy. The European Commission reports that

265 IPCC, *Renewable Energy* (n 250) at 8.
266 Ibid at 71.
267 Ibid at 76.
268 EC, *Clean Planet* (n 17) at 6.
269 Ibid.
270 Ibid.
271 Ibid.
272 Ibid at 9.
273 Ibid at 6.
274 Ibid at 8.
275 Ibid, planning to reduce oil and gas imports, which were 55 per cent in 2018 to 20 per cent by 2050.

competitive deployment of renewable electricity also provides a major opportunity for the decarbonization of other sectors such as heating, transport, and industry, either through direct use of electricity or indirectly through the production of e-fuels such as e-hydrogen.[276]

The European Commission is developing 'power-to-X', whereby synthetic fuels can be stored and used in multiple ways across different economic sectors that are otherwise hard to decarbonize.[277] Power-to-X technologies refer to technologies that allow transforming electricity into synthetic liquids and gases (hydrogen, methane, or other gases). Hydrogen produced with carbon-free electricity combined with CO_2 from sustainable biomass or direct air capture can make a carbon-neutral alternative of the same molecules as natural gas or oil; and thus, can be distributed via existing transmission systems and used by existing installations and applications.[278] However, in the EU, a biomass-based transition is limited by the availability of land.[279] The European Commission reports that sustainable biomass has an important role to play in a net zero GHG emissions economy, for heat supply, biofuels, substitutes for carbon intensive building materials; and when used in power generation, CO_2 emitted can be captured and stored, creating negative emissions.[280]

Grasslands and marginal or degraded lands unsuited for conventional food crops have potential for supporting substantial bioenergy production, but biodiversity considerations and water shortages limit this potential, the IPCC noting that conversion of such lands to biomass plantations has the potential to reduce downstream water availability.[281] The IPCC also cautions that the impact of bioenergy on social and environmental issues such as health, poverty, and biodiversity may be positive or negative depending on local conditions and the design and implementation of specific projects.[282] While these biomass technologies are attractive in respect of generating abundant electricity from carbon-free sources, the European Commission reports that a drawback is that their production is energy intensive.[283]

There are initiatives to develop smaller and more powerful batteries in many countries. One example is a collaboration of scientists and other scholars in Canada with the private sector, who are working on the next generation of lithium-tellurium batteries, a metal by-product of copper and lead-zinc smelting, which are miniature, high energy, have extended storage capacity, and have a high safety rating.[284]

The European Commission reports that carbon capture and storage was previously viewed as a major decarbonization option for energy intensive industries, but by 2018, this potential appeared lower, considering the rapid deployment of renewable energy technologies, other options to reduce emissions in industrial sectors, and issues concerning social acceptance of the technology itself.[285] Carbon capture and utilization

276 Ibid at 9–10.
277 Ibid at 10.
278 Ibid.
279 Ibid at 14.
280 Ibid.
281 Ibid at 232.
282 Ibid at 215.
283 Ibid at 10.
284 University of British Columbia, 'Next-generation battery' (UBC Trek 2019) at 35.
285 EC, *Clean Planet* (n 17) at 145.

in industry refers to processes where CO_2 is captured and then converted into a new product.[286] However, the European Commission suggests that carbon capture can serve as a transition strategy for energy-intensive industries, capturing CO_2 emissions from biomass-based energy and industrial plants to be stored to create negative emissions.[287] It notes that, to date, capture and storage technology has not yet reached the commercialization stage; it requires research of successful applied use, and it faces limited public acceptance.[288] The European Commission also notes that soil carbon sequestration has co-benefits with agriculture and is cost-effective, but its potential feasibility and cost-effectiveness at the global scale appear to be more limited.[289]

Another major platform is the decentralization of power systems based on renewables, including consumers' involvement, increased interconnectivity, improved energy storage deployed on a large scale, demand side response, and management through digitalization.[290]

Under Mission Innovation, Canada, the EU, and twenty other governments have agreed to double their respective investments in transformative, clean energy research and development over five years, encourage private sector investment in clean energy technology, and increase collaboration among participating countries.[291]

ii. Net Zero Emissions Buildings and Low Carbon Retrofit of Buildings

Another major strategy towards net zero is reconceptualizing buildings for industrial, commercial, and residential use, including low carbon retrofitting, rigorous climate conscious building codes, green roofs, building-specific solar energy, and water collection and use within buildings.

The World Green Building Council and the Green Building Council, collaborating in the Advancing Net Zero project, are dedicated to supporting market transformation towards 100 per cent net zero carbon buildings by 2050.[292] They recognize that in most situations, net zero energy buildings, i.e. buildings that generate 100 per cent of their energy needs on-site, are not feasible, and suggest that buildings that are energy efficient and supply energy needs from renewable sources (on-site and/or off-site) is a more appropriate target for the mass scale required to achieve Paris Agreement levels of global emission reductions.[293]

[286] Ibid at 11, citing e-fuels as an example where the CO2 gets released again when the fuel is combusted, displacing emissions of fossil fuels.

[287] Ibid.

[288] Ibid.

[289] IPCC, 'Global Response 2018' (n 14) at 316.

[290] EC, *Clean Planet* (n 17) at 10.

[291] Smart Prosperity Leaders' Initiative (March 2018), 'Report from Clean Technology Economic Strategy Tables (CTEST): The Innovation and Competitiveness Imperative' (September 2018); as well as sector-specific reports.

[292] World Green Building Council, 'What is Net Zero Carbon' (2019), <https://www.worldgbc.org/advancing-net-zero/what-net-zero>.

[293] World Green Building Council, 'From Thousands to Billions: Co-ordinated Action towards 100% Net Zero Carbon Buildings By 2050' (31 May 2017), <https://www.worldgbc.org/news-media/thousands-billions-coordinated-action-towards-100-net-zero-carbon-buildings-2050>.

In the EU, given that most of the housing stock for 2050 already exists, most of the required reduction in energy use needs to occur in existing buildings, both residential and business.[294] The European Commission's strategies include retrofitting buildings with improved materials for insulation, sustainable renewable heating such as electricity, district heating, renewable gas or solar thermal efficient appliances, smart buildings, and appliance management systems.[295]

In 2018, thirty-seven major European banks launched a new energy efficiency mortgage pilot scheme.[296] With 97 per cent of Europe's buildings currently deemed inefficient, reducing fossil-fueled energy use in buildings through greater energy efficiency and renewable energy is key to tackling climate change.[297] The operation of buildings is a major contributor to the EU's carbon footprint, responsible for over a third of carbon emissions and 40 per cent of the total energy used in Europe. The initiative includes an Energy Efficient Mortgages Action Plan, with the aim of creating a European energy efficient mortgage, to incentivize borrowers to improve the energy efficiency of their buildings or acquire highly energy efficient properties.[298] The World Green Buildings Council's Europe network has undertaken extensive research to develop and define building performance assessment criteria for energy efficient mortgages in a way that will meet the expectations of the different market actors.[299] Mortgages account for around €7 trillion, or a third of the European banking sector's assets, and are the best-known form of property finance for consumers, which means that energy efficient mortgages could become a powerful economic tool in tackling the risks from poor performing buildings.[300]

The UK government has committed to cutting the energy use of new buildings in half by 2030.[301] The UK enacted the Smart Meters Act 2018, with over 12 million smart and advanced meters operating to help people to take control of their energy use and save money on their bills.[302] Its goal is to bring down the cost of building low energy, low carbon buildings, and to drive lower carbon, lower cost, and higher quality construction techniques.[303]

The UK government's Clean Growth Strategy works with lenders to develop green mortgages to incentivize people to make their homes more energy efficient. The premise is that banks might be willing to offer more favourable terms, such as lower interest rates, to owners of energy-efficient homes, if they are less likely to default on their mortgage payments because they have considerable cost savings on energy bills. However, the Grantham Institute notes that while the reasoning behind promoting

294 EC, *Clean Planet* (n 17) at 8.
295 Ibid.
296 Europe Regional Network, 'Creating an Energy Efficient Mortgage for Europe: Towards a New Market Standard' (2018), <https://www.worldgbc.org/sites/default/files/Creating%20an%20Energy%20Efficient%20Mortgage%20for%20Europe%20-%20Towards%20a%20New%20Market%20Standard%20-%20Web_2.pdf>.
297 Ibid at 8.
298 Ibid at 9. See also EeMAP, <https://www.energyefficientmortgages.eu>.
299 Ibid at 13.
300 Ibid.
301 'Delivering Clean Growth Progress' (n 26) at 2.
302 Ibid at 13.
303 Ibid at 25.

green mortgages is intuitive, there is not yet a lot of evidence to draw from, and it could be that higher income people are more likely to buy energy efficient homes and their lower default rate is because of that higher income.[304] In the US, one study of 71,000 ENERGY STAR and non-STAR homes found that default risks are on average 32 per cent lower in energy-efficient homes, controlling for other loan determinants.[305] It found that the lower risks associated with energy efficiency should be taken into consideration when underwriting mortgage risks.[306]

In Canada, the City of Vancouver has a suite of innovative green building policies. In 2014, the City established a long term goal that all new and existing buildings in Vancouver, British Columbia will run on 100 per cent renewable energy by 2050.[307] The city subsequently developed the Zero Emissions Building Plan to ensure that all new buildings will emit zero operational GHG emissions by 2025, and net zero GHG emissions overall by 2030. The vast majority of the city's new homes are being built to meet the standard. Under the BC Energy Step Code, municipalities in the province are committing to higher energy performance for new buildings, aimed at net zero carbon by 2032.[308]

The government of Canada committed to reducing GHG emissions from its own buildings and fleets by 40 per cent below 2005 levels by 2030 or earlier, and by 80 per cent by 2050.[309] The federal government announced the Low Carbon Cities Canada network in its 2019 budget, which will provide end-to-end retrofit project facilitation and market development, to boost project activity and crowd in private investment.[310] Retrofits allow property owners to simultaneously improve the life span, operating income, and value of their buildings, while creating safer, healthier, working and living environments. The Canadian government's Investing in Canada plan has committed Cdn $186 billion over twelve years to upgrading infrastructure in communities across the country, at an average spend of over Cdn $15 billion per year. Its Canada Infrastructure Bank is to mobilize private sector financing.

iii. Transportation

In order to meaningfully move away from fossil-fuel-based transportation, we need massive expansion of charging infrastructure for electric vehicles and strategies to support remote off-grid communities or operations in transitioning toward cleaner energy sources and renewables.[311] Strategies are also needed to increase electrification

[304] Sini Matikainen, 'What Are Green Mortgages and Could They Increase the Energy Efficiency of UK Homes?', Grantham Research Institute on Climate and the Environment (17 January 2018), <https://www.lse.ac.uk/GranthamInstitute/news/do-green-mortgages-work/>.

[305] Nikhil Kasa, Roberto Quercia, and Chao Yue Tian, *Home Energy Efficiency and Mortgage Risks* (Institute for Market Transformation, March 2013), <https://www.imt.org/wp-content/uploads/2018/02/IMT_UNC_HomeEEMortgageRisksfinal.pdf>.

[306] Ibid at 2.

[307] City of Vancouver, Green Vancouver, <https://vancouver.ca/green-vancouver/zero-emissions-buildings.aspx>.

[308] Vancouver Economic Commission, 'Shift' (2019), <https://shift.opentech.eco/>.

[309] Government of Canada, '2016–2019 Federal Sustainable Development Strategy'.

[310] Canada Expert Panel (n 31) at 42.

[311] See UK Government, Decarbonization and Energy Efficiency Roadmap Action Plans in October 2017.

in industrial processes, including transportation of production supply inputs and final product distribution.

Transport is responsible for over one quarter of GHG emissions in the EU.[312] The European Commission reports, therefore, that all transport modes need to contribute to decarbonization: electric vehicles, efficient and sustainable batteries, highly efficient electric powertrains, biofuels for heavy-duty vehicles, and electrification of short sea shipping and inland waterways.[313] Since 75 per cent of the EU's population lives in urban areas, the EU proposes smart cities that embrace innovations in mobility, safe cycling and walking paths, clean local public transport, the introduction of new delivery technologies such as drones, underpinned by behavioural changes by individuals and companies.[314] The European Commission reports that a net zero emissions economy can only be achieved with smart infrastructure, ensuring optimal high-speed train interconnection and sectoral integration across Europe, including timely completion of the Trans-European Transport and Energy Networks, and smart charging or refuelling stations that enable seamless, cross-border services.[315] Only then will there be a real alternative to aviation for short and medium distance passenger travel within the EU.[316]

In the UK, transport accounts for 27 per cent of the country's GHG emissions.[317] Heavy goods vehicles, cars, and vans contribute 87 per cent of that total.[318] The UK's Road to Zero strategy sets out long term ambitions and pathway to zero emission vehicles, alongside plans for the expansion of charging infrastructure and reducing emissions from existing vehicles.[319] The UK government's target is that more than half of the cars produced in the country will be ultra-low emission by 2030.[320] Under its Automated and Electric Vehicles Act 2018, the UK government announced a £400 million public-private Charging Infrastructure Investment Fund to increase chargepoints across the UK from the current 14,000 public chargepoints.[321]

The UK Energy Transitions Commission recently concluded that reaching net zero carbon emissions from heavy industry and heavy-duty transport sectors is technically and financially possible by 2060, earlier in developed economies, and could cost less than 0.5 per cent of global GDP.[322] Its report outlines the possible routes to fully decarbonize cement, steel, plastics, trucking, shipping, and aviation, which together represent 30 per cent of UK energy emissions today.

[312] EC, *Clean Planet* (n 17) at 10.

[313] Ibid.

[314] Ibid at 11.

[315] Ibid at 13.

[316] Ibid at 11–12, citing the International Maritime Organization ('IMO') and the International Civil Aviation Organization ('ICAO').

[317] Department for Business, Energy and Industrial Strategy, Final UK Greenhouse Gas Emissions National Statistics (2020), https://data.gov.uk/dataset/9568363e-57e5-4c33-9e00-31dc528fcc5a/final-uk-greenhouse-gas-emissions-national-statistics.

[318] Ibid.

[319] 'Delivering Clean Growth Progress' (n 26) at 40.

[320] UK Government, 'The Road to Zero' (2018), <https://www.gov.uk/government/news/government-launches-road-to-zero-strategy-to-lead-the-world-in-zero-emission-vehicle-technology>.

[321] 'Delivering Clean Growth Progress' (n 26) at 43.

[322] UK Energy Transitions Commission, 'Reaching Net-Zero Carbon Emissions: Mission Possible' (2019), <http://www.energy-transitions.org/mission-possible>.

In Canada, vehicle electrification through hydrogen fuel cell technology is being developed for trucking companies, and a consortium has secured Cdn $15 million in investment for a pilot project to test the ability of hydrogen to fuel Alberta's heavy-duty freight transportation sector.[323] The Alberta Zero-Emissions Truck Electrification Collaboration project, scheduled to run until mid-2022, involves the design and manufacture of two heavy-duty, extended-range, hydrogen fuel cell electric hybrid trucks that will be pilot tested by moving freight year-round between Edmonton and Calgary under Canada's harshest road conditions.[324] If successful, it will seek financing to scale-up the technology, addressing a significant source of GHG emissions in Canada.

China leads the world in deployment of electric vehicles, using 45 per cent of all electric cars globally and 99 per cent of all electric buses, with 92,000 sold in 2018 alone. It also dominates global markets for low-speed electric vehicles and electric two-wheelers.[325] The Chinese central government's policy is to require each Chinese vehicle manufacturer and importer to make or import at least 12 per cent electric vehicles in 2020.[326] These regulations apply to any company that manufacturers or imports more than 30,000 vehicles in China. The Chinese government provides subsidies to manufacturers of electric vehicles: all-electric plug-in cars with a range over 400 km are eligible for subsidies of RMB 25,000 (about US $3,600); all-electric plug-in cars with a range of 250 km–400 km are eligible for subsidies of RMB 18,000 (about US $2,600); plug-in hybrid cars are now eligible for subsidies of RMB 10,000 (US $1,500), with a schedule for elimination of carbon-emitting cars in the future.[327]

There are also growing opportunities provided by digital technology and consumer behavioural shifts, such as digitally enabled car-sharing models, which have grown exponentially globally. An example is peer-to-peer car rental ATzuche in China, which is a mobile application allowing individuals to rent out their vehicles, 100,000 registered cars in fourteen Chinese cities, including Beijing, Shanghai, and Shenzhen;[328] Drivezy is India's car and two-wheeler sharing marketplace; and MOIA is a ride-sharing app and programme in Germany.[329] While relatively nascent, the World Economic Forum suggests that these service-based businesses have great potential to radically reduce emissions, better deploy cars that currently exist, and decouple resource development from economic growth.[330]

Air travel may also not be completely doomed because of its large carbon footprint. In 2019, one Canadian seaplane operator announced plans to electrify its fleet, having tested a very short-haul flight of five minutes.[331] Norway has announced that it wants

[323] Transition Accelerator, 'Freight as the Anchor Tenant for a Canadian Hydrogen Economy' (2019), <https://www.transitionaccelerator.ca/>.

[324] Alberta Zero-Emissions Truck Electrification Collaboration (12 March 2019), <https://www.cesarnet.ca/blog/15-million-project-test-hydrogen-fuel-alberta-s-freight-transportation-sector>.

[325] Sandalow (n 263) at 92–3.

[326] Ibid at 95.

[327] Ibid.

[328] Atzuche, 'Company overview' (2019), <https://www.crunchbase.com/organization/atzuche#section-overview>.

[329] MOIA, 'MOIA Meets You' (2019), <https://www.moia.io/en>.

[330] WEF, *Next Frontier* (5) at 12.

[331] Josh Petri, 'Fossil Fuel-Free Air Travel Gets Closer with a Short Electric Flight from Vancouver', *Bloomberg News* (11 December 2019), <https://www.bnnbloomberg.ca/fossil-fuel-free-air-travel-gets-closer-with-a-short-electric-flight-1.1360890>.

all domestic flights to be electric by 2040.[332] It marks the very first steps in replacing fossil fuel-powered aircraft, and while electric airplanes on a commercial basis seem a long way off, as one news story observed, 'the time between the Wright brothers' first 120-foot flight and John Alcock and Arthur Brown's first nonstop trans-Atlantic flight was just 16 years'.[333]

iv. Transforming Water Use

As discussed in Chapter 2, clean and safe water is becoming an urgent issue, with water availability becoming unpredictable in many parts of the world. In addition to water scarcity, inundation of salt water and flooding threaten to contaminate fresh water sources. The UN observes that growing demand for water increases the need for energy-intensive water pumping and treatment, which has contributed to the degradation of critical water-dependent carbon sinks such as peatlands. It notes that some climate change mitigation measures, such as the expanded use of biofuels, are further exacerbating water scarcity.[334]

The UN suggests that national and regional climate policy and planning must take an integrated approach to climate change and water management, because increased water stress and future demand will require increasingly tough decisions about how to allocate water resources among competing water uses, including for climate change mitigation and adaptation activities.[335] It suggests that there is a unique opportunity to improve water management practices in ways that will allow communities to make confident, risk-informed decisions that can help increase climate resilience and improve ecosystem health.[336] For example, in 2018, ABP bought over €110 million in green government bonds issued by Ireland for the funding of sustainable water and waste management projects aimed at reducing the consequences of climate change.[337]

Norges Bank Investment Management has focused on water investments since 2009. It manages the assets of the Norwegian Government Pension Fund Global, currently more than US $1 trillion.[338] Norges Bank Investment Management observes that water challenges may give rise to risks and opportunities for companies, and their responses may influence long term returns for the fund.[339] It has also observed that externalities from unsustainable water use may present a risk to its portfolio's long term value, thus it is interested in sustainable water management and efficient water regulation across different sectors and geographies.[340] The CDP reports:

[332] Umair Irfan, 'Forget Cars. We Need Electric Airplanes', *VOX* (9 April 2019), <https://www.vox.com/2019/3/1/18241489/electric-batteries-aircraft-climate-change>.

[333] Ibid.

[334] UN Water, 'UN-Water Policy Brief: Climate Change and Water' (2019), <https://www.unwater.org/unwater-policy-brief-on-climate-change-and-water/>.

[335] UN Water, 'UN-Water launches Policy Brief on Climate Change and Water' (11 September 2019), <https://www.unwater.org/unwater-policy-brief-on-climate-change-and-water/>.

[336] Ibid.

[337] ABP, 'Sustainable Investment' (n 247) at 28.

[338] CDP, *Treading Water, Corporate Responses to Rising Water Challenges* (2018) at 6, <https://www.cdp.net/en/research/global-reports/global-water-report-2018>.

[339] Ibid.

[340] Ibid.

> Companies will not achieve the transformations needed until water is meaningfully embedded into corporate governance. Environmental and sustainability professionals can make incremental improvements to a company's water performance, but it is the strategic decisions taken by the CEO and the Board that will truly transform outcomes for a water secure future. Decisions, for example, associated with product development, market expansion, or resource allocation, all have the potential to significantly reduce or even eliminate a company's negative environmental impacts. And increasingly, investors are looking to hold C-Suite decisionmakers accountable for their performance on water-related issues.[341]

There is also need for infrastructure to deliver sustainable water and to support urban agriculture.[342]

v. Agricultural Practices and Reforestation

Changing agricultural practices can be an effective climate adaptation strategy, reducing emissions intensity of food production, including mixed crop livestock production systems, improving irrigation efficiency, and water efficiency, in turn improving food production and enhancing food security. Regenerative agriculture can build farm fertility and resilience over time, which in turn can increase productivity and reduce reliance on chemicals needed to combat stressors on food crops such as pests, crop diseases, and nutrient deficiencies. Organic crops reduce the use of pesticides that produce carbon emissions when they are manufactured and they reduce the amount of pollutants that enter fresh water sources. Healthy soil can hold more water, enhance plant nutrients, and increase resilience to floods and droughts. Food producers are working with farmers to advance the sustainability of water use in farm operations that are their supply sources.

The European Commission suggests that agroforestry and other techniques that efficiently use nutrient resources will enhance soil carbon, biodiversity, and improve resilience of farming to climate change.[343] It advocates afforestation and restoration of degraded forest lands and other ecosystems to further increase absorption of $CO_{2,}$ while also benefiting biodiversity, soils, and water resources, recognizing that carbon sinks are as important as reducing emissions, and that further increasing the natural sink of forests, soils, agricultural lands, and coastal wetlands is crucial for the success of the EU's net zero strategy.[344]

China's Natural Forest Conservation Plan is the largest reforestation programme in the world, with massive tree-planting programmes, expansion of forest reserves, and a ban on logging in primary forests, the Chinese government spending more than three times the global average per hectare.[345]

[341] Ibid at 16.

[342] IPCC, 'Global Response 2018' (n 14) at 316.

[343] EC, *Clean Planet* (n 17) at 14.

[344] Ibid.

[345] Sandalow (n 263) at 115, citing China, *National Afforestation and Greening Plan* (2016–2020); China, *National Forest Management Plan* (2016–2050); China, *Action Plan for Climate Change in Forestry in the 13th Five-Year Plan*; and China, *Action Plan for Forestry to Adapt to Climate Change* (2016–2020).

The Canadian government has pledged to plant two billion trees over the next ten years as part of its Cdn $3 billion effort to deploy natural climate solutions.[346] It has committed to taking action to conserve and restore Canada's forests, grasslands, agricultural lands, wetlands, and coastal areas, support 3,500 seasonal jobs in tree planting, help cities expand and diversify their urban forests, and rebuild forests after wildfires.[347]

The IPCC observes that the large potential of afforestation and reforestation to neutralize emissions may be technically and geophysically feasible if implemented appropriately in terms of biodiversity, but cautions that soil quality will diminish over time as forests saturate.[348] It reports that options to reduce absolute emissions are limited unless paired with demand-side measures.[349]

In addition to these efficiency measures is the need to radically reduce waste. Measures such as the EU Fluorinated Greenhouse Gases Regulation that require a 79 per cent reduction in the use of hydrofluorocarbons ('HFC') across the EU by 2030;[350] the UK government's programme to radically reduce the amount of biodegradable waste sent to landfill;[351] and the Ellen MacArthur Foundation efforts to convert 20 per cent of plastic packaging into reuse models[352] are all aimed at the circular economy. They offer some hope that we can shift economic activities in time to prevent crossing any additional planetary boundaries. However, that transition needs to recognize the particular challenges for micro and small businesses, the subject of the following chapter.

346 Justin Trudeau, 'Planting Two Billion Trees and Using the Power of Nature to Fight Climate Change' (27 September 2019), <https://2019.liberal.ca/wp-content/uploads/sites/292/2019/09/Planting-two-billion-trees-and-using-the-power-of-nature-to-fight-climate-change.pdf>.

347 Ibid.

348 IPCC, 'Global Response 2018' (n 15) at 316.

349 Ibid.

350 'Delivering Clean Growth Progress' (n 26) at 60.

351 Ibid at 61.

352 Ellen MacArthur Foundation, 'Reuse, Rethinking Packaging' (13 June 2019), <https://www.ellenmacarthurfoundation.org/publications/reuse>.

9

Climate Governance for Micro, Small, and Medium Enterprises

Micro, small, and medium businesses ('MSME') comprise more than 99 per cent of all businesses globally and generate approximately 70 per cent of jobs worldwide. They play a pivotal role in stimulating economic growth and producing a broad range of goods and services, and are an essential part of the supply chain in many sectors. They are also instrumental in providing employment for vulnerable groups such as women, young entrepreneurs, racialized people, Indigenous peoples, and poor communities.[1] The European Commission reports that microenterprises, defined as enterprises employing fewer than ten people and having an annual turnover or annual balance sheet total or maximum of €2 million represent over 90 per cent of European enterprises.[2] In the United Kingdom ('UK'), MSME account for 99.3 per cent of all private sector business and provide 60 per cent of all private sector employment.[3] In the United States ('US'), small and medium enterprises make up 99 per cent of all firms.[4]

Of the 'formal MSME', i.e. those businesses that are registered with company registries or tax authorities, 83 per cent are microenterprises.[5] Formal small and medium enterprises ('SME') contribute up to 40 per cent of gross domestic product ('GDP') in emerging economies.[6] In most emerging countries, there are also a huge number of informal micro and small businesses, far outnumbering formal MSME. For example, in 2007 in India, there were fewer than 1.6 million registered MSME, but an estimated 26 million unregistered.[7] Thus MSME contribute to global economies. The United Nations' Sustainable Development Goals recognize the importance of MSME and have called for action to improve their access to finance, value chains, and markets.

This chapter briefly examines challenges for MSME in addressing climate change. It highlights lack of infrastructure and financing to address climate change financial risk. It offers initial ideas for designing policy and norms for small businesses and proposes

[1] United Nations ('UN'), 'MSME' (27 June 2019), <http://www.intracen.org/MSME-day/2019/>.

[2] European Commission, 'Supporting Entrepreneurs and the Self-Employed: Microfinance' (2019), <https://ec.europa.eu/social/main.jsp?catId=952&intPageId=3510&langId=en>.

[3] UK Department for Business, Energy and Industrial Strategy, *Business Population Estimate for the UK and Regions: 2018 Statistical Release* (11 October 2018), <https://assets.publishing.service.gov.uk/government/uploads/system/uploads/attachment_data/file/746599/OFFICIAL_SENSITIVE_-_BPE_2018_-_statistical_release_FINAL_FINAL.pdf>.

[4] S Firoozmand et al, 'State of SME Finance in the United States in 2015', Tradeup and Nextrade Group (March 2015).

[5] Khrystyna Kushnir, Melina Laura Mirmulstein, and Rita Ramalho, *Counting MSMEs across the World* (World Bank and IFC, 2010) at 2 (hereafter Kushnir et al).

[6] World Bank, 'Small and Medium Enterprises Finance' (2019), <https://www.worldbank.org/en/topic/smefinance>.

[7] Kushnir et al (n 5) at 2.

From Ideas to Action. Janis Sarra, Oxford University Press (2020). © Janis Sarra. DOI: 10.1093/oso/9780198852308.003.0009.

ways in which international and regional development banks can use these ideas in their advancing of finance and standards to address climate-related financial risk.

I. Climate-Related Risks Can Be Particularly Challenging for MSME to Address

Often micro and small businesses are capitalized by personal funds, or funds from friends and family. Often secured credit is not available, or if it is, it must be secured against the personal assets of the entrepreneur or founder of the business and her or his family. Thin capitalization means that there is usually not excess capital to address disasters arising from acute climate events such as flooding or wildfire, aside from insurance if the businesses have coverage. As discussed in earlier chapters, acute events due to climate change result in destruction of productive assets, tools of the trade, inventory, or the facility in which the business is located. This conflation of personal and business assets has been found to be a principal reason for micro and small business failure, even without calculating in climate risks.

There may not even be a governance structure in place in the MSME that can identify and respond to climate-related financial and other risks. For the sole proprietor, micro business, or small business, the only legal and practical decision-makers are likely the founder/entrepreneur and sometimes a few involved family members. Often the only time that financial records are up to date is when the business files its annual income taxes. For medium-sized companies, at least in emerging countries, any notion of a board of directors is often family members appointed to fulfil the requisite legal requirements for company registration. They often lack internal governance mechanisms or risk management expertise.[8] Even if the board is duly constituted with outside directors, there is often not an infrastructure in place that performs audit functions, human resources management, and strategic planning.

In addition to lack of governance structure, there are also often not resources to seek outside professional help in respect of climate governance. Given the myriad types of businesses, there are not yet standard templates that the MSME could adopt to identify and address climate-related risks, and to monitor progress towards net zero carbon emissions.

As noted earlier, the vast majority of insurance policies do not cover flooding and many exclude extreme weather events from the policy. Some countries have disaster relief funds, but even with this assistance, a MSME may not survive an acute event. Given that credit is often only available to a MSME on the basis of encumbering personal assets, where an acute event occurs and the business cannot operate, a secured creditor may refuse new credit and realize on the original loan, causing the loss of the family home.

For example, even as micro and small businesses in California, United States were trying to recover from harms caused by wildfires, they were being hit with new

[8] Ronald Davis, Stephan Madaus, Alberto Mazzoni, Irit Mevorach, Rizwaan J Mokal, Barbara Romaine, Janis Sarra, and Ignacio Tirado, *Micro, Small, and Medium Enterprise Insolvency: A Modular Approach* (OUP, 2018) at 13–14 (hereafter Davis et al, *MSME*).

hardships.[9] In order to cope with fire risk and new fires, the utility company PG&E cut power to 179,000 customers in October 2019, closing small businesses, jeopardizing perishable goods, and seriously diminishing their ability to earn revenue.[10] MSME businesses were experiencing mounting losses from loss of customers and loss of production time. Grocery stores were among the hardest hit, losing up to US $100,000 of perishable inventory from one blackout.[11]

While resources to operate many MSME may be limited, there are still ways in which MSME can take action to proactively address climate-related financial risk, prior to any acute or chronic event. The remainder of this chapter explores how this governance and financing could occur.

II. Regulatory and Infrastructure Support for MSME in the Transition

An important first goal is to provide some infrastructure support to help MSME transition to decarbonization and increase circular economy approaches to production and service delivery. That includes information and financial support to adopt energy efficient technologies, reduce energy consumption, and shift to renewable energy sources. It means providing resources to retrofit buildings in which MSME operate, making them more efficient and strengthening their capacity to withstand acute events. It can include information regarding locating supply chain sources nearer to location of the business, and it can facilitate partnership with other businesses to design waste out of productive processes.

The European Union ('EU') has recognized that it can only meet its international commitments to fight climate change if small businesses, 'as main drivers of competitiveness and prosperity', are fully integrated in its climate strategy.[12] The EU is leading in global efforts to recognize particular challenges for small and medium-sized enterprises ('SME') as they try to mitigate the effects of climate change. The European Commission's Green Action Plan for SME is aimed at helping them take advantage of the opportunities offered by the transition to a green economy, make them aware of resource efficiency improvements and the potential of the circular economy for productivity and business opportunities, and to inform them about EU resource efficiency actions and support for 'green entrepreneurship'.[13] It has initiated efforts to support the transition of SME to a greener economy, including information, financing, and infrastructure support.[14]

[9] R Gold, K Blunt, and T Ansari, 'PG&E Reels as California Wildfire Burns', *The Wall Street Journal* (26 October 2019).

[10] J Carlton, J Kang, and T Ansari, 'Blackouts Lash Small Businesses', *The Wall Street Journal* (25 October 2019).

[11] Ibid.

[12] SME United, 'Circularity Helps SMEs Reach Climate Targets' (26 August 2019), <https://smeunited.eu/news/circularity-helps-smes-reach-climate-targets>.

[13] European Commission, 'Green Action Plan for SMEs', <https://ec.europa.eu/growth/smes/business-friendly-environment/green-action-plan_en>.

[14] European Commission Staff Working Document, 'List of EU actions supporting SMEs in a green economy Accompanying the document Communication from the Commission to the European Parliament, the Council, the European Economic and Social Committee and the Committee of the Regions

A primary focus of the European Commission strategy is to improve SME resource-efficiency, in order to increase their competitiveness and contribution to a greener economy. The European Commission Resource Efficiency Excellence Centre provides advice and support on SME resource efficiency performance, technological options to increase resource-efficiency in the sector, and financing advice, adopting a modular approach and using the Enterprise Europe Network ('EEN') agreed taxonomy.[15]

The European Resource Efficiency Excellence Centre will assess the economic impact of resource efficiency measures on SME, offer user-friendly information on available resource-efficiency technologies, liaise with national and regional partners to develop advisory services, and build a database to support arguments for financing SME resource efficiency.[16] It seeks to inform SME of the positive benefits and opportunities, encouraging them to take-up green technologies, providing a practical toolbox, and offering examples of successful projects. The European Commission guide will also provide information on the specificities of the circular economy, such as the role of treating waste as a resource for industry and the need for further developing collaborative business approaches such as industrial symbiosis.[17]

One example of a collaborative effort is R2π ('tRansition from linear 2 circular'), which is a collaboration of a number of governments, academic institutions, and private sector businesses to encourage MSME to move to circular economic activities.[18] It is funded under the European Commission's Research and Innovation programme. R2π has created business tools and policy packages that are practical guides to shifting to more sustainable business practices. It has created an online toolkit that offers step by step advice for MSME in moving to circular economic activity, and has generated research on making the transition for six sectors: construction, chemicals, food, water, plastics, and textiles.

i. Financing for the MSME Sector in Respect of Climate Action

Micro and small businesses can increase their climate resilience by increasing their insurance, installing green roofs or bioswales for water retention, adding onsite energy resources like combined heat and power systems or rooftop solar installations, developing acute event or disaster recovery plans, identifying backup supply and distribution chains, and communicating preparedness information to employees.[19] All of

Green Action Plan for SMEs, enabling SMEs to turn environmental challenges into business opportunities', SWD/2014/0213 final, <https://eur-lex.europa.eu/legal-content/EN/TXT/?uri=CELEX:52014SC0213>.

[15] Ibid. One module is the Resource Efficiency Self-Assessment Tool for SMEs (COSME 2014). The European Resource Efficiency Excellence Centre (COSME 2015) will integrate data from, and encourage data provision by the EEN sector groups, as well as from other relevant EU initiatives.

[16] Ibid.

[17] Ibid. See also <http://ec.europa.eu/enterprise/policies/sme/regional-sme-policies>.

[18] R2π Project, Circular Economy Business Models Toolkit (2019), <<https://smeunited.eu/news/circularity-helps-smes-reach-climate-targets>. The 'R' represents the linear 'radius' while the π symbolizes the circle.

[19] Center for Climate and Energy Solutions, 'Business Action on Resilience' (2019), <https://www.c2es.org/content/business-action-on-resilience/>.

these initiatives require financing, yet MSME frequently have limited access to capital or have no access at all. It continues to be difficult to raise financing for any expansion of the business, let alone financing to transition to circular economic activity. Often private sector green finance does not finance small businesses because of the high costs of pre-project due diligence and high monitoring costs on loans given.

One important support for MSME in addressing climate mitigation and adaptation is therefore to develop new financing models that expressly recognize the challenges facing MSME. It involves conceptualizing new ways in which public and private finance can collaborate to direct resources to MSME seeking to decarbonize, while at the same time ensuring that the benefits of transition accrue largely to the businesses and not solely to private capital funders.

The European Commission's action plan is also aimed at facilitating access to finance for SME energy efficiency, including EU funding available for resource efficiency improvements.[20] The European Investment Bank is to provide financing through financial intermediaries for resource efficiency improvements linked to ecosystem services and climate change adaptation. The European Commission and the European Investment Bank are developing the Natural Capital Financing Facility ('NCFF'), an instrument that will establish replicable, bankable natural capital projects to demonstrate to private investors the attractiveness of natural capital projects for the longer term, and leverage funding to SME from private investors through the use of EU funds.[21]

From 2015 to 2019, the European Fund for Strategic Investments mobilized €439.4 billion in additional investment across the EU, allocated to more than one million start-ups and small businesses.[22] To date it has created more than 1.5 million jobs, built or renovated 531,000 affordable flats, installed 28.3 million smart energy meters, brought renewable energy to 10.4 million households, and improved waste treatment for 33.3 million people.[23]

The European Commission's InvestEU Fund in 2019 announced €11.25 billion in financing for SME to address climate-related risks and opportunities.[24] The European Investment Fund ('EIF') is part of the European Investment Bank group, its central mission is to support Europe's SME by helping them to access finance. It designs and develops venture and growth capital, guarantees, and microfinance instruments that specifically target SME, and seeks to support innovation, research and development, entrepreneurship, growth, and employment.[25]

[20] Ibid, citing the 'European Small Business Portal' (funding section), the 'Access to Finance Portal', the EEN website, and 'Your Europe-Business'.

[21] Ibid. See also EU Business @ Biodiversity Platform; European Maritime and Fisheries Fund.

[22] EU Investment Plan for Europe, 'The Junker Plan's Impact on Jobs and Growth' (October 2019), <https://ec.europa.eu/commission/sites/beta-political/files/juncker-plan-impact-jobs-growth_en.pdf>.

[23] Ibid. See also Kate Whiting, 'This is what a Green New Deal for Europe could look like', World Economic Forum (21 May 2019), <https://www.weforum.org/agenda/2019/05/this-is-what-a-green-new-deal-for-europe-could-look-like/>.

[24] European Commission, The InvestEU Programme (5 June 2018), https://ec.europa.eu/commission/presscorner/detail/en/MEMO_18_4010.

[25] European Commission, 'Investment Plan for Europe: €2 billion in fresh loans for 20,000 businesses in Spain' (22 February 2016), <https://ec.europa.eu/commission/commissioners/2014-2019/katainen/announcements/investment-plan-europe-eu2-billion-fresh-loans-20000-businesses-spain_en>.

For example, the 'Innovfin SME guarantee programme' facilitates loans to SME to stimulate sustainable activities. Its first initiative was in Spain in 2016, aimed at leveraging a portfolio of €150 million of loans to benefit over 750 companies in Spain from 2016 to 2018. The idea is that an entity in the Member State, for example, Compañía Española de Reafianzamiento ('CERSA'), part of the Spanish Ministry of Industry, provides counter-guarantees to regional mutual guarantee schemes that will enable them in turn to provide guarantees to banks financing innovative companies in Spain, with the guarantees having the support of a counter-guarantee provided by the EIF. The arrangement is expected to support more than 19,000 financially underserved SME in Spain.[26]

Another example is the EIF and Raiffeisenbank EAD (Bulgaria) guarantee agreement to increase lending to innovative SME in Bulgaria, allowing the bank to provide €35 million of loans to innovative companies in Bulgaria over two years.[27] The loans will be enabled by an EIF guarantee under the EU InnovFin Finance for Innovators initiative, with financial backing from the European Commission's Horizon 2020 programme, allowing Raiffeisenbank to offer innovative companies additional financing at favourable conditions.[28]

The European Commission's Programme for Employment and Social Innovation ('EaSI') microfinance initiative is aimed at increasing access to, and the availability of, microfinance for vulnerable groups that want to set up or develop their business and microenterprises. It is aimed at building up the institutional capacity of microcredit providers and supporting development of social enterprises, in particular by facilitating access to finance.[29] In 2019, €96 million was available for interested microcredit providers and social enterprise investors through the EaSI guarantee, aimed at enabling microcredit providers and social enterprise investors to reach out to entrepreneurs they would not have been able to finance otherwise due to risk considerations, with the EIF implementing the EaSI guarantee.[30]

The European Commission is developing financial instruments specifically targeting SME. It has said that recipients of Private Finance for Energy Efficiency instruments ('PF4EE') will be defined in the context of Member States' national energy efficiency action plans ('NEEAP') and will primarily be those SME targeted by the national/regional schemes developed by Member States to implement their NEEAP.[31] It has announced establishment of an EU-wide network of public and private financiers and investors that support eco-innovation, creating a 'one-stop-shop' web platform for eco-innovation business projects, providing information, guidance, tools, and a financing matchmaking platform to link SME with investors.[32]

[26] Ibid.
[27] European Commission, 'Investment Plan for Europe: second agreement for SMEs in Bulgaria' (2 February 2016), <https://ec.europa.eu/commission/commissioners/2014-2019/georgieva/announcements/investment-plan-europe-second-agreement-smes-bulgaria_en>.
[28] Ibid.
[29] European Commission, 'EaSI microfinance initiative', <https://ec.europa.eu/social/main.jsp?catId=1084&langId=en>.
[30] Ibid.
[31] European Commission, The InvestEU Programme (n 24).
[32] Ibid, citing Network of Eco-Innovation Investors Network.

The European Regional Development Fund ('ERDF') will also be used to promote energy efficiency and renewable energy use in SME.[33] The European Commission is expressly promoting green entrepreneurship and new business models for energy efficiency, including support of eco-innovative business ideas.[34] Priority is being given to models establishing resource efficiency practices in SME, focusing on durability, reuse, repair, and recycling of their products and processes, and reduction in material use and/or energy and water use.[35]

The European Commission plan is also aimed at addressing systemic barriers to cross-sectoral and cross-national value chain collaboration, by facilitating models that reuse materials, products, and waste, incentivizing cross-sectoral and cross-regional co-operation of resource-efficient value chains.[36] This initiative is important to developing circular economy strategies, since one sector's waste is another's supply inputs, as was illustrated in Chapter 8 in respect of China's circular economy initiatives. The European Commission's goal is to promote a greener European internal market and facilitating access to international markets for green entrepreneurs.[37]

Another objective is green technology transfer action from Europe to South Mediterranean countries to help entrepreneurs and SME from these countries build new entrepreneurial activities based on green technologies, such as clean-tech services that support the greening of industry and business solutions in support of resource efficiency, through co-operation with European SME.[38] A guidebook on improving resource efficiency in SME was published in 2016.[39]

Many MSME contribute to the EU adaptation and mitigation strategy by performing circular economy activities.[40] For example, they are manufacturing and providing eco-friendly products and services, are active in the sustainable renovation of existing buildings, and are contributing to prolonging product life by repairing products and ensuring their maintenance.[41] The European Commission is directing resources to investments in SME innovation, research, and development, and increased policy co-ordination and public-private partnerships to advance sustainable, circular solutions to SME productive activities.[42] The European Commission also observes that the path to decarbonization should include international co-operation. MSME should be supported in their efforts to export eco-friendly products and services. The

[33] Ibid. See also <http://ec.europa.eu/regional_policy/thefunds/regional/index_en.cfm> and <http://ec.europa.eu/regional_policy/sources/docgener/informat/2014/fiche_sme_en.pdf>.

[34] Ibid, stating: 'The new SME Instrument under Horizon 2020 will encourage SMEs to put forward their most innovative ideas with an EU dimension.' Funding will be provided in the form of a lump sum of €50,000 for six months. See also <http://ec.europa.eu/regional_policy/sources/docgener/informat/2014/fiche_low_carbon_en.pdf>.

[35] Ibid.

[36] Ibid.

[37] Ibid.

[38] Ibid.

[39] European Commission, 'Improving Resource Efficiency in SMEs', Volume 10: Guidebook Series: How to support SME Policy from Structural Funds (September 2016), <http://ec.europa.eu/DocsRoom/documents/18343>.

[40] SME United, 'Circularity Helps SMEs Reach Climate Targets' (26 August 2019), <https://smeunited.eu/news/circularity-helps-smes-reach-climate-targets>.

[41] Ibid.

[42] Ibid.

European Commission has stated that the 2050 long term strategy can only succeed in turning the EU into a net zero economy if it results in a combination of measures based on boldly moving towards a circular economy.

Some pension funds have recognized the importance of MSME in the transition to net zero carbon. Dutch €399 billion pension fund ABP launched the Netherlands Energy Transition Fund in 2018, focusing on local small projects and companies involved in the generation, distribution, and usage of energy. It immediately committed €50 million to the fund, known as ANET, observing that 'We want to be a social partner for the local energy transition and take our responsibility for tackling climate change'.[43] It will invest in relatively small companies and projects that focus on innovative solutions and technologies for the energy transition.[44]

France's le Programme d'investissements d'avenir ('Investment for the Future Programme') includes 'SME Initiatives' funds, up to €200,000 granted over three years; and the Ecotechnologies Fund, which is an SME equity investment fund worth €150 million. The Green Loans programme, which provides loans for green finance up to €5 million, with low interest rates and requiring no guarantee, is being directed towards financing energy efficient or less polluting productive processes or manufacturing eco-products.[45]

In the UK, the government announced a programme to assist SME to improve energy efficiency, given that they account for 50 per cent of UK business energy use.[46] Its goal is to develop peer-to-peer networks and financial support, to raise awareness of the benefits of energy efficiency to SME, and to enhance finance options available to SME to invest in energy efficiency.[47] It is designing innovation funding to support business models that scale-up energy efficiency projects from SME.

The International Finance Corporation ('IFC'), an arm of the World Bank, has been using blended financing to enable MSME green projects to demonstrate viability and then pave the way for financing on fully commercial terms.[48] It blends concessional funds—typically from development partners—alongside its own commercial funding, to mitigate early-entrant costs or project risks, helping re-balance risk-reward profiles for pioneering investments in climate finance. Concessional financing is where loans are given on more generous terms than market loans, either through lower interest

[43] L Preesman et al, 'Dutch Roundup: ABP Launches Energy Transition Fund', *IPE News* (January 2019), <https://www.ipe.com/countries/netherlands/dutch-roundup-abp-launches-energy-transition-fund/www.ipe.com/countries/netherlands/dutch-roundup-abp-launches-energy-transition-fund/10029215.fullarticle>.

[44] ABP, 'Sustainable and Responsible Investment 2018' (ABP 2019) at 5, <https://www.abp.nl/images/responsible-investment-report-2018.pdf>.

[45] S Hampton and T Fawcett, 'Challenges of Designing and Delivering Effective SME Energy Policy' (2017) Foundations of Future Energy Policy at 193, <https://ora.ox.ac.uk/objects/uuid:1c373218-9abf-42ce-84d8-d7d2c056a5fb> (hereafter Hampton and Fawcett); and le gouvernement de France, Les Rapports du Programme d'investissements d'avenir, (2020), https://www.gouvernement.fr/rapports-divers.

[46] UK Government, 'Helping Business to Improve the Way They Use Energy' in 'Delivering Clean Growth Progress Against Meeting Our Carbon Budgets' (October 2018) at 31, <https://assets.publishing.service.gov.uk/government/uploads/system/uploads/attachment_data/file/748296/delivering-clean-growth.pdf> (hereafter 'Delivering Clean Growth Progress').

[47] Ibid at 32.

[48] IFC, 'Climate Finance' (2019), <https://www.ifc.org/wps/wcm/connect/CORP_EXT_Content/IFC_External_Corporate_Site/Solutions/Products+and+Services/Blended-Finance/>.

rates or grace periods in terms of timelines for repayment. It can facilitate development of MSME businesses that are aimed at circular economic activity.

The Climate Investment Fund ('CIF') was established by fourteen donor countries that contributed over US $8 billion in support of scaling-up mitigation and adaptation action in seventy-two developing and middle income countries. The CIF is aimed at accelerating climate action by empowering transformations in clean technology, energy access, climate resilience, and sustainable forests in developing and middle income countries.[49] The resources of the CIF are held in trust by the World Bank, and funds are disbursed as grants, highly concessional loans, and risk mitigation instruments to recipient countries through multilateral development banks. The CIF seeks to scale-up low-cost, long term financing to lower the risk and cost of climate financing. Examples include sustainable forest management in Guatemala,[50] sustainable urban infrastructure in Ukraine,[51] scaling-up renewable energy in Lesotho, Sub-Saharan Africa,[52] and financial instruments for energy efficient cities in Brazil.[53]

One example of the CIF financing for MSME is a solar rooftop initiative in India. The MSME sector accounts for almost a third of India's gross domestic product and accounts for approximately 25 per cent of the total energy consumed in the industrial sector.[54] Thus, a shift to solar energy is a key strategy for shifting to renewable energy sources. However, the CIF initiative revealed a number of barriers to this energy shift. Operational barriers include MSME lacking the capacity and knowledge to maintain the equipment installed on their premises, and reluctance of distribution utilities to promote rooftop solar systems as they fear losing their high-revenue generating consumers.[55] Financing barriers include that many MSME do not have any credit history; the installation of rooftop solar systems requires high upfront investment; and MSME face difficulty in meeting their collateral requirements as existing plants and machinery are already pledged as collateral for existing loans.[56] Going forward, one strategy that has been identified is to focus on financing clusters of MSME that are most likely to benefit from financing of solar rooftop energy, such as auto components and pharmaceutical businesses. They have high energy requirements, have longer term business potential, and their production facilities tend to have ample rooftop space available for system installation.[57] The example illustrates that not only must new financing be directed towards MSME transition, but the structural and financial barriers need to be systemically addressed as well.

[49] Climate Investment Funds, 'Accelerating Climate Action' (2019), <https://www.climateinvestmentfunds.org/>.

[50] See <https://www.climateinvestmentfunds.org/projects/sustainable-forest-management>.

[51] See <https://www.climateinvestmentfunds.org/projects/dpsp-iii-sustainable-urban-infrastructure>.

[52] See <https://www.climateinvestmentfunds.org/projects/lesotho-renewable-energy-and-energy-access-project>.

[53] FinBRAZEEC, <https://www.climateinvestmentfunds.org/projects/dpsp-iii-financial-instruments-brazil-energy-efficient-cities-finbrazeec>.

[54] Deloitte, 'Scaling up of rooftop solar in the SME sector in India' (2019), <https://www.climateinvestmentfunds.org/sites/cif_enc/files/knowledge-documents/final_scaling_up_rooftop_solar_in_sme_in_india.pdf?hootPostID=b8ff02a27dc240f956f83f6e487b0aa9>.

[55] Ibid at 7.

[56] Ibid.

[57] Ibid at 10.

The IFC-Canada Climate Change Program is a partnership between the Canadian government and the IFC to promote private sector financing for clean energy projects in emerging countries, through the use of concessional funds to catalyse investments in renewable, low carbon technologies. The Canadian government contributed Cdn $291.6 million, which was then leveraged to US $1.8 billion in IFC and private sector climate financing in emerging markets.[58] The funds, invested at concessional or below market terms, were blended with IFC funds to enable climate change investments that would not otherwise happen due to market barriers.[59] The objective was to demonstrate the viability of similar projects that can later be financed on fully commercial terms.[60] For example, The IFC-Canada Climate Change Program provided sustainable energy financing, incentivizing banks in six countries to enter new lines of business in climate finance. Funding from the programme helped offset some of the early entrant costs associated with building a new portfolio, resulting in nine projects and enabling over 150 smaller scale renewable or energy efficiency investments, including run-of-river hydro in Bosnia, biomass generation in Honduras, energy service company leasing projects in Lebanon, and energy efficiency and renewable energy projects for MSME in thirteen emerging nations.[61]

In many cases, MSME lack the technical, financial, and institutional capacity to identify the best ways to build climate resilience.[62] For example, temperatures in Africa are projected to rise faster than the global average during the twenty-first century, with drought in many areas and a profound loss of agricultural land. Yet six out of ten of the one billion people in Africa rely on agriculture for their livelihoods.[63] How these micro businesses will survive is a critically important question. The UN reports that the least developed countries in Africa are among the most vulnerable to climate change, yet the least able to adapt. With US $1.3 billion of voluntary contributions from donors, the Global Environment Facility Least Developed Countries Fund holds the largest portfolio of adaptation projects in the least developed countries.[64] While the people of Africa have much to lose from climate impacts, they contributed very little to the massive amounts of greenhouse gas emissions that have caused global warming. This reality was recognized in the Paris Agreement's commitment to support the nations of Africa in promoting low carbon development.[65]

Hampton and Fawcett have observed that a significant challenge in the design of effective SME energy policy is that European SME are often exempted from regulation, taxes, and market-based mechanisms to promote energy efficiency, as they are

[58] IFC-Canada Climate Change Program, 'End-of-Investment Period Report' (2019), <https://www.ifc.org/wps/wcm/connect/e42ee4af-0d9b-479a-b323-bc1c58fe86d0/ifc-climate-change-program-canada-062018.pdf?MOD=AJPERES&CVID=mtX0VE6>.

[59] IFC-Canada Climate Change Program, <https://www.ifc.org/wps/wcm/connect/topics_ext_content/ifc_external_corporate_site/climate+business/blendedfinance_ifccanada>.

[60] Ibid.

[61] IFC-Canada Climate Change Program, 'End-of-Investment Period Report' (n 58) at 18.

[62] IFC-Canada Climate Change Program (n 59) at 5.

[63] Global Environmental Facility, 'Climate Change Adaptation in Africa: UNDP Synthesis of Experiences and Recommendations' (30 November 2018), <https://www.thegef.org/publications/climate-change-adaptation-africa-undp-synthesis-experiences-and-recommendations>.

[64] Ibid.

[65] Ibid at 6.

considered to have limited capacity for economies of scale; to suffer from lack of information, time, or expertise to deal with regulations or administrative rules; and find it more difficult or expensive to access capital than larger organizations.[66] They observe that the UK's more market-focused approach to policy design can increase complexity, and result in SME being exempted from policy initiatives such as recycling of packaging and government regulatory standards. Hampton and Fawcett argue that the energy and emissions savings from these policies are not included in national targets, resulting in little pressure from central government to rigorously evaluate and aggregate impacts, and that 'carrot approaches' alone are not sufficient to achieve the scale of carbon reductions required to meet the EU's emissions reductions targets.[67]

In contrast, other countries are creating regulatory incentives for small business transition to sustainable low carbon activities. In France, for example, under the EU scheme administering compliance and collecting fees from producers to subsidize the recycling of packaging waste, companies of all sizes handling packaging are required to register and contribute towards the recycling subsidy, whereas SME are excluded from the regulation in the UK.[68]

Hampton and Fawcett suggest that universal approaches such as building regulations and product standards present opportunities for extending energy efficiency throughout the economy, but usually involve hard-fought legislation. They observe that approaches that focus on smart technologies, building tenancy infrastructures, and green business practices may help policy-makers at the national level to target policies at SME in ways that avoid additional administrative burden.[69] They suggest policy changes to address smaller scale opportunities for intervention, giving the example of 'green leases', potentially introduced through government building portfolios, which may help to address the 'split-incentive problem', often cited as limiting the capacity for SME building tenants to implement efficiency savings. It could promote the practice of working from home.[70]

It is clear that there are a number of challenges to designing and implementing effective energy and other carbon reducing policies for SME, and Hampton and Fawcett have suggested that addressing this group as a whole may not offer the best solutions; that there is a clear need for the improved evaluation and monitoring of local energy efficiency programmes to generate data necessary for informed policy-making.[71]

III. MSME Governance of Climate Risk and Opportunity

Given the lack of governance infrastructure in most MSME, an ideal approach would be to develop governance tools that allow MSME to apply the tools to their particular business, accessible online at no cost. There need to be some resources directed towards building capacity of MSME to identify and respond to climate change risk,

[66] Hampton and Fawcett (n 45) at 189–90.
[67] Ibid at 194.
[68] Ibid at 192.
[69] Ibid.
[70] Ibid at 196–7.
[71] Ibid at 197.

and to explore the upside opportunities. It means that some of the above financing should be directed towards governance if MSME are to mitigate and adapt over the longer term.

There also needs to be educational resources directed towards effective climate governance of MSME. For example, as noted in Chapter 5, the Canadian Climate Governance Experts programme involves fifty-five governance experts who are donating their time to conduct educational and information exchange sessions with corporate boards, decision-makers of small businesses, and pension boards, offering *pro bono* advice on getting started in effective climate governance.[72] Use of templates, sector guidelines, and finance portals would also assist in creating easy access to accurate and relevant advice on transitioning to net zero carbon.

i. Women Will Help Lift Up Micro and Small Businesses

Although women face barriers to equal participation in climate governance, as discussed earlier, they also offer the greatest potential for lifting up micro and small businesses in the transition to net zero carbon and the circular economy.

An example of effective governance and climate mitigation for a MSME is Solar Sister in Africa, focused on renewable energy, in turn increasing women's income and economic security, shielding them from harmful health effects of indoor pollution, and making them agents of climate change mitigation through their involvement in renewable energy deployment.[73] Indoor smoke from solid fuels is responsible for more than 1.6 million deaths annually and 3.6 per cent of the global burden of disease, worse than annual deaths associated with poor sanitation.[74] Solar Sister trains and supports women to deliver clean energy directly to homes in rural African communities, providing training that enables women entrepreneurs to build sustainable businesses in their own communities. Solar Sister's network of 4,300 women entrepreneurs has delivered solar lighting and clean cookstoves to over 1.5 million people in hard to reach markets. Families benefit from better health and economic stability thanks to use of clean cookstoves and solar light delivered by Solar Sister, including children having reliable lighting to study by at night.[75] Families who switch to clean cookstoves significantly reduce time spent collecting wood, money spent on solid fuels, and suffer fewer respiratory issues from smoke output, significantly improving the health of women and children.[76]

The income earned through Solar Sister allows women to contribute to household earnings and gain confidence, financial independence, and respect from their

[72] Canadian Climate Governance Experts, Canada Climate Law Initiative, Janis Sarra and Cynthia Williams, University of British Columbia and York University, <https://ccli.ubc.ca/>.

[73] Solar Sister, 'Our Impact' (2019), <https://solarsister.org/what-we-do/our-impact/>.

[74] Intergovernmental Panel on Climate Change ('IPCC'), D Arvizu, P Balaya, L Cabeza, T Hollands, A Jäger-Waldau, M Kondo, C Konseibo, V Meleshko, W Stein, Y Tamaura, H Xu, and R Zilles, 'Direct Solar Energy' in O Edenhofer, R Pichs-Madruga, Y Sokona, K Seyboth, P Matschoss, S Kadner, T Zwickel, P Eickemeier, G Hansen, S Schlömer, and C von Stechow (eds), *IPCC Special Report on Renewable Energy Sources and Climate Change Mitigation* (CUP 2012) at 337 (hereafter 'Direct Solar Energy').

[75] Solar Sister (n 73).

[76] Ibid.

families. Seventy-five per cent of their solar entrepreneurs live in rural or last-mile communities, 83 per cent are women, and 60 per cent live on less than US $2 a day.[77] Training and ongoing mentoring equip entrepreneurs with important skills, such as financial management and technical product knowledge. As women gain confidence, they are role models and change agents in their communities. Solar Sister helps women entrepreneurs adopt useful business skills, and sustain or grow their income over time. In 2018, the programme replaced 238,372 kerosene lamps with solar and helped 15,251 people switch to clean cookstoves, generating US $46 million in energy-related customer savings.[78] 15,251 clean cookstoves is the equivalent carbon sequestration of 600,000 trees growing for ten years.[79] By starting and growing clean energy businesses, its entrepreneurs both bring home extra income and put away savings.

In summary, MSME support the global economy. It is important, therefore, to embed considerations of their unique challenges and contributions in the design of measures to transition to a net zero carbon circular economy. They need financial and infrastructure support that is attuned to their thinly-capitalized businesses, their limited or non-existent governance structures, the systemic barriers to their viability given the region, country, or market in which they are operating, and their huge potential, from sheer numbers of MSME globally, to contribute to the United Nations' Sustainable Development Goals. Financial support for the transition to net zero must recognize and ameliorate gender and race discrimination in the allocation of resources.

[77] Solar Sister, *Light the Way: Outcomes 2018* (1 August 2019), <https://solarsister.org/wp-content/uploads/2019/09/2018-annual-report-1.pdf>.
[78] Ibid.
[79] Ibid at 9.

10
Conclusion

As this book goes to press, the world is in 'lockdown' from the coronavirus pandemic, with no immediate end in sight. Most governments are trying to devise programmes to protect the health and safety of their populations and to direct financial resources towards shelter and food, given that millions of their citizens cannot go to work. Businesses are closed, air travel is largely halted, corporate boardrooms have become virtual, and courts are shut down save for urgent virtual hearings. Expected financial and social losses are not yet calculable, but gross domestic product in the short term has dropped several percentage points and economic recovery will depend on whether countries globally can bring the pandemic under control within the next year.

Carbon dioxide ('CO_2') emissions dropped by 17 per cent in the first four months of 2020, as the pandemic spread and economic and social activity was suspended.[1] Over one third of the reduced emissions came from reduced surface transport, which accounts for 20 per cent of global emissions,[2] highlighting the direct link between business activity—such as the transport of goods, services, and people—and carbon emissions. A recent study estimates that global emissions will fall 4 per cent overall this year if world economies open up, or possibly 7 per cent if lockdowns persist in parts of the world for the second half of 2020.[3] The authors observe that most changes in emissions are likely to be temporary, as they do not reflect structural changes in the economic, transport, or energy systems.[4]

Therein lies the key to our policy choices going forward. Even with almost full lockdown of economies globally, we are still at 83 per cent of our usual CO_2 emissions, painting a stark portrait of the massive amount of effort that needs to occur if we are not going to cross more planetary boundaries, beyond which the damage will be irreversible. We know that CO_2 can stay in the atmosphere for decades and that a temporary drop in emissions is unlikely to shift our global climate trajectory.

It is a critically important moment in history. Once we are past the most urgent needs of the pandemic, governments will need to make policy choices about economic recovery. They should be directing all their resources toward economic activity that shifts us rapidly towards decarbonization. Economic recovery must be closely attuned to our commitments to move to net zero carbon emissions and a

[1] Compared with the mean 2019 levels. See C Le Quéré, R B Jackson, M W Jones, A J P Smith, S Abernethy, R M Andrew, A J De-Gol, D R Willis, Y Shan, J G Canadell, P Friedlingstein, F Creutzig, and G P Peters, 'Temporary reduction in daily global CO2 emissions during the COVID-19 forced confinement' (2020) 10 *Nature Climate Change* 647–53 at 648. The study used a combination of energy, activity, and policy data from sixty-nine countries, fifty US states, and thirty Chinese provinces, which represent 85 per cent of the world population and 97 per cent of global CO_2 emissions.

[2] Ibid.

[3] Ibid at 652.

[4] Ibid.

From Ideas to Action. Janis Sarra, Oxford University Press (2020). © Janis Sarra. DOI: 10.1093/oso/9780198852308.003.0010.

circular economy. Any economic stimulus needs to be 'green', whether it is public investment or allocating capital or tax incentives to encourage private investments. Resources given by governments or loans by financial institutions need to be conditional on companies shifting their businesses towards circular economic activities and a serious reduction in carbon emissions. We need to shift to renewable energy as quickly as possible for heating, transport, and production processes. Economic recovery measures need to be aimed at financially supporting sustainable economic activity. That means, for example, that funding in the energy sector should be directed solely to renewable energy, incenting legacy fossil fuel energy companies to develop new business plans. As discussed in this book, there needs to be massive retrofit of commercial, institutional, and residential buildings to achieve net zero emissions. Agriculture needs to become sustainable from the first seeds planted to getting food to our families.

This idea of 'green recovery' is starting to receive some attention, even at the height of the pandemic. The European Union, for example, has announced that it will borrow and then leverage €750 billion in the next year towards economic recovery, a substantial amount of that capital directed to circular economic activity.[5]

The pandemic lockdown does not change the vast majority of observations and recommendations in this book, because addressing climate change is an absolute imperative. The pandemic is an *unexpected* catastrophe, climate change is an *expected* one. We have seen the early effects of global warming on land and water ecosystems, economic systems, human morbidity and mortality, food and water security, and productivity.

Unfortunately, it no longer takes imagination to envision what a climate tipping point looks like, the pictures are everywhere: loss of homes and businesses due to hurricanes, wildfire, flooding, and sea level rise; premature deaths from pollution, extreme heatwaves, and water scarcity; and the commencement of massive migration necessitated by extreme heat and lack of water and arable land.

However, the pandemic has also revealed that governments can move very rapidly and co-operatively when risks to life are urgent, including allocating capital to support people and taking measures to lockdown businesses and production processes that are spreading harm. Climate change is also an urgent risk to life if the trajectory of greenhouse gas emissions is not radically altered. Effective control of these threats requires both a fundamental reconsideration of the harmful effects of conducting business as usual, and reliance on the knowledge provided by science to determine what alterations to our conduct will allow us to gain control in each case.

The transition to a circular economy is an ongoing project, engaging the entire timeframe of immediate to long term. It is a dynamic process, in that as information develops, we need to continually adjust strategies. The technologies to transition exist today, but with new developments, they should become even more effective and, hopefully, more accessible to broader numbers of people.

The ideas are all there, the actions have commenced, but business needs to seriously step up and take its share of responsibility for the transition to net zero carbon

[5] European Commission, 'Europe's moment: Repair and prepare for the next generation' (May 2020), <https://ec.europa.eu/commission/presscorner/detail/en/ip_20_940>.

emissions. Thinking has evolved from lower carbon, to low carbon, to net zero, to net positive climate, as scientists globally urge us to act now to prevent irreparable harm to the planet.

Situating businesses in this picture is fairly clear. Companies and investors have the capital to shift the trajectory of global warming. They have responsibility to act as part of their social licence to operate. Never have the best interests of the company and best interests of pension beneficiaries aligned so well with the public interest.

Failure to act will place businesses at risk. This book challenges directors, officers, pension fiduciaries, and investment managers to move from ideas to action, to recognize that they have been the beneficiaries of high carbon emissions, and the costs of those emissions are now going to adversely affect the health of their businesses, pension funds, and asset portfolios. As corporate and pension fiduciaries, they need to exercise effective oversight and management of climate change, framed in the larger context of the planet at risk. This book has suggested that fairness and equity should be guiding principles, for regulatory intervention, for effective climate governance, for remedies awarded in lawsuits, and generally in the move to a climate positive circular economy.

Companies and investors should also take note of the leadership of some investors in linking effective climate governance to the United Nations' Sustainable Development Goals in terms of how we conceptually think about corporate obligations in our own countries and internationally. We need to ensure that all participants in the economy - corporations, investors, portfolio managers, asset managers, financial intermediaries, credit rating agencies, and institutional lenders, place climate governance at the top of their strategic planning. Micro, small, and medium enterprises are important in this transition to a net zero carbon economy, as they comprise the vast majority of businesses globally.

Regulators also need to act in a manner that is fair and equitable in terms of how they conceptualize carbon pricing and other regulatory interventions to shift corporate behaviour. Partnerships between the public and private sectors are essential to shifting financial activity towards a circular economy. While the strategies and tools are at a nascent stage, they are critically important to effective governance going forward. Where public resources are expended in direct investment, loans or partnerships, there need to be structures in place that ensure the benefits accrue fairly and equitably to a wider range of people, particularly Indigenous and racialized people and women, for all the reasons discussed throughout this book.

Protection of biodiversity needs to be embedded into government policy and private actions at every stage of design and production. At the current rate of biodiversity loss, we are likely to pass more planetary boundaries from which humanity will not be able to recover. That means new and innovative thinking as to how we build natural capital protection into everything from climate governance best practices to tax and regulatory oversight policy.

There is an urgent need for a healthy infrastructure to support the move to a sustainable circular economy. The resources are there if there is the political and social will. During the 2008 financial crisis, the US government provided a US $700 billion bailout for domestic banks, and the US Federal Reserve provided US $5 trillion in liquidity and loan guarantees to large non-American banks and almost US $10 trillion to foreign central banks through currency swaps.[6] Most of this massive amount of money was made available almost immediately, and most was eventually paid back, with interest. There is no reason why capital cannot be mobilized on an immediate and massive scale to deal with an even more fundamental challenge—*the future of our planet*.

Innovative and forward looking business plans that transition away from high emissions must provide income support, meaningful retraining, and job opportunities for the large number of employees dependent on work in high-carbon-emitting sectors. This book has offered examples of successful shifts to wind, solar, and other renewable energy; the potential for new uses of minerals such as copper and bitumen; and the development of new climate-friendly technologies that can contribute to the path to net zero and can be scaled-up to commercial success.

A green recovery also means allocating public resources directly, or in partnership, to regions globally that are particularly suffering hardship from the pandemic and climate change. It means full partnership with Indigenous peoples, as discussed throughout this book. Transition must be just and equitable.

My interest in effective climate governance commenced eight years ago, when I worked with scientists who had been researching, thinking, and acting on climate change issues for decades. It seemed that the corporate governance and corporate finance piece of the puzzle was missing, which, at the time, it was. There was little talk of legal and governance strategies for mitigation and adaptation except in the insurance sector. I was inspired to act because of my granddaughter—I worry about the world we are leaving her and all future generations. Since that time, I have three more granddaughters, but also since that time, a large segment of the financial world has become alert to the urgency of these issues and the need to act through every avenue that we can. That action has started, we need to seriously scale-up financing of the transition.

Countries in the global north, which have caused the vast majority of emissions, need to direct significant resources to the global south, which is experiencing the most devastating impacts of climate change. Such financial support can produce positive synergies for all countries, but cannot be structured in a manner that fails to empower emerging nations to make their own decisions, control their own resources, benefit from circular economy innovations, and protect their own populations. The allocation of financial resources needs to recognize and empower disadvantaged groups, peoples, and communities. It needs to embed fairness and equity in the distribution of costs and benefits of the transition. It needs to develop pathways that recognize the boundaries of our planet's capacity, preventing us from crossing them further. It needs a massive shift to the circular economy, to literally save our planet. It requires that all of us become stewards of the Earth. We owe it to ourselves, our children, our grandchildren, and future generations.

[6] Adam Tooze, *Crashed: How a Decade of Financial Crises Changed the World* (Allen Lane, 2018); see also Janis Sarra and Cheryl Wade, *Predatory Lending and the Destruction of the African-American Dream* (CUP, 2020).

APPENDIX

Governance Checklist for Directors and Pension Fiduciaries

There are a growing number of resources for companies and institutional investors that allow directors, officers, and pension fiduciaries to ask the questions and then develop the business plans to meaningfully address climate change. The questions in this Appendix are drawn primarily from the Canadian Climate Governance Experts programme of the Canada Climate Law Initiative, with the help of governance resources from the World Economic Forum, the Taskforce on Climate-related Financial Disclosures ('TCFD'), and Canadian securities regulators.[1]

Checklist of questions for corporate directors and officers

1. **Does the company have a climate plan?**
   i. Does the board of directors consider the risks and opportunities associated with climate change to be an integral part of its accountability for the long term stewardship of the organization?
   ii. To what extent does the board have a robust understanding of how climate change may affect the company? Do board members understand sector-specific climate change-related issues?
   iii. What information does the board need to gather to understand impacts on the business and to prioritize strategies to mitigate or control risks?
   iv. Has the board been provided sufficient information, including management's materiality assessments in respect of the organization's climate change-related risks, to appropriately oversee and consider management's assessment of these risks?
   v. Is climate considered in company-wide assessments of material risks and opportunities in the short, medium, and long term?
   vi. Does the climate plan set specific targets to reach net zero and does it include effective monitoring of implementation of the strategy against goals and targets?
   vii. Does the climate plan address protection of biodiversity?
   viii. Has the board considered assessing its climate plan by comparing it to the United Nations' Sustainable Development Goals?

[1] Sources: Janis Sarra, Canadian Climate Governance Experts (2019), https://ccli.ubc.ca/; TCFD Implementation Guide; Dr Janis Sarra and Professor Cynthia Williams, *Time to Act: Response to questions posed by the Expert Panel on Sustainable Finance on Fiduciary Obligation and Effective Climate-related Financial Disclosures* (CCLI, 2019), and studies cited therein, https://ccli.ubc.ca/publications/; the World Economic Forum, 'How to Set Up Effective Climate Governance on Corporate Boards: Guiding Principles and Questions' (2019), <https://www.weforum.org/whitepapers/how-to-set-up-effective-climate-governance-on-corporate-boards-guiding-principles-and-questions>; and CSA, 'Staff Notice 51-358 Reporting of Climate Change-related Risks' (1 August 2019), <https://www.osc.gov.on.ca/en/SecuritiesLaw_csa_20190801_51-358_reporting-of-climate-change-related-risks.htm>.

2. **Does the board have effective oversight of its climate strategy, including identifying climate-related risks that are emerging or increasing in significance for the company?**
   i. Does the board have climate expertise and knowledge in its matrix of board composition/director skills? If not, is it hiring non-conflicted expertise to advise it?
   ii. Which board committees and directors are taking the lead on, and responsible for, climate-related issues?
   iii. What are the processes by which the board and/or board committees are informed on a timely basis about new or emerging climate -related issues facing the company?
   iv. Has the board received appropriate training on climate change?
   v. Is accountability for climate risks and opportunities considered during internal evaluations of the board and its members?
   vi. Is oversight and management of climate change-related risks and opportunities integrated into the organization's strategic plan, and if so, to what extent?
   vii. Is the board aware of how the organization's investors are factoring climate-related risks into their investment and voting decisions?

3. **Has the board identified strategic opportunities for the business over the short, medium, and long term, and embedded climate opportunity priorities in its strategic planning, performance objectives, policies, annual budgets, business plan, and enterprise risk management system?**
   i. Has the board ensured that climate systemically informs strategic investment planning and decision-making processes and is embedded into the management of risk and opportunities across the organization?
   ii. Are risks and opportunities informed by scenario analyses?
   iii. Are the board's deliberations integrated into strategic planning, business models, financial planning and other decision-making processes?
   iv. How are climate-related materiality assessments conducted and are they integrated into budget or operating cycle planning?
   v. How does the board hold management accountable for implementing the regulatory requirements for climate-relevant disclosure and for maintaining oversight of emerging regulation?
   vi. How does the board hold management accountable for any biodiversity loss or protection due to the productive activities of the organization?

4. **Who in the company is responsible for climate-related risk and accountable for implementing the company's strategy?**
   i. Are the managers responsible for climate-related risks and opportunities communicating effectively to the board?
   ii. Do directors undertake decisions that are informed by the best available information on climate risks and opportunities?
   iii. Is there a 'lead climate director' (of chair of the board) to whom the executive officer responsible for implementing the company's climate plan is directly reporting, in order to ensure no gaps between board committee in devising, implementing and monitoring the climate plan?
   iv. Is implementation of the climate strategy being monitored effectively against goals and targets?
   v. Is the company's management compensation incentivization scheme designed to promote and reward sustainable value creation over time?
   vi. Is the board confident that the company is positioned and has dedicated sufficient resources to effectively identify, mitigate, manage, and monitor material climate-related risks?

5. **Is the board approving the disclosure of the company's efforts to manage climate change to investors and stakeholders, including integrating disclosure in its financial reporting?**
    i. Does the organization report on the material financial risks and opportunities associated with climate change?
    ii. Does the organization report in line with the TCFD framework?
    iii. How does the board verify that the company has embedded effective materiality assessment processes in relation to climate risks and opportunities?
    iv. Is the board aware and informed about potential mandatory climate-related reporting requirements in jurisdictions in which it has operations?
    v. Does the board feel prepared to explain its disclosures on climate in response to investor-led challenges?

Checklist of Select Questions for Management

1. Does management have expertise or have access to the appropriate expertise to understand and manage material climate-related risks that may affect the organization?
2. Has management appropriately considered how each of the different categories of climate-related risks may affect the organization?
3. Has management considered which units and individuals in the organization have responsibility for identifying, disclosing and managing material climate-related risks and what their reporting lines are to senior management?
4. To what extent are climate responsibilities integrated with mainstream business processes and decision-making?
5. Is management aware of current climate-related litigation that may pose a financial or reputational risk now or in the future?
6. Has management implemented effective systems, procedures and controls to gather timely and accurate climate-related information for purposes of management analysis, decision-making, and disclosure to regulators and stakeholders?
7. Has management appropriately assessed the current and future financial impacts of material climate-related risks on the organization's assets, liabilities, revenues, expenses and cash flows over the short, medium, and long term?
8. Do regulatory filings contain the required disclosures in respect of material climate-related risks, and are they detailed and not boilerplate?
9. What is the organization's exposure to the potential effects of extreme weather events and how does it ensure the resilience of its supply networks and services to the impact of severe weather events?
10. What is the exposure of the organization's properties and other assets to risks, such as flooding or fires?
11. What are the major risks associated with the organization's water use, particularly in water stressed regions, including compliance with regulation?
12. What is the organization's exposure to supply chain disruption climate change-related risks?
13. What is the organization's plan to protect and enhance biodiversity?
14. In implementing the organization's climate plan, is management considering the differential impacts on stakeholders based on race and gender, and correcting for any inequitable impacts?
15. How does the organization incorporate emissions regulations and climate change considerations into its asset valuations?

16 How does climate change regulation impact capital expenditure strategy for exploration and development of assets?
17. How is the organization managing energy consumption and related price and supply risks?

Checklist of Questions for Pension Fiduciaries

In undertaking due diligence in investment decisions, five questions regarding climate change that pension funds should want answered by companies in which they invest:

1. Does the company have a climate business plan to sustain itself in a net zero or 1.5°C world, bearing its share of carbon mitigation; and does the plan assign clear responsibility for implementing the company's climate strategy and effective monitoring against goals and targets?
2. Where climate risk is material, does the company have an effective climate strategy, integrating the business and financial impacts in its balance sheet and access to capital consideration of risks?
3. Has the company identified strategic climate opportunities for the business over the short, medium, and long term, and embedded them in its strategic planning, performance objectives, policies, annual budgets, and business plan, and directions to service providers that undertake its engagement and voting?
4. Does the board have effective oversight of the company's climate strategy, including designating the audit and/or risk committee to take the lead and clear processes by which the board is informed on a timely basis about climate change-related issues?
5. Is the company effectively reporting its efforts to manage climate change to investors in line with the TCFD framework, and is the board approving these reports?

Five questions the pension board should ask its investment managers where assets are being externally managed and its service providers are conducting engagement activities

1. Does the investment manager have an effective climate strategy that can be sustained in a net zero or 1.5°C world, integrating climate change factors into investment decision-making and ongoing management with a view to generating investment returns to meet fund liability obligations within a prudent level of risk, over a timescale that matches the objectives of the pension fund?
2. In investment decisions, is the manager considering whether a company has adopted an effective climate strategy to sustain itself in a net zero or 1.5°C world; has undertaken efforts to identify and manage material risks and opportunities to the business from climate change?
3. Has the manager assessed effectiveness of an investee company's oversight of its climate strategy, including monitoring and accountability mechanisms?
4. Where engagement is delegated to the fund manager or service provider, is the manager/service provider undertaking engagement and proxy voting in line with the pension fund's goals of sustainability and managing climate risk? Is the service provider or manager effectively reporting engagement efforts to the pension board?
5. Is the investment manager effectively reporting its efforts to manage climate change to the pension fund, including integrating climate risk and return in its financial and investment reporting?

Five questions the board should ask itself regarding its own best practices for climate change:

1. Does the pension board have a climate plan, including setting targets for decarbonizing its portfolios?
2. Does the board have effective oversight of its climate strategy, including identifying climate-related and biodiversity risks that are emerging or increasing in significance for the pension fund?
3. Has the board identified strategic opportunities for the business over the short, medium, and long term, and embedded climate opportunity priorities in its strategic planning, performance objectives, policies, annual budgets, business plan, and enterprise risk management system?
4. Who in the organization is responsible for climate-related risk and accountable for implementing the pension fund's strategy?
5. Is the board approving the disclosure of the pension fund's efforts to manage climate change to beneficiaries and other stakeholders, including integrating disclosure in its financial reporting?

Index

For the benefit of digital users, indexed terms that span two pages (e.g., 52–53) may, on occasion, appear on only one of those pages.

Figures are indicated by *f* following the page number